HEROIC TRANSFORMATION:
HOW HEROES CHANGE THEMSELVES
AND THE WORLD

First published 2019
by Palsgrove

Library of Congress Cataloging in Publication Data
Name: Allison, Scott T., Editor

Title: Heroic Transformation: How Heroes Change Themselves
and The World
Edited by Scott T. Allison

Description: 1 Edition | Richmond: Palsgrove, 2019 | Includes bibliographical references
Identifiers: ISBN-10: 0-9983440-2-8 | ISBN-13: 978-0-9983440-2-7

ISBN-10: 0-9983440-2-8

ISBN-13: 978-0-9983440-2-7

Cover design by Scott T. Allison assisted by Canva: https://www.canva.com

COVER IMAGE: The person holding the world was drawn by a Portuguese student of Mariana Reis Barbosa - https://www.linkedin.com/in/mariana-reis-barbosa-a4b5a780/

PG Palsgrove

HEROIC TRANSFORMATION:
HOW HEROES CHANGE THEMSELVES
AND THE WORLD

EDITED BY
SCOTT T. ALLISON

Praise for 'Heroic Transformation'

"Heroic Transformation is an insightful volume containing wisdom about the metamorphosis of the classic hero in film and literature. The book is truly a compelling collection of student scholarship at its finest."

-- *Dr. Robert A. Giacalone, Ray Smiley Chair in Business Ethics and Director of the Ginn Institute for Social Responsibility at John Carroll University.*

"Professor Scott T. Allison has edited another superbly crafted book of student-authored essays that shed light on our understanding of heroism science. This volume is a must-read for scholars of heroism and heroic leadership."

-- *Dr. James K. Beggan, Professor of Sociology, University of Louisville*

"The rapidly developing field of heroism science reminds us that a range of circumstances can transform potential heroes into actual heroes, and that those personal transformations can transform all that surrounds them. Scott T. Allison is a pioneer in this new scholarly domain. With great care and generosity he has enabled his best students to transform themselves into skilled thinkers and writers. The result is wonderfully far reaching study of thirty-one transformed and transforming heroes. This is a stimulating read for anyone who loves heroes or studies heroes."

-- *Dr. George R. Goethals, E. Claiborne Robins Distinguished Professor of Leadership Studies, University of Richmond*

"From Malala to Mulan, and Dexter to Frodo, this volume contributes to our understanding of heroic psychological transformation in an informative, entertaining, and comprehensive way. These student-authors provide a clear and compelling synthesis of theory and research in heroism science."

-- *Dr. Jeffrey D. Green, Professor of Psychology, Virginia Commonwealth University*

Contents

SECTION 3 • CIVIL RIGHTS HEROES

SECTION 4 • ENTERTAINMENT HEROES

Acknowledgements

This book is the third in the Palsgrove series of student-authored books that my team and I have edited over the past few years. It was made possible by many sources of support from a variety of generous individuals. Foremost, I thank my student-authors for their enthusiastic participation in this enterprise. These gifted young people have taught me much about heroism and they give me bright hope for the future of humanity and for our planet.

This volume could not have been produced without the encouragement and support from several key corners of the University of Richmond. My heartfelt thanks go out to Ronald Crutcher, President of the University of Richmond; Patrice Rankine, Dean of Arts & Sciences; and Cindy Bukach, Chair of the Psychology Department. These terrific individuals have provided the inspiration to continue this series of student-authored books on heroism.

I am also grateful to Greg Smith, my friend and colleague for the past 14 years. Greg's help with the technical aspects of publishing these books has been invaluable. Additional thanks go to Karyn Kuhn, one of the best academic administrators in the history of the University of Richmond. Whenever I need any kind of assistance, Karyn is always there with the perfect answer, always delivered with kindness and wisdom.

Perhaps the one person most responsible for my interest in heroism is my dear friend and colleague, Al Goethals. Al and I have been buddies and research collaborators since 1985. For many years now, the two of us have enjoyed biweekly lunches at *The Tavern*, during which we exchange ideas about leadership and heroism. These lunches have nourished our thoughts and have served as the genesis of our many co-authored books and articles. I owe a huge debt of gratitude to Al for his generous spirit and wisdom.

This work would never have happened without my loving wife and partner Connie Allison, who for reasons I'll never understand has tolerated the many unsavory aspects of my character. Connie's gentle demeanor, steadfast warmth, and sweet companionship have inspired and sustained me more than she'll ever know. Thank you, my dear Constance Rae.

As is my custom, my final thanks are reserved for you, dear reader. The universe has conspired to place this book in your hands, and I suspect that you're reading these words because heroism is calling you and a heroic life awaits you. I hope you take this calling very seriously. Every human being is designed to become a hero in myriad ways, and your job is to remain awakened to the call and to allow the journey to transform you in ways you can't even imagine. If you remain open to going on the metamorphic journey, I promise it will happen.

- Scott T. Allison, January 2019
Richmond, Virginia

FOREWORD

Transformation is everywhere – as day morphs into night and back again, as the seasons change, and as ageing, disease, and repair are occurring constantly inside our bodies. Transformation is perhaps most obvious and predictable in nature. And it is equally ingrained in us humans, though our stubbornness and sometimes slow to change habitual patterns can cloud this universal fact of life.

As an ethnographer and observer of the wonders of life, human beings, and the universe, Joseph Campbell knew this better than most. It is no wonder that transformation lies at the heart of his most famous edict, the hero's journey. From before we could even speak and write we gathered in front of a fire and would communicate in non-verbal ways; by drawing on the sand, carving images on stone walls, looking deep into each other's eyes. And when we developed complex systems of language and writing the power of story evolved to new heights. Through these stories we were able to convey the magic of the world around us, and within us.

Civilizations and our own life stories are filled with highs and lows, and everything in between. Their countless cycles of transformations are not neat, orderly, or systematic. Yet, there is a pattern, as Joseph Campbell outlined. When we are in the thick of it, they are unsettling, intertwined, painful, surprising, with few periods of calm that seem to be fleeting. Other times, they can be lacklustre and mundane – but never predictable. Life is chaos. Life is messy. And so too are the stories that are produced by this turbulent and beautiful human existence.

In this book, prolific author, respected psychologist, and renowned heroism expert, editor Scott T. Allison, together with his talented legion of young authors remind us of this truth. Its astonishing breadth of fictional and non-fictional heroes spanning film and television, epic narratives and legends, civil rights, and the entertainment industry will take you on a winding, but never dull journey of the tales we have created throughout history and continue to this day. I say 'we', because they truly belong to all of us; they are part of us in the deepest sense.

But what makes us even more unique as a species is our ability to reflect back onto the page, the computer screen, the television – whatever 'mirror' we may choose – the hidden meanings behind these stories. It is by grappling with and attempting to decode the many complex layers of these characters, their heroic and at times not so heroic exploits, that we may achieve ever expanding states of understanding of what we are capable of and a deeper consciousness of our supra-humanity.

Having been on this journey of the birth of the field of heroism science for a few years now, there is nothing more gratifying than seeing students weave their own meaning into the beautiful tapestries that their ancestors and contemporaries have created. And in so doing, they are recreating them and breathing new life into these tales that we may have heard numerous times; but perhaps never fully understood.

We are presently in a turning point as a species and as a field. We see products of culture recycled, but told in different ways. We see mistakes of the past being repeated on many fronts, as if a déjà vu has set in. And we also see messages of hope that seem familiar from the recent past, or maybe ages of old, revived. Everything is returned – the oldest spiritual traditions speak of the primordial cycle of birth-death-rebirth. It is the same pattern, yet it never occurs in the same way twice, as with the hero's journey. Buddhists have long stated that life is impermanence; the only thing we can truly count on is change.

As you delve into the adventures of this book, its heroines and heroes, keep this universal truth in mind. As you take a walk through the transformations of these characters, their trials, suffering, strengths, and twists through the fresh eyes of these bright up-and-coming authors, take a moment to think about how their magic exists within you. What character echoes most for you, and why?

Malala Yousafzai, Muhammad Ali, Eleanor Roosevelt, Oskar Schindler, Audrey Hepburn, Siddhārtha Gautama? Or perhaps James "Sawyer" Ford, Harry Potter, Batman, or Daenerys Targerean?   How have you been deeply transformed in your own life? If you haven't, why not? What events in your life moulded you, broke you, elevated you? Who are you on life's eternal stage?

French philosopher Paul Ricœur spoke of a "second naïveté" – as children, we were able to see with clear heart and mind a certain wonder and awe all around us. We took that without question. We inevitably lost that as adulthood set in and we learnt to distance ourselves from 'fairytales', 'myths', and 'child's play'.

Well, I say to you, the reader, it takes deep courage to dive into these pages and the lives of these heroines and heroes. It takes deep courage to revisit your everyday life anew, to dare to see the magic that has been lost. It takes deep courage and risk – so fundamental to heroism – to believe. Because to admit that the choices we make, the words we speak, the movements we make, are deeply interconnected with a higher purpose is intimidating, and even overwhelming.

Transformation and heroism are fundamentally embodied at their core, meaning we must breathe in, smell, taste, sense, intuit, touch, listen, feel our way through a new adventure that awaits us, not just think our way through it. The same goes for this book.

Go on – I dare you. Let's take this heroic journey into our second childhood together.

Dr. Olivia Efthimiou, Postdoctoral Associate
School of Arts, Murdoch University, Australia
Summer 2018

INTRODUCTION

THE METAMORPHOSIS OF THE HERO: WHAT IT IS, HOW IT HAPPENS, WHY IT'S IMPORTANT

SCOTT T. ALLISON

"The measure of intelligence is the ability to change."

— Albert Einstein

One of the most revered deities in Hinduism is Ganesha, a god symbolizing great wisdom and enlightenment. Ganesha's most striking attribute is his unusual appearance. In images throughout India and southeast Asia, he is shown to be a man with an ordinary human body and the head of an elephant. According to legend, when Ganesha was a boy, he had the habit of making foolish, immature decisions. Shiva realized that his son needed an entirely new way of thinking, a new and broader way of seeing the world. To achieve this aim, Shiva cut off Ganesha's human head and replaced it with that of an elephant, an animal representing unmatched wisdom, intelligence, reflection, and listening. Ganesha was transformed from a naïve boy, operating with narrow and limited conscious awareness, into a strong, wise, and fully awakened individual.

This book is about how people undergo dramatic, positive change. In short, it's about heroic transformation – what it is, how it comes about, and why it's important. The guiding principle underlying this book is that an understanding of the nature of personal transformation may hold the key to nothing less than the future well-being of the entire human race. Yes, you read that correctly. The premise of transformation is that the modern world, with its capability of self-destruction, cannot survive without a revolution of consciousness.

Unlike Ganesha, one need not undergo a literal decapitation to experience heroic transformation. One only needs to travel the hero's journey, which sounds simple but is actually the most daunting task facing any human being. There is one piece of good news and two pieces of bad news about the hero's journey. The good news is, of course, that anyone who completes the path emerges a brand-new person, a much-improved version of one's previous self. Transformation, after all, means "to change form", which precisely describes the massive alteration undergone by Ganesha. With his new head, Ganesha now sees the world with greater clarity and broader insight. The bad news is that the hero's journey inevitably involves setback, suffering, and a death of some type. What dies is usually the former self, the untransformed version of oneself that sees the world "through a glass darkly" (Bergman, 1961). What happened to Ganesha happens to us all metaphorically; the journey marks the death of a narrow, immature way of seeing the world and the birth of a wider, more enlightened way of viewing life.

The second piece of bad news is that one cannot engineer the journey for one-self. Doing so only makes the journey ego-driven, and as we will see, one of the primary purposes of the hero's journey to tame or eliminate the ego. The hero's journey "happens" to us, usually against our will. A tornado hurls Dorothy into the land of Oz. Ilsa's arrival at Casablanca sends Rick down his heroic path. The death of Bambi's mother completely alters Bambi's destiny. Heroes do not go on the transformative journey on their own volition any more than caterpil-lars make a decision to transform into a butterfly. All of us are thrown into the hero's journey, often kicking and screaming in protest. It is the only way most of us will ever change.

A unique feature of this series of books, called the Palsgrove Series, is that each volume in the collection is authored by undergraduate students at the

University of Richmond. This particular book is authored by 31 first-year Richmond students, all of whom were instructed to compose a 4,000-word paper illuminating the origins, processes, and consequences of heroic transformation. Each chapter in this book describes a single case-study of a hero with emphasis on how that hero transformed him or herself on their heroic journey. As a collection we can see some extraordinary patterns of transformation that repeat themselves across many relevant dimensions. These identifiable patterns emerge for heroes of both fiction and heroes of non-fiction; for heroes of both antiquity and of the present day; and for heroes from across the globe, including Asia, Europe, North America, and the Middle-East. Heroic transformation appears to be a prized and universal phenomenon that is cherished and encouraged in all human societies (Allison & Goethals, 2017; Efthimiou & Franco, 2017; Efthimiou, Allison, & Franco, 2018a, 2018b).

The hero's transformation is the most central yet most overlooked element of Joseph Campbell's (1949) hero monomyth. This monomyth consists of the epic journey that every hero undergoes in classic mythology, literature, film, and real life. Allison and Goethals (2017) describe in great detail the purpose, origins, dimensions, processes, and consequences of the hero's transformation. The goal of this introductory chapter is to briefly review these various elements of heroic metamorphosis and offer some additional insights about their significance to human experience. Moreover, I will provide a brief overview of seven barriers to heroic transformation, and I will suggest ways for overcoming these barriers so that as many of us as possible can reach our full potential as human beings.

OVERVIEW OF HEROIC TRANSFORMATION

Until the past decade, there has been virtually no scholarship on the topic of heroic transformation. Two early seminal works in psychology offered hints about the processes involved in dramatic change and growth in human beings. In 1902, William James addressed the topic of spiritual conversion in his classic volume, *The Varieties of Religious Experience*. These conversion experiences bear a striking similarity to descriptions of the hero's transformation as reported by Campbell (1949) and Allison and Goethals (2017). These experiences included feelings of peace, clarity, union with all of humanity, newness, happiness, generosity, and being part of something bigger than oneself. James emphasized the pragmatic side of religious conversion, noting that the mere belief and trust in a deity could bring about significant positive change independent of whether the deity actually exists. This pragmatic side of spirituality is emphasized today by Thich Nhat Hanh, who observes that transformation as a result of following Buddhist practices can occur in the absence of a belief in a supreme being. Millions of Buddhists have enjoyed the transformative benefits described by James by practicing the four noble truths, the noble eightfold path, and many other spiritual practices (Hanh, 1999, p. 170).

The second early psychological treatment of human transformation was published in 1905 by Sigmund Freud. His *Three Essays on the Theory of Sexuality* described life-altering transformative stages in childhood involving oral, anal, phallic, and latent developmental patterns. Although Freud suggested that people tend to resist change in adulthood, all subsequent major schools of psychological thought have since proposed mechanisms for transformative change throughout the lifespan. Humanistic theories, in particular, have embraced the idea that humans are capable of a long-term transformation into self-actualized individuals (Maslow, 1943). Developmental psychologists have proposed models of transformative growth throughout human life (Erikson, 1994). Recent theories of self-processes portray humans as open to change and growth under some conditions (Sedikides & Hepper, 2009) but resistant under others (Swann, 2012). In the present day, positive psychologists are uncovering key mechanisms underlying healthy transformative growth in humans (Lopez & Snyder, 2011).

An important source of transformation resides in tales of heroism told throughout the ages. These mythologies reflect humanity's longing for transformative growth, and they are packed with wisdom and inspiration (Allison & Goethals, 2014). Just reading, hearing, or observing stories of heroism can stir us and transform us. According to Campbell (2004, p. xvi), these hero tales "provide a field in which you can locate yourself" and they "carry the individual through the stages of life" (p. 9). The resultant transformations seen in heroic stories "are infinite in their revelation" (Campbell, 1988, p. 183). Otto Rank (1909) observed that "everyone is a hero in birth, where he undergoes a tremendous psychological as well as physical transformation, from the condition of a little water creature living in a realm of amniotic fluid into an air-breathing mammal" (p. 153).

This transformation at birth foreshadows a lifetime of transformative journeys for human beings.

According to Allison and Goethals (2017), hero stories reveal three different targets of heroic transformation: A transformation of setting, a transformation of self, and a transformation of society. These three transformations parallel Campbell's (1949) three major stages of the hero's journey: departure (or separation), initiation, and return. The departure from the hero's familiar world represents a transformation of one's normal, safe environment; the initiation stage is awash with challenge, suffering, mentoring, and transformative growth; and the final stage of return represents the hero's opportunity to use her newfound gifts to transform the world. The sequence of these stages is critical, with each transformation essential for producing the next one. Without a change in setting, the hero cannot change herself, and without a change in herself, the hero cannot change the world. Our focus here is on the hero's transformation of the self, but this link in the chain necessarily requires some consideration of the links preceding and following it. The mythic hero must be cast out of her familiar world and into a different world, otherwise there can be no departure from her status quo. Once transformed, the hero must use her newly enriched state to better the world, otherwise the hero's transformation lacks social significance.

The hero's transformation is essential for the hero to achieve her goal on the journey. During the quest, "ineffable realizations are experienced" and "things that before had been mysterious are now fully understood" (Campbell, 1972, p. 219). The ineffability of these new insights stems from their unconscious origins. Jungian principles of the collective unconscious form the basis of Campbell's theorizing about hero mythology. As Le Grice (2013) notes, "myths are expressions of the imagination, shaped by the archetypal dynamics of the psyche" (p. 153). As such, the many recurring elements of the mythic hero's journey have their "inner, psychological correlates" (Campbell, 1972, p. 153). The hero's journey is packed with social symbols and motifs that connect the hero to her deeper self, and these unconscious images must be encountered, and conflicts with them must be resolved, to bring about transformation (Campbell, 2004). Ultimately, the hero's outer journey reflects an inner, psychological journey that involves "leaving one condition and finding the source of life to bring you forth into a richer or mature condition" (Campbell, 1988, p. 152).

Allison and Smith (2015) identified five types of heroic transformation: physical, emotional, spiritual, mental, and moral. Allison and Goethals (2017) proposed a sixth type: motivational transformation. These six transformation types span two broad categories: physical transformation, which we call *transmutation*, and psychological transformation, which we call *enlightenment*. Physical transmutations are endemic to ancient mythologies involving gods that transform humans into stars, statues, and animals. Transmutation also pervades superhero tales of ordinary people succumbing to industrial accidents and spider bites that physically transform them into superheroes and supervillains. These ancient and modern tales of transmutation are symbolic of hidden powers residing within each of us, powers that emerge only after coaxing from environmental forces. Efthimiou and her colleagues have written at length about the power and potential of biological transformation to change the world (Efthimiou, 2015, 2017; Efthimiou & Allison, 2017; Franco, Efthimiou, & Zimbardo, 2016). Epigenetic changes in DNA and the science of human limb regeneration are two examples of modern day heroic transmutations (Efthimiou, 2015). The phenomenon of neurogenesis refers to the development of new brain cells in the hippocampus through exercise, diet, meditation, and learning. This transformative healing and growing can occur even after catastrophic brain trauma. Efthimiou (2017) discusses how the hero organism can engage in regeneration or restoration processes, referring to an organism's ability to grow, heal, and re-create itself.

The other five types of transformation – moral, motivations, mental, emotional, and spiritual – comprise the second broad category of transformation that we call enlightenment. Emotional transformations refer to "changes of the heart" (Allison & Smith, 2015, p. 23) involving growth in empathic concern for others. We call this transformation *compassion*. Spiritual transformations refer to changes in belief systems about the spiritual world and about the workings of life, the world, and the universe; we call this change *transcendence*. Mental transformations refer to leaps in intellectual growth and significant increases in illuminating insights about oneself and others; we label this *wisdom*. Moral transformations occur when heroes undergo a dramatic shift from immorality to morality; we call this *redemption*. Finally, a motivational transformation refers to a complete shift in one's purpose or perceived direction in life; we label this a *calling*.

The purpose of the hero's journey is to provide a context or blueprint for human metamorphic growth. Why do we need such life-changing growth? Allison and Setterberg (2016) argue that people are born "incomplete" psychologically and will remain incomplete until they rise above challenges that enable them to realize their full potential. Transcending these challenges enables the hero to "undergo a truly heroic transformation of consciousness," requiring them "to think a different way" (Campbell, 1988, p. 155). This shift provides a new "map or picture of the universe and allows us to see ourselves in relationship to nature" (Campbell, 1991, p. 56). Buddhist traditions and twelve-step programs of recovery refer to transformation as an awakening. In a similar manner, Campbell (2004) described the journey's purpose as a much-needed voyage designed to "wake you up" (p. 12). The long-term survival of the human race may depend on such an awakening, as it becomes increasingly clear that the unawakened, pre-transformed state is unsustainable to us at the level of the individual level as well as collectively. As individuals, transformation is necessary for our psychological, emotional, social, and spiritual well-being. Collectively, the survival of our planet may depend on broader, enlightened thinking from leaders who must be transformed themselves if they are to make wise decisions about human rights, climate change, peace and war, healthcare, education, and myriad other issues.

Below I offer five reasons why transformation is such a key element in the hero's journey, and why it is essential for our own and others' welfare.

1. Transformations foster developmental growth. Early human societies recognized the value of initiation rituals in promoting the transition from childhood to adulthood (van Gennep, 1909). A number of scholars, including Campbell, have lamented the failure of our postmodern society to recognize the psychological importance of rites and rituals (Campbell, 1988; Le Grice, 2013; Rohr, 2011). Coming-of-age stories are common in mythic hero tales about children "awakening to the new world that opens at adolescence" (Campbell, 1988, p. 167). The hero's journey "helps us pass through and deal with the various stages of life from birth to death" (Campbell, 1991, p. 56).

2. Transformations promote healing. Allison and Goethals (2014, 2016, 2017) claim that the simple act of sharing stories about hero transformations can deliver many of the same benefits as group therapy (Yalom & Leszcz, 2005). These benefits include the instillation of hope; the relief of knowing that others share one's emotional experiences; the fostering of self-awareness; the relief of stress; and the development of a sense of meaning about life. A growing number of clinical psychologists invoke hero transformations in their practice to help their clients develop the heroic traits of strength, resilience, and courage (Grace, 2016). Recent research on post-traumatic growth demonstrates that people can overcome severe trauma and even use it to transform themselves into stronger, healthier persons than they were before the trauma (Ramos & Leal, 2013).

3. Transformations cultivate social unity. Campbell (1972) argued that hero transformations "drop or lift [heroes] out of themselves, so that their conduct is not their own but of the species, the society" (p. 57). The transformed hero is "selfless, boundless, without ego." The most meaningful transformations are a journey from egocentricity to sociocentricity, from elitism to egalitarianism (Campbell, 1949; Rohr, 2011; Wilber, 2007). No longer isolated from the world, transformed individuals enjoy a feeling of union with others. Describing the hero's journey, Campbell (1949) wrote, "where we had thought to be alone, we shall be with all the world" (p. 25).

4. Transformations advance society. The culmination of the hero's journey is the hero's boon, or gift, to society. This gift is what separates the hero's journey from simply being a test of personal survival. For the voyage to be heroic, the protagonist in myth must use her newly acquired insights and gifts to better the world (Campbell, 1949; Rohr, 2011). The heroic boon to society follows the successful completion of the individual quest, and so we can say that the social boon is entirely dependent upon the hero's personal transformation that made the personal quest a success. Hero mythology, according to Campbell (1972), is designed to teach us that society is not a "perfectly static organization" but represents a "movement of the species forward" (p. 48).

5. Transformations deepen spiritual and cosmic understanding. Campbell (1988) observed that the hero's transformation involves learning "to experience the supernormal range of human spiritual life" (p. 152). Myths, he said, "bring us into a level of consciousness that is spiritual" (p. 19). In every hero tale, the hero must "die spiritually" and then be "reborn to a larger way of living" (p. 141), a process that is the enactment of a universal spiritual theme of death being the necessary experience for producing new life (Campbell, 1991, p. 102). Hero transformations supply cosmological wisdom. Famed ethnographer van Gennep (1909) observed that transformative rituals in early human tribes have "been linked to the celestial passages, the revolutions of the planets, and the phases of the moon. It is indeed a cosmic conception that relates the stages of human existence to those of plant and animal life and, by a sort of pre-scientific divination, joins them to the great rhythms of the universe" (p. 194).

INTERNAL AND EXTERNAL SOURCES OF TRANSFORMATION

Allison and Goethals (2017) distinguished between sources of transformative change that come from within the individual and sources that originate from outside the individual. There are at least four internal sources of transformation. First, transformation can arise as a result of natural human development. An initial transformative event, a sperm cell fertilizing an egg, leads to a zygote transforming into an embryo, which then becomes (in order) a fetus, a baby, a toddler, a child, an adolescent, a young adult, a mid-life adult, and an elderly adult. A second internal source of change resides in people's needs and goals. According to Maslow's (1943) pyramid of needs, an individual is motivated to fulfill the needs at a particular level once lower level needs are satisfied. Once the needs at the four lower levels are satisfied, one is no longer concerned with them or driven by them. In effect, one transitions to higher levels and eventually achieves self-actualization, during which one might enjoy peak experiences of having discovered meaning, beauty, truth, and a sense of oneness with the world -- a transformative state reminiscent of James' (1902) description of the religiously converted individual.

A third internal source of transformative change is human transgression and failure. People often undergo significant change after being humbled by their "fallings and failings" (Rohr, 2011, p. xv). Joseph Campbell (2004) acknowledged that not all heroic quests end with glorious, heroic success. "There is always the possibility for a fiasco," he said (p. 133). Such fiascos can serve as the grist for a larger transformative mill, producing a kind of suffering needed to fuel a greater hero journey. It is a general truth that for substance abusers to be sufficiently motivated to seek recovery from their addictions, they must reach a profound level of pain and suffering, commonly referred to as "hitting rock bottom." Suffering, according to Rohr (2011), "doesn't accomplish anything tangible but creates space for learning and love" (p. 68). This space has been called liminal space (van Gennep, 1909; Turner, 1966), defined as the transitional space between one state of being and an entirely different state of being. In liminal space, one has been stripped of one's previous life, humbled, and silenced. Transgressions, and the liminal space that follows them, are the fertile soil from which heroic transformations may bloom.

Finally, a fourth internal source of transformation is what Allison and Goethals (2017) call an enlightened dawning of responsibility. This dawning is captured in a simple phrase, composed of ten two-letter words, "If it is to be, it is up to me" (Phipps, 2011). There is a long history of social psychological work devoted to studying the forces at work that undermine the dawning of responsibility in emergency settings (Latane & Darley, 1969). Research has shown that in a crisis a small but courageous minority of people do step up to do the right thing even when there are strong pressures to avoid assuming responsibility. These fearless social aberrants, most of whom are ordinary citizens, are able to transcend their circumstances and transform from ordinary to extraordinary. Whistleblowers are a notable example; they demonstrate the mettle to step up and do right thing at great potential cost to themselves (Brown, 2017). Bystander training is now available to cultivate this dawning of responsibility in situations where transformative leadership is needed (Heroic Imagination Project, 2018).

External situational forces can also evoke transformative change. Situations, for example, can trigger emotional responses that transform us. William James (1902) noted that in the context of religious conversion, "emotional occasions... are extremely potent in precipitating mental rearrangements" (p. 77). Emotions need not be negative to induce change. Feelings of elevation can transform people psychologically and behaviorally (Haidt, 2003). People become elevated after witnessing a morally beautiful act, and this elevated feeling has been shown to produce altruistic acts (Thomson & Siegel, 2013). A second external source of transformation is the series of trials that all heroes must undergo during their journey. Suffering can be an internal cause of transformation when it results from self-destructive actions, but suffering caused by outside forces can serve as an external source of transformation. Campbell (1988) believed that "trials are designed to see to it that the intending hero should be really a hero. Is he really a match for this task?" (p. 154). The point of greatest danger for the hero is when she enters the belly of the whale (Campbell, 1949). The belly can be entered literally as in stories of Jonah and Pinocchio, but usually the belly is a metaphorical place along the journey in which the hero's darkest inner-demons must be "disempowered, overcome, and controlled" (p. 180). For Campbell, the hero's journey truly is an inner task of conquering one's fears and slaying one's dragons. Positive psychologists today refer to this transformative process as post-traumatic growth, during which people convert the worst thing that ever happened to them into the best (Rendon, 2015).

A third external source of transformation is the vast hero literature and mythology to which we are exposed throughout our lives. Allison and Goethals (2014, 2016, 2017) have long argued that narratives about heroes, pervasive in all of storytelling from Gilgamesh to the present day, serve as a nourishing catalyst for transformative change. The central premise of the *Heroic Leadership Dynamic* is that our consumption of heroic tales takes place within an interactive system or process that is energizing, always in motion, and drawing us toward rising heroes and repelling us from falling ones. The HLD framework proposes two transformative functions of hero stories: an epistemic function and an energizing function. Hero narratives supply epistemic growth by offering scripts for prosocial action, by revealing fundamental truths about human existence, by unpacking life paradoxes, and by cultivating emotional intelligence. The epistemic value of hero tales is revealed in Campbell's (1988) observation that hero mythology offers insights into "what can be known but not told" (p. 206) and that "mythology is the womb of mankind's initiation to life and death" (Campbell, 2002, p. 34). Hero tales also offer energizing benefits, providing people with agency and efficacy. Narratives of heroism promote moral elevation, heal psychic wounds, and inspire psychological growth (Allison & Goethals, 2016; Kinsella, Ritchie, and Igou, 2015, 2017).

The fourth external source of transformation is the social environment of the hero. In hero narratives and classic mythology, the hero's journey is populated by numerous friends, companions, lovers, parent figures, and mentors who assist the hero on her quest (Campbell, 1949). The hero is always helped along the journey by the actual, imagined, or implied presence of others. Campbell also discussed the importance of encounters with parental figures; male heroes seek atonement with father figures, and female heroes with mother figures. Campbell also described the hero's brush with lovers and temptresses, who can either assist, distract, or do harm to the hero. The majority of people who are asked to name their heroes mention a mentor or coach who had a transformative effect on them (Allison & Goethals, 2011).

The temporal sequencing of mentorship is an important element of the hero's journey. Mentors help heroes become transformed, and later, having succeeded on their journeys, these transformed heroes then assume the role of mentor for others who are at earlier stages of their quests. In short, "transformed people transform people" (Rohr, 2014, p. 263). Mentors can have a transformative effect with their words of advice, with their actions, or both. Words can fall on deaf ears but one's actions, attitudes, and lifestyle can leave a lasting imprint. St. Francis of Assisi expressed it this way: "You must preach the Gospel at all times, and when necessary use words" (Rohr, 2014, p. 263). A mentor can be viewed as a type of hero who enhances the lives of others (Kinsella, Ritchie, & Igou, 2015).

The hero's journey prepares people for leadership roles by offering a transformative experience that can be shared later with others. Burns (1978) argued that transforming leaders make an effort to satisfy followers' lower needs (e.g., survival and safety), thereby elevating them for the important work that they – leaders and followers -- must do together to produce significant higher-level changes. Burns described transforming leadership as individuals engaging each other "in such a way that leaders and followers raise one another to higher levels of motivation and morality" (p. 20). Both leaders and followers will be "elevated" such that the leaders create a "new cadre of leaders" (p. 20). This conception is consistent with Campbell's ideas about the role of mentorship during the hero's journey, with the mentor elevating the hero and preparing her for future mentoring duties. Burns' framework also makes explicit a notion that is largely implicit in Maslow's (1943) model, namely, that the self-actualized person has become an elder, a mentor figure, and a moral actor who wields transformative influence over others. Erik Erikson's (1994) theory of lifelong development makes the similar claim that older generative individuals, having been given so much early in life, are now in a position to give back to younger people.

Other theories also point to the transformative effect of mentoring and leadership. Hollander (1995) has proposed a two-way influence relationship between a leader and followers aimed primarily at attaining mutual goals. Hollander defined leadership as "a shared experience, a voyage through time" with the leader in partnership with followers to pursue common interests. For Hollander, "a major component of the leader–follower relationship is the leader's perception of his or her self relative to followers, and how they in turn perceive the leader"

(p. 55). Tyler and Lind (1992) have shown that these perceptions are critically important in cementing good follower loyalty. Followers will perceive a leader as a "legitimate" authority when she adheres to basic principles of procedural justice. Leaders who show fairness, respect, and concern for the needs of followers are able to build followers' self-esteem, a pivotal step in Maslow's (1943) pyramid, thereby fostering followers' transformative movement toward meeting higher-level needs.

Mentors and leaders can also use their charisma to exert a transformative effect on their followers. Goethals and Allison (2014) reviewed the transforming leadership of three heroic leaders from the 20th century whom they dubbed "the three kings": Muhammad Ali, Elvis Presley, and Martin Luther King, Jr. These kings radiated powerful charisma that transformed their followers. All three kings had exceptional personas. All three made an emotional connection with their audiences. All three related and embodied compelling stories. All three enacted theatrical leadership that gave people what they wanted and needed. Two of them, King and Ali, used words, delivered in riveting styles, often touching on religious precepts, to influence their followers' thoughts, feelings, and behavior. The three kings used their charisma to transform others, through both their words and their example.

THE THREE TRANSFORMATIVE ARCS OF HEROISM

Allison and Goethals (2017) identified three deficits of the hero at the outset of her journey. The untransformed hero is missing (1) a sociocentric view of life; (2) an autonomy from societal norms that discourage transformation; and (3) a mindset of growth and change. Below we explain why the arc of metamorphosis bends toward sociocentricity, autonomy, and growth.

Egocentricity to Sociocentricity

Campbell (2004) believed that one of the central functions of hero mythology is to "get a sense of everything – yourself, your society, the universe, and the mystery beyond – as one great unit" (p. 55). He claimed that "when we quit thinking primarily about ourselves and our own self-preservation, we undergo a truly heroic transformation of consciousness" (Campbell, 1988, p. 155). In most hero narratives, the hero begins the journey disconnected from the world. She is a self-centered, prideful individual whose sole preoccupation is establishing her identity, her career, and her material world. The entire point of her hero journey is to awaken her to the larger, deeper task of thinking beyond herself, to developing communion with everyone and with everything (Friedman, 2017). To the extent that we spend the first stages of our lives selfishly building our personal identities and careers, we may be designed to awaken in later stages to our original predisposition toward sociocentricity (Rohr, 2011). Campbell (2001) urged us all to cultivate this greater purpose of forming compassionate unification with all of humanity. He believed this awakening is the central function of hero mythology.

Dependency to Autonomy

A person's willingness to deviate from the dominant cultural pattern is essential for heroic transformation. Heroes do the right thing, and do what they must do, regardless of authority, tradition, and consequence. Maslow (1943) called this characteristic autonomy. "There are the 'strong' people," wrote Maslow, "who can easily weather disagreement or opposition, who can swim against the stream of public opinion and who can stand up for the truth at great personal cost" (p. 379). Fulfillment of the lower needs in the pyramid is essential for autonomy to develop in individuals. "People who have been made secure and strong in the earliest years tend to remain secure and strong thereafter in the face of whatever threatens" (p. 380). Zimbardo (2008) has championed the idea that heroes are people with the ability to resist social pressures that promote evil, and that such resistance requires the moral courage to be guided by one's heart rather than by social cues. Zimbardo and other hero activists drive home the point that "the opposite of a hero isn't a villain; it's a bystander" (Chakrabortty, 2010; Langdon, 2016). While the transformed hero enjoys "union with the world," she remains an autonomous individual who can establish her own path in the world that is unfettered by pressures to conform to social pressures.

Stagnation to Growth

One can be autonomous but not necessarily growing and stretching toward realizing one's full potential. The pre-transformed hero naturally resists change, and thus severe setbacks may be her only impetus to budge. Without a prod, she will remain comfortable in her stagnation, oblivious to the idea that anything needs changing. The hero's journey marks the death of pretense and inauthenticity, and the birth of the person one is meant to be. Campbell (1988) described the process as "killing the infantile ego and bringing forth an adult" (p. 168). Sperry (2011) has argued that people are so attached to their false selves that they fear the death of the false self even more than they fear the death of their physical self. Our growth can also be inhibited by a phenomenon called the crab bucket syndrome (Simmons, 2012). This syndrome describes the consequences of our entrenchment with our families, our friends, and our communities, and they with us. Any attempt we make to crawl up and out of the bucket is met with failure as the crabs below us pull us back down. For most of us, the hero's journey represents the best way, and perhaps the only way, to escape the bucket and discover our true selves. Campbell (1991) argued that a healthy, transformed individual accepts and embraces her growth and contradictions. "The psychological transformation," wrote Campbell, "would be that whatever was formerly endured is now known, loved, and served" (p. 207).

EIGHT BARRIERS TO TRANSFORMATION

We now turn to eight factors that can stand in the way of people undergoing a positive transformative experience in life. There are no doubt many more barriers than those mentioned here, but I highlight these as especially important. These blockages include (1) self-ignorance; (2) an impoverished environment; (3) a history of untreated trauma; (4) a victim mentality; (5) poor mentorship; (6) narcissism; (7) severe illness; and (8) psychological inflexibility. Removing or overcoming these impediments is easier in some cases than in others, as we'll note below:

1. Self-Ignorance

A recurring theme in psychological research is that people are unaware of much of their own psychological functioning (Alicke, 2017; Bargh & Morsella, 2008; Nisbett & Wilson, 1977; Wegner, 2002). This lack of self-awareness may explain people's resistance to transformative growth. Early psychoanalytic theories of Freud, Adler, and Horney were the first to point to the destructive effects of behaving unconsciously. Carl Jung (1956) described the shadow as the dark, unknown aspects of our personalities that prevent us from transforming into our full potential. Building on Jung's work, Campbell observed that all "the images of [hero] mythology are referring to something in you," and that our shadow impedes our ability to make the best use of these images (p. 68). The solution to self-ignorance resides in therapeutic intervention and in good mentoring.

2. Impoverished Environment

Maslow's (1943) model of hierarchical needs suggests that people can get stuck at lower stages of the hierarchy that focus on satisfying basic biological and security needs. Heroic potential may be suppressed when individuals are afflicted by poverty or safety concerns that thwart their ability to progress upward in the hierarchy toward higher-level goals. Resolving this problem is easy in theory but extremely difficult in practice, as most world societies either lack the will or the means to eliminate poverty.

3. History of Trauma

Related to the above is the possibility that exposure to traumatic events can impede people's ability to undergo transformative growth. Trauma disrupts people's sense of safety and their ability to cope with the overwhelming threat and danger, damaging their physical, emotional, and cognitive functioning processes (Keck et al., 2017). Safety and security needs become paramount to the traumatized individual, rendering higher level needs unimportant. The good news is that most people can show great progress in recovering from the deleterious effects of trauma. This recovery is the basis of the hopeful phenomenon of post-traumatic growth (Rendon, 2015).

4. Victim Identity

People who have been harmed and who derive their entire personal identity from being a victim of harm may find it difficult to grow and transcend their victimhood. I am not making the claim that there are no legitimate victims; there most certainly are people who have been harmed and have real grievances. My argument here is adopting a strong and permanent victim identity is a sure way of avoiding growth and moving beyond the pain of having been harmed. Once again, the solution to resolving the victim identity problem resides in one's willingness to seek therapeutic interventions that focus on re-framing one's identity.

5. Dark Mentorship or No Mentorship

Another obstacle to one's ability to transform may be the absence of good mentor figures who can offer guidance through the transformative process. Social sources of wisdom, inspiration, and change are critical elements of the hero monomyth as described by Campbell (1949). These social sources appear in the form of friends, mentors, peers, and allies, all of whom represent rich and essential sources of transformation. There are times, moreover, when people encounter the wrong mentor whose advice does more harm than good. Allison and Smith (2015) used the term dark mentors to describe these damaging guides who undermine people's ability to walk the heroic path. The solution to this problem is for people to choose their mentors wisely – a tall order when, ironically, it may require good mentorship to steer us away from the bad kind. Trusted friends and companions can help us distinguish among the good and bad social sources of influence.

6. Narcissism and Egocentricity

Psychologists believe that roughly 6% of US adults are afflicted with narcis-sistic personality disorder (Bressert, 2018), which means that at least 15 million Americans may be narcissists. The characteristics of narcissism are a grandi-ose sense of importance, a preoccupation with unlimited success, a belief that one is special and unique, exploitation of others, lack of empathy, and arro-gance. Narcissists are unlikely to undergo heroic transformation because they don't believe they need one and thus avoid it entirely (Worthington & Allison, 2018). The narcissist assigns blame for his problems to others, leading the him to believe that other people need to change rather than the narcissist himself. Narcissism is a difficult condition to therapeutically remedy but some research suggests that in rare cases it can happen (Malkin, 2013).

7. Severe Mental and Physical Illness

People who suffer from acute illness may lack the ability to experience heroic transformation. It is true that some people with monumental health challenges can sometimes use those challenges to achieve a miraculous enlightenment.

These are rare but notable exemplars of change under dire circumstances (see Allison & Goethals, 2011). Most individuals facing severe mental or physical disability are unable to reap the benefits of the hero's journey because they are preoccupied with managing their condition. Physical and emotional therapies can help, as can time, patience, spiritual practices, and mentoring.

8. Psychological Flexibility

People show individual differences in psychological flexibility, defined as an individual's ability to adapt to fluctuating situational demands. Those classified as low in psychological flexibility have been shown to experience less growth and development (Kashdan & Rottenberg, 2010). To help people overcome inflexibility, Hayes, Strosahl, and Wilson (2011) developed a therapeutic approach called acceptance and commitment therapy (ACT). The goal of ACT is to increase the ability to contact the present moment more fully as a conscious human being, and to change behavior when doing so serves valued goals. Psychological flexibility is established through six core ACT processes, several of which sound like mindful pathways to Buddhist enlightenment. The six elements of ACT are acceptance, cognitive defusion, being present, self as context, values, and committed action. All of these processes are viewed as positive psychological skills that enable people to grow and evolve into healthy adaptive human beings. They also resemble Franco, Efthimiou, and Zimbardo's (2016) skillset of heroic eudaimonia, which includes mindfulness, autonomy, and efficacy (see also Jones, 2017).

CONCLUSION

This chapter has reviewed the functions, processes, and consequences of the hero's transformation. William James once observed, "Whenever one aim grows so stable as to expel definitively its previous rivals from an individual's life, we tend to speak of the phenomenon, and even wonder at it, as a transformation" (James, 1902/2013, p. 70, italics added). James' use of the word "wonder" implies that people are moved by the transformations they see in people, and also that these transformations are a rare occurrence. As did James, we suspect that many people spend their entire lives resisting change, denying the need for it, and suffering as a result of avoiding it. As Jung (1945) observed, "There is no coming to consciousness without pain. People will do anything, no matter how absurd, in order to avoid facing their own soul. One does not become enlightened by imagining figures of light, but by making the darkness conscious" (p. 335).

The transformed hero represents the zenith of human maturity, the state of well-being that allows people to flourish (Seligman, 2011), achieve "bliss" (Campbell, 1988), and experience eudaimonia (Franco et al., 2016). As a result of their journey, heroes acquire wisdom about themselves and the world; they develop the courage to face their inner dragons; they are in union with all of humanity; they pursue justice even at a cost to themselves; they are humbled and tempered; and they embark on a journey that "opens the world so that it becomes transparent to something that is beyond speech, beyond words, in short, to what we call transcendence" (Campbell, 2014, p. 40; see also Friedman, 2017). The wisdom of writers and philosophers, from Homer in 800 BCE to Phil Zimbardo today, tells us that we are all called to lead a heroic life. Yet most people are unaware of this fact, or they face impediments that thwart the realization of their heroic potential. If the ultimate goal of the hero's journey is for the hero to bestow the world with transformative gifts, then one would think that the world would be doing everything possible to promote the hero's journey for everyone. Yet the hero's transformation remains a secret, avoided by many or most people, perhaps because it clashes with our Western notion of linear, unabated "progress" from cradle to grave (Rohr, 2011).

I offer one final thought with which to conclude this chapter. Central to the phenomenon of transformation is the principle of *transcend and include*. Higher stages of transformation do not discard the values of the lower stages; they include them. When we were young and held strong opinions that later seem naïve to us, we were not wrong at the time. We were merely incomplete. To illustrate this idea, my dear friend George Goethals has mused many times about his childhood baseball hero, Willie Mays. Goethals freely admits that his taste in heroes has evolved and matured since the 1950s, yet if you ask him if that means that Mays is no longer his hero, Goethals will quickly tell you that Mays remains his hero to this very day. This exemplifies the principle of transcend and include. Transformation to a higher level of consciousness always transcends but also includes the lower levels (Rohr, 2011). Joseph Campbell's (1949) understanding of this phenomenon is seen in the phrase, "master of both worlds". At the end of their transformative journey, heroes are comfortable navigating in their original world as well as in the new world order that they help create.

REFERENCES

Alicke, M. (2017). Willful ignorance and self-deception. Psychology Today. Retrieved from https://www.psychologytoday.com/us/blog/why-we-blame/201709/willful-ignorance-and-self-deception

Allison, S. T. (2015). The initiation of heroism science. Heroism Science, 1, 1-8.

Allison, S. T., & Goethals, G. R. (2011). Heroes: What they do and why we need them. New York: Oxford University Press.

Allison, S. T., & Goethals, G. R. (2013). Heroic leadership: An influence taxonomy of 100 exceptional individuals. New York: Routledge.

Allison, S. T., & Goethals, G. R. (2014). "Now he belongs to the ages": The heroic leadership dynamic and deep narratives of greatness. In Goethals, G. R., Allison, S. T., Kramer, R., & Messick, D. (Eds.), Conceptions of leadership: Enduring ideas and emerging insights. New York: Palgrave Macmillan. doi: 10.1057/9781137472038.0011

Allison, S. T., & Goethals, G. R. (2016). Hero worship: The elevation of the human spirit. Journal for the Theory of Social Behaviour, 46, 187-210.

Allison, S. T., & Goethals, G. R. (2017). The hero's transformation. In S. T. Allison, G. R. Goethals, & R. M. Kramer (Eds.), Handbook of heroism and heroic leadership. New York: Routledge.

Allison, S. T., Goethals, G. R., Marrinan, A. R., Parker, O. M., Spyrou, S. P., Stein, M. (2019). The metamorphosis of the hero: Principles, processes, and purpose. Frontiers in Psychology.

Allison, S. T., & Setterberg, G. C. (2016). Suffering and sacrifice: Individual and collective benefits, and implications for leadership. In S. T. Allison, C. T. Kocher, & G. R. Goethals (Eds), Frontiers in spiritual leadership: Discovering the better angels of our nature. New York: Palgrave Macmillan.

Allison, S. T. & Smith, G. (2015). Reel heroes & villains. Richmond: Agile Writer Press.

Bargh, J. A., & Morsella, E. (2008). The unconscious mind. Perspectives on Psychological Science, 3, 12-30.

Bergman, I. (1961). Through a glass darkly. Stockholm: Janus Films.

Bressert, S. (2018). Narcissistic Personality Disorder. Psych Central. Retrieved on May 21, 2018, from https://psychcentral.com/disorders/narcissistic-personality-disorder/

Brown, A. J. (2017). Whistleblowers as heroes. In S. T. Allison, G. R. Goethals, & R. M. Kramer (Eds.), Handbook of heroism and heroic leadership. New York: Routledge.

Burns, J. M. (1978). Leadership. Harper & Row, New York.

Campbell, J. (1949). The hero with a thousand faces. New York: New World Library.

Campbell, J. (1972). Myths to live by. New York: Viking Press.

Campbell, J. (1988). The power of myth. New York: Anchor Books.

Campbell, J. (1991). Reflections on the art of living. New York: HarperCollins.

Campbell, J. (2004). Pathways to bliss. Novata, CA: New World Library.

Campbell, J. (2014). The hero's journey. San Francisco, CA; New World Library.

Chakrabortty, A. (2010). Brain food: The psychology of heroism. Retrieved on September 15, 2015 from http://www.theguardian.com/science/2010/mar/09/brain-food-psychology-heroism

Davis, J. L., Burnette, J. L., Allison, S. T., & Stone, H. (2011). Against the odds: Academic underdogs benefit from incremental theories. Social Psychology of Education, 14, 331-346.

Efthimiou, O. (2015). The search for the hero gene: Fact or fiction? International Advances in Heroism Science, 1, 1-6.

Efthimiou, O. (2017). The hero organism: Advancing the embodiment of heroism thesis in the 21st century. In S. T., Allison, G. R., Goethals, & R. M. Kramer (Eds.), Handbook of heroism and heroic leadership. New York, NY: Routledge.

Efthimiou, O., & Allison, S. T. (2017). Heroism science: Frameworks for an emerging field. Journal of Humanistic Psychology. 10.1177/0022167817708063

Efthimiou, O., & Franco, Z. E. (2017). Heroic Intelligence: The Hero's Journey as an Evolutionary and Existential Blueprint. Journal of Genius and Eminence, 2(2), 32-43.

Efthimiou, O., Allison, S. T., & Franco, Z. E. (2018a). Heroism and wellbeing in the 21st century: Recognizing our personal heroic imperative. In O. Efthimiou, S. T. Allison, & Z. E. Franco (Eds.), Heroism and wellbeing in the 21st Century: Applied and emerging perspectives. New York: Routledge.

Efthimiou, O., Allison, S. T., & Franco, Z. E. (2018b). Definition, synthesis, and applications of heroic wellbeing. In O. Efthimiou, S. T. Allison, & Z. E. Franco (Eds.), Heroism and wellbeing in the 21st Century: Applied and emerging perspectives. New York: Routledge.

Erikson, E. H. (1994). Identity and the life cycle. New York: W. W. Norton & Company.

Franco, Z. E., Efthimiou, O., & Zimbardo, P. G. (2016). Heroism and eudaimonia: Sublime actualization through the embodiment of virtue. In J. Vittersø (Ed.), Handbook of eudaimonic wellbeing. New York: Springer.

Freud, S. (1905/2011). Three essays on the theory sexuality. Eastford, CT: Martino Fine Books.

Friedman, H. L. (2017). Everyday heroism in practicing psychology. Journal of Humanistic Psychology. https://doi.org/10.1177/0022167817696843

Goethals, G. R. & Allison, S. T. (2012). Making heroes: The construction of courage, competence and virtue. Advances in Experimental Social Psychology, 46, 183-235. doi: 10.1016/B978-0-12-394281-4.00004-0

Goethals, G. R., & Allison, S. T. (2014). Kings and charisma, Lincoln and leadership: An evolutionary perspective. In Goethals, G. R., Allison, S. T., Kramer, R., & Messick, D. (Eds.), Conceptions of leadership: Enduring ideas and emerging insights. New York: Palgrave Macmillan. doi: 10.1057/9781137472038

Grace, J. (2016). Heroic counseling. Retrieved on September 10, 2015 from http://heroiccounseling.com/

Haidt, J. (2003). Elevation and the positive psychology of morality. In C. L. M. Keyes & J. Haidt (Eds.), Flourishing: Positive psychology and the life well-lived (pp. 275-289). Washington DC: American Psychological Association.

Hanh, T. N. (1999). The heart of the Buddha's teaching. New York: Broadway Books.

Hayes, S. C., Strosahl, K. D., & Wilson, K. G. (2011). Acceptance and commitment therapy: The process and practice of mindful change. New York: The Guilford Press.

Heroic Imagination Project (2018). Retrieved from https://www.heroicimagination.org/

Hollander, E. P. (1995). Ethical challenges in the leader–follower relationship. Business Ethics Quarterly, 5, 55–65.

James, W. (1902). The varieties of religious experience. Boston, MA: Bedford

Jones, P. (2017). Mindfulness-based heroism: Creating mindful heroes. Journal of Humanistic Psychology. https://doi.org/10.1177/0022167817711303

Jung, C. (1945). Alchemical studies. Princeton, NJ: Princeton University Press.

Jung, C. (1956). The archetypes and the collective unconscious. Princeton: Princeton University Press.

Kashdan, T., & Rottenberg, J. (2010). Psychological flexibility as a fundamental aspect of health Clinical Psychology Review, 30 (7), 865-878

Keck, B., Compton, L., Schoeneberg, C., & Compton, T. (2017). Trauma recover: A heroic journey. Heroism Science, 2, 1-17.

Kinsella, E.L., Ritchie, T.D., & Igou, E.R. (2015). Lay perspectives on the social and psychological functions of heroes. Frontiers in Psychology, 6, 130. doi: 10.3389/fpsyg.2015.00130

Kinsella, E.L., Ritchie, T.D., & Igou, E.R. (2017). Attributes and applications of heroes: A brief history of lay and academic perspectives. In S. T. Allison, G. R. Goethals, & R. M. Kramer (Eds.), Handbook of heroism and heroic leadership. New York: Routledge.

Langdon, M. (2016). The hero construction company. Retrieved September 15, 2015 from http://www.theherocc.com/

Latane, B., & Darley, J. (1969). Bystander "Apathy". American Scientist, 57, 244-268.

Le Grice, K. (2013). The rebirth of the hero: Mythology as a guide to spiritual transformation. London: Muswell Hill Press.

Lopez, S. J., & Snyder, C. R. (Eds.) (2011). The Oxford handbook of positive psychology. New York: Oxford University Press.

Malkin, C. (2013). Can narcissists change? Psychology Today. Retrieved from https://www.psychologytoday.com/us/blog/romance-redux/201309/can-narcissists-chang%C3%A9

Maslow, A. (1943.) A theory of human motivation. Psychological Review, 50, 370–396.

Nisbett, R., & Wilson, T. D. (1977). Telling more than we can know. Psychological Review, 84, 231-259.

Phipps, R. (2011). My trip to Melbourne. Retrieved September 8, 2015 from http://quotationsbook.com/quote/35768/

Rank, O. (1909). Der mythus von der geburt des helden. Berlin, Germany: Franz Deuticke.

Ramos, C., & Leal, I. (2013). Posttraumatic growth in the aftermath of trauma: A literature review about related factors and application contexts. Psychology, Community & Health, 2, 43–54, doi:10.5964/pch.v2i1.39

Rendon, J. (2015). Upside: The new science of post-traumatic growth. New York: Touchstone.

Rohr, R. (2011). Falling upward. Hoboken, NJ: Jossey-Bass.

Rohr, R. (2014). Eager to love. Cincinnati, OH: Franciscan Media.

Sedikides, C. & Hepper, E. G. D. (2009). Self-improvement. Social and Personality Psychology Compass, 3, 899-917.

Seligman, M. E. P. (2011). Flourish. New York: Atria Books.

Simmons, A. (2012). The crab syndrome. San Antonio, TX: Antuan Simmons.

Sperry, L. (2011). Spirituality in clinical practice. New York: Routledge.

Swann, W. B., Jr. (2012). Self-verification theory. In P. Van Lang, A. Kruglanski, & E.T. Higgins (Eds.), pp 23-42. Handbook of Theories of Social Psychology. London: Sage.

Thomson, A. L., & Siegel, J. T. (2013). A moral act, elevation, and prosocial behavior: Moderators of morality. The Journal of Positive Psychology, 8, 50-64.

Turner, V. W. (1966). The ritual process: Structure and anti-structure. Ithaca, NY: Cornell University Press.

Tyler, J. & Lind, (1992). A relational model of authority in groups. Advances in Experimental Social Psychology, 25, 115-191.

van Gennep, A. (1909). The rites of passage. Paris: Émile Nourry.

Wegner, D. (2002). The illusion of conscious will. Cambridge: MIT Press.

Wilber, K. (2007). Integral spirituality. Boulder, CO: Hambhala.

Worthington, E. L, & Allison, S. T. (2018). Heroic humility: What the science of humility can say to people raised on self-focus. Washington. DC: American Psychological Association.

Yalom, I. & Leszcz, M. (2005). Theory and practice of group psychotherapy. New York: Basic Books.

Zimbardo, P. (2008). The Lucifer effect: Understanding how good people turn evil. New York: Random House.

SECTION 1: FILM AND TELEVISION HEROES

1

From Little Princess to Mother of Dragons: Daenerys Targaryen's Heroine's Journey

HALLIE M. WHITING

In the Temple of the Dosh Khaleen, Dothraki warriors speak in their native tongue about the fate of the pretty, pale, white-haired girl standing before them. "Don't you want to know what I think?," she calmly questions. The towering pillars, burning goblets of fire, and patronizing gazes are no sources of intimidation to Daenerys. "You are small men. None of you are fit to lead the Dothraki. But I am. So I will." Laughter erupts from the men, but their ridicule and insults are nothing to Daenerys when she takes one hand on the burning goblet and effortlessly pushes it over to set fire to the entire building, burning all the men inside. The wooden temple burns to the ground, but Daenerys Targaryen emerges from the ashes. She is not a little princess, a widow, or slave. She is the Mother of Dragons (Benioff, 2016).

Shakespeare posed an important question centuries ago: "What's in a name?" (Shakespeare, 1597/1985). In *Game of Thrones*, Daenerys Targaryen's name contains almost all of her life: Daenerys of the House Targaryen, the First of Her Name, The Unburnt, Queen of the Andals, the Rhoynar and the First Men, Queen of Meereen, Khaleesi of the Great Grass Sea, Protector of the Realm, Lady Regnant of the Seven Kingdoms, Breaker of Chains, and Mother of Dragons (Daenerys Targaryen, 2017). While the lengthiness of her name certainly speaks to her ability as a conqueror and ruler, it does not do her life story justice. Daenerys serves as a heroine to not only the fictional world which she lives in but also to the reality in which we admire her. The purpose of this chapter is to offer an analysis of the heroine's transformation of Daenerys Targaryen, drawing from the literature of heroism science.

THE HEROINE'S JOURNEY

Joseph Campbell identified a pattern of narrative that exists in the dramas, stories, myths, and religious rituals of all time periods and named it, "The Hero's Journey" (Campbell, 1949). The journey is partitioned into three stages: departure, initiation, and return. Within those three stages are five to six "mini stages" which the hero takes on before moving into next stage. The hero's journey exists within every ancient and modern story because it reflects our human unconscious wishes and dreams, and it calls us to go on the same journey.

The hero's journey exists in *Game of Thrones* just as much as it exists in the Bible or Star Wars. Daenerys Targaryen's journey is significant for several reasons. The first is that she holds the most potential to take control of the Iron Throne and -- both metaphorically and literally -- win the Game of Thrones. The second reason is that her story is significant to a large audience that, for many centuries, has been and is still overlooked: women. The path of men and women's lives are drastically different, especially in patriarchal societies where men are taken much more seriously in social, political, and economic battles. From the day she was born, Daenerys was certainly not raised nor expected to become the powerful political player and moral heroine she is now. The term "hero" is technically masculine and, the research done on heroes often does not account for the heroine's journey. While many of the stages are similar to those of the hero's journey, the heroine's journey is certainly not identical because of the additional battles of sexism that heroines must fight. The heroine's journey begins as all hero's journeys do when she is summoned with a call to adventure.

Departure

Joseph Campbell describes the first step of the hero's journey as the "call to adventure" (Campbell, 1949). This call can either be accepted or refused, but the multitude of heroic stories indicate that the hero's response often does not affect the continuance of the journey. At the beginning of *Game of Thrones*, Daenerys was a naive pawn used by the men in her family battling in a political war. She was forced on her heroine's journey when her older brother, Viserys, sold her in an arranged marriage to Khal Drogo of the Dothraki clan in exchange for the Dothraki army. At this time, her future appeared very bleak as she was forced to abandon her home and be dehumanized into a tool of reproduction for the Dothraki clan. On her wedding night, she receives three dragon eggs as a gift. Dragons had been extinct for decades, and the eggs would not hatch, so the present initially seemed useless and would only exist as decor. However, she eventually discovers that the eggs begin to hatch when they come into her ownership. The abrupt marriage arrangement is important to her journey because the departure stage of the heroine's journey awakens the heroine to a growth mindset (Allison et al., 2017; Worthington & Allison, 2018), meaning she learns that her identity is not fixed, and "the old concepts, ideals, and emotional patterns no longer fit" (Krucli, n.d.). At the beginning of the journey, Daenerys learns that she has not fully developed her identity and sense of self within her world.

Daenerys as an Underdog

On her wedding night, the youthful Daenerys is raped by the aggressive Khal Drogo. This moment was disheartening to watch because Daenerys is an underdog in the series. Underdogs are defined as "disadvantaged parties facing advantaged opponents and unlikely to succeed" (Vandello et al., 2017). Daenerys is an underdog because she is young, naive, and alone. The numbers favor her captors because they are both stronger physically and numerically as a group.

Daenerys doesn't know how to defend herself until a Dothraki woman becomes her mentor in that moment and teaches her how to come into contact with her inner Khaleesi, or "queen" through taking advantage of Drogo's carnal urges. By taking control in the bedroom, Daenerys shows Drogo that she refuses to be his submissive. It is in this moment that their relationship drastically changes from one of slave and slave-keeper, to husband and wife. The transformation within this relationship once again reflects Daenerys' growth mindset.

The heroine can never complete her journey alone; it often takes at least one guide to teach her lessons that her current self cannot learn on her own. The writer's choice to make Daenerys' aid a woman is intentional because female power and women helping women is a significant aspect of the heroine's journey that shapes Daenerys' perspective on her own heroine's journey. Without the unnamed woman's help, Daenerys would have lived an unsatisfying life of submissive wife. One could argue that the unnamed woman was a heroine herself. There are three categories in which heroes fall: enhancing, moral modeling, and protecting (Kinsella et al., 2017). The unnamed woman certainly falls into the enhancing category because she uplifts Daenerys and enriches her life, even for a short period of time. The woman's identity, or lack thereof, also contributes to her heroism because she does not gain anything out of the situation which is typical of heroism.

Belly of the Whale

The "belly of the whale" stage refers to the point in the heroine's life that, "rather than conquering what lies beyond, the heroine is swallowed into the unknown" (Sargeant, 2013). As soon as the heroine thinks she knows what the journey will look like, her entire world is flipped upside down. The tumultuous journey out of the heroine's comfort zone is pushed further as the heroine "find herself trapped in the antagonist's backyard" (Sargeant, 2013). The purpose of the "belly of the whale" stage is to foreshadow the path of the heroine's journey. In Daenerys' case, her moment is when Khal Drogo and their first born child dies of infection and she is locked away in the widow's hut where she will spend her days praying. Her moment as a worshipped Khaleesi halts when Khal Drogo dies because, up until this point, he had essentially served as her bodyguard against the oppressive expectations that the Dothraki society places on women who are not associated with men of high status. Daenerys is able to use her intelligence and other heroic attributes to escape the widow's hut, her journey's "belly of the whale." This stage foreshadows her heroic path by revealing her life's purpose as a woman of power and independence.

Initiation

The initiation stage is the longest period of Daenerys' life, and arguably, is the most important stage of the heroine's journey. During this time, Daenerys' identity is solidified as she ascends to power. She slowly gains armies, earns allies, and makes enemies not by conquering with a fist of fury and rage, but by showing she is to be trusted and taken seriously.

The stereotypically-viewed feminine aspects of her identity are remarkably important to why she is arguably the most pivotal character in *Game of Thrones*. In the entertainment industry, masculinity is reserved for male characters and femininity is for female characters. In Game of Thrones, the lack of gender diversity in the royal realm causes many of the male rulers to use the same strategies because the traditionally masculine methods are all they know. In other words, the men are not accustomed to non-masculine methods of leadership or war, so they rise to power just as they fall from power. The women in *Game of Thrones* are arguably smarter rulers because have the capacity to choose strategies from both the masculine and feminine categories. Daenerys favors strategies that enact cooperation, independence, and mutual benefit because she was denied these qualities for most of her life. Unlike many of her counterparts, Daenerys does not lose the essence of herself as she becomes more powerful. While she does abandon her naive, little girl identity behind, her empathy for the oppressed and passion for justice only grows stronger.

Man as the Tempter

One of the "sub-steps" of the initiation stage is referred to as the "man as the tempter." This stage is when the heroine faces temptations, often of a physical or pleasurable nature, that may lead her to abandon or stray from her quest (Campbell, 1949). Daenerys is tempted to abandon her quest when a warlock creates an illusion of her late husband, Khal Drogo, who asks her to join him in the afterlife with their son. She escapes the dream because she knows that her true destiny is not wifehood or motherhood, but something much greater. Like many other heroes, Daenerys' has an epiphany that reveals her destiny to avenge her family and those like her by taking the Iron Throne. Daenerys now has a new-found purpose for living, and everything she does after this point will focus on the steps she must take to fulfill her duty. After realizing her destiny, it is not long until the audience finds them watching the "little, naive princess" burning down a hut of Dothraki leaders, as described at the beginning of this chapter.

Return

The latest season of *Game of Thrones* encapsulates Daenerys' beginning steps in the "Return" stage of the hero's journey. She returns to her home in Dragonstone for the first time since she was born, and she is officially identified as a major player in the game in the eyes of the Iron Throne. Daenerys also teams up with the great male hero from the north, Jon Snow, who shows her that there is not just one war being fought in Westeros.

The next season is the final season of the series which means the audience will finally see the precise nature and shape Daenerys' return stage of her heroine's journey. Many critics question Daenerys' sanity, going as far as to say she is turning into her father who was known as "the mad king." This begs the question: Will next season's events shape Daenerys into a hero or a villain? With all of her new power, will she be able to maintain her morals and use her dragons for overall good? It's important to emphasize "overall" because while the basis of Daenerys' campaign is to free the people that the ruling family, the Lannisters, put into slavery and avenge the oppressed, she has to make some very difficult decisions that could be seen as evil. The idea of someone watching the scene where Daenerys kills the Dothraki men in the hut with no context and then labelling Daenerys as evil is known as "consequentialism" (Li, 2015). Knowing the entirety of the story leads the viewer to adapt a "bad deed for overall good" point of view. Daenerys may be killing men, but she is doing it to rid the world of a few oppressors and continue her journey to create a more just and equal Westeros.

TYPES OF TRANSFORMATIONS

Daenerys begins her journey as a naive young girl and will likely end as a strong, powerful, queen. In both the hero's and heroine's journeys, transformations do not typically occur overnight. The time it takes to grow as a person is referred to as a "journey" for good reason. Allison and Smith (2015) identified several types of transformations that heroes undergo such as moral, emotional, intellectual, and physical.

Moral Transformation

Heroes who experience a moral change must overcome a personal value that prevents them from reaching their greatest potential (Allison & Smith, 2015). For Daenerys, a moral transformation that she undergoes is one operating from a sense of entitlement and power to one deriving from a sense of duty and justice (G.E., 2017). As a princess turned Khaleesi, power runs through her veins which leads to a recurring close-call between lust for burning her enemies alive in dragon fire and passion to undo injustices. Daenerys' critics who predict she will morph into the mad king that her father was usually point to her moral transformation as being incomplete. While notions of her moral transformation being incomplete are valid because the journey is not complete, the previous seasons allow viewers to infer that Daenerys is not on the same path as her father. Unlike her father, Daenerys undertook a journey from princess to slave, and now that she understands what it is like to be patronized and abused, her identity will never revert back to one of entitlement. The essence of Daenerys' return will be one of reestablishing justice in Westeros.

Emotional Transformation

The emotional transformation refers to "transformations of the heart, and they include heroes who, through adversity, grow into courage, resilience, and empathy" (Allison et al., 2017). As mentioned previously, Daenerys emotionally transforms from being naive and weak to compassionate and strong. The season one plotline follows Daenerys' transformation from being a terrified obedient to a total independent. The emotional transformation is extremely prevalent in the heroine's journey in comparison to the hero's journey. In the words of Richard Rohr, "if you do not transform your pain, you will transmit it" (Rohr, 2011). Daenerys allows herself to accept pain and transform it to strengthen her relationships instead of allowing her pain to foster her motivation to avenge her family and the oppressed.

Intellectual Transformation

An intellectual transformation refers to a change in mental abilities or fundamental insights about the world (Allison et al., 2017). Coming-of-age stories are perfect examples of such transformations. Many heroic journeys feature a hero or heroine as a child or adolescent, a time of development when growing into wisdom becomes paramount. Daenerys is forced to mature very quickly when she is married to Khal Drogo. The audience can relate to Daenerys' initial fear and hesitations because of moments in their own lives that forced them to grow up, moments such as moving from home and going to college. The intellectual transformation is important to the heroine's journey because it was vital for Daenerys to mature in order to understand her role in changing her society. If Daenerys did not mature enough to accept the role as Khal Drogo's wife and transform it into a position of personal power, she never could have continued on the heroine's journey because she wouldn't have acquired the mental strength to do so.

Physical Transformation

The fourth transformation is the physical transformation, which refers to the heroine's bodily or physical change. Physical transformations are more prevalent in hero's journeys than in heroine's journeys. This male bias may exist because traditionally men use physical strength as a means of bringing about change while women use other strategies such as communication. Daenerys experiences a physical metamorphosis by becoming impervious to fire. More importantly, she often refers to the hatching of the dragons as the birth of her children. Although Daenerys was not literally pregnant with dragons, her connection with them is so strong that she feels like their hatching was a birth she labored. This physical transformation is significant to her heroine's journey because it resulted in her newfound sense of responsibility. Daenerys must take great caution in her decisions throughout her journey because her death doesn't only affect her. If Daenerys is reckless and is imprisoned or killed, her dragons will be motherless and likely enslaved. The physical transformation heightens the stakes of her journey, and it pushes Daenerys to improve her response to pressure, hence, strengthening her role as a heroine.

Gender Significance in the Hero's Journey

Brief references to the significance of Daenerys' gender as a heroine do not do justice to the importance of this demographic variable. Traditional gender stereotypes have been injurious to women and have followed the mindset that "women take care" and "men take charge" (Hoyt, 2014). Historically, women have been restricted to the homely realm, while men have had the freedom to move autonomously throughout life. The media and entertainment industries have been no exception to this patriarchal rule. In the top 100 films of 2016, women represented

29% of all protagonists (2016 Statistics, n.d.). Daenerys' womanhood is not only important to the other women in Game of Thrones, but also to the society in which her audience admires her.

Dimensional Characters

Increasing the number of female protagonists in the entertainment industry is important, but an important aspect of creating female characters is promoting dimensional women like Daenerys. Her identity is not entirely shaped by her relationships with men in the show. She has qualities that stereotypically reside in both the masculine and feminine categories such as strength, determination, compassion, and love. Hoyt writes that Hillary Clinton claims she personally experienced society working tirelessly at labeling women as either "a hard working professional woman or a conscientious and caring hostess" (Hoyt, 2014). By creating female characters with multiple dimensions, *Game of Thrones* allows the audience to relate much more profoundly to the character of Daenerys.

Daenerys acknowledges her gender, but does not let it define her. Many of her obstacles include convincing men that she is not their submissive princess. Instead of taking the insults men hurl at her, she throws them right back at these men. "Woman? Is that meant to insult me? I would return the slap if I took you for a man" (Martin, 2000).

Burning down a hut of men who want to enslave her is extremely satisfying to watch for feminist viewers who sometimes wish they could do the same. Another example of Daenerys teaching men that beauty is not to be confused with naivety occurs when she is making a trade to free 'The Unsullied', an army of elite warriors. The slave owner agrees to trade his massive army for one of her dragons. After Daenerys takes possession of the army, she frees them, and after witnessing her genuine passion for justice, the army unanimously decides to serve her despite their newfound ability to live freely. Daenerys outwits the slave owner because he underestimates the loyalty she has cultivated with her dragons which are historically perceived to be untamable. The dragon burns the slave owner to ashes, and Daenerys is soon recognized as a major player in the war to win the game of thrones.

Women Helping Women

Daenerys personally experiences the effects of a patriarchal society, so whenever an opportunity to uplift a woman presents itself, she does not ignore it. Missandei was originally a slave until she was freed by Daenerys and offered a high position as Daenerys' trusted advisor. Another example of women helping women is seen when Daenerys meets Yara Greyjoy. The female characters saw bits of themselves in each other, for they both had terrible fathers and are both battling the same battles against sexism while working to maintain their position in a much grander war.

Women helping women is an important theme in the heroine's journey that the hero's journey lacks. In the heroine's journey, there is more of an emphasis on community growth, an essential but often overlooked consequence of heroic action (Efthimiou, Allison, & Franco, 2018). In the hero's journey, the men may be fighting similar battles, but they are ultimately working towards different goals. In the heroine's journey, an undercurrent of a gender-based battle exists within every story. All the women in Westeros experience sexism, so they all have something common between them that unites them in a way that the men cannot fathom. Daenerys couldn't have continued on her journey without the help of other women, and she understands that she has a duty to help uplift other women as well.

CONCLUSION

While *Game of Thrones* is set in a fictional land, themes of power and gender ultimately connect the audience to reality. The world we live in is far from achieving equality among genders. For example, the United States has yet to elect a woman as President, women in Saudi Arabia only recently earned the right to drive, and there are more CEOs named John than there are CEOs that are women (Wolfers, 2015). Like many female political figures today, Daenerys has to work twice as hard to get to the same place as her male counterparts. The entertainment industry's role is to entertain its audience, and it does so by holding up a mirror to society and picking out different themes and issues on which to focus.

Daenerys is the perfect example of the entertainment industry dipping its toes into creating dynamic, powerful female protagonists. This movement is important because showing powerful women on television can motivate people to achieve gender equality in the real world. Dimensional female characters that people can relate to can drastically impact the perceptions of women as leaders. When Daenerys ascends to power and finishes the heroine's journey by changing her society into a more equal world, a ripple effect can be set in motion. Daenerys' success as a woman and as a character has challenged the entertainment industry to create more dimensional female protagonists, thus challenging women in the real world to model these powerful characters' behaviors. The media definitely influences people's decisions, and *Game of Thrones* poses the question: Could Daenerys' success as a heroine inspire real women to take on their own heroine's journey? Time will tell.

REFERENCES

Allison, S. T. (2015). The initiation of heroism science. Heroism Science, 1, 1-8.

Allison, S. T., & Goethals, G. R. (2017). The hero's transformation. In S. T. Allison, G. R. Goethals, & R. M. Kramer (Eds.), Handbook of heroism and heroic leadership. New York: Routledge.

Allison, S. T., Goethals, G. R., & Kramer, R. M. (2017). Setting the scene: The rise and coalescence of heroism science. In S. T. Allison, G. R. Goethals, & R. M. Kramer (Eds.), Handbook of heroism and heroic leadership. New York: Routledge.

Allison, S. T., Goethals, G. R., & Kramer, R. M. (Eds.) (2017). Handbook of heroism and heroic leadership. New York: Routledge.

Allison, S. T., Goethals, G. R., Marrinan, A. R., Parker, O. M., Spyrou, S. P., Stein, M. (2019). The metamorphosis of the hero: Principles, processes, and purpose. Frontiers in Psychology.

Benioff, David.; Weiss, D.B. (Writers), & Sackheim, Daniel. (Director). (2016). Book of the Stranger [Television series episode]. In D. Benioff (Producer), Game of Thrones. New York: HBO Home Entertainment.

Campbell, J. (1949) The hero with a thousand faces. Princeton, NJ: Princeton University Press.

Davis, J. L., Burnette, J. L., Allison, S. T., & Stone, H. (2011). Against the odds: Academic underdogs benefit from incremental theories. Social Psychology of Education, 14, 331-346.

Daenerys Targaryen. (n.d.). In Game of Thrones Wiki. Retrieved October 4, 2017, from http://gameofthrones.wikia.com/wiki/Daenerys_Targaryen

Efthimiou, O., Allison, S. T., & Franco, Z. E. (Eds.) (2018). Heroism and wellbeing in the 21st Century: Applied and emerging perspectives. New York: Routledge.

Eylon, D., & Allison, S. T. (2005). The frozen in time effect in evaluations of the dead. Personality and Social Psychology Bulletin, 31, 1708-1717.

G.E. (2017, July). What is the moral compass of "Game of Thrones"?. The Economist. https://www.economist.com/blogs/prospero/2017/07/how-westeros-won

Gray, K., Anderson, S., Doyle, C. M., Hester, N., Schmitt, P., Vonasch, A., Allison, S. T., and Jackson, J. C. (2018). To be immortal, do good or evil. Personality and Social Psychology Bulletin.

Hoyt, C. L. (2014). Social identities and leadership: The case of gender. In Goethals, G. R., et al. (Eds.), Conceptions of leadership: Enduring ideas and emerging insights. New York: Palgrave Macmillan.

Krucli. (n.d.). Joseph Campbell's "The Hero Journey". [PDF] Retrieved October 6, 2017, from http://www.krucli.com/Joseph_Campbell_Hero_Journey.pdf

Li, Yi. (2015). Consequentialism in Game of Thrones. Retrieved from https://winteriscoming.net/2014/12/16/explain-noble-kill-10000-men-battle-dozen-dinner-consequentialism-game-thrones/

Sargeant, J. (2013, October, 20). The Hero's Journey: The Belly of the Whale [Blog post]. Retrieved from https://mastersarge.wordpress.com/2013/10/20/1651/

Shakespeare, W. (1597/1985). Romeo and Juliet. Woodbury, N.Y: Barron's.

Statistics 2016. (n.d.). Retrieved from https://womenandhollywood.com/resources/statistics/2016-statistics/

Vandello, J. A., Goldschmied, Nadav; & Michniewicz, Kenneth. (2017). Underdogs as heroes. In S. T. Allison, G. R. Goethals, & R. M. Kramer (Eds.), Handbook of heroism and heroic leadership. New York: Routledge.

Walker, W. T. (2011). Men's Pain and Transformation [Blog post]. Retrieved from http://www.beamsandstruts.com/articles/item/608-on-mens-pain#startOfPageId608

Wolfers, J. (2015, March 2). Fewer Women Run Big Companies Than Men Named John. The New York Times. Retrieved from https://www.nytimes.com/2015/03/03/upshot/fewer-women-run-big-companies-than-men-named-john.html

Worthington, E. L, & Allison, S. T. (2018). Heroic humility: What the science of humility can say to people raised on self-focus. Washington. DC: American Psychological Association.

2

ELLE WOODS, LEGALLY BLONDE, AND THE HERO'S JOURNEY: WHAT, LIKE, IT'S HARD?

REGHAN J. RUF

"I'm never going to be good enough for you, am I?" asks Elle Woods, dressed in hot-pink fishnet tights, a playboy bunny costume, hot pink peep-toe wedges, and matching satin bunny ears. Elle commands the attention of any and every room, but in this instance, she commands the attention of a room full of people who want nothing to do with her. They are wearing cable knit sweaters featuring varying shades of beige and eggshell white, pantyhose, collared shirts, and pleated skirts ending just above the knee. They are glancing at each other while sipping glasses of hundred-dollar Merlot, tightly crossing their legs, sitting up straight, and smirking at Elle. She holds her ground, throws an insult or two at the ring leader, and sashays out of the room, heading directly to collect what she came for. She sees him, talks to him even, but her face begins to change. She loses the signature light in her eyes, the gold radiating off of her person dims, and she shrinks into herself. She has lost, and they, he, has won; unsurprisingly, she is not content with this outcome, and she is prepared to fight.

Elle Woods, a Bel-Air native and daughter of two very successful parents, is quite accustomed to standing out in a room full of people who are dulled by her radiance. She is not, however, accustomed to standing out in a negative context; in fact, humiliation, especially socially, is a phenomenon completely foreign to her. She is excluded not only physically, but in every aspect of her life: her presence is unwanted, she is gazed at under disapproving eyes, and she is regarded across the room as a simple, air-headed blonde with no substance to her whatsoever. Elle has no allies: she is alone in this battle, despite the fact that she worked just as hard as every other player to make it to the field.

Elle is a seasoned player, however, and she remains unscathed when faced with humiliation on the grounds that she is dressed completely differently than everyone else in the room; it is not until she is rejected that she truly begins to falter. It is quite clear that Elle, especially in this situation, is the underdog. She is put up against the judgmental, clique-ish Harvard Law students, and no one truly expects her to even make it through a semester at Harvard, let alone somehow come out on top. It is this very attitude, this preconceived idea that, based on her appearance and her different socialization, she will completely and utterly fail at Harvard, that causes her to transform motivationally and intellectually in a manner consistent with underdog heroes.

OVERVIEW OF HEROISM SCIENCE

Heroism science is a relatively new field in psychology. Focused primarily on determining the journey of a hero, motivations of a hero, the impact of the hero, and the transformation of the hero as well as other facets, heroism science aims at analyzing the plethora of heroes both past and present. Based largely on Joseph Campbell's (1949) hero monomyth, which describes the prototypical heroic path of departure, initiation, and return, the hero's journey is one that is largely subject to various interpretations and has been debated among researchers ever since the emergence of the field (Allison, Goethals, & Kramer, 2017). The heroic actor, described as "a functioning biological organism that can perceive, move within, respond to, and transform its environment", is a fairly broad definition that is applicable to a wide variety of situations and people, thus leading to the overall study of heroism science to be extremely subjective (Johnson, 2008).

This subjective definition allows for the argument to be made that nearly any person can be a hero, so long as someone, somewhere, believes that they did something heroic. Regardless of the specifics of the heroic act, however, there are constants in this field that apply to nearly every single heroic story: the hero is summoned on a journey, is missing some sort of inner quality, experiences sets of trials and tribulations, receives assistance from others, finds the missing quality, successfully completes the mission, and returns home in order to bestow some sort of boon to better the community from which he/she came (Allison, Goethals, & Kramer, 2017). In the case of Elle Woods, these constants are extremely applicable.

Elle Woods' Hero's Journey

Elle's story begins in Los Angeles, California, where she is in her senior year at the California University of Los Angeles, is the president of her sorority Delta Nu, and is expecting a proposal of marriage by her longtime boyfriend Warner Hunnington III. Her world is turned upside down, however, when instead of proposing, Warner ends his relationship with Elle on the grounds that he needs someone more "serious" if he plans on attending Harvard Law School in the coming fall and becoming a senator by the time he is thirty. It is this rejection, this romantic failure, that causes Elle to undergo her first motivational transformation and sets her on the path of her hero's journey. Characterized by Allison and Goethals to be brought about by tragedy, this type of transformation can "beget motivational changes in people who heroically use these tragedies to transform entire societies" (Allison & Goethals, 2017). In Elle's case, her tragedy in this instance is simple: her heart is broken, her world ripped from under her feet, and her character utterly destroyed by the notion that she is not serious enough to support her partner in a stressful career path. At this point in her journey, Elle is completely dependent on Warner for her sense of self-worth, and when he so blatantly rejects her, she is completely lost.

To cope with this tragedy, Elle completely shifts her focus. Instead of pursuing a career with her major (fashion merchandising), she decides to attempt to prove to Warner that, contrary to his belief, she can be serious, and she makes plans to attend Harvard Law with him and become a lawyer as well. Here, her motivation is driven still by her dependence to Warner; she yearns for his approval and is continuing to base her self-worth on it. This decision to move from her friends, family, and home, which is linked directly to her romantic failure, marks the beginning of the first phase of her hero's journey: departure.

As mentioned previously, Elle's departure is clear cut: she picks herself up, prepares to leave her family, friends, and the safety and support she has known her whole life, to pursue a career in which she had originally no interest. While the departure itself is self-evident, the process leading up to it was not; consistent with her underdog status, she was doubted the entire way by those around her. The underdog, described by Franco, Blau, and Zimbardo (2011) as "individuals who overcame handicap or adverse conditions and succeed in spite of such negative circumstances", and the underdog described by Vandello et al. (2017) as "disadvantaged parties acing advantaged opponents and unlikely to succeed" describes Elle perfectly. After first making the decision to pursue Harvard and after purchasing books on the LSAT, Elle informs her parents of her decision. At this time, Elle is swimming in her family's pool, talking to her father, who is standing up outside of the pool and looking down at her as he speaks. After telling him that she plans to go to Harvard, and that Harvard is a "perfectly acceptable place", her mother first responds with "honey, you were first runner up at the Miss Hawaiian Tropics contest... why are you going to throw that all away?" (Legally Blonde, 2001), thus exemplifying just how little her parents expect of her based solely on her appearance.

To make matters worse, her father follows up with "sweetheart, you don't need law school. Law school is for people who are boring, and ugly, and serious. And you, Button, are none of those things" (Legally Blonde, 2001), illustrating even further how little Elle's parents truly think of her. Additionally, the positioning of Elle and her parents is significant to the scene in that her parents are physically looking down on her as they speak, which simply exemplifies even more so how she is being looked down upon.

Elle's parents are very clearly unconvinced that she is capable of not only being admitted to Harvard, but also that she is capable of being "serious". These sexist views are consistent with what Crystal Hoyt (2014) describes in her analysis of gender stereotypes: "The particular stereotypes that influence the perception and evaluation of individuals in leadership are those maintaining that 'women take care' and 'men take charge'." Elle is an attractive, charismatic, intelligent young woman, but it is these very characteristics that lead those around her to assume that she will fail in a position where she must take charge and be a leader: for instance, a lawyer.

Initiation

Once she is accepted into Harvard, Elle experiences what is perhaps the most difficult and trying time of her life. She is completely unaccustomed to the life of the east coast: she arrives to her new school in a black convertible with two moving trucks following closely behind, dressed in hot pink leather, with her dog Bruiser wearing a matching outfit. Unsurprisingly, she is judged immediately. As Elle attempts to navigate Harvard and become re-socialized to the social norms of her new school, she experiences a number of failures that push her along her motivational transformation. One such repetitive failure is her failure to make friends and establish a social life, which proves to be one of the most damaging issues for her. She is not well-liked at Harvard; she is excluded from groups, picked on, and judged by everyone around her for sticking to herself and refusing to completely surrender her individuality to the east coast. It is these failures, however, that push her to undergo her second motivational transformation.

Her second, and most important, motivational transformation is brought about yet again by romantic failure. Elle's beloved Warner is at this point engaged to a snobby New England girl named Vivian who does everything in her power to make Elle's life a living hell. After inviting Elle to a "costume party" which is really just a typical party hosted for the purpose of humiliating Elle, Vivian begins to go out of her way to dehumanize Elle. It is not this, however, that catalyzes Elle's transformation; rather, it is rejection, once again, from Warner. After discussing with Warner her concerns about balancing a summer internship with the well-regarded Professor Callahan, Warner tells Elle, "oh you'll never get the grades to qualify for one of those spots...you're just not smart enough, sweetie" (Legally Blonde, 2001), thus prompting Elle to finally see the reality. Despite the fact that she was accepted into the same law school, is taking the same classes, and is engaged in the same workload as Warner, she is forced to accept that she will never be good enough for him. It is this realization that not only catalyzes her second motivational transformation, where she shifts from being motivated primarily by her need for Warner's approval and acceptance to her desire to prove to everyone "just how valuable Elle Woods can be" (Legally Blonde, 2001), but also marks the beginning of her transformation from dependence to autonomy.

Once Elle makes the conscious decision to put no further stock in the opinions of Warner, her transformation of dependence to autonomy is complete. Autonomy is defined by Phil Zimbardo as the idea that "heroes are people with the ability to resist social pressures that promote evil, and that such resistance requires the moral courage to be guided by one's heart rather than by social cues" (Allison & Goethals, 2017). Such autonomy is reflected by Elle Woods in her newly acquired ability to stand her ground against the many, many negative social pressures at Harvard and remain true to herself, an idea that also coincides with Dik et al.'s (2017) social cognitive career theory.

Social Cognitive Career Theory and Elle Woods

Social cognitive career theory (SCCT) consists of three person variables: self-efficacy (i.e., confidence in one's ability to successfully execute particular tasks), outcome expectations (i.e., beliefs regarding the results of successful completion of particular tasks), and personal goals. The theory describes how these three person variables' interactions "influence the development of vocational interests, educational and career choice, and work-related performance", all of which translate fairly clearly to Elle Woods' hero's journey (Dik et. al., 2017). In terms of self-efficacy, Elle never once wavered in her own personal confidence in her ability to not only be admitted into Harvard Law, but also in her ability to succeed there, despite everyone else's doubts of her doing so. Elle's outcome expectations were originally that if she succeeds in going to Harvard, Warner will realize his mistake and take her back; however, after undergoing her second motivational transformation, her outcome expectations shift to instead focus on becoming a successful lawyer. While it is true that her outcome expectations shift, her personal goals do not change; rather, they remain the same throughout her journey. Whether it be in the form of Warner's acceptance, or whether it is quantified into a grade point average at Harvard, or it is measured simply in the looks of those around her, Elle, above all else, just wants to be taken seriously.

Initiation as a Serious Law Student

Once Elle becomes fairly well-acquainted with law school, and once she is able to successfully thrive without Warner's (or anyone's) approval, Elle embarks on the second part of her initiation: her initiation as a serious law student. At this point, Elle has experienced two motivational transformations as well as a transformation from dependence to autonomy, and she is well-versed and prepared to fight for a spot in Professor Callahan's internship. This internship, different from a position as a summer associate, is being offered to four first year students on the grounds that he has too large of a case load to handle with his more seasoned graduate students only. After studying relentlessly, actively engaging in class, and impressing Professor Callahan with her resume, Elle earns a spot, along with Vivian and Warner, in Callahan's internship. At this point, Elle has begun to befriend Vivian, despite the fact that Vivian had spent so much time attempting to ruin Elle's Harvard experience. It seems, to a third-party observer, that Elle's success in securing the internship was well deserved, and that she is finally on the path to succeeding as an underdog. However, it soon becomes clear that the opposite is actually at work.

During a late night working on the case, and after a successful day of Elle proving herself to be an excellent law student, Professor Callahan reveals that he is both sexually and romantically attracted to Elle, and makes it clear that she will be able to secure a summer associate position if she has some sort of sexual intercourse with him. Callahan turns out to be a sexual predator (Beggan & Allison, 2018). Disgusted, and humiliated, Elle decides to quit; she has just been dehumanized and objectified, and it has been made known that all of her hard work in class was nothing compared to the pull of her appearance. This failure, however, is unlike other failures experienced by Elle over the course of her journey. This time, instead of being motivated to work even harder and to prove that she is capable of being taken seriously, she resorts to quitting and wallowing in her suffering. Consistent with the underdog hero is the presence of a mentor; in this case, Professor Callahan represents the dark mentor who attempts to lead the hero, Elle, astray. Fortunately, however, a bright mentor places Elle on the right track.

One of the ten dimensions of transformation is external situational forces; one such external source of transformation is a mentor (Allison & Goethals, 2017). According to Joseph Campbell (2004), "the mentor may be some little wood sprite or wise man or fairy godmother or animal that comes to you as a companion or as an advisor, letting you know what dangers are along the way and how to overcome them." For Elle, this mentor is Professor Stromwell, a female professor who until this point had not shown any particular interest in her. At the point of her advising, Elle is in a nail salon, saying her final goodbyes to her friends before leaving to go back to Los Angeles. Professor Stromwell, who is also in the nail salon and coincidentally (and fortuitously) overhears Elle's rendition of the happenings between herself and Professor Callahan, tells Elle, "if you're going to let one prick ruin the rest of your life, you're not the girl I thought you were" (Legally Blonde, 2001).

This simple vote of confidence, this simple reassurance that someone in an authority position, and especially a woman, believes in her, is enough to transform Elle once again, but this time, it is intellectual. An intellectual or mental transformation is defined by Allison and Goethals (2017) as "featuring a change in mental abilities or fundamental insights about the world". Professor Stromwell's words allow Elle to have the realization that there will always be people, and especially men, that will refuse to take her seriously because of her appearance; however, once that fact is accepted, it can be overcome. Professor Stromwell is the quintessential example of a mentor who helps heroes "become transformed", thus allowing those transformed heroes to later help other heroes, specifically other underdog heroes, transform as well (Rohr, 2014).

Return

After completing her initiation, Elle is finally tested one last time, and at this point the stakes are high. After bringing to light the disgusting actions of Professor Callahan, his client, Brooke Taylor Windham, who is accused of killing her husband, fires him and hires Elle to represent her in his place. Here, Elle has replaced Professor Callahan as the leading defense attorney and is attempting to prove that the defendant, Brooke Taylor Windham, did not shoot and kill her husband, Hayworth. While cross examining a witness, Chutney, who is Windham's step-daughter and biological daughter of the deceased, Elle uses her Cosmopolitan knowledge of hair care to find the hole in Chutney's story, exploit it, and prove that it was she, not Windham, who killed Hayworth.

The fact that Elle won the case based on the conjunction of her newly acquired law skills and her previous knowledge of hair care brings Elle's transformation into full circle: she has transcended herself in the sense that she is no longer concerned with needing the approval of men (or anyone), and she has gained an entire new set of skills and knowledge, but she has not let go of the old Elle Woods, the one who thrives on knowing obscure facts about beauty; Elle has transcended herself, but included her old self, and both parts were necessary in order for her to successfully complete her hero's journey. Campbell (1949) would describe Elle as have been transformed to the point of being the "master of both worlds", and she is now capable of promoting well-being in both worlds (Efthimiou, Allison, & Franco, 2018).

One of the most significant facets to the hero's journey is the hero's return to his/her old world, accompanied by a 'boon' or reward to bestow on the community. In this case, Elle's boon is that she has demonstrated to everyone that a person, let alone a female who already has gender stereotype-related odds stacked up against her, can successfully integrate into a new world, experience dozens of failures, and still succeed. Elle's journey, simply put, is inspiring, and that alone is a great enough boon that Elle's best friend, Paulette, vows to name her unborn baby Elle in her honor. Elle graduates Harvard Law with honors, with offers to join one of Boston's most prestigious law firms, and with a boyfriend (not that she needs one). Her astounding accomplishments, her overwhelming overcoming of all the odds that were stacked up against her, lead to her journey being the quintessential underdog story.

An Analysis of Elle Woods' Heroic Transformation

There is no doubt that Elle Woods, while completing her hero's journey, experienced suffering. This suffering, however, is leads to beneficial consequences. According to Allison and Setterberg (2016), there are six benefits to suffering: suffering is redemptive, suffering signifies a crossover point in life, suffering encourages humility, suffering stimulates compassion, suffering promotes social union, and suffering instills meaning and purpose. For Elle Woods, nearly all of these six are relevant. Elle's extreme suffering during the initiation phase most certainly signified a crossover point in life: by the time she had completed that phase, she had been "through the fire", and her motivational and intellectual transformations that came about during this phase speak to the wisdom and maturity gained.

Additionally, even though Elle was being personally attacked by Vivian, her suffering left room for learning and love, thus allowing her to forgive Vivian and eventually befriend her, therefore encouraging humility and stimulating compassion. Elle's suffering also instilled meaning and purpose into her life: she was determined to not let her suffering control her life; instead, she took her suffering in stride and used it to propel her forward into her transformations, which ultimately led to the completion of her hero's journey.

Despite her heroic transformation, Elle Woods is a reluctant hero. Originally, she did not choose to change, but was instead cast onto the track by her romantic failure with Warner. Aligning with the stagnation to growth transformation, Elle naturally resisted the change, and was perfectly comfortable remaining in stagnation (in her fashion merchandising major, studying the history of polka-dots and living in LA), but was forced to change when she failed romantically (Allison & Goethals, 2017).

CONCLUSION

Elle Woods, throughout her hero's journey, transforms both motivationally and intellectually in a manner consistent with underdog heroes. Throughout her heroic quest, she experiences suffering and failure, both of which aid in her transformations both from dependence to autonomy and stagnation to growth, along with receiving help from a mentor along the way. Her story speaks to the very real, very painful issues of sexism that were present in the early twenty-first century, but also to the sexism that is present event today. It is still remarkably difficult for women to be taken seriously in leadership positions, and especially for those women who align closely with Elle's personality or appearance. Additionally, the issue of needing approval from another person is extremely relevant for people of all ages, but specifically for the adolescents who are most likely to watch this film. Elle Woods' story teaches adolescent chidren that anything is possible, and that, most importantly, no approval is needed in order to be successful. This powerful message undoubtedly speaks to kids and teenagers all over the world. Elle's story is one that is inspiring, thought provoking, and important, and emphasizes to everyone who witnesses it that just about anyone can wake up and say, "I think I'll go to law school today" (Legally Blonde, 2001).

REFERENCES

Allison, S.T., Goethals, G. R., & Kramer, R. M. (2017). The rise and coalescence of heroism science. In S. T. Allison, G. R. Goethals, & R. M. Kramer (Eds.), Handbook of heroism and heroic leadership. New York: Routledge.

Allison, S. T., & Goethals, G. R. (2017). The hero's transformation. In S. T. Allison, G. R. Goethals, & R. M. Kramer (Eds.), Handbook of heroism and heroic leadership. New York: Routledge.

Allison, S. T., & Goethals, G. R. (2016). Hero worship: The elevation of the human spirit. Journal for the Theory of Social Behaviour, 46, 187-210.

Allison, S. T., Goethals, G. R., Marrinan, A. R., Parker, O. M., Spyrou, S. P., Stein, M. (2019). The metamorphosis of the hero: Principles, processes, and purpose. Frontiers in Psychology.

Allison, S. T., & Setterberg, G. C. (2016). Suffering and sacrifice: Individual and collective benefits, and implications for leadership. In S. T. Allison, C. T. Kocher, & G. R. Goethals (Eds), Frontiers in spiritual leadership: Discovering the better angels of our nature. New York: Palgrave Macmillan.

Beggan, J. K., & Allison, S. T. (Eds.) (2018). Leadership and sexuality: Power, principles, and processes. Northampton, MA: Edward Elgar.

Campbell, J. (2004). Pathways to bliss. Novata, CA: New World Library

Campbell, J. (1949). The hero with a thousand faces. NewYork: New World Library

Davis, J. L., Burnette, J. L., Allison, S. T., & Stone, H. (2011). Against the odds: Academic underdogs benefit from incremental theories. Social Psychology of Education, 14, 331-346.

Dik, B. J., O'Connor, W., & Shimizu, A. B. (2017). Career development and a sense of calling. In S. T. Allison, G. R. Goethals, & R. M. Kramer (Eds.), Handbook of heroism and heroic leadership. New York: Routledge.

Efthimiou, O., Allison, S. T., & Franco, Z. E. (Eds.) (2018). Heroism and wellbeing in the 21st Century: Applied and emerging perspectives. New York: Routledge.

Franco, Z. E., Blau, K., & Zimbardo, P. G. (2011, April 11). Heroism: A Conceptual Analysis and Differentiation Between Heroic Action and Altruism. Review of General Psychology. Advance online publication. doi: 10.1037/a0022672

Goethals, G. R., & Allison, S. T. (2016). Transforming motives and mentors: The heroic leadership of James MacGregor Burns. In G. R. Goethals (Ed.), Politics, ethics and change: The legacy of James MacGregor Burns (pp. 59-73). Northampton, MA: Edward Elgar Publishing.

Goldschmied, N., Michniewicz, K., & Vandello, J. A. (2017). Underdogs as heroes. In S. T. Allison, G. R. Goethals, & R. M. Kramer (Eds.), Handbook of heroism and heroic leadership. New York: Routledge.

Hoyt, C. L. (2014). Social Identities and Leadership: The Case of Gender. In (pp. 71-91).

Hoyt, C. L., Allison, S. T., Barnowski, A., & Sultan, A. (2019). Implicit theories of heroism and leadership: The role of gender, communion, and agency. Basic and Applied Social Psychology.

Johnson, M. (2008). "What makes a body?" The Journal of Speculative Philosophy, 22, 159–169. doi: 10.1353/jsp.0.0046

Legally Blonde (2001). Metro-Goldwyn-Mayer.

Luketic, R. (Director). (2001). Legally Blonde [Motion picture on DVD]. Santa Monica, CA: MGM Home Entertainment.

Rohr, R. (2014). Eager to love. Cincinnati, OH: Franciscan Media.

Worthington, E. L, & Allison, S. T. (2018). Heroic humility: What the science of humility can say to people raised on self-focus. Washington. DC: American Psychological Association.

3

James "Sawyer" Ford: The Man Who Had to Become Lost to Find the Hero Within

LEO S. TROIK

"Dear Mr. Sawyer, You don't know who I am but I know who you are and I know what you done. You had sex with my mother and then you stole my dad's money all away. So he got angry and he killed my mother and then he killed himself, too. All I know is your name. But one of these days I'm going to find you and I'm going to give you this letter so you'll remember what you done to me. You killed my parents, Mr. Sawyer" ("Pilot, Part 2" Lost, 2006). On the steps of the church in which his parent's funeral is being held, 8-year old James Ford writes a letter to the con-man who drove his family into oblivion and changed his life forever. James would spend the next eleven years slowly transforming himself into the very man who had caused the demise of his parents, eventually even taking the name Sawyer for himself.

From the moment he took upon the name Sawyer to the point that Oceanic 815 crashed onto the sandy shore of The Island, the place which served as the "New World" setting for his heroic transformation (Allison & Goethals, 2017; Campbell, 1949), "Sawyer" lived a life consumed by greed, pride, and deception. Sawyer religiously bound himself to a competitive lifestyle in which he sought personal gain at the expense of others. His own unwavering will to kill the man who had destroyed his childhood, coupled with an unbreakable shell built up over years, created an impediment to heroism for Sawyer. However, Sawyer's innermost humanity shone through during one of his final 'long' cons before his arrival on The Island. During the con he gained the trust of a woman with a wealthy husband and 'accidentally' revealed a large sum of money to her, eventually admitting that it is for an opportunity of gargantuan monetary gain, prompting her to talk her wealthy husband into joining him on the economic endeavor. However, upon discovering that the couple he had been conning had a young boy, Sawyer decided to not go through with the con, despite the sizable potential personal gain. This glimpse of Sawyer's humanity and self-restraint would serve as one of the first cracks in Sawyer's shell of villainy and baseless-ness -- a crack that would widen over his time on The Island and bring more inner heroic virtues and character strengths to the surface.

Ever since the fateful night that took the lives of both of Sawyer's parents, Sawyer was an underdog (Vandello et al., 2017). During every step of his jour-ney, he had to fight and suffer to fulfill the newfound purpose he had found on The Island. The trauma and suffering Sawyer endured upon seeing his par-ents die and having to carry on afterwards led him initially down a very dark tunnel and almost caused him to transform into a villain. However, evidenced by glimpses of persevering morality and goodness, Sawyer never truly committed to a life of villainy and was therefore able to undergo a heroic transformation. In the aforementioned case of Sawyer discontinuing his con upon seeing that the couple had a young son, he showed that his suffering stimulated compassion within him. "We identify with struggle precisely because we know struggle, both firsthand at the level of personal experience, and also at the deeper arche-typal level" (Allison & Goethals, 2017, p. 213) Sawyer closely identified with the struggle he was so close to putting the young boy through, because he experi-enced something so similar in his own childhood.

Before his transformation, Sawyer was overcome with greed, wrath, and pride. However, one of the most notable changes that he underwent as a result of his transformation was a shift from pride to humility and moderation, as well as one from egocentricity to sociocentricity (Allison, 2015; Allison & Goethals, 2017). He demonstrated these changes in his behavior throughout his time on The Island. For example, Sawyers's earliest instinct on The Island was to hoard as many materials for himself as he could, frequently stealing from others and taking more than his fair share to give himself a higher survival edge. This pattern reflects the competitive nature of life that he had come to fully embrace previous to The Island.

Initially upon arriving on The Island, Sawyer would act in ways that would reveal slight of masochistic tendencies. When one of the survivors lost their asthma inhaler, Sawyer refused to tell the truth that would exonerate him of any blame; instead, he would subject himself to physical torture. Sawyer had no personal gain invested in this, encouraging the idea that he acted purely out of a twisted sense of masochism and trickery. Also, upon being treated for a near-fatal wound by Jack, the doctor and 'leader' of the crash survivors, Sawyer crudely remarked that he would not save him if their roles were reversed. This remark runs contrary to the perspective of self-gain and benefit, because it would be in Sawyer's best interest to befriend and be gregarious to the only doctor on The Island for the purpose of pure self-preservation. Also, while these words eventually prove to be divergent from his actions, they dichotomously stray from many of "The Great Eight" attributes of heroism (Allison & Goethals, 2011). The statement demonstrates a lack of selflessness, charisma, care, and reliability, thereby creating conflict between himself and the leader, undermining a sense of trust in himself from the others, and identifying him as an overall reprobate individual.

THE INITIATION OF SAWYER'S PATH TO HEROISM

Sawyer's involuntary hero journey was initiated both by internal purpose and transcendent summons (Dik et al., 2017). The apex of Sawyer's villainy and the inner morality and heroism that Jacob, the ageless protector of The Island, saw within him put him on the Oceanic Flight 815. The mammoth contrast in the good and evil sides of Sawyer which came together to put him on The Island highlight the vast transformation that he would undergo there. The villainy that put him on the plane stemmed from his pre-transformative purpose of getting revenge on the real Sawyer and the illusion of bliss that it would bring him. This thirst for revenge took him to Australia in the first place and ended with him committing the evil act of killing an innocent man, bringing him no peace or happiness whatsoever. This represented the peak of Sawyer's darkness, which began to peel away as he began his journey on The Island. Sawyer's transcendent summons came from Jacob, a godlike figure on The Island who represented preservation of all that is good and pure on The Island and the world beyond. Jacob's influence over The Island coupled with the extent of the influence that The Island had on Sawyer indirectly made Jacob Sawyer's mentor over his time on the island. By influencing the events on the island and continually testing the survivors of the crash, Jacob attempted to draw the goodness and heroism out of everyone to see who would succeed him as protector of The Island.

Due to the nature of The Island, Sawyer's acts of heroism were unavoidably high risk, high velocity, and full of barriers. In fact, the level of risk and difficulty that Sawyer subjected himself to make his actions heroic as opposed to merely altruistic as noted by Franco, Blau and Zimbardo (2011). One of the earliest and most stark examples of this pattern occurs when Sawyer risked his life and his chance to potentially leave The Island by trying to save Walt, a young boy and fellow survivor of Oceanic 815, from 'The Others'. Not only was Sawyer vastly outnumbered by 'The Others'; he was also unarmed and unequipped, showing that he completely looked past personal risk to selflessly save someone else. The polarity and significance of the choices Sawyer was forced to make early in his tenure on The Island forced him to choose to either take the dark road and remain in his shell or allow himself to be put in danger and risk to help others.

THE EVOLUTION OF SAWYER'S PURPOSE

Sawyer's own internal purpose and meaning were reshaped as a part of his transformation. Initially, his mission in life was to exact revenge on the man who had caused the demise of his parents, doing almost anything and everything that had to be done to accomplish this goal. However, after undergoing certain transformative events on The Island, it became clear that a new purpose took over his being. The newfound purpose was brought onto him by three distinct entities: Jacob, the other survivors of Oceanic 815, and the death of the real Sawyer.

Because Jacob first spotted Sawyer sitting on the steps of the church at his parents' funeral, he had designated him as one of his potential replacements for caretaker of The Island. As mentioned above, Jacob hand-picked everyone on the Oceanic 815 crash to potentially replace him, but had to mentor them both directly and indirectly to impose his own will on them. In this way, mainly by means of indirect influence and oversight, he was able to push Sawyer closer to his newfound purpose. The influence that the other survivors of Oceanic 815 had on Sawyer was paramount in the transformation of his purpose. Despite his initially harsh, bitter, and selfish actions, he still receives a certain degree of kinship and aid from the others which makes him feel an unfamiliar warmth that enhanced his prosocial sentiments (Kafashan et al., 2017). In the initial stages of his journey, Sawyer transitions from pure egoism to some 'expected levels of helping' such as reciprocity and vested interest as noted in Kafashan et al. (2017). Finally, upon killing the real Sawyer, he was finally able to fully move on to his new purpose and leave the old one behind. While the death of the real Sawyer did not provide absolution or resolve for Sawyer, it allowed him to get a sense of closure for his old purpose, allowing him to fully undertake his new goal.

Soon after his role as leader was unofficially confirmed by his companions, he was faced with a situation in which a woman was being held at gunpoint by two men, pleading for mercy. Instantly, despite personal risk and discouragement from some of his companions, Sawyer stepped in and managed to save the woman. Sawyer's pure, inner compulsion to save a woman he did not know for absolutely no personal gain, coupled with his willingness to place his own safety at huge risk, defines his act as that of pure heroism. "Heroism is an extreme form of pro-sociality, a category of behavior that involves benefiting another. By definition, "typical" pro-sociality involves the actor delivering average – or expected -- levels of benefits to others. Here we define heroes as those who incur costs (e.g., risk of injury or death; or significant sacrifices such as time, money, or other forms of personal loss) to deliver greater-than-expected benefits to others" (Baumard & Boyer, 2013).

PROSOCIAL ELEMENTS OF SAWYER'S HEROIC EVOLUTION

A tremendous contrast from the beginning of his journey to this point in the series involved how people around him viewed him and treated him. In his very first notable scene, Sawyer was seen blaming Sayid, a fellow survivor of Oceanic 815, for the crash purely because of his Arabic appearance, quickly placing Sawyer in a very negative and villainous light. This act of racism toward Sayid not only formed a negative precedent for the way the others saw Sawyer but also succeeded in surrounding him in an antagonistic light. Furthermore, instead of attempting to redeem himself in the eyes of the others, Sawyer continued to act in a manner that temporarily solidified his status as the (self-admittedly) most disliked member of Oceanic 815 survivors.

"Ain't that just like a woman? She keeps the house, you get the cheap-ass apartment. Man, I thought these people hated me, but I gotta hand it to you... Stealing a baby, trying to drown it, now that's a new low. You even made Locke take a swing at you. Hell, that's like getting Ghandi to beat his kids." - Sawyer ("The Long Con" Lost, 2006)

Had Sawyer not mended his ways and acted in a heroic way, he would not have ever been able to   get the support and trust that he eventually received as a leader. "We define heroes as symbols, and leaders as agents. We see heroism as a perception in the eyes of followers, one that symbolizes the desires and values of the collective they represent" (Decter-Frain et al., 2017).

Falling in love on The Island proved to be a catalyst for Sawyer's evolution into a hero. The principle of "kin selection" (Kafashan et al., 2017) can be used to explain this positive correlation between Sawyer's love for another and his will to do good. From an evolutionary standpoint, by helping and ensuring the safety of a woman he loves, he is acting in the best interest of his potential children. However, his love for Kate and, eventually, for Juliette, did not just engender noble actions toward them, but helped invoke a certain sense of compassion into his life, allowing him to cast aside more of the dark armor that he stubbornly held on to for so long. The strong feelings he had for Kate forced him into action, where he might acted more selfishly otherwise. When put into captivity with Kate at the hands of 'The Others', Sawyer acted atypically when Kate's well-being was threatened. This is significant because prior to this incident, Sawyer's stubborn, prideful, and hard-headed nature ensured that no number of threats could push him to act or say something he was not compelled to.

Sawyer's rivalry with a Jack helped him grow as a leader and realize much about the nature of the importance of interaction with groups and society in relation to heroism. Through the multitude of frequent conflicts between Sawyer and Jack, there was no doubt that Jack usually had the support of the majority, the moral high ground, and the status of the de-facto leader, constantly ensuring that Sawyer would always come out second best. The most notable direct conflict between Jack and Sawyer revolved around Kate; their individually strong feelings of love for her solidified their rivalry and ensured that there would be a continuous competition between them. Also, much of Sawyer's growth as a hero is seen in contrast to Jack, who, as opposed to Sawyer, took upon the role of the leader and the hero the moment he stepped on The Island. Due to coming to The Island already possessing so many of 'The Great Eight' attributes of a hero (Allison & Goethals, 2011) as well as instantly using his skills as a doctor to save others and contribute to the well-being of the survivors, Jack was quickly designated as the leader and protagonist.

Meanwhile, Sawyer was busy clinging to his old, dark ways and quickly came to obtain the reputation as the most hated of the survivors. Sawyer's growth and transformation relative to both Jack and himself is highlighted by the scene in which Sawyer jumped out of Lapidus's helicopter in order to slightly increase the chance that Kate, Jack, Hurley, Aaron, and Lapidus survive, due to the helicopter not having enough fuel to carry all of them. When it was made evident that the helicopter did not have enough fuel to carry the amount of weight that was on it, Sawyer did not hesitate to jump out of the helicopter, sacrificing himself for everyone else, while Jack sat motionless, unable to do anything. In this moment Sawyer's heroism purely overshadows Jack's and shows, more than anything else, how far he had come.

SAWYER'S JOURNEY AND HOW HE TRANSFORMED

Sawyer's moral and emotional transformation from a sardonic, egocentric, con man to a caring, courageous, leader is spotlighted by his physical transformation into Jim LaFleur: the head of security of the Dharma Initiative. Not only did his role as the head of security of The Dharma Initiative propel him into a role where he had no choice but to lead people in a wise and disciplined manner, but Jack's departure from The Island solidified Sawyer as arguably the most prominent and important character left on The Island at this time. His role as primary decision maker and leader was confirmed shortly after the final time shift when his plan, despite being admittedly risky and stupid, was quickly accepted by almost everyone. Not only did this confirm the people's trust and confidence in Sawyer, but it also reaffirmed his own willingness to assume the role of a leader when one was so desperately needed.

Sawyer's transformation journey follows Joseph Campbell's (1949) original description of the classic hero's journey: "A hero ventures forth from the world of common day into a region of supernatural wonder: fabulous forces are there encountered and a decisive victory is won: the hero comes back from this mysterious adventure with the power to bestow boons on his fellow man" (Campbell, 1949, p. 30). However, Sawyer falls under more than one subcategory of heroes as described by Goethals and Allison (2012), making him a transcendent hero of sorts. Much of the suffering Sawyer undergoes throughout his journey -- largely brought about by himself on himself -- causes him to grow and develop in some way. However, even after Sawyer shifts almost entirely to a heroic persona, tragedy and suffering still follow him. Most notably demonstrated by the death of Juliet, the woman whom Sawyer had come to love. Her demise came at a time during which Sawyer was no longer at the negative end of any of the interpersonal conflicts, as he had shifted to a purely protagonist role. Unlike many of his previous tragedies and calamities, this one played no role in his positive transformation, but instead acted to reinforce the tragedy and suffering that heroes often endure.

Sawyer's willingness and bravery in sacrificing himself for the safety and wellbeing of others demonstrated the degree of heroic martyrdom that he embodied. This martyrdom was made most evident in the aforementioned scene in which Sawyer jumped out of Lapidus's helicopter to save everyone else in it. This act of martyrdom was not only heroic because it helped save the lives of others, but also included the highest degree of personal risk. Not only did Sawyer risk his own life by jumping out of a moving helicopter, but he also condemned himself to losing Kate, whom he cared for and loved more than anything else. This ultimate act of selflessness in what could have easily been his last moment alive, brought to light the new purpose he had developed in his heroic transformation.

The antithesis between what Sawyer said and what he did showed that his acts of heroism were not rooted in self-acclaim and self-promotion, but were genuinely based on his desire to promote the good of others. Often, Sawyer even saw himself as a bad man due to the bad things he had done in the past, but he had no interest in hiding the misdeeds of his past from others. He even encouraging them to view him in a dark light:

"Sawyer, this idea, all of this, what we did, what made... How does someone think of something like that?" [Charlie asks]
[Sawyer has a flashback]
"I'm not a good person, Charlie. Never did a good thing in my life." [Sawyer replies]
-- From "The Long Con" (Lost, 2006)

Sawyer's abrasive, witty, and harsh manner of communication initially had the effect of portraying him as a villain. However, as Sawyer developed and transformed, his harsh demeanor and attitude worked to redefine him partially as a 'Tragic Hero' (Kinsella et al., 2017).

Sawyer did not complete 'the return' aspect of the hero's journey as described by Joseph Campbell (1949) in the traditional sense. However, by opposing and fighting against The Man in Black, Sawyer benefited society on account of the fact that The Man in Black represented everything evil and dark on The Island, and, if successful, this dark entity would extend its influence past The Island to ultimately turn the world into a dark place.

Sawyer's transformation demonstrates the epitome of the notion that all people, no matter how seemingly evil and irrevocably afflicted by their past, have the capacity to transform into a hero. Sawyer's transformation also shows how invaluable relationships and interactions with other people are to one's innermost development. No matter how independent and distrustful of the world Sawyer was upon coming to the island, the relationships he forged with his fellow islanders brought the inner aspects of his heroism out into the light and allowed him to develop traits such as leadership. Sawyer's transformation brings hope for humanity in the sense that even the most unlikely underdogs have the potential of becoming remarkable individuals who can make the world a better place. The message of hope for humanity can be found in the message that great good can be found in some of the most seemingly villainous individuals.

Allison, S. T. (2015). The initiation of heroism science. Heroism Science, 1, 1-8.

Allison, S. T., & Goethals, G. R. (2011). Heroes: What they do and why we need them. New York: Oxford University Press.

Allison, S. T., & Goethals, G. R. (2017). The hero's transformation. In S. T. Allison, G. R. Goethals, & R. M. Kramer (Eds.), Handbook of heroism and heroic leadership. New York: Routledge, Taylor & Francis Group.

Allison, S. T., Goethals, G. R., & Kramer, R. M. (Eds.) (2017). Handbook of heroism and heroic leadership. New York: Routledge.

Allison, S. T., & Goethals, G. R. (2013). Heroic leadership: An influence taxonomy of 100 exceptional individuals. New York: Routledge.

Allison, S. T., Goethals, G. R., Marrinan, A. R., Parker, O. M., Spyrou, S. P., Stein, M. (2019). The metamorphosis of the hero: Principles, processes, and purpose. Frontiers in Psycholo-gy.

Allison, S. T., & Setterberg, G. C. (2016). Suffering and sacrifice: Individual and collective benefits, and implications for leadership. In S. T. Allison, C. T. Kocher, & G. R. Goethals (Eds), Frontiers in spiritual leadership: Discovering the better angels of our nature. New York: Palgrave Macmillan.

Bender, J. (Director), & Abrams, J. J., & Williams, S. (Writers). (2006, February 08)."The Long Con". In LOST. Harrisonburg, Virginia: ABC.

Baumard, N. & Boyer, P. (2013). Explaining moral religions. Trends in Cognitive Sciences, Volume 17, Issue 6, 272–280.

Campbell, J. (1971). Man & Myth: A Conversation with Joseph Campbell. Psychology Today, July 1971.

Campbell, J. (1949). The hero with a thousand faces. New World Library.

Davis, J. L., Burnette, J. L., Allison, S. T., & Stone, H. (2011). Against the odds: Academic underdogs benefit from incremental theories. Social Psychology of Education, 14, 331-346. Eylon, D., & Allison, S. T. (2005). The frozen in time effect in evaluations of the dead. Personality and Social Psychology Bulletin, 31, 1708-1717.

Franco, Z. E., Blau, K., & Zimbardo, P. G. (2011, April 11). Heroism: A Conceptual Analysis and Differentiation Between Heroic Action and Altruism. Review of General Psychology. Advance online publication. doi: 10.1037/a0022672

Gray, K., Anderson, S., Doyle, C. M., Hester, N., Schmitt, P., Vonasch, A., Allison, S. T., and Jackson, J. C. (2018). To be immortal, do good or evil. Personality and Social Psychology Bulle-tin.

Kafashan, S., Sparks, A., Griskevicius, V., & Barclay, P. (2014). Prosocial behaviour and social status. In J. T. Cheng, J. L. Tracy, & C. Anderson (eds) The Psychology of Social Status (pp. 139–158). New York: Springer.

Kafashan, S., Sparks, A., Rotella, A., & Barclay, P. (2016). Why Heroism Exists: Evolutionary Perspectives on Extreme Helping. In S.T.Allison, G.R.Goethals, & R.M.Kramer (Eds.) The Handbook of Heroism and Heroic Leadership, pp. 36-57. Routledge.

Kinsella, E. L., Ritchie, T. D., & Igou, E. R. (2015). Zeroing in on heroes: A prototype analysis of hero features. Journal of Personality and Social Psychology, 108, 114- 127.

Vandello, J. A., Goldschmied, N. P., & Richards, D. A. R. (2007). The appeal of the underdog. Personality and Social Psychology Bulletin, 33, 1603-1616.

4

"Let's Get Down to Business": A Handbook of Heroic Transformation in Mulan

YUN-OH PARK

American media has few popular films and TV shows that showcase strong Asian or Asian American representation. Among the limited list are Joy Luck Club (1993), Rush Hour (1998), and Fresh Off the Boat (2017). Walt Disney's Mulan (1998), adds to this list the heroic story of Fa Mulan, whose unique character is both female and Asian. Mulan, who is kind hearted, brave, and easy to relate to, has since become an international hero that continues to inspire an appreciation for and to highlight Asian culture in the media. The story is based on the legend of Hua Mulan, which was originally told as a poem known as the Ballad of Mulan. Since the legend has been passed down from as far back as the sixth century, thousands of people have recognized Hua Mulan as a hero. Today, Disney's Mulan inspires us, especially young women and girls to awaken the heroic qualities that lie within ourselves. These qualities may then be applied to fighting against our society's sexism and confining gender roles as well as to finding our true personal identities. Using recent research on heroism, we can better understand and utilize Mulan's heroic example.

Mulan's story closely follows the hero's journey, or Joseph Campbell's mon-omyth of the hero. The journey includes departure, initiation, and return (Campbell, 1949). Departure, or the separation of the hero from their normal world, begins with a "call to adventure." While in the "normal world," Mulan is devoted to bringing honor to her family. Although she sincerely desires to make her family proud, her free-spirited personality and her inability to con-form and to follow tradition makes it difficult for her to do so. Mulan strug-gles to fit into the stereotypically feminine gender roles set by the patriarchy in the film and clashes with the expectation that she must try and secure a marriage. After disappointing her family through failing her meeting with the matchmaker, the situation seems bleak. Suddenly, a call to adventure creates for her an opportunity to depart from the world that she cannot fit into nor thrive in. This opportunity presents itself when the Huns invade China, caus-ing the Imperial City of China to call for a man from each family to serve in the war against the Huns. When Mulan's old and injured father is drafted, she resolves to save his life by dressing up as a man and taking his place. Mulan responds to her call to adventure by taking off during the night with her father's armor, a haircut, and her horse.

Initiation, or "the challenges, obstacles, and foes that must be overcome for the hero to prevail," (Allison, Goethals, & Kramer, 2017) begins once Mulan's meeting with the matchmaker turns into a disaster. The matchmaker says to Mulan, "you may look like a bride, but you will never bring your family honor!" (The Matchmaker, Disney, 1998) After having disappointed her family, Mulan is then faced with difficult questions concerning her own iden-tity, purpose, and role. As initiation continues, Mulan is faced with more adversities after arriving at the training camp. Her first task is to learn how to resemble and act as she and her companion, Mushu, believe a man would. With a slightly humorous, rocky, and misguided start, she is able to become "Ping" for her time spent undercover. In addition, she must also endure the physically arduous training required to become a strong and competent soldier.

At the end of the film, Mulan makes a return to her family's home. Her jour-ney was extremely successful, having have been able to defeat Shan Yu and the rest of the Huns with the entire Imperial City of China and emperor to witness. Although the emperor awards her with gifts of appreciation and recognition for her service, she is more grateful to have been able to find peace within herself and to return to her loving family. Her father welcomes her back with a heart full of gratitude, pride, and relief. By the end of the film, Mulan not only succeeds in bringing honor to her family, but she has also been able to uncover truths about herself and an identity that she embraces.

As part of the hero's transformation, Joseph Campbell (1949) discusses death, whether it be a physical or spiritual death. One of the more specific deaths in the film occurs after Mulan's departure from her old life. This leads to the "death" of her old character, who is without greater responsibility and feels lost in her role in life and society. Once arrived at the training camp, a birth to a new character, "Ping", sparks the beginning of an even broader transformation, during which Mulan grows from the lost individual to a brave, intelligent, and defiant hero.

To further analyze Mulan's heroic transformation, it is useful to invoke Allison and Goethals' (2017) "three missing pieces of the neophyte hero". The first piece, which details a shift from egocentricity to sociocentricity, is embodied by Mulan's transformation throughout the film. At the start of the movie, Mulan is focused mainly on personal challenges such as the desire to complete her chores and responsibilities, as well as to make her family proud. By the end, however, Mulan's goals and focus have shifted outward and toward protecting her friends, as well as toward protecting the people of China. The change from egocentricity to sociocentricity is also seen through her gain in companions. Although initially Mulan had few companions besides her family members, she eventually becomes surrounded by friends, family, and allies. Similarly, Mulan achieves sociocentricity as an additional effect of gaining respect and recognition from the citizens of China.

The second piece, which is achieved by moving away from dependency and towards autonomy (Allison & Goethals, 2017), explains that the hero must be independent, willing to move against society, and able to pioneer new paths. This idea draws from Joseph Campbell's (2004) wisdom that we must all "follow our bliss", meaning that we must pursue what is most important, fulfilling, and valuable to ourselves. Expanding upon this thought, Allison and Goethals (2017) state that "we do not find our bliss by following a trail blazed by others." Mulan, who is at first unable to identify, much less "follow" her bliss, eventually discovers that her journey is meant to be one full of trail blazing and autonomy. Mulan develops a strong sense of autonomy by the end of the film, allowing her to defy the expectations set in her society that women cannot and should not fight, speak up, or act independently.

Mulan's developmental growth follows the third transformational arc described by Allison and Goethals (2017): the arc from stagnation to growth. From merely trying to live up to what was expected of her as a subdued young woman to enduring and thriving from training and battle, we observe as Mulan grows as a person and transforms into a hero. Mulan herself is able to learn, reflect upon, and consequently gain from her experiences, as well.

Additional components of the research on heroic transformation include questions of whether the journey is voluntary or involuntary and from who or what the hero receives help (Allison & Goethals, 2017; Allison et al., 2019).

Mulan's journey is both voluntary and involuntary – it is involuntary because she had no choice in that the war would come to her home and family, but at the same time, voluntary because she had chosen to take her father's place. On her journey she is given both physical and spiritual help. Her companions, Mushu, Cri-Kee, and her horse, Khan, provide physical help while her ancestors provide her spiritual help. The ancestors, who sent Mushu to Mulan, also help Mulan by protecting and watching over her and her family. Her main sidekick Mushu is helpful in many instances, and sometimes even saves her life. He gives her advice, provides companionship, and often works behind the scenes to ensure her success. For example, Mushu plays a crucial role in saving China and Mulan's life when he sets off the firework that defeats Shan Yu.

TAXONOMY OF HEROES

Based on Franco, Blau, and Zimbardo's (2011) situation-based taxonomy of heroes, we can define Mulan as a civil hero and a military hero. Although many of her heroic actions are implemented through saving others in battle, her brave decision to take her father's place as a mere citizen, and on top of that as a woman in her society, shows her civil heroism. Mulan is also an example of the classic underdog – viewers want to see her succeed, even if her chances are unlikely.

Using Allison and Goethals' (2012) taxonomy of heroes, we can define Mulan as a traditional hero, or a hero that is moral, competent, or complete, and makes exceptional contributions over time. Mulan does not only display these characteristics, but makes an exceptional contribution to the people of China by saving lives and by defeating the Huns.

Lastly, Mulan is a cultural hero to people across the world, regardless of race or gender. At the University of Richmond, Asian American, Non-Asian American, and international students from China were asked how they felt about Mulan as a hero. The general consensus among Asian American students was that Mulan's Asian heritage helps make her into a more personal and relatable hero. After asking international students about the reputation and impact of Mulan in China, it was generally said that the movie is well-appreciated and popular like it is in America.

"The Great Eight" Traits

"The Great Eight" attributes heroes (Allison & Goethals, 2011) can be used to describe Mulan's heroic characteristics. Allison and Goethals surveyed people's descriptions of heroes and identified the eight most commonly used attributes used to describe them. These attributes are: smart, strong, selfless, caring, charismatic, resilient, reliable, and inspiring. It is easy to find instances of all these traits throughout the movie, starting with intelligence. Part of what makes Mulan a successful hero and warrior is her ability to make up for a lack of pure strength with intelligence and wit. During training, Mulan is the first to be able to retrieve the arrow from the top of a pole – a test created by general Li Shang. The soldier is supposed to have on one wrist a heavy medallion that symbolizes strength, and on the other, one that symbolizes discipline.

Although the task seemed impossible and none of the stronger soldiers were able to retrieve the arrow, Mulan is the first to retrieve the arrow by tying the two medallions together and using them to make climbing easier. Upon reaching the top, she has proven herself and has gained the respect of the other soldiers, including Shang. In another scene, Mulan wittingly causes an avalanche which wipes out most of the Hun soldiers, saving her allies and winning the battle. In the final battle scene, Shan Yu, the leader of the Huns, says to Mulan, "it looks like you're out of ideas," after cornering her on the roof (Shan Yu, Mulan, 1998). Of course, Mulan is able to think quickly and with the help of Mushu, she cleverly uses a firework to defeat Shan Yu. At the imperial city, Mulan's leadership amongst Yao, Ling, Chien Po, and Shang as well as her inspiring determination, courage, and loyalty make the group successful in saving the emperor and defeating the Huns.

The non-battle related defining traits within Mulan's character become apparent through her relationships with others. Her high capacity for love and compassion are evident when she risks her life to join the army to save her father's life. In the avalanche scene, Mulan risks her life again to save Shang from being swept away by the snow. Although she has the opportunity to take cover and save herself, she pulls herself and Khan back into the powerful snow to go back for Shang. Later, we see Mulan's loyalty and selfless personality when, even after having been exiled by Shang and the rest of the army, she returns to warn him and the other soldiers that the Huns are going to attack. Mulan's strong sense of morality and dedication to her homeland drove her to hurry back to the city and fight the Huns even after having been abandoned.

In addition, Mulan's charismatic personality earns followers that appreciate and respect her for her heroic actions, whether they be friends, family, or the citizens of China. By the end of the story, Shang falls in love with Mulan, becoming enamored by her ability to fight well, her kindness and morality, and her bold spirit. We as viewers also find Mulan to be likable because she is genuinely kind and easygoing, and at times even has a great sense of humor. For example, towards the start of the film, we watch as Mulan completes her chore of feeding the chickens by attaching a bone on a string to the back of her dog's collar. This laid-back and playful way to complete her chores makes her likable and relatable to the viewers. By the end of the film, we are glad to see that Mulan's relaxed, warm, and cheerful personality at the start of the film does not diminish because of her transformation into a warrior. Her character satisfies all the traits of "The Great Eight," surely defining her as a hero.

Missing Inner Quality

Although they may have great traits, heroes are often missing an inner quality at the beginning of their heroic journey, according to Allison and Goethals (2017). One of the central themes that the film is built around is Mulan's search for her missing inner "quality." Allison and Goethals define this as "a fundamental truth about oneself or the world" that the hero may be lacking. In this situation, Mulan's missing quality is her lack of self-understanding and her obliviousness about why she does not fit into her society. It is only after she matures through her inner challenges and battle experiences that she truly grows into herself. Her struggle with her identity begins with the matchmaker scene. Her sorrow and fear are told explicitly through the song "Reflection," in which she sings the lyrics, "... I will never pass for a perfect bride Or a perfect daughter... Why is my reflection someone I don't know Somehow I cannot hide Who I am Though I've tried" (Lea Salonga, 1998). After her hero's journey, she returns with more knowledge about herself; she knows that she is strong, independent, and intelligent. Mulan comes back with the understanding that her ability to be the "perfect daughter" and to follow the social norms that did not fit well with her did not define her worth. Mulan was able to prove to herself that she could find a truer and greater purpose, identity, and version of herself.

More on the Hero's Transformation

Mulan's transformation begins with a literal one. A montage in the film shows her cutting her hair, tying it up, putting on her father's armor, and taking his sword. Although she transforms physically into a male soldier, her real hero's transformation had just begun. The mental and figurative part of her transformation begins when she arrives at the training camp, at which her perseverance and determination are tested. Although at first she is seen struggling with the physically demanding and arduous tasks of the training, she succeeds in becoming a physically competent soldier. By the end of training, she is able to run with heavy buckets of water on her back, fight with a staff, fish by hand, and shoot arrows. Other types of experiences, such as suffering and hardships, transformed her, as well. After Mulan and the others arrive as reinforcement only to find that the previous troops had already been killed in battle, Mulan must overcome the devastating emotions brought on by war and death. By the time she reaches her final stage of transformation, she has been strengthened emotionally and physically by her training and experiences, and she is ready to step up to become the hero that saves the day.

Suffering

Suffering plays a critical role in the hero's transformation (Allison & Setterberg, 2016). The benefits of suffering are that it is redemptive, signifies a crossover point in life, encourages humility, stimulates compassion, promotes social union, and instills meaning and purpose. Mulan suffers at first, from struggling with her identity, to withstanding tough training, to being expelled from the army. "Reflection" shows an internal suffering that signified a crossover point in Mulan's life – the realization that where she was in life was not the right place, and that it did not align with who she felt like she was. The training camp scenes exhibit physical suffering, and her expulsion shows again emotional suffering that stimulates compassion from viewers. The culmination of the low points at which we see Mulan is a crucial step of her hero transformation. These low points lead us to sympathize with her, strengthening our feelings toward her as a hero, as well as add to the glory of her eventual redemption. After the emperor is saved by Mulan, he compares her to a flower, saying that "the flower that blooms in adversity is the most beautiful and rare of them all" (The Emperor of China, Mulan, Disney, 1998).

HEROES AND UNDERDOGS

Mulan's role as an underdog is highlighted by the strong correlation between heroes and underdogs. Throughout the film, the audience is encouraged to root for Mulan because she is a woman who is told that she cannot do what a man can do. As an underdog fighting against sexism, we appreciate the rebelliousness that makes Mulan an advocate for feminism in the story. We need her to survive the war and save china in order to gain the respect of her family and friends, to love and become at peace with herself, and to represent and empower women.

As previously mentioned, Mulan is an underdog of a few different groups. At the beginning of the film, she is an underdog in her society at home. She does not fit in with the other women and constantly receives backlash and reprimand when trying to move against the norm. We watch as Mulan struggles to become the traditional woman preparing to be married in imperial China, and we sympathize with her throughout her disastrous meeting with the matchmaker. Likewise, Mulan finds herself as a physical underdog in the army. As a woman, Mulan's feminine physical and nonphysical characteristics make it difficult for her to fit in with the other men. Immediately upon arriving at the training grounds, Mulan (as Ping) starts a brawl by accident, causing the soldiers to already alienate her. Through the course of a montage and a catchy song, viewers are glad to see Mulan overcome the various adversities and eventually succeed while earning the trust and respect of her peers. From the very beginning, the audience roots for her due to a combination of her greatness as a character and having formidable odds stacked against her.

CONCLUSION

Mulan presents to us a fight against societal norms, a journey of finding and proving oneself, and an inspiring story of bravery and love. Drawing upon different avenues of heroism science research, we have been able to define and analyze Mulan's character and transformation, and we have shown how these two elements impact real people in the story. Mulan inspires people across different backgrounds, genders, and ages to be defiant and to be unforgiving of one's own self. Mulan's story instills in us the courage to defy and break through the constraints that society often imposes upon us, which in turn may lead to social progress and even an increased understanding of self-identity.

In addition, Mulan is one of few pop culture heroes in America to be of Asian descent. Hopefully, we will see more and more Asian representation in the media as time progresses – with great stories of not just Chinese Americans, but of Korean Americans, Japanese Americans, and other Asian American heroes and heroines. We could apply the examples of heroism from Mulan and possibly benefit ourselves by breaking through and progressing beyond the many social forces set upon us. We can all work toward eliminating gender stereotypes, prejudices, and sexism by taking with us the lessons from this great heroine and by becoming similar heroes ourselves.

REFERENCES

Allison, S. T., Eylon, D., Beggan, J.K., & Bachelder, J. (2009). The demise of leadership: Positivity and negativity in evaluations of dead leaders. The Leadership Quarterly, 20, 115-129.

Allison, S. T., & Goethals, G. R. (2012). Personal versus cultural heroes. Retrieved from https://blog.richmond.edu/heroes/2012/09/12/personal-versus-cultural-heroes

Allison, S. T., & Goethals, G. R. (2013, May 17). Heroes: What They Do & Why We Need Them. Retrieved October 06, 2017, from https://blog.richmond.edu/heroes/2013/05/17/10-reasons-why-we-need-heroes/

Allison, S. T., Goethals, G. R., & Kramer, R. M. (2017). Setting the scene: The rise and coalescence of heroism science. In S. T. Allison, G. R. Goethals, & R. M. Kramer (Eds.), Handbook of heroism and heroic leadership. New York: Routledge.

Allison, S. T., & Goethals, G. R. (2017). The hero's transformation. In S. T. Allison, G. R. Goethals, & R. M. Kramer (Eds.), Handbook of heroism and heroic leadership. New York: Routledge.

Allison, S. T., Goethals, G. R., Marrinan, A. R., Parker, O. M., Spyrou, S. P., Stein, M. (2019). The metamorphosis of the hero: Principles, processes, and purpose. Frontiers in Psychology.

Allison, S. T., & Setterberg, G. C. (2016). Suffering and sacrifice: Individual and collective benefits, and implications for leadership. In S. T. Allison, C. T. Kocher, & G. R. Goethals (Eds), Frontiers in spiritual leadership: Discovering the better angels of our nature. New York: Palgrave Macmillan.

Disney Wiki. (2017) Fa Mulan. [online] Available at: http://disney.wikia.com/wiki/Fa_Mulan [Accessed 6 Oct. 2017].

Disney Wiki. (2017). Mulan. [online] Available at: http://disney.wikia.com/wiki/Mulan [Accessed 6 Oct. 2017].

Franco, Z. E., Blau, K., & Zimbardo, P. G. (2011, April 11). Heroism: A Conceptual Analysis and Differentiation Between Heroic Action and Altruism. Review of General Psychology. Advance online publication. doi: 10.1037/a0022672

Goethals, G. R., & Allison, S. T. (2014). Kings and charisma, Lincoln and leadership: An evolutionary perspective. In Goethals, G. R., et al. (Eds.), Conceptions of leadership: Enduring ideas and emerging insights. New York: Palgrave Macmillan

Goethals, G. R., & Allison, S. T. (2016). Transforming motives and mentors: The heroic leadership of James MacGregor Burns. In G. R. Goethals (Ed.), Politics, ethics and change: The legacy of James MacGregor Burns (pp. 59-73). Northampton, MA: Edward Elgar Publishing.

Hua Mulan. (2017, September 29). Retrieved October 06, 2017, from https://en.wikipedia.org/wiki/Hua_Mulan

Klimczak, N. (2016, January 1). The Ballad of Hua Mulan: The Legendary Warrior Woman Who Brought Hope to China. Retrieved October 06, 2017, from http://www.ancient-origins.net/history-famous-people/ballad-hua-mulan-legendary-warrior-woman-who-brought-hope-china-005084

Lea Salonga (2014). Reflection. Mulan: An Original Walt Disney Records Soundtrack. (Recorded 1997-1998).

Vandello, J. A., Goldschmied, N., and Michniewicz, K., (2017). Underdogs as Heroes. In S. T. Allison, G. R. Goethals, & R. M. Kramer (Eds.), Handbook of heroism and heroic leadership. New York: Routledge.

5

Jack Bauer: The Heroic Transformation of the Ultimate Moral Rebel

ETHAN LIBO

In December 1955 in Montgomery, Alabama, Rosa Parks broke the law by saying one word: "No." When Parks refused to give up her seat in protest of segregation, she was arrested for her defiance. Today Parks is remembered as a hero and looking back one can see she had the moral high ground. What's interesting is that at the time Rosa Parks was treated like criminal for exercising a basic right. This leads to the ethical question: Is it wrong to break the law no matter how unjust it may seem? People will argue that no matter how unjust the law, it is still wrong to break it in protest because doing so will set a dangerous precedent. The counter-argument to this idea is that we as a society aren't going to break a law in mass protest unless some part of that law is deeply unjust. This idea was proposed by Henry David Thoreau and has been coined as "civil disobedience." Thoreau argued that as a society we have a responsibility to put pressure on our lawmakers if a law is unjust, and if they ignore us than we have no choice but to take matters into our own hands.

Jack Bauer, played by Kiefer Sutherland in Fox's hit TV series 24, took the idea of "civil disobedience" to a new extreme through eight seasons of thrilling and at times cheesy drama and action. The basic mechanism underlying 24 was that events occurred in real time. A 24 season consisted of 24 episodes in which each episode was an hour long in air time, but also an hour long in the show; therefore each season consumed one day. During each of these days Jack Bauer had to stop a terrorist attack by the end of the day, but with so many lives on the line Jack Bauer had to cross the line of the law. As Bauer put it himself, "I will do whatever it takes to save them and I mean whatever it takes." During his career Jack Bauer saved millions of lives but in doing so he disobeyed superiors (including the President at times), but more importantly he tortured people and violated the constitution.

Many characters in the show and many viewers call Jack Bauer a sociopath, but in this chapter I am arguing to dispel this notion. This chapter will also examine the type of hero Jack Bauer is by examining his key attributes, his journey and the transformation he went through during his journey, and his journey's ultimate impact on society.

BAUER AND HERO TAXONOMY

Jack Bauer may occupy two places in the hero situation-based taxonomy proposed by Franco, Blau, and Zimbardo (2011). The first and most obvious classification would be a "military and other duty-bound physical risk heroes" (Franco et. al, 2011). As a field agent for the Los Angeles Counter Terrorist Unit, Jack Bauer put his life on the line every day while chasing potential terrorist leads. Bauer exceeded his call of duty like it was a part of his call of duty. There were many instances where he was ready to give his own life even when there were other options on the table. Bauer often found himself in a situation where he had to choose between saving his family and saving thousands of innocent lives, but somehow he always managed to evade these ultimatums and save everyone.

As mentioned earlier, Jack Bauer could also be a social hero because he broke the law in situations where he needed to do it for the greater good of the American people. The reason why Jack Bauer doesn't quite fit into the social hero category is because he is not breaking the law due to its unjust nature but rather because it is inconvenient given the urgency of the matter. According to the United States constitution, people shall not be subject to cruel and unusual punishment. One would not be going out on a limb to say that some of Bauer's punishment methods were cruel and unusual. One of Bauer's favorite moves for interrogation was shooting people and then sticking his gun into their open wounds.

This raises the question about whether it is appropriate for Bauer to obstruct due process of law and torture a terrorist on U.S. soil for the greater good of possibly saving millions of innocent citizens. Jack Bauer understands it is not ethical; he does not view what he does as appropriate. Bauer realizes that he doesn't have time to play philosopher because something terrible must be done to stop something catastrophic from happening. Jack Bauer is a hero because he is willing to dirty his own conscience to save others. Bauer has succumbed to a phenomenon called the "hindsight bias" in that looking back and seeing how everything worked out it is easy to say Bauer was a hero. At the time, however, he was criticized for his methods. Thus, Bauer has been anointed the nickname of "The Ultimate Moral Rebel" (Mouw, 2010).

Bauer and the Attributes of a Hero

Joseph Campbell (1949), who could be called the parent of heroism studies, said "Heroes have an irresistible and mysterious power" (Franco et al., 2011). For Jack Bauer, this power was both a blessing and a curse. Bauer was able to withstand some of the most dangerous situations and overcome insurmountable odds in dramatic ways. This irresistible and mysterious power was also the same thing that dragged Bauer's loved ones into situations they had no business being in (Franco et al., 2011). Bauer would be told later in the series, "You're cursed, Jack. Everything you touch, one way or another, ends up dead." When Bauer absorbed this truth, it struck a nerve with him because he knew it was true. Almost every person and relationship in his life had been sacrificed for the greater good of society. This sacrifice was a unique attribute of Jack Bauer, but he also displays all the standard attributes of a hero.

Bauer and the "Great Eight" Traits

Allison and Goethals (2011) conducted a study of people's perceptions of the common attributes associated with being a hero. These perceived traits were compiled into eight parent attributes, and this group of attributes was dubbed "the great eight" traits of heroes. The great eight consists of the traits of smart, strong, caring, selfless, charismatic, resilient, reliable, and inspiring (Allison & Goethals 2011). Bauer displays all of these attributes in a unique fashion. He has an intelligence for his job as a field agent that is unmatchable in his world. Bauer finds creative ways to kill his enemies, such as when at one point he threw an enemy into a dishwasher where the knives were pointing outwards. Bauer's enemies fear his strength. At certain points in the series when Bauer is being hunted down, his enemies often warn each other about how highly trained and competent Bauer is. He also displays brute strength as he never loses a fist fight during the entire series.

Compassion is definitely not the first trait that people think of when considering Jack Bauer. Bauer does care deeply about his loved ones, but because his job takes them away from him he shows no compassion towards his enemies because he blames them for what he has lost. It is to Jack's benefit that he does not take mercy on his enemies because it makes him more effective at his job of saving as many lives as possible. Selflessness is Bauer's most defined trait, as everyone knows he does not do what he does for the fame. Bauer sacrifices everything he has so others can keep everything they have, and yet the series ends with him as a fugitive of the United States government. He saves millions of lives, sacrificed his own and never receives recognition for it; this is most certainly heroism with a capital "H".

People who are charismatic tend to draw people towards them like a magnet. Jack Bauer's charisma stems from his bluntness. Out of all the candidates people want Bauer to work for them because they know he will find some way, no matter what, to get the job done. This relentlessness is reminiscent of his irresistible and mysterious charisma mentioned earlier. If there is one thing that Jack Bauer is not, it is a quitter, and no one would blame him if he did quit. After losing his wife, his best friend, and the relationship with his daughter, Bauer is able to work his way out of dark depressions.

Often a season will open with Bauer in a depression, a new terror threat will surface and Bauer will be forced out of his retirement or firing. This new challenge pulls him out of his depression because he needs to be his best self to get the job done. If Jack Bauer is not reliable then the United States in the world of "24" would be decimated. Jack's bosses jump through hoops to get Bauer involved with the newest threat. Bauer gets pulled into a crisis by the FBI while being indicted by them at the same time. Jack Bauer is certainly not considered an inspiration to society but he should be. From the little glimpse we get of normal civilians on the show, we see that they view Bauer as deranged and dangerous. However, if they knew what he went through they would see him as the inspiration that we, the audience, know him to be.

BAUER'S JOURNEY AND TRANSFORMATION

Introduction to the Hero's Journey

According to Joseph Campbell, the hero's journey consists of three stages encompassed into the hero's "monomyth" (Campbell, 1949). These three stages are departure, initiation and return. Each season of 24 could be considered a different hero's journey for Jack Bauer, yet this would ignore the overarching transformation that takes place across eight seasons and a reboot series. At the end of the last series Bauer is still alive, which raises the question: Is Jack Bauer's transformation complete? The short answer is yes and this is due to the to some of the non-traditional features of Bauer's heroic transformation. Let's now examine each stage of Bauer's journey.

Departure

Before the departure of a hero even begins, the hero usually has a calling (Dik et al., 2017). When choosing his career Bauer found his calling by making an environment-fit choice. To make this choice effectively, he had to understand himself and the opportunities the world had to offer (Dik et al., 2017). By understanding this idea, Bauer was able to choose a role that optimized his skills to the benefit of society. In the P-E fit chart Bauer fits under the role of the police detective (Dik et al., 2017). The core value of this role is independence, which is a core attribute of Bauer. Many times in the series Bauer goes rogue because he need to circumvent government restraints on him to get the job done. Bauer is arguably more dangerous on a mission alone than in the group because his level of intuition is so far above everyone else that other allies will slow him down. There are three dimensions of calling, and Bauer mostly fulfills the third. This third dimension of a calling is "the sense that one's work is not principally carried out for personal happiness or fulfillment but rather to advance the well-being of others, or the greater good" (Dik et al., 2017). This is the story of Jack Bauer's life.

Before a hero departs on their journey, they are living in a state of comfort and are familiar with their world. The first season of 24 opens with Bauer at home with his wife and daughter. Bauer's wife and daughter aren't getting along, but in the same way that all families don't always get along. It is apparent that Bauer feels comfortable and is happy with his home life. Like many heroes, Bauer does not leave his world of comfort by choice. Bauer gets called into work late at night for something that seems to be routine. It turns out that it's not routine and a terrorist group is trying the assassinate a presidential candidate. While this is escalating, Bauer's daughter gets kidnapped. Bauer is now in a situation where terrorist are blackmailing him to not do his job. At the end of the first season Bauer reaches the breaking point of his world of comfort.

After rescuing his daughter and stopping the terrorists, Bauer watches his wife bleed to death right in front of him. With Bauer's wife now dead and his relationship with his daughter strained, the two loving constants in his life are gone. As a tragic as this situation was, the pain was necessary for Bauer to undergo his transformation and become the hero the world needed.

Campbell (1949) describes the hero's transformation as: follows: "A hero ventures forth from the world of common day into a region of supernatural wonder: fabulous forces are there encountered and a decisive victory is won: the hero comes back from this mysterious adventure with the power to bestow boons on his fellow man." During this journey, three transformations are said to take place: A transformation of setting, a transformation of self, and a transformation of society (Allison & Goethals, 2017; Allison, Goethals, & Kramer, 2017; Ross, 2019). We have mentioned the hero venturing from the common world, which is the transformation of setting (Campbell, 1949). Let's now look at the transformation of self.

Initiation

Usually the initiation stage and transformation of oneself requires a mentor to guide the experience. For Bauer, there is not any one individual who guides his transformation but rather a group of people. Bauer is transformed into someone who uses unconventional methods to do his job, and adopt his unorthodox ways he needs the support of his work colleagues. Bauer is able to gain the trust of people within an hour after meeting them. Bauer's energy gravitates people towards him and he gains trust fast. This is where the argument of Bauer being a sociopath should be put to rest. Bauer makes genuine friendships, and he shows time and time again that he would put his life on the line for these people. If he were a sociopath he would have sacrificed them for his own benefit.

During a hero's initiation, the hero encounters the toughest obstacles they will have to face (Campbell, 1949). For Bauer, this initiation featured the death of everyone he got close to, the countless terror threats he put down, and being imprisoned by the Chinese for three years. Ultimately initiation ends when the hero slays "the dragon" (Campbell, 1949). This is not a literal dragon, but rather an enemy that encompasses the trial one needs to overcome to fulfill the heroic transformation. Part of the dragon theory is that a portion of the hero lives within their dragon, so when they destroy the dragon they are not only vanquishing their enemy but also vanquishing something that lives inside them to complete their transformation. Jack Bauer's dragon was president Charles Logan. Logan was a true sociopath willing destroy anyone to cement his legacy. Some of Logan's sociopathic tendencies lived inside Bauer, but in the moment when Logan is ultimately brought down by Bauer in the 8th season the distinction between the two of them is clear. Bauer is a hero fighting for the people he loved, while Logan only fights for himself.

Return

The final stage of the monomyth is the return, in which the hero uses the transformation they have received to transform society. It could be argued that Bauer's transformation of society didn't happen, or hasn't happened yet, as Bauer was never able to give what he gained back to society. Most people probably wouldn't be able to relate to what Bauer learned anyway. In many hero's journeys, the hero returns to their world as the "master of both worlds.", and for Bauer this is not the case. Despite not achieving this dual identity, Bauer is still a hero because he spent his entire career sacrificing himself to save society, and thus it would be foolish to say that he is not a hero just because he did fully complete Campbell's return phase of the journey. Every hero's transformation will differ in a multitude of ways. These deviations will be examined in the next section.

Characterizing Bauer's Transformation

No hero journeys are identical, and in fact there are ten common ways that journeys can differ: subject; scale; speed; duration; timing; direction; type; depth; openness; and source (Allison & Goethals, 2017). Bauer's Journey differs with a few of these characteristics. Arguably the most important is Bauer's type of transformation. Bauer's type of transformation differs because he is already highly competent and trained when the series begins. Bauer has already been transformed physically, motivationally, and intellectually. During the series Bauer will undergo a moral transformation and an emotional transformation. Bauer's moral transformation could ironically be described as an immoral transformation. His transformation was a paradox because he used unethical methods to save lives, and saving lives is usually considered ethical. In other words, Bauer needed to become immoral to do something moral, with his means justifying his ends. Bauer's emotional transformation is intriguing because it is a dynamic transition. When the series begins, Bauer is emotionally in touch with himself and the people around him. Bauer almost becomes a tragic hero and falls from grace emotionally after his wife dies (Allison & Goethals, 2017). Bauer is emotionally out of synch for a while, but as the series moves on and he forms new relationships, these insensitivities disappear and once again he is transformed emotionally.

There is no doubt that there is also a great depth in Bauer's heroism because there is nothing superficial about what he does. A hero who is superficial should not be considered a hero; the motivation should matter, as heroism cannot be a facade. For Bauer, heroism is not a pretense because he gains nothing and sacrifices everything, The speed of transformation is another characteristic of transformation that is very interesting in the case of Jack Bauer. While Bauer's transformation ultimately takes roughly 15 years of time in the series (about two years pass between each of the 8 seasons), Bauer only transforms on the specific day that is the focus of each season. While the transformation happens over a long period time, it also happens in speedy clusters. This is not an unusual pattern in hero's transformations (Allison, 2015; Williams, 2018; Worthington & Allison, 2018).

CONCLUSION

Jack Bauer is a hero because he sacrificed most of his personal life to achieve aims that were much larger than himself. Critics argue that Bauer tortured people, and torture is never justifiable. This chapter has argued that Bauer's heroism demands a more nuanced understanding of his complex life. Bauer tortured a few lives to save millions, a fact that demonstrated Bauer's awareness of the bigger picture. When the going got tough and Jack Bauer had to make a tough decision with limited time and resources, he put ethics to the side. It is the "act now pray for forgiveness later" attitude. No human is perfect, which means no hero can be perfect either.

The series 24 has not been discussed much throughout this chapter, but there are some relevant aspects of the series that offer insight into Jack Bauer's character. Some series have multiple main characters, or a main character with really strong supporting characters, but 24 could be called "The Jack Bauer Show". Eight seasons and a reboot were all built around one iconic character. Many people who have never even seen the series know the name Jack Bauer because he is such a developed and dynamic character. People joke about his grumpiness, or his catchphrase "dammit" (you can't drop f-bombs on Fox), but at the end of the day everyone admired him. This is the only thing that matters in the debate over whether Bauer is a hero or not. There is no real objective way to define heroism. One can study the taxonomy, the attributes, the journey, and then transformation, but in the end the judgement of heroism is up to people's perceptions. If one is viewed as the hero, then that is the truth of those viewers; similarly, people who do not view Bauer as a hero are also expressing a subjective truth. Heroism, like beauty, is in the eye of the beholder (Allison & Goethals, 2017). If one concludes that Jack Bauer is not a hero after 15 years of devoting every shred of himself to the betterment of society, then heroism is not a quality that is attainable by humans.

REFERENCES

Allison, S. T. (2015). The initiation of heroism science. Heroism Science, 1, 1-8.

Allison, S. T., & Goethals, G. R. (2017). The hero's transformation. In S. T. Allison, G. R. Goethals, & R. M. Kramer (Eds.), Handbook of heroism and heroic leadership. New York: Routledge.

Allison, S. T., Goethals, G. R., & Kramer, R. M. (2017). Setting the scene: The rise and coalescence of heroism science. In S. T. Allison, G. R. Goethals, & R. M. Kramer (Eds.), Handbook of heroism and heroic leadership. New York: Routledge.

Allison, S. T., Goethals, G. R., & Kramer, R. M. (Eds.) (2017). Handbook of heroism and heroic leadership. New York: Routledge.

Campbell, J. (1949) The hero with a thousand faces. Princeton, NJ: Princeton University Press.

Davis, J. L., Burnette, J. L., Allison, S. T., & Stone, H. (2011). Against the odds: Academic underdogs benefit from incremental theories. Social Psychology of Education, 14, 331-346.

Decter-Frain, Ruth Vanstone, & Jeremy A. Frimer (2017) Why and how groups create moral heroes. In S. T. Allison, G. R. Goethals, & R. M. Kramer (Eds.), Handbook of Heroism and Heroic Leadership. New York: Routledge.

Dik, Adelyn B. Shimizu, & William O'Connor (2017) Career development and a sense of calling contexts for heroism. In S. T. Allison, G. R. Goethals, & R. M. Kramer (Eds.), Handbook of Heroism and Heroic Leadership. New York: Routledge.

Eylon, D., & Allison, S. T. (2005). The frozen in time effect in evaluations of the dead. Personality and Social Psychology Bulletin, 31, 1708-1717.

Franco, Z. E., Blau, K., & Zimbardo, P. G. (2011). Heroism: A conceptual analysis and differentiation between heroic action and altruism. Review of General Psychology.

Gray, K., Anderson, S., Doyle, C. M., Hester, N., Schmitt, P., Vonasch, A., Allison, S. T., and Jackson, J. C. (2018). To be immortal, do good or evil. Personality and Social Psychology Bulletin.

Hoyt, C. L. (2014) Social Identities and Leadership. In G. Goethals (Ed.), Conceptions of Leadership. New York: Palgrave MacMillan.

Kafashian, Adam Sparks, Amanda Rotella, & Pat Barclay (2017). Why heroism exists evolutionary perspectives on extreme helping. In S. T. Allison, G. R. Goethals, & R. M. Kramer (Eds.), Handbook of Heroism and Heroic Leadership. New York: Routledge.

Kinsella, Timothy D. Ritchie, & Eric R. Igou (2017). Attributes of heroism. In S. T. Allison, G. R. Goethals, & R. M. Kramer (Eds.), Handbook of Heroism and Heroic Leadership. New York: Routledge.

Mouw, R. J. (2010). The moral work of watching. Retrieved from https://perspectivesjournal. org/posts/24-the-moral-work-of-watching/

Parks, C. (2017). Accidental and purposeful Impediments to heroism. In S. T. Allison, G. R. Goethals, & R. M. Kramer (Eds.), Handbook of Heroism and Heroic Leadership. New York: Routledge.

Ross, S. L. (2019). Who put the super in superhero? Transformation and heroism as a function of evolution. Frontiers in Psychology.

Vandello, Nadav Goldschmied, & Kenneth Michniewicz (2017) Underdogs as Heroes. In S. T. Allison, G. R. Goethals, & R. M. Kramer (Eds.), Handbook of Heroism and Heroic Leadership. New York: Routledge.

Williams, C. (2018). The hero's journey: A mudmap to wellbeing. In O. Efthimiou, S. T. Allison, & Z. E. Franco (Eds.), Heroism and wellbing in the 21st century. New York: Routledge.

Worthington, E. L, & Allison, S. T. (2018). Heroic humility: What the science of humility can say to people raised on self-focus. Washington. DC: American Psychological Association.

6

The Heroic Transformation of Dexter Morgan, Killer of Killers

S. S. Diaz

Serial killers have been viewed as evil by practically every sane person in history. Yet is it possible for a serial killer to be viewed as a hero rather than a villain? The answer, quite surprisingly, is yes. The Federal Bureau of Investigation defines a serial murder as the unlawful killing of two or more victims by the same offender, in separate events (Morton, 2010). A common question arises over the discussion of serial killers: what could possibly cause an individual to kill multiple innocent victims? Several factors, such as childhood upbringing, genetics, and life experiences, can cause a person to transform into a serial killer. Different serial killers exhibit different behaviors as well as motives for their killings. However, there are a few distinct traits that are common among serial murderers, including impulsiveness, a lack of remorse for their actions, sensation seeking tendencies, and a need to be in control (Morton 2010). Serial murder is not a new phenomenon, as serial killers have existed for centuries.

Many even go unnoticed, killing dozens, potentially even hundreds of victims without ever being caught by authorities.

The purpose of this chapter is to describe the heroic life and transformation of a prominent television character Dexter Morgan, during seasons one through four of Dexter, a serial killer of killers. This chapter first reviews the hero's journey as described by Joseph Campbell (1949).

Creation of Dexter and the Summoning of His Journey

The Hero's Journey is the basis of all great stories and consists of three main phases: the call to adventure and departure from the hero's ordinary world, test, and trials in the supernatural world and the return back to the familiar world (Campbell, 1949). Dexter Morgan's heroic transformation began at a very young age. When he was just a toddler, he witnessed the gruesome killing of his own mother. She was murdered by three men in a storage unit, while Dexter and his older brother, Brian, helplessly sat there and watched. The killers left both boys in the storage unit alone with their dead mother, the two young children sitting in their mother's blood for days before they were found by police. Police officer Harry Morgan was the one to carry Dexter out of the dark and gloomy storage unit. The memories of the killing stayed with Dexter for his whole life but remained dormant until he reached adulthood. He carries that memory with him every day of his life, and evidently those horrid memories are responsible for his need to kill, which Dexter refers to as his "dark passenger" (Cerone, 2006).

Harry Morgan saw something in Dexter the day he pulled him from the crime scene. He saw potential in Dexter's youth and believed that Dexter had a good chance of not remembering the terrible things he had witnessed. Harry treated Dexter like his own child and years later adopted him. Growing up, Dexter had a normal life. He had two stepparents and a stepsister, Debra, that loved him unconditionally. However, as Dexter got older he started having certain aggressive tendencies. These urges were eating away at him. He initially dealt with these feelings by killing small animals or rodents. However, his father Harry caught on to him when their neighbors' dog went missing. He confronted his son, and Dexter tried to justify the killing with the fact that the dog was keeping his sister and mother up all night long, promising he would never do something like that again. However, the dark passenger returned, and when Harry found blood on Dexter's clothes he realized his son was troubled.

Dexter's tendencies only got stronger as he got older, but Harry still loved his son despite his unconventional desires. Soon enough, Dexter's urges escalated. He was no longer satisfying his dark passenger by killing rodents and other animals, he needed to kill people. Harry realized that Dexter would never be able to change the way he feels, so instead of discouraging his impulses, he decided to come up with a rigid code that would help Dexter cope with his issues.

Harry's code was a simple set of guidelines, designed as a framework for survival. The code prevented Dexter from getting into trouble and gave him a way to channel his impulses while simultaneously ridding the world of people who he deemed deserved to die. The first rule of the code, and arguably the most important to Harry, is never get caught. No father wants to see their own son be sent to jail for life, or even potentially be put to death, because of a feeling they cannot control. The second rule of the code, which has greater meaning to Dexter than the first, is never kill an innocent. Dexter is not an immoral human being because of his tendencies. He is always aware that killing innocent human beings is wrong. When Dexter chooses a victim, he devotes however many hours it takes to researching and spying on his victims until he is one hundred percent positive that the victim is a killer, someone who instills pain on innocent people. The remaining rules of the code exist to ensure the first rule and are as follows: never make a scene, fake emotions and normality in order to fit in, never get emotionally involved, don't leave any traces, and never make things personal (Dexter Wiki, 2017).

Being given this set of rules at such a young age had quite an impact on Dexter. He began spending more time with his father and learning essential lessons. Harry taught Dexter how to hunt, fight, kill, target, and do everything else he needed to know in order to live his life as a serial killer. It is quite ironic that one of the most respected police officers in Miami was teaching his own son how to kill and get away with murder; however, Harry was abetting Dexter in "following his bliss" (Campbell, 1949). Dexter spent several years practicing the code and training before he ever made his first human kill. It wasn't always easy for Dexter; he was forced to conceal his tendencies until Harry was absolutely positive that Dexter was ready to begin his life-long journey.

As Dexter approached adulthood, his beloved father began getting sick and was hospitalized due to a heart attack. Dexter spent all of his free time by his father's side, going straight from school to the hospital. However, Harry's treatment was only causing him to get sicker. Dexter and Harry discovered that it was because the nurse was injecting him, along with numerous other patients, with poison rather than real medicine. It was at that instant, when Dexter and his father realized what was really going on, that Harry gave Dexter the command to make his first kill. Dexter Morgan killed the nurse and he was never the same after that. He crossed the first threshold of his heroic transformation when he made his initial kill.

A year later, Harry's heart gave out and Dexter was alone. No other living human knew about his dark passenger and about what he had done. However, Harry's influence and code remained with him past his existence.

Dexter's Departure

A hero's departure begins in an ordinary world where they are called to an adventure. Initially, the hero refuses to follow that call, but with the help of a mentor they begin their journey of departing the world they have known their whole lives (Campbell, 1949). Since birth, Dexter has been lacking an inner quality. He is unable to develop real human connections. The only person he really connected with was his father because of Harry's acceptance of the dark passenger. Without Harry, the only family Dexter has left is Debra. The siblings are both employed by the Miami Metro Police Department: Dexter works as a blood splatter analyst, following his passion for forensics, and Debra, following the footsteps of their late father, works as a Detective for the homicide department.

Dexter begins his journey by gaining intelligence, resilience, and strength, only three of the great eight characteristics of a hero (Allison & Goethals, 2013, 2017). Over the years, Dexter has mastered faking human interactions. He brings donuts to work to share with his colleagues, he flashes a smile when someone says hello to him, he is an avid member of the Miami Metro bowling team, and he dates women he's not truly interested in to make it seem like he is living a normal life. Initially Dexter was seemingly soulless, a quality common among serial killers, showing no remorse or concern for the effect of his actions on others. Meanwhile, he murders rapists, torturers, and pedophiles once the sun sets. No one knows what he does and no one can ever know.

Working with the police department, Dexter has a huge advantage in finding his next targets. Criminals who are let go due to mistrials or accomplices of criminals that go unnoticed make the perfect victims for Dexter. He cleans the streets by disposing of bad guys, when the police can't catch them or when the law interferes with police work. Franco, Blau, and Zimbardo (2011) differentiate heroic action from general altruism by stating that heroism is a way to unify several courageous actions, involving risk, that are selfless and for the greater good of society. From this definition, we can say with confidence that Dexter is a hero, not simply an altruist.

Dexter's Initiation and Positive Female Influences

Mentors are crucial to a hero's transformation. Other than Harry, Dexter has two influential women in his life that help him obtain additional heroic traits: Debra and Rita show Dexter how to be compassionate, which is a communal characteristic that is commonly associated with women leaders (Hoyt, 2014). Dexter cares very deeply about his sister but has difficulty connecting with her because he conceals his emotions. She is the only living person Dexter loves, initially. However, he cannot be completely honest with her and if she ever found out about his dark passenger, she would never love him again. They are quite bonded by the considerable amount of time they spend together at work and outside of work as well.

Debra was involved in arresting an abusive husband and befriended the wife, Rita, who had dealt with the abuse for years before they put the terrible man behind bars. She introduced Dexter to Rita, and they began dating. Rita is initially very reserved due to her past relationship, which Dexter respects and understands. At first, their relationship contains no real substance because Dexter is using her to help maintain his fake persona. Realizing the relationship is peculiar, Dexter says, "I have to play the game, and after years of trying to look normal I think I met the right woman for me" (Cerone, 2006). However, as their relationship progresses throughout the series, Dexter begins to truly care about Rita and her two children. He is constantly spending time with them, going to the park with them, or making them pancakes before school in the morning; he begins to assume the role of a father figure. For the first time in his life, he cares about people other than Harry and Debra. The new relationships that Dexter engages in contribute to his moral and emotional transformation.

Dexter's Turbulences

During a hero's journey the hero is frequently pushed out of their comfort zone with difficult challenges and obstacles (Campbell, 1949). Dexter's journey is far from smooth; there are several instances where he almost blows his cover. One morning, two scuba divers were swimming at the bottom of the ocean in Bay Harbor, Miami. They noticed a few black trash bags sitting in the sand. They swam over and pulled at them, causing the knot to become undone. Human limbs emerged from the open bag and began rising to the water's surface. Within an hour, detectives, professional scuba divers, and forensics workers, including Dexter himself, arrived at the scene, discovering hundreds of trash bags containing dozens of bodies at the bottom of the ocean. It was the biggest case Miami Metro had ever seen.

Dexter became fearful that the truth would emerge not because he was afraid he would end up in an electric chair, but because he didn't want the people he loved and cared about to know the truth about him. He feared that the truth would alter their lives forever, preventing them from continuing to live normal lives. It would ruin both Debra and Rita if they knew the man who they loved was a serial killer.

For months, both the FBI and Miami Metro Police worked on the case, trying to find the person who killed all of these people. As they started identifying the bodies, they noticed something odd. All of the victims were criminals, specifically killers. The killer received the nickname, "The Bay Harbor Butcher."

To keep Dexter's identity a secret, he was forced to trick the police several times. He broke the air conditioning of the room that was refrigerating all of the bodies they found, destroying practically all of the evidence. Dexter came out of the case unscathed because it was pinned on another cop within the same department who was very corrupt and had killed several people himself. Dexter was content with this result because that cop was not an innocent person, and he was able to continue his life. His dark passenger lived on. From this upsetting incident, Dexter came out on top as he discovered his missing inner quality of compassion. He realized what was really important in life: his loved ones.

Introduction to Innocence

Rita and Dexter's relationship becomes complicated when Rita discovers that she is pregnant. She decides to keep the baby, leaving Dexter's role in the child's life completely up to him. Dexter is troubled with this decision, reflecting on his relationship with his father. He fears his son will end up like himself, troubled by a dark passenger. With Debra's help, Dexter realizes that all he wants is to be a part of his son's life, and most importantly, to have a family once again. He proposes to Rita, and they are married shortly after. Dexter fell in love with his son, Harrison, at first glance. He was perfect, entirely innocent, something Dexter never thought he would have in his life.

The Ultimate Boon

Dexter makes a pivotal mistake when he becomes too personally involved with one of his targets. The police discover three different type of murders recurring every few years in large cities all over the country. They name the man responsible "The Trinity Killer," but are unable to find him. Dexter becomes interested and begins hunting for the killer himself, finding him quite easily. Using an alias, Dexter befriends The Trinity Killer, named Arthur, due to their similar life-styles. Like Dexter, The Trinity Killer lives a perfectly normal life with his wife in kids outside of Miami.

Dexter is finding it difficult to juggle work, family, as well as his dark passenger, so he continues to spend time with Arthur because he believes he could learn how to handle his new life while keeping his dark side a secret from his family. Dexter is troubled when Arthur discovers Dexter's true identity and is forced to make Dexter kill with his cover blown. To keep his family safe, Dexter sends the kids to Disney World with their grandparents and plans a honeymoon weekend with Rita and their baby. With Rita and Harrison leaving for the trip a day early, Dexter has only one night to successfully kill Arthur Mitchell. Within hours of his wife's departure, Dexter has Trinity on his table.

While conversing with Arthur moments before Dexter takes his life, Dexter makes an essential realization about himself. He says to Arthur, "'I can't believe there was a time I actually thought I could learn something from you.'" Almost humored by his remark, Arthur questions back, "you think you're better than I am?" To which Dexter replies, "No, but I want to be." As Dexter stabs Arthur in the chest, Arthur mutters back, "you can't control the demon inside of you anymore than I can control mine" (Cerone, 2006).

Dexter's Altered Life

Relieved that the threat Trinity posed on his family was gone, Dexter returns home, excited to be reunited with his family shortly. He notices Rita's purse sitting on the kitchen table, which she had taken with her earlier that morning when she left for the airport. The faint sound of Harrison's cry sends shivers down Dexter's spine. He walks into his bathroom, following his son's cries, and sees his ten-month old baby sitting in a pool of his own mother's blood. Born in blood, just like Dexter. Dexter looks to his right and sees his wife in the bathtub, dead. Earlier that day, Rita returned home when she realized she had forgotten something, and Trinity was there waiting for her. He killed her exactly like he killed every other victim of his vicious cycle, by slitting her femoral artery and leaving her to bleed and out and die almost instantly.

Dexter's Return and Refusal

Dexter initially has a very difficult time coping with his beloved wife's death. He loses his temper on several occasions which results in him bludgeoning a man to death in a public restroom. He becomes careless, disregarding the code he had been following for decades. However, the grief he feels never interferes with the relationship he has with his son. After Rita's death, Astor and Cody, Dexter's stepchildren, go to live with their grandparents in Orlando, but they frequently come back to Miami to visit Dexter and their brother. The sense of family is still present in Dexter's life, yet he is left feeling hollow from Rita's demise and tremendously guilty because his dark passenger was responsible for her murder. A redeemed hero begins as a neutral or positive character, then descends into villainy and ultimately returns to a protagonist in the end (Allison, 2015; Allison & Goethals, 2017; Allison & Smith, 2015). Dexter is well aware that he is responsible for his wife's death, and he even mutters "it was me" when the police officer asked him what had happened when first arriving at the scene of the crime (Cerone, 2006). Guilt is an emotion Dexter has never encountered before, and thus he is unable to handle himself.

MASTER OF THE TWO WORLDS

Joseph Campbell describes the road back as the first step in a hero's return to his original world. The opposite of the call to adventure, the road back is where the hero must return home with their reward (Campbell, 1949). With Rita's passing and the departure of Astor and Cody, Dexter is left alone with his son. Dexter and Harrison's bond only gets stronger; Dexter would do anything to protect his son. Harrison is Dexter's light during a time of grief and sorrow. Although Dexter will never forgive himself for Rita's death, because of Harrison he transforms into a more responsible, compassionate, and careful man. When his dark passenger emerges again, Dexter executes every step of the kill flawlessly. He no longer makes careless mistakes; in order to be a good father he has to be an even better serial killer. Dexter can never break the first rule of the Code because that would result in Harrison growing up parentless. Through all of Dexter's trials and losses, he is able to return home with the biggest prize of all, his son.

Dexter's return from his journey is unique in the sense that he arrives home to an unfamiliar world. He began his journey as an introvert, caring about only one other human in the world. Through the relationship he develops with Rita, Dexter learns the importance of genuine human interactions. He sees that a life with loved ones is far better than living life alone. Although Dexter never had a fairy tale ending with his whole family, Dexter carried the lessons he learned from Rita with him for the rest of his life. Dexter identified the sacred value of his life through his son: family. Harrison became the most important part of Dexter's life, replacing his dark passenger. However, he masters balancing his two separate lives. Dexter is able to satisfy his dark passenger without it interfering with his relationships and work. In a way, Dexter was given a fresh start. With his past behind him, Dexter was given freedom to live. Through the completion of his journey and transformation, Dexter acquired additional heroic traits. At the beginning of the series Dexter only carried intelligence, resilience, and strength; however, throughout his transformation, he acquired compassion, selflessness, charisma, and reliability.

CONCLUSION

It is hard to imagine a serial killer as anything other than wicked, but through Dexter's transformation as a hero, it is shown that a murderer can actually be an asset to society and can do good rather than evil. He underwent a transformation of self as well as a transformation of society (Allison, 2015; Allison & Goethals, 2017). He began his journey not out of the desire to better society, but rather the need to kill. Throughout his evolution, this seems to change. His transformation advances society by ridding the world of the monsters that exist. Although his need to kill remains present, his reasons for doing so come from a need to protect his family, no longer from his need to take lives. Dexter himself changes from being one of the monsters he usually sought out to kill, into a hero, serving society in the only way he knows how.

Although "Dexter" is a fictional TV series, the story of a serial killer who kills killers may not be that unique. Miranda Barbour was 19 years old when she received the nickname the "Craigslist Killer." She has confessed to killing at least 22 people (Smith, 2010). Her cause for her killings dates back to her childhood when she was repeatedly sexually assaulted by her uncle. All of her confirmed victims seemed to follow a similar pattern: they were rapists (Lysiak, 2016). One of her closest friends said, "I think she has been through a lot of painful things, and while I would never say that justifies taking lives, it's important to understand what might be motivating her" (Smith, 2010). It is difficult to justify the act of murder, but in the case of Dexter, and possibly Miranda as well, killing was not out of cruelty but rather with an intention to better the world and with the hope that with the end of a life a greater world will be born.

REFERENCES

Allison, S. T. (2015). The initiation of heroism science. Heroism Science, 1, 1-8.
Allison, S. T., & Goethals, G. R. (2011). Heroes: What they do and why we need them. New York: Oxford University Press.
Allison, S. T., & Goethals, G. R. (2013). Heroic leadership: An influence taxonomy of 100 exceptional individuals. New York: Routledge.
Allison, S. T., & Goethals, G. R. (2016). Hero worship: The elevation of the human spirit. Journal for the Theory of Social Behaviour, 46, 187-210.
Allison, S. T., & Goethals, G. R. (2017). The hero's transformation. In S. T. Allison, G. R. Goethals, & R. M. Kramer (Eds.), Handbook of heroism and heroic leadership. New York: Routledge.
Allison, S. T., Goethals, G. R., & Kramer, R. M. (2017). Setting the scene: The rise and coalescence of heroism science. In S. T. Allison, G. R. Goethals, & R. M. Kramer (Eds.), Handbook of heroism and heroic leadership. New York: Routledge.
Allison, S. T. & Smith, G. (2015). Reel heroes and villains. Richmond: Agile Writer Press.
Cerone , D., Colleton, S., & Eglee, C. H. (Producers), & Manos, J. (Writer). (2006, October 1). Dexter [Television series]. Miami, Florida : Showtime .
Dexter Wiki. (n.d.). Retrieved from https://en.wikipedia.org/wiki/Dexter_(TV_series)
Franco, Z. E., Blau, K., & Zimbardo, P. G. (2011, April 11). Heroism: A Conceptual Analysis and Differentiation Between Heroic Action and Altruism. Review of General Psychology.
Frese, S. (2014, June 23). - Crime and Forensic Blog. Retrieved October 06, 2017.
Goethals, G. R., Allison, S. T., Kramer, R., & Messick, D. (Eds.) (2014). Conceptions of leadership: Enduring ideas and emerging insights. New York: Palgrave Macmillan.
Hoyt, C. L. (2014). Social identities andlLeadership: The case of gender. In Goethals, G. R., Allison, S. T., Kramer, R., & Messick, D. (Eds.), Conceptions of leadership: Enduring ideas and emerging insights. New York: Palgrave Macmillan.
Kinsella, E. L., Ritchie, T. D., & Igou, E. R. (2017). Attributes and Applications of Heroes. In S. T. Allison, G. R. Goethals, & R. M. Kramer (Eds.), Handbook of heroism and heroic leadership. New York: Routledge.
Lysiak, M. (2016, February 16). 'I Didn't Hurt Anyone Who Didn't Deserve It'. Retrieved November 02, 2017.

Morton, R. J. (Ed.). (2010, May 21). Serial Murder. Retrieved October 04, 2017.

Solomon, P. T. (Director). (2011). Finding Joe [Motion picture]. The United States of America .

Smith, J. M. (2010). Relating rape and murder,. New York: Palgrave Macmillan.

Vandello, J. A., Goldschmied, N., & Michniewicz, K. (2017). Underdogs as Heroes . In S. T. Allison, G. R. Goethals, & R. M. Kramer (Eds.), Handbook of heroism and heroic leadership. New York: Routledge.

Section 2: Heroes in Epic Novels and Stories

7

How Frodo Baggins Became a Hero: An Analysis of a Hobbit's Heroic Transformation

LEE M. TYLER

"All we have to decide is what to do with the time that is given us."
~J.R.R. Tolkien

Gandalf reveals both his fatalism and his heroism in this conversation with Frodo in Tolkien's *The Fellowship of the Ring*. Gandalf explains the truth behind the ring -- that it is the "one ring to rule them all," and that the dark lord Sauron hunts it with ringwraiths. He is saying that even though men cannot control the problems or opportunities that are given them, everyone has the choice to take action, for good or for evil. Anyone can be a hero if they seize the day and choose to perform heroic actions. Frodo's transformation is important because he represents the ordinary person the everyman. Frodo is surrounded by characters who are immortal, are great warriors, have unimaginable power, or are descended from kings -- all qualities of the traditional epic hero -- while he is a sheltered hobbit and is about the size of a human nine-year-old. Nevertheless, Frodo is the hero of *The Lord of the Rings*. Tolkien chooses a hobbit due to their small stature and sheltered lives to show that anyone can become a hero if they wish to do good and are able to endure whatever hardships they face. This is consistent with Franco and Zimbardo's (2006) seminal analysis of heroism which argues that everyone is capable of performing small acts of everyday heroism.

The mission statement of Zimbardo's *Heroic Imagination Project* is: "To encourage and empower individuals to take heroic action during crucial moments in their lives. We prepare them to act with integrity, compassion, and moral courage, heightened by an understanding of the power of situational forces." The banality of heroism concept, as the name suggests, emphasizes the everyday aspects of heroism. It removes two basic tendencies that people have to resist heroic action. One is the belief that only special people, the "heroic elite," can do heroic things. The other is the "bystander effect," a phenomenon that occurs when many people witness an event that requires action, but each person assumes that someone else will perform it. Franco and Zimbardo (2006) aspire to discover what spurs people out of inactivity and into heroism, which they refer to as the "high watermark" of human behavior. Franco and Zimbardo also ask if it is "possible to foster what we term 'heroic imagination,' or the development of a personal heroic ideal" which will provide moral clarity in times of trouble.

In addition to possessing a considerable amount of heroic imagination, Frodo Baggins is a worldwide hero who transcends cultural influence and who possesses many universal qualities, even if he is fictional. As a character, he touches many people at some point in both the books and the movies in the *Lord of the Rings* franchise. Analyzing Frodo's heroic journey and transformation, as well as his characteristics that allow him to complete his journey, reveal that ordinary beings are capable of acquiring the traits of a hero, and that choosing to act heroically and embark on the journey can bring about significant heroic transformation.

In *The Hero with a Thousand Faces*, Joseph Campbell (1949) found that most myths follow a common archetypal pattern which he called the hero's journey. This quest contains three parts: initiation, departure, and return. Most heroes who follow this journey are traditional heroes. Traditional heroes are a hero subtype proposed by Goethals and Allison (2012) along with transforming, transfigured, transparent, transposed, tragic, transitional, transitory, and trending. These nine hero subtypes display different types of heroism at different times and for different people. They can range from epic heroes, to sports figures, and to political activists, depending on the time, place, and situation.

Frodo Baggins is a traditional hero, indicating that he follows the archetypal hero monomyth very closely. During the hero's journey, there are "three distinct transformations: A transformation of setting, a transformation of self, and a transformation of society" (Allison & Goethals, 2017). Frodo's story begins in the Shire, a peaceful farmland where the hobbits live. Frodo departure stage of the journey involves leaving the shire and visiting many faraway places, each with its own trials. This transformation of setting and these many trials lead to a transformation of self. The Shire is disconnected from the wars and dealings of Middle-earth. It is so far removed that many of the characters in *The Two Towers* and *The Return of the King* (the Ents, the people of Rohan, and the people of Gondor) have never even heard of hobbits or have thought them to be myths. Frodo experiences his call to adventure when Bilbo passes on his ring to Frodo. Later, Gandalf tells Frodo that his ring will lead to the destruction of Middle Earth if it is not destroyed. Not only is Frodo called to adventure by this threat, but he is also chased by ringwraiths, or Black Riders, who are hunting the ring. When Frodo and his companions cross into Bree, they cross the first threshold by leaving behind their homeland. Frodo must abandon the safety of the Shire to transform into the kind of person who can save Middle-earth by climbing Mount Doom.

Frodo and his friends cross the threshold again when they leave Rivendell with the rest of the fellowship of the ring. Along the way, Frodo has many helpers and mentors. Gandalf, Aragorn, and the Fellowship are all helpers in his journey. Once the Black Riders are following Frodo, he has to fight the will of the ring to resist wearing it. The ring wants to be found and not destroyed. At times, Frodo does give into this temptation and he almost dies in most of these instances. Frodo also has to fight the temptation to put the burden of the ring on someone else -- someone who is stronger, more powerful, and worldlier (like Aragorn, Gandalf, or Galadriel). After Gandalf first tells Frodo that he owns the ring, Frodo says to Gandalf, "But I have so little use of these things! You are wise and powerful. Will you not take the Ring?" (Tolkien, 1954). At this point Frodo learns that those who are more powerful than he is will be far too tempted to wield the power of the ring. Only a humble being can carry the weight of the ring and not wield it.

Frodo experiences another transformation with several near-death experiences. In *The Fellowship of the Ring*, Frodo gets stabbed by a ring wraith and when he wakes up, he notices how he has changed physically and mentally since he left the shire. Another death-like event serves as the death phase for the trilogy as a whole is when the members of the fellowship are underground in Shelob's lair and Frodo is poisoned. Again, after destroying the ring he falls into a death-like sleep and awakens transformed. In the end, Frodo saves Middle-earth and returns to the Shire profoundly changed by his journey.

The transformation of society is the natural consequence of the hero's own personal transformation, and it is aimed at augmenting the well-being of the hero's larger community (Efthimiou, Allison, & Franco, 2018). For Frodo, society transformation occurs at two different points: when the fellowship is created and when Frodo destroys the ring. By eliminating the ring, Sauron falls and the age of men begins. Frodo's mentor and friend Aragorn claims his birthright to the throne of Gondor, and Frodo returns to the shire and writes his story in Bilbo's book -- the story that we have been discussing. These societal changes are the restoration of order and the reward part of the journey. After he finishes his portion of the book, Frodo leaves the Shire and sails with Bilbo to the Haven across the sea. Frodo's transformation is so great that he cannot remain in the Shire. He is experiencing the apotheosis -- by sailing away, Frodo will experience eternal peace. It is a place where the elves, who are immortal, go. Frodo's heroism has earned this elixir.

There are ten main dimensions of transformation, according to Allison and Goethals (2017). These dimensions are subject, scale, speed, duration, timing, direction, type, depth, openness, and source. Each of the dimensions of transformation as they relate to Frodo Baggins are listed below.

Subject

The subject as a dimension of transformation refers to who is transformed by the heroic action. In *The Lord of the Rings*, Frodo Baggins is the primary beneficiary of transformation; however, his actions do lead to a change in society by his act of saving Middle-earth from the wrath of Sauron, marking the beginning of the age of men. Frodo becomes strong and brave, but he also is deeply wounded by his journey. When Frodo makes the decision to leave the Shire, he says to Sam, "But I have been too deeply hurt, Sam. I tried to save the Shire, and it has been saved, but not for me" (Tolkien, 1956).

Scale

The number of heroic actors who are transformed represent a measurement of scale. Frodo is one of the most transformed characters in the franchise because he is the ring bearer; however, he was surrounded by other heroic actors throughout his journey. In *The Fellowship of the Ring*, Frodo is always part of a group, including the other hobbits from the shire and the fellowship. In *The Two Towers* and *Return of the King*, Frodo and Sam form a dyad that undergoes transformation. Sam even carries Frodo up mount Doom when the ring is too much for Frodo to bear. "'Come, Mr. Frodo!' he cried. 'I can't carry it for you, but I can carry you and it as well'" (Tolkien, 1955).

Speed

Heroic transformations vary along the dimension of the speed of the transformation. Frodo is able to instantly transform when he puts on the ring because the wearer of the ring is rendered invisible. In a bar in Bree, Frodo accidentally slips on the ring which causes him to "simply vanish" (Tolkien,

1954). This heroic transformation occurs instantaneously. Frodo also undergoes much slower transformations that take the length of the journey to transpire. These transformations were intellectual, emotional, and physical in nature. Frodo learned more about Middle-earth outside of the Shire. He becomes more empathetic towards Smeagol while being the ring bearer, and he is changed physically by walking to Mordor and by his various injuries.

Duration

The effects of heroic transformations can last from anywhere between a very short amount of time to a very long amount of time. Most of the heroic transformations that Frodo experiences are long-lasting, except for his physical transformation of becoming invisible when he wears the ring; as soon as Frodo removes the ring he becomes visible again. Frodo is so transformed by his journey that he feels that he cannot even remain in the Shire after he has saved it and written his book. This leads him to the decision to sail across the sea to live with the elves in the Haven.

Timing

Timing refers to when in one's life the heroic transformation occurs. Heroic transformations may occur at any point during the hero's lifetime. Frodo does not experience any heroic transformations until after he has reached adulthood. Bilbo passes on the ring to Frodo on Frodo's thirty-third birthday, which is the Hobbits' coming of age. Because Frodo is an adult when he receives the ring he is more prepared to handle these heroic transformations than someone who is still a child. This developmental element is demonstrated by other characters of the book as we see how much Pippin, a much younger hobbit, struggles on the journey. While the Fellowship is traveling through the mines of Moria, Pippin causes a disturbance by dropping a stone down a well. Gandalf growls at him, "Fool of a Took! This is a serious journey, not a Hobbit waling-party. Throw yourself in next time, and then you will be no further nuisance. Now be quiet!" (Tolkien, 1954).

Direction

Heroic transformations usually follow one of four arcs. Allison and Smith (2015) identified and distinguished among these four heroic transformational arcs, which include the classic hero arc, the enlightened hero arc, the redeemed hero arc, and the non-transformational hero arc. Frodo Baggins follows the classic hero arc during which an ordinary person traverses the classic journey and emerges as a hero at the end. Frodo was an ordinary hobbit with no exceptional powers and he blossoms into a hero because he was able to carry the ring to Mount Doom where it was destroyed.

Type

Allison and Smith (2015) also identified five types of transformations that heroes undergo. These five transformations are a moral transformation, an emotional transformation, a spiritual transformation, an intellectual transformation, and a physical transformation. Allison, Goethals, and Kramer (2017) added a sixth transformation which they called a motivational transformation. Frodo Baggins experiences emotional, intellectual, and physical transformations. Throughout his journey to destroy the ring, Frodo becomes brave and resilient out of necessity. He also learns to feel empathy for Sméagol. Frodo undergoes an intellectual transformation when he acquires important insights about the world outside of the shire. Frodo experiences his first physical transformation on his journey to Rivendell. "Looking in a mirror he was startled to see a much thinner reflection of himself than he remembered: it looked remarkably like the young nephew of Bilbo who used to go tramping with his uncle in the Shire; but the eyes looked out at him thoughtfully" (Tolkien, 1954).

Gollum follows Frodo to the edge of Mount Doom where Gollum bites off Frodo's finger with the ring on it. "Gollum, dancing like a mad thing, held aloft the ring, a finger still thrust within its circle. It shone now as if verily it was wrought of living fire" (Tolkien, 1955). Frodo never fully recovers from the Black Rider's stab wound so he always feels the pain in his shoulder at the spot he was stabbed. After his journey, Frodo is unable to live out the rest of his life in the shire because he is never fully healed; in fact, it causes him to get sick on the anniversary of the injury. Frodo tells Sam after informing him of his decision to leave, "It must often be so, Sam, when things are in danger: someone has to give them up, lose them, so that others may keep them" (Tolkien, 1955). This leads to Frodo to sail off to the Haven with Bilbo and the elves.

Depth

Heroic transformations can be either shallow or deep. Frodo's invisibility is a shallow transformation, but the wounds that he receives while wearing the ring cause deep transformations. Frodo Baggins undergoes mostly deep transformations from his journey. He is willing to risk his life to destroy the ring, exclaiming to Sam, "I must carry the burden to the end. It can't be altered. You can't come between me and this doom" (Tolkien, 1955). Frodo is never able to fully recover from this injury, although he is psychologically transformed by it.

Openness

A subject must be open to transformation to undergo heroic transformation. Being open means having the ability and motivation to change. Frodo accepts the burden of the ring, but at first he is pushed into initiating his journey because of the ringwraiths. One of the Black Riders questions Sam's grandfather-the-Gaffer and he describes it like this: "I told him Mr. Baggins had left his home for good. Hissed at me, he did. It gave me quite a shudder. I don't know (what sort of fellow he was), says he; but he wasn't a Hobbit. He was tall and black like, and he stooped over me. I reckon it was one of the Big Folk from foreign parts. He spoke funny." The appearance of a ringwraith in the Shire is enough to spur Frodo to action. In Rivendell, Frodo decides to be the ring bearer and a member of the Fellowship saying, "I will take the Ring, [. . .] though I do not know the way" (Tolkien, 1954). Frodo's openness to change and willingness to take heroic action is key to his heroic transformation.

Source

Frodo experiences both internal and external sources of transformative change. The internal source that he feels represents his intrinsic motivation to change and "an enlightened dawning of responsibility" (Allison & Goethals, 2017; Davis et al., 2011). Frodo feels that the ring is his responsibility and that therefore it is his responsibility to be the ring bearer. Frodo also experiences external sources of transformation, one of which is a series of trials by which he is transformed through suffering as a result of dealing with arduous outside forces. Another, less obvious external source of transformation that the experiences are the influence of being raised by Bilbo and hearing of his adventures.

Social Sources of Transformation

Frodo has other people helping him through every step in his journey. At the beginning, he has the other hobbits and Aragorn. Then Frodo benefits from travelling with the Fellowship and Gandalf. Along the way, they encounter many helpful characters who take care of them and gift them. First, they meet Tom Bombadil, and Elrond in Rivendell. Later, the lady Galadriel gives them gifts that are crucial to the success of the quest. She presents him with a "small crystal phial" and said to him, "May it be a light to you in dark places, when all other lights go out" (Tolkien, 1954).

The Great Eight: How Frodo Acquires These Qualities

Allison and Goethals (2011) conducted research into people's perceptions of heroes and uncovered eight major trait categories of heroes: smart, strong, caring, selfless, charismatic, resilient, reliable, and inspiring. Below I describe how Frodo Baggins possesses each of the "Great Eight" traits and how he acquires them throughout his journey.

1. **Smart**: Frodo is often acknowledged as being intelligent by his companions before and during the journey. He is more bookish than the other hobbits and his knowledge of the Elvish language earns the respect of the Elves. Frodo thanks Gildor Inglorion and the other elves in the high-elven speech at the beginning of his journey, and in turn they call him "Elf-friend" and "a jewel among hobbits" (Tolkien, 1954).

2. **Strong**: Frodo is very brave before his heroic transformation and his bravery only increases from his journey. He first demonstrates his bravery by

choosing to be the ring bearer, saying to Gandalf, "But this would mean exile, a flight from danger to danger, drawing it after me. And I suppose I must go alone, if I am to do that and save the Shire. But I feel very small, and very uprooted, and well-- desperate. The Enemy is so strong and so terrible" (Tolkien, 1954). Throughout the series, Frodo faces many trials head on, such as entering Moria and fighting Shelob.

3. **Selfless**: Frodo was selfless before embarking on his quest. Indeed, he leaves his home and life behind in the Shire to go on his heroic quest. He also knows that he will most likely die, even if he succeeds in his task. When he and Sam are discussing the amount of food that they have left, Frodo says to Sam, "If the One goes into the fire, and we are at hand? I ask you, Sam, are we ever likely to need bread again? I think not" (Tolkien, 1955). Frodo acknowledges that they most likely won't survive even if they succeed, showing that Frodo is so selfless that he is willing to die to save Middle-earth.

4. **Caring**: Frodo always shows love for his companions -- especially Sam, whom he calls his "dearest hobbit, friend of friends" (Tolkien, 1955). Frodo learns to show empathy for Sméagol, a cruel little creature that found and held the ring for many years until Bilbo stole it from him. Frodo and Sam capture Sméagol, who had been following them, and Frodo says, "For now that I see him, I do pity him" (Tolkien, 1955).

5. **Charismatic**: Frodo is very eloquent and almost poetic before his journey even begins. He randomly sings and recites poetry throughout his journey. Frodo is also described as being "taller than some and fairer than most" hobbits (Tolkien, 1954).

6. **Resilient**: Frodo has to become resilient while on his journey. Before he left the Shire, his resilience was never tested. Frodo keeps on pushing through the quest, even though he faces many obstacles. Some of the most notable obstacles are being chased and stabbed by Black Riders, the Balrog in Moria, Boromir's attack, and Shelob poisoning him. In addition, he has the carry the ring and fight its will constantly. Frodo becomes more resilient emotionally and physically with every trial he overcomes.

7. **Reliable**: Frodo's reliability was never tested before he began his transformation, however he is very loyal to Gandalf, Bilbo, and the rest of the fellowship. Frodo proves his reliability by succeeding in his mission of destroying the ring.

8. **Inspiring**: Frodo is inspiring before, during, and after his transformation. Before his transformation, Frodo inspires Sam, Merry, and Pippin to join him on his journey. During his transformation he motivates the rest of the fellowship to keep fighting Sauron and his forces, even when all hope seemed lost. He also remains humble throughout his journey (Worthington & Allison, 2018).

CONCLUSION

By completing his journey and achieving his heroic transformation, Frodo integrates both what fate has given him and what he could achieve through his own heroic efforts and imagination. He acknowledges that he has been presented with an impossible task, yet he maintains the courage and the friendships to complete the cycle and bring the elixir to himself, his friends, and society at large. He has many strikes against him; for example, his diminutive size and his sheltered existence. Frodo knows nothing of the world or danger or evil. Hobbits are generally fun-loving and somewhat lazy, and while Frodo is smarter than most, he is still young and inexperienced. Not only that, but his mission is a near impossible one and would be impossible to do alone. He is an everyday hero who achieves a great success by doing his part and allowing the heroic journey to unfold organically. In this way, Frodo inspires us all.

REFERENCES

About Us. (2017, July 20). Retrieved from http://heroicimagination.org/about-us/

Allison, S. T. (2015). The initiation of heroism science. Heroism Science, 1, 1-8.

Allison, S. T., & Goethals, G. R. (2011). Heroes: What they do and why we need them. New York: Oxford University Press.

Allison, S. T., & Goethals, G. R. (2017). The hero's transformation. In S. T. Allison, G. R. Goethals, & R. M. Kramer (Eds.), Handbook of heroism and heroic leadership. New York: Routledge, Taylor & Francis Group.

Allison, S. T., Goethals, G. R., & Kramer, R. M. (Eds.) (2017). Handbook of heroism and heroic leadership. New York: Routledge.

Allison, S. T., & Setterberg, G. C. (2016). Suffering and sacrifice: Individual and collective benefits, and implications for leadership. In S. T. Allison, C. T. Kocher, & G. R. Goethals (Eds), Frontiers in spiritual leadership: Discovering the better angels of our nature. New York: Palgrave Macmillan.

Allison, S. T., & Smith, G. (2015). Reel heroes & villains. Richmond: Agile Writer Press.

Campbell, J. (1949). The hero with a thousand faces. New York: Pantheon Books.

Davis, J. L., Burnette, J. L., Allison, S. T., & Stone, H. (2011). Against the odds: Academic underdogs benefit from incremental theories. Social Psychology of Education, 14, 331-346.

Efthimiou, O., Allison, S. T., & Franco, Z. E. (Eds.) (2018). Heroism and wellbeing in the 21st Century: Applied and emerging perspectives. New York: Routledge.

Franco, Z. E., & Zimbardo, P. G. (2006). The banality of heroism. The Greater Good, 3, 30–35.

Fuller, S. C. (n.d.). The Lord of the Rings. Retrieved from https://www.cliffsnotes.com/ literature/l/the-lord-of-the-rings/about-the-lord-of-the-rings-trilogy?lcitation=true

Goethals, G. R., & Allison, S. T. (2012). Making heroes. The construction of courage, competence, and virtue. Advances in Experimental Social Psychology, 46, 183–235.

Tolkien, J.R.R. (1954). The Fellowship of the Ring. New York: Ballantine Books.

Tolkien, J.R.R. (1955). The Two Towers. New York: Ballantine Books.

Tolkien, J.R.R. (1955). The Return of the King. New York: Ballantine Books.

Worthington, E. L, & Allison, S. T. (2018). Heroic humility: What the science of humility can say to people raised on self-focus. Washington. DC: American Psychological Association.

8

Bruce Wayne's Heroic Journey: The Everlasting Quest for Justice

Michael D. Loughran

At approximately 12:22 in the morning on August 31, 1997 there was a high-speed automobile accident in Paris. A black Mercedes-Benz crashed into the 13th pillar of the Alma tunnel near the Seine River causing three passengers to suffer fatal injuries with one managing to escape alive but severely damaged. Found in the wreckage was Diana, Princess of Wales. Pronounced dead only a few hours later, the world lost the iconic figure of elegance, beauty, and gentle determination. More tragically, her children Prince William, aged 15, and Prince Harry, aged 12, lost their mother. It is impossible to imagine the depth of their misery following the loss of the person who cared for them since birth.

It is commonly believed, however, that pain creates room for growth and inspires perseverance. On the 20th anniversary of the accident, Prince William and Prince Harry were finally able to reveal their emotions and continuous struggle after the passing of their mother as young adults. In a new documentary, Diana, 7 Days, Prince William acknowledges that "When you have something as traumatic as the death of your mother when you're 15...it will either make or break you." He continues: "And I wouldn't let it break me. I wanted it to make me. I wanted her to be proud of the person I would become...." (Singer, 2017). The death of Princess Diana caused the United Kingdom and the world alike to feel desolate and somber and her two sons to bear unspeakable pain. Ultimately, it was this pain that triggered the boys' motivation to seek an improved world.

From a heroic perspective, Prince William and Prince Harry demonstrated an extraordinary degree of courage and strength at a very young age. To help console the saddened hearts of thousands of people watching, William and Harry presented themselves as emotionally strong while walking behind their mother's casket at the funeral procession only six days after her death. While wanting to release their emotions of anger and misery, they conquered their inner struggles in order to show the world what it means to be strong in the face of utter despair. Prince William and Prince Harry are not unlike fictional icon Bruce Wayne, who at a very young age lost both of his parents. An important similarity between Bruce Wayne and Prince William is that their personal tragedies inspired them to strive for a world filled with peace and prosperity for their community and others around them. On the other hand, an important difference between both situations is that Bruce essentially blamed himself for their deaths due to his unappeasable fear as a young boy, but it is this trauma and his fear which allows him to grow into a hero.

Throughout this chapter, I provide an analysis of Bruce Wayne's heroic transformation from a young boy filled with fear to the masked man called "Batman" who conquers injustice. While there are many variations of the character since Batman first appeared in comics in 1939, created by Bob Kane, I will focus primarily on Christopher Nolan's interpretation in *The Dark Knight Trilogy* and *Batman Begins* to decipher Bruce Wayne's transformative journey. I describe how this heroic transformation commences, what allows it to prosper and what concludes his heroic tale. An important aspect of Bruce Wayne's journey to heroism is that it is almost exclusively internal as he continuously fights his inner demons of morality and fear. The concluding thoughts will focus primarily on the importance of Bruce Wayne's heroic transformation as it pertains to the greater good of society, in this case Gotham City, in the face of villainous threats.

Heroes are widely considered the peak of human evolution. It is also commonly believed that only the greatest of humankind are able to earn the title of 'hero.' Comparative mythologist Joseph Campbell (1949) provided the prototypical evolution of heroic behavior that describes the journey that one must embark on to become a hero in his iconic book, *The Hero with a Thousand Faces*. This heroic journey is called the hero monomyth, and it consists of three primary parts: departure, initiation, and return (Campbell, 1949). Ultimately, the hero sets out on a journey in an unknown, dangerous situation and is charged with performing a daunting task. The hero always needs to find a missing quality within himself to accomplish his mission, and to find this missing truth the hero usually must endure great suffering. These painful trials will eventually enable him to transform into a hero capable of delivering a great boon to society (Allison & Goethals, 2017).

Suffering is crucial to the hero's journey. Suffering is redemptive, encourages humility, inspires compassion, and most importantly it endows the hero with a sense of meaning and purpose (Allison & Setterberg, 2016). Without this suffering, the heroic transformation may never occur. It is important to note that all heroes begin their journey 'incomplete' and only during pivotal moments on the journey do they begin to process of obtaining the missing inner quality. While attempting to discover their true and complete self, the hero faces significant obstacles, which explains why a helpful mentor is essential. The mentor assists the hero in finding himself and allows the hero to complete his journey by defeating a villainous obstacle (Allison & Smith, 2015).

Although there are numerous understandings and nuances to the definition of heroism that could fill pages, the definition of heroism that is most useful comes from Franco et al. (2011) who state, "Heroism is the willingness to sacrifice or take risks on behalf of others or in defense of a moral cause." According to Allison and Goethals (2011), there are distinct character traits needed for heroism. These eight characteristics, called "The Great Eight," are as follows: smart, strong, self-less, caring, charismatic, resilient, reliable, and inspiring. Heroism is very subjective, meaning that what can be called heroism lies in the eye of the beholder as Joseph Campbell made very clear in *The Power of Myth* (1988). However, the journey to become a hero is an inward one dependent on the hero's ability to conquer inner demons in order to transform into an extraordinary individual capable of transforming society.

CALL TO JUSTICE AND EXPOSURE TO TRAUMA

As a young child, Bruce Wayne grows up as heir to the most powerful family in Gotham City. His father, Thomas Wayne, is the owner of Wayne Enterprises and an illustrious billionaire determined to use his wealth and status as a means for good in his city. He seeks to provide affordable public transformation for all citizens as well as aid in the clean-up of the city's deteriorated areas. Along with focusing on the betterment of society, he and his wife Martha care deeply for their only child, Bruce. As a boy with the most wealthy and powerful parents in Gotham City, Bruce appears destined to coast through life effortlessly under the wing of his father, one day taking charge of Wayne Enterprises himself. Although life is relatively easy for adolescent Bruce, he struggles with a fundamental element of human nature: fear. Bruce is deathly afraid of bats which provides great insecurities as it is demoralizing for him to feel weak and submissive to an outside force. This fear is so great that it causes him to have painful nightmares and panic at the mere sight of the flying creature. Bruce relies heavily on his father Thomas Wayne to help alleviate his worries and phobia, as many children do.

This becomes clear when one day, while exploring the vast property owned by his family, Bruce accidentally plummets down into an old water well. Of course, his father eventually comes to the relief of his son and pulls him out of the dark abyss. While carrying him back to their mansion and doctoring the minor injuries suffered by Bruce, Thomas says, "And why do we fall Bruce? So we can learn to pick ourselves up" (Nolan, 2005). Bruce becomes accustom to the fact that whenever he is afraid or whenever he is in trouble, his father will be there to offer assurance, protection, and diminish his worries.

However, after one tragic incident, this steady influence will be no more. While enjoying a casual night out, Thomas accompanied by his wife, takes Bruce to see a theatrical production. Unfortunately, unbeknownst to Thomas, the performance includes the depiction of actors dressed as bats terrifying the protagonist, as well as Bruce. The sight of fictional bats becomes too much for Bruce to handle so his father suggests they leave through a back door and proceed home. Inauspiciously, while exiting the theater and heading down a grim alley, a man holds the Wayne family at gunpoint, demanding money in exchange for their lives. Thomas Wayne attempts to save his family by reaching for his wallet, however the criminal, clearly unstable, fires his weapon striking two bullets into Thomas and Martha. While bleeding out on the decrepit street, Thomas' last words to his son are as follows: "Bruce, it's okay, don't be afraid" (Nolan, 2005).

Until this moment, Bruce had never truly fallen and had never truly been affected by his fears because of his privileged upbringing. Now he is required to pick himself up. Throughout the introduction to Batman and Bruce Wayne, Nolan relies heavily on fear as a motivating factor for his protagonist. This becomes clear when Bruce says to his butler and now only parental figure, "Alfred, it was my fault. I made them leave the theater. If I hadn't gotten scared..." (Nolan, 2005). Langley states that research indicates that losing parents for kids old enough to understand is the single most stressful common life event that a child can experience (Langley, 2012). Bruce experiences the most stressful situation a child can endure, not to mention his tremendous guilt for indirectly causing their deaths.

With the loss of his parents, Bruce's call to a heroic journey begins at an early age. His guilt suffocates him because he believes his parents would still be alive if he didn't allow his to fear to control him. This pain and anger is Bruce's motivation as it spurs his heroic transformation when he begins to search inward to conquer his inner demons, primarily fear. He will also have to learn that contrary to his father's advice, it is okay for him to be afraid as long as he doesn't let it become debilitating and controlling.

Psychologist Phil Zimbardo provides a checklist of the chief features of a heroic act, including that it must be engaged voluntarily and it must involve physical risk or potential sacrifice (Zimbardo, 2007). A person's "calling" in life is generally voluntary and is directed toward improving the welfare of others compared to being driven by self-interest motivation (Dik & Duffy, 2009). There are obvious connections between such a calling and heroism. It becomes clear that Bruce Wayne experiences a calling as a young man attempting to live in a world without his parents. He is determined to make his parents proud, although his personal sentiment clouds his judgement. Before his call to defeat injustice can be fully realized, he must realize himself the importance of morality and the difference between revenge and justice.

Fourteen years after the death of Thomas and Martha Wayne, their murderer attends a sentencing hearing with the possibility of release for cooperating in a major criminal case. In attendance is Bruce Wayne with a pistol in his jacket and the intent to kill the man who brought him terrible amounts of pain. Due to the murderer's role in the criminal case, someone else fires a bullet into his chest thereby denying Bruce the opportunity. Bruce stares intensely at this dying man because his desire for closure and revenge which he has focused on for 14 years has been taken from him. After this incident, Bruce says to his lifelong friend Rachel Dawes, "My parents deserved justice," while she responds, "You're not talking about justice, you're talking about revenge.... They're never the same. Justice is about harmony, revenge is about you making yourself feel better" (Nolan, 2005). Bruce then confesses his potential sin: "I'm not one of your good people, Rachel. All these years, I wanted to kill him. And now I can't." Rachel then slaps Bruce across the face for his evil intentions, saying curtly, "Your father would be ashamed of you" (Nolan, 2005).

Bruce finally realizes how different his definition of justice is from his father's, the man he admires so deeply. He almost destroys the possibility of being a symbol of good as his father had been, and this recognition motivates Bruce to transform his beliefs and morals. This is an example of a metaphorical fall from which Bruce must recover to attain heroic status. Alone in the world, lost emotionally, Bruce throws the pistol he intended to use into the river, signifying his readiness and willingness to pursue justice instead of revenge. Randall M. Jensen argues in *Batman and Philosophy: The Dark Knight of the Soul*, that

"Bruce wants not only to atone for their deaths, but also give meaning to their lives by ensuring that their legacy doesn't die with them.... Batman isn't just trying to defeat and destroy the evil forces of Gotham, he's trying to build something as well" (White, 2008). His morals begin to align with his father's ideals but first he must begin the first part of his heroic journey: departure.

Departure: The Call to Adventure

Aware of his mistakes for desiring revenge and aware of the criminal activity occurring in the underbelly of Gotham City, Bruce Wayne voluntarily seeks out the means to conquer his goals of bettering himself to improve society. Allison et al. (2017) describe departure as the phase which begins the hero's journey and is necessary for a hero to acquire the important quality that he lacks. In this case, Bruce lacks the ability to control his fear, he lacks the ability to fight injustice, and he lacks the ability to represent his family's name. This departure is often characterized by an internal source of transformative change involving human transgression and failure. After "fallings and failings," people often undergo drastic change due to being humbled (Rohr, 2011; Worthington & Allison, 2018). This is the case for Bruce Wayne who, after hitting "rock bottom," leaves his wealthy inheritance and popular name behind and seeks resolution. As previously stated, suffering instills the hero with meaning and purpose (Allison & Setterberg, 2016), and Bruce's purpose now centers on avenging his parents' death by seeking justice for his community.

Mentorship

Bruce travels half-way across the world due to an identity crisis and encounters Henry Ducard, or Ra's al Ghul, master of the League of Shadows, a society intending to restore balance to the world through purges. Henry Ducard becomes pivotal to Bruce's transformation as he helps Bruce understand how controlling himself is the key to helping him control others. One of the most important aspects of the heroic transformation is the arrival of a mentor (Allison & Goethals, 2017). Tom Landry, former football coach for the Dallas Cowboys, clearly states that a mentor is someone "who tells you what you don't want to hear, who has you see what you don't want to see, so you can be who you have always known you could be" (Farcht, 2007, p. 294). Mentors retain the capability of benefiting the hero by guiding them, but the wrong mentor can also cause a hero to fail by leading them down a malicious path (Allison & Smith, 2015). It becomes clear that Henry Ducard is an already transformed person, helping Bruce transform himself, but his mentorship requires Bruce to be morally inclined and deviate from the villainous aspects of the League of Shadows.

When Bruce arrives, Henry Ducard realizes that "...a man like you is only here by choice, or because he is truly lost" but Bruce responds by clearly identifying his goals: "I seek the means to fight injustice. To turn fear against those who prey on the fearful" (Nolan, 2005) but he doesn't know how to accomplish this yet. Through training, Ducard manipulates Bruce's fear, anger, and guilt in order to teach him how to control them, rather than let them control him. Wisely, Ducard says, "Your anger gives you great power. But if you let it, it will destroy you..." along with, "...and what you really fear is inside yourself. You fear your own power. You fear your anger...Now you must journey inwards... Breathe in your fears. Face them. To conquer fear, you must become fear...Feel terror cloud your senses. Feel its power to distort. To control. And know that this power can be yours. Embrace your worst fear" (Nolan, 2005).

Ducard serves a very important role as Bruce's mentor because he identifies Bruce's insecurities and exposes them therefore creating room for growth. He says, "You are afraid...but not of me. Tell us, Mr. Wayne, what do you fear?" (Nolan, 2005) and proceeds to engage him in combat to provoke his mental fears as well as the physical fear of death. He enlightens Bruce; he demonstrates that fear can be used advantageously, but only if mastered and used correctly. Thomas Wayne taught his son that the elimination of fear is crucially important in finding peace, and Bruce naively follows his instructions. Contrary to this notion, Ducard reveals that "to manipulate the fears in others, you must first master your own" (Nolan, 2005).

Initiation

The second component of the Hero's journey is initiation, which requires the hero to prevail in overcoming obstacles, challenges, and enemies (Allison et al., 2017). A famous example of initiation comes from Star Wars (1977) during which the protagonist hero Luke Skywalker, without mentorship from Obi-wan Kenobi, faces battle against the evil Empire to save Princess Leia. In Batman Begins (Nolan, 2005), Bruce's initiation requires him to face his mentor, Henry Ducard, in order to maintain his definition of justice and avoid a path of self-destruction.

After learning to control his fears and channel his anger to something positive, Bruce becomes aware of the villainous aspect of the League of Shadows. Henry Ducard claims to desire worldly justice, just as Bruce does, but the means by which he seeks to accomplish this goal is far different than Bruce's. In order to become a member of the League of Shadows, Ducard commands Bruce to execute a criminal convicted of stealing. Ducard says, "We have purged your fear. You are ready to lead these men. You are ready to become a member of the League of Shadows. But first, you must demonstrate your commitment to justice," and he hands Bruce a sword with which to strike the felon. After Bruce refuses, Ducard claims, "Your compassion is a weakness your enemies will not share." This is a rather momentous moment as Bruce is required to truly define what his definition of justice is compared to his mentors. He states, "That's why it's so important. It separates us from them" (Nolan, 2005), 'them' implying criminals and villains. This is the most essential aspect to Bruce's journey towards becoming the hero known as Batman. The League of Shadows rests on the fundamental belief that in order to conquer injustice, societal destruction is required to rebuild. Ducard explains that Gotham, due to its resounding injustice, is beyond saving. Bruce, on the other hand, recognizes that their interpretation of justice is villainy. Doing what he claims is necessary, Bruce sets fire to the League of Shadows and combats his former mentor, eventually saving his life before he dies.

This aspect of Bruce's transformation is critical because he clearly evolves as a hero. He conquers all three of his inner demons: fear, anger and morality. Interestingly enough, it is his mentor who provides him with the ability through training, and opportunity to become a hero after he becomes a threat. Bruce returns to Gotham City and puts on the cowl for the first time in order to fight injustice and face his former mentor once again to save his famed city.

Return

The final aspect of the heroic journey is the return, defined as when the hero, upon returning to their original world, delivers a great benefit to their society. After completing their personal transformation, the hero now focuses on wider ambitions of benefiting their community (Allison et al., 2017). Drawing once again from Star Wars (Lucas, 1977), Luke Skywalker's return occurs when he finally faces Darth Vader and uses the force he gained through his personal transformation to destroy the infamous Death Star.

A powerful manifestation of Bruce Wayne's heroic transformation is seen when he puts on the cowl and finally becomes Batman. He explains the reasoning behind why he dons the cowl: "People need dramatic examples to shake them out of apathy. I can't do that as Bruce Wayne. As a man...I'm flesh and blood, I can be ignored, destroyed. But as a symbol...as a symbol I can be incorruptible. I can be everlasting. Something elemental...something terrifying" (Nolan, 2005). We first witness Batman help defeat injustice when he raids a drug trade regularly executed by criminals but he instills fear in his enemies to accomplish something that the proper authorities were not able to accomplish before. Although some might consider this vigilantism, Batman provides aid to a city in desperate need of ridding criminals, which is the most important criterion in determining whether or not he is heroic. Alfred instructs Bruce that his plan for saving Gotham cannot be with the intentions of thrill seeking or to prove he's a hero: "For Thomas Wayne, helping others wasn't about proving anything to anyone, including himself...It can't be personal, or you're just a vigilante" (Nolan, 2005). After returning to society, Bruce becomes distracted by his prominent wealth and newly gained power but Alfred helps him remember why he initially desired transformation: to defeat injustice like his father before him.

Although Bruce's return never fully concludes, the first indication of his benefitting Gotham City occurs when Ducard arrives. Ducard has the intent to drive the citizens insane using a hallucinogen which would essentially cause them to destroy themselves while intoxicated. Before Ducard is able to initiate the machine that will spread this hallucinogen across the entire city, Bruce, or rather Batman, faces him. One important aspect of Bruce's morality is that he doesn't execute criminals; this mercy is what separates himself from evil. So when faced with the decision to either kill his mentor or let his city perish he relies on his father's influence. At the mercy of Batman, his former mentor Ducard exclaims, "Have you finally learned to do what is necessary?" Bruce responds, "I won't kill you...but I don't have to save you" (Nolan, 2005). The train carrying the machine capable of destroying Gotham, along with Ducard, proceeds to crash thus saving the city.

Bruce's return to Gotham City includes his realization that Batman is a symbol of justice in a way that bears similarity to his father's reputation as a helpful philanthropist. Bruce determines that he must always put Gotham City before his personal satisfaction. He recognizes that he must not sacrifice his morality at any cost. This allows him to be truly heroic and benefit Gotham City by protecting the citizens from all villainous threats.

CONCLUSION

Joseph Campbell's (1949) monomyth is the most famous and influential depiction of the hero's evolution and development. When Batman, revered for his physical prowess, defeats villains such as the Joker who is known for his masterful plans, or Bane with his domineering stature, we witness the finished product of this heroic transformation. Batman solely desires justice for Gotham City, a desire spurred by his father's reputation. The man behind the mask is essentially the product of the suffering child standing over his parents' dead bodies. Although this transformed hero gains all the glory, Bruce Wayne's long journey of suffering endowed him with meaning and purpose dedicated to justice that is the root of all his heroic behavior. His painful journey also promoted his mental and physical well-being (Efthimiou, Allison, & Franco, 2018). Bruce, much like Prince William and Prince Harry, relies on the transformative gift of suffering to perform greats acts of altruism and bravery concerning the betterment of society.

It is important for the hero to never forget what spurred their transformation. Heroism is not a final product, but rather a continuous display of bravery and selflessness for the greater good of society. And it is tenuous. If Batman were ever to forget the child who lost both of his parents, the transformation would be unwound and Gotham City would lose its famed hero.

REFERENCES

Allison, S. T., & Goethals, G. R. (2011). Heroes: What they do and why we need them. New York: Oxford University Press.

Allison, S. T., & Goethals, G. R. (2016). Hero worship: The elevation of the human spirit. Journal for the Theory of Social Behaviour, 46, 187-210.

Allison, S. T., & Goethals, G. R. (2017). The hero's transformation. In S. T. Allison, G. R. Goethals, & R. M. Kramer (Eds.), Handbook of heroism and heroic leadership. New York: Routledge.

Allison, S. T., Goethals, G. R., & Kramer, R. M. (2017). Setting the scene: The rise and coalescence of heroism science. In S. T. Allison, G. R. Goethals, & R. M. Kramer (Eds.), Handbook of heroism and heroic leadership. New York: Routledge.

Allison, S. T., Goethals, G. R., Marrinan, A. R., Parker, O. M., Spyrou, S. P., Stein, M. (2019). The metamorphosis of the hero: Principles, processes, and purpose. Frontiers in Psychology

Allison, S. T., & Setterberg, G. C. (2016). Suffering and sacrifice: Individual and collective benefits, and implications for leadership. In S. T. Allison, C. T. Kocher, & G. R. Goethals (Eds), Frontiers in spiritual leadership: Discovering the better angels of our nature. New York: Palgrave Macmillan.

Allison, S. T., & Smith, G. (2015). Reel heroes & villains. Richmond: Agile Writer Press.

Campbell, J. (1949). The Hero with a Thousand Faces. New World Library.

Campbell, J. (1988). The power of myth. New York: Anchor Books.

Christopher Nolan. Perf. Christian Bale. (2005-2012) "The Dark Knight Trilogy," Warner Home Video

Davis, J. L., Burnette, J. L., Allison, S. T., & Stone, H. (2011). Against the odds: Academic underdogs benefit from incremental theories. Social Psychology of Education, 14, 331-346.

Dik, B. J., Duffy, R. D., & Eldridge, B. (2009). Calling and vocation in career counseling: Recommendations for promoting meaningful work. Professional Psychology: Research and Practice, 40, 625–632.

Efthimiou, O., & Allison, S. T. (2017). Heroism science: Frameworks for an emerging field. Journal of Humanistic Psychology.

Efthimiou, O., Allison, S. T., & Franco, Z. E. (Eds.) (2018). Heroism and wellbeing in the 21st Century: Applied and emerging perspectives. New York: Routledge.

Farcht, J. (2007). Building personal leadership. Hampton, VA: Morgan James Publishing.

Hoyt, C. L., Allison, S. T., Barnowski, A., & Sultan, A. (2019). Implicit theories of heroism and leadership: The role of gender, communion, and agency. Basic and Applied Social Psychology..

Langley, T. (2012) Batman and Psychology: A Dark and Stormy Knight. Wiley, 2012.

Rohr, R. (2011). Falling upward. Hoboken, NJ: Jossey-Bass.

Singer, H. (2017) Diana, 7 Days. United Kingdom: BBC.

White, M. D., and Robert Arp. (2008) Batman and Philosophy: The Dark Knight of the Soul. Hoboken, NJ: John Wiley & Sons.

Worthington, E. L, & Allison, S. T. (2018). Heroic humility: What the science of humility can say to people raised on self-focus. Washington. DC: American Psychological Association.

Zimbardo, P. (2007). The Lucifer effect: Understanding how good people turn evil. New York: Random House.

9

BATMAN'S REMARKABLE HERO'S JOURNEY: THE DARK KNIGHT TRILOGY

DECLAN H. SCANLON

Bruce lands on the cold soil of the well. He slowly rises and looks into the dark abyss in front of him. Suddenly loud screeches and the flapping wings are all he can hear; then blackness. Nolan's trilogy of Batman is quite unique because it takes a comic book hero, places him in the real world, and presents him with real world problems. The villains that Batman faces throughout the sequence are not silly or unrealistic; they are human. Instead of making Bruce the powerful and mighty Batman who is perfect and always stands for good, Nolan shows the human side of the hero. A man who is broken, scarred, and truly flawed. Nolan delivers a realistic version of a hero who is terribly damaged, yet he manages to become a masked vigilante that Gotham city relies on to keep the streets safe.

The purpose of this chapter is to describe the journey and transformations that turn an ordinary man, Bruce Wayne, into a civil-hero (Franco, Blau & Zimbardo, 2011). Bruce takes three specific pathways to transformation: dependence to autonomy, egocentricity to sociocentricity, and stagnation to growth. Through his journey he experiences multiple transformations that are moral, intellectual, emotional, and physical in nature (Allison & Goethals, 2017; Goethals & Allison, 2014). With each pathway taken and transformation completed, Bruce becomes more than just a man; he becomes a legend. His journey has three main stages: departure, initiation, and return (Allison, Goethals & Kramer, 2017). With the completion of each phase in his expedition, Bruce grows further from ordinary and gets closer to achieving true heroism.

The Departure from the Ordinary World

This first phase of the journey repesents the period in the hero's life where the audience is introduced to the character's normal world before his adventures begin (Campbell, 1949). Bruce is shown in his true nature and crucial details about him are revealed. The audience can relate to his life, which helps us later sympathize with him when he is enduring his plight (Campbell, 1949). The journey begins when Bruce is a mere child. While he and best friend and love interest, Rachel Dawes, are playing outside the Wayne Mansion, an accident occurs. Bruce falls down a well in his garden that leaves him stranded about 20 feet below the surface. Rachel runs for help as Bruce lies at the bottom of the well, at the mouth of a small underground cave. He looks into the empty darkness as he waits in fear for what is to come. Suddenly a colony of bats flies out and surrounds him. Afterwards, they escape the darkness into the light. Bruce lets out terrifying screams but is not heard until he falls unconscious. When he wakes up his father, Thomas Wayne, is descending into the well reaching his hand out to grab his son. This incident sparks Bruce's fear of bats and is the true start of his journey to heroism (Nolan, 2005).

The Call to Adventure

This stage of the journey occurs when the hero receives a metaphorical call that casts the character out of his ordinary world (Campbell, 1949). This departure challenges the hero to take action and make strides toward accomplishing his mission.

In *Batman Begins,* the city of Gotham is stricken by poverty and is overrun by crime. From low level robberies to intricate organized crime groups, the city is in shambles. While attending the local theater with his parents, Bruce is reminded of his biggest fear. The acrobatic performers come from the sky like bats and he has flashbacks of being terrorized by the innocent creatures. He becomes so fearful of the play that he asks his father if they can leave the theater. Being a sympathetic man, Thomas does not bat an eye and takes both Bruce and his wife to the back exit (Nolan, 2005). However, as the three leave, they are confronted by a robber, Joe Chill. The man takes out a gun and tells the family to give him all their valuables. Thomas Wayne stays serene and tells the man to calm down while he hands him his wallet. Chill then tries to steal Martha Wayne's pearl necklace but is distracted by Thomas trying to stop him. He then shoots both of Bruce's parents. He looks at a young Bruce and runs away to escape the crime scene. Bruce is devastated and sits by both his dead parents and cries.

Years later, Bruce gets word of Chill's release from prison and decides to make an appearance at the court hearing. He is determined to avenge his parents' death even if it means he will be put into jail himself. Bruce comes to the Gotham City courthouse in a trench coat with a gun at his side, ready to kill the man that shattered his world so many years before. While Chill is leaving the courtroom, he is surrounded by crowds of reporters and citizens. As Bruce gets ready to finally shoot the man, someone else does the deed for him. Bruce is happy that Joe Chill is dead, but he is unsatisfied with the way it happened. This drives Bruce to meet with the leader of the mob in Gotham, Carmine Falcone (Nolan, 2005). He realizes he has much less control over his life than he thought, propelling him into a life of crime and fighting.

While this appears to be a giant step backwards, it is actually a small step forward. Bruce's pathway from dependence to autonomy is complete at this point in the trilogy (Allison & Goethals, 2017). He is stripped of his innocence when his parents are killed and he can no longer depend on them to help him with his needs. Although he has Alfred, the family's longtime butler, no kid should have to grow up without their parents. Bruce is forced to be independent, and he does not handle it well (Allison & Goethals, 2017). However, his journey toward heroism continues without him realizing it.

The Refusal of the Call

When the protagonist of a story suffers a tragedy in his life, he may decide to refuse the call and turn to a life of crime, or he may simply isolate himself from society. The challenges ahead that are involved in becoming a hero may seem unimportant to him and he may have doubts of ever being the same man again (Campbell, 1949). Sure enough, while his city struggles, Bruce disappears to escape his horrible past.

He finds himself halfway across the world in a Bhutanese prison for stealing electronics. With nothing to lose, Bruce spends his time provoking other inmates and fighting groups of them. He is an excellent fighter and is never defeated by the malicious men around him, but he continues to stay hidden from the world he once came from and has no intentions of ever returning (Nolan, 2005). The fear and doubt that surrounds Bruce ensure that he can feel content just being a prisoner.

Meeting of the Mentor

During the challenging parts of the journey, the hero becomes in desperate need of guidance from anyone (Campbell, 1949). Whether the mentor provides an item, knowledge, or even self-confidence, it is all Bruce needs to transform his fears and doubts into something more positive and special (Allison & Goethals, 2017; Gray et al., 2018).

After a prison gang tries to kill Bruce, he is put into solitary confinement where he is left to rot away. That is until Henri Ducard comes to him and offers him a chance to train with the League of Shadows (Nolan, 2005). This opportunity would allow him to overcome and master his greatest fears. After little convincing, Bruce decides to join him. Ducard shows him that he is meant for much more than he ever imagined and that he is truly the decider of his own fate. While he is training, he slowly begins to understand his path to greatness and altruism.

Crossing the First Threshold

At this stage, the hero finally understands the path that must be taken and chooses to accept the challenge. During this process, the hero will undergo a transformation that pushes him out of is comfort even more and allows him to enter the new world (Campbell, 1949).

After intense training with Ducard and other members of the League of Shadows, Bruce finally learns his path and discovers his true potential. His last test to become a member of the league is to execute a man who stole from a village (Nolan, 2005). While this may seem like justice to many, Bruce decides to leave his mentor and the League of Shadows because of their immoral views. He escapes the base of operations and leaves it in flames with a person he believes to be Ra's al Ghul. The only man Bruce saves is his mentor Ducard, but little does he know, the man he saved has not been honest about his true identity (Nolan, 2005).

Bruce goes through his first hero transformation while he is training with the League of Shadows, and this metamorphosis is an intellectual one (Allison & Goethals, 2017). He understands his life in a worldlier view and changes his opinions about his true purpose. He sees that hiding away from his fears is selfish when his city needs a hero to make the world safe. This idea helps him build his self-confidence to do the right thing, every time.

Once he leaves the League of Shadows, Bruce understands that his purpose is to help the city of Gotham and rid the streets of its petty crime. While he was a self-centered prisoner who only a few months earlier had nothing to live for, he decides to put his past behind him and help the people. His transformation from egocentricity to sociocentricity is just beginning (Allison & Goethals, 2014, 2017).

After being absent for almost seven years, Bruce returns to Gotham city where he begins to fight crime after the sun falls. He dresses entirely in black and looks like a bat because of his mask and spiked cape. After this "job" becomes more important to Bruce, he becomes known as "the Batman", the cities vigilante. Even the Gotham Police Department works with Batman because he never kills the people he takes out. His strict moral code calls for him to leave his victims tied up or stuck for the police to apprehend (Nolan, 2005). This further proves Batman's heroic mentality and dedication to keeping the city safe in a way unlike that of the League of Shadows. His character follows a similar mentality of the Buddhist teachings of bodhicitta, which speaks of an awakened mind "'that inspires a promise, a vow to advance step by step to help others'" (Allison & Goethals, 2017; Mercer, 2016).

Belly of the Whale

The stage can be seen as the hero's final commitment to become more than an ordinary person (Campbell, 1949). By entering this portion of the quest, Bruce shows his willingness to undergo a complete metamorphosis. Toward the end of Batman Begins, Bruce is at the height of his skillset and ability to fight crime. Now he is forced to face something much greater: his old mentor. Henri Ducard travels to Gotham to release a toxin into the city's water supply. This poison causes hallucinations of people's worst fears if exposed to it. Bruce is forced to overcome the toxin's harsh effects while also attempting to stop Ducard (Nolan, 2005). The people of Gotham begin destroying the city and Ducard reveals himself to Bruce as Ra's al Ghul. Batman has a final showdown with his old mentor and leaves him on a train that crashes and explodes. This act also stops the toxin from being released fully, which saves the city. The destruction and chaos almost swallows Gotham whole, but with the help of Batman, the city lives to see another day.

The Initiation and the Road of Trials

After surviving the initial obstacle in the "Belly of the Whale," the hero is tested rigorously through a series of trials (Campbell, 1949). In Batman's case, these trials appear in the form of criminals who try to disturb the peace and safety of the city of Gotham. Batman has been fighting crime for quite a while when The Dark Knight begins, and he has continued to help the city thrive while he sweeps the streets of criminals every night. Harvey Dent, the new district attorney, has stepped up as Gotham's newest crime fighting powerhouse and is even coined the name "The White Knight" by some (Nolan, 2008). His position as a public figure puts him in harm's way, but he does not seem affected by this potential threat. The coming of Harvey incentivizes Batman to retire from his life as a vigilante because Bruce believes that Gotham deserves a new hero "with a face" (Nolan, 2008). However, he has yet to meet his newest threat, whose presence is now being felt throughout the city.

The hero understands that unlike his previous tests, this one is different. A villain that the Batman cannot take down alone has risen to power. Bruce is forced to make allies and work together with other people in order to defeat the new criminal mastermind (Campbell, 1949). Bruce soon learns more about the man known as the Joker, a fiendish villain who has been running the city's crime and is only growing stronger. He has a bizarre disposition and belongs in an insane asylum due to his rough past. Eventually the Joker proposes an ultimatum: either Batman reveals his true identity, or the he is going to kill someone every night (Nolan, 2008).

While questioning mob boss Sal Maroni for more information about the Joker, Batman is told, "You got rules.... the Joker, he's got no rules.... if you want this guy you got one way, but you already know what that is...." (Nolan, 2008). Bruce is torn between hanging up his cape and continuing his mission as Gotham's dark knight. After the judge and police commissioner are assassinated by the Joker, the men who should have been locked up by Harvey run free because sources are terrified of what will happen to them if they stand as a witness. When Bruce asks Alfred what he should do, he replies with, "Endure.... they will hate you for it, but that's the point of Batman; he can be the outcast, he can make the choice...the right choice" (Nolan, 2008). After hearing this advice, Bruce is able to see the broader picture and understands that he must stop the Joker and remain as the Batman. Being a leader and being a hero are two independent roles. Bruce understands this concept but is unsure of what he will become if he proceeds (Decter-Frain, Vanstone & Frimer, 2017).

Batman reaches out to Detective Gordon who had helped him with Ra's al Ghul. The two men work together to stop the Joker from killing Harvey Dent, while Dent is transported to the Police Department. Luckily Batman is there and deters the Joker from actually doing any harm, but his men still manage to take both Rachel and Harvey. Detective Gordon captures the Joker as he is unveiling Batman's identity and places him in a cell until further questioning (Nolan, 2008).

The Ordeal

The hero is forced to face his greatest fear yet: losing the love of his life (Campbell, 1949). Bruce has loved Rachel since he was a child and would do anything to save her, but he must also ensure Harvey's safety due to Bruce's strong belief that if Dent falls, the city will follow (Nolan, 2008).

Batman interrogates the Joker on the whereabouts of the two-missing people with his own strategy: force. After suffering multiple head slams and punches to the face, the Joker tells Batman where the victims are an is put back into a cell at the police department. Gordon leads the police department to go save Rachel from one warehouse, while Batman attempts to save Harvey at a separate warehouse. Both of the victims are surrounded by gasoline and a small bomb that will ignite everything when it blows. With most of the force out looking for Rachel, the Joker blows up a cell and escapes the prison (Nolan, 2008). The police department fails to get to Rachel on time, but Batman is able to save Harvey. However, Harvey's face has gasoline on it, which ignites after they leave the building. This causes half of his face to burn off. After the news of Rachel's death reaches the two men, they both are devastated. Bruce becomes extremely depressed and almost loses his mind. This is mostly due to the fact that he could have been with Rachel if he had hung up his cape earlier. Harvey, unfortunately, takes a turn for the worst (Nolan, 2008).

While Dent is in the hospital recovering from his burn wounds, he is visited by the Joker disguised as a nurse. He corrupts Harvey's clearly vulnerable and weak mind, which reminds the audience of an earlier scene in the movie. At a fancy dinner the District Attorney tells Rachel and Bruce that, "You either die a hero, or live long enough to see yourself become a villain" (Nolan, 2008). This foreshadows Harvey's transformation from a hero to Gotham's new villain. He becomes known for flipping a coin to decide his victims fate. Harvey eventually captures Detective Gordon's family because he believes he is at fault for

Rachel's death. While he prepares to kill members of Gordon's family, he is stopped by Batman. He tackles Harvey over a ledge where Harvey drops to his death.

The Reward

At this point in the story the hero must become more than just a man after facing a near death situation (Campbell, 1949). He is forced to play the role of the villain in order to give his city the peace it has been waiting for.

The Joker has been captured by the police after a standoff that almost left numerous innocent people killed. Although his fate is never explicitly stated, it is inferred that the Joker is put in the newly built insane asylum ("The Dark Knight Trilogy," 2012). Batman has killed the public hero of Gotham and understands that in order to keep the city from losing faith, he must present himself as a villain and Harvey as a hero. He tells Gordon to say that Harvey died trying to defend the detective's family. He then runs away from the police and retires his suit for the greater good of the city. Harvey is praised for being a hero who died protecting his city, while Batman is now seen as nothing but a vicious outlaw (Nolan, 2008).

Batman undergoes a moral transformation when he decides to take the blame for everything that Harvey had done. He demonstrates that a hero is someone who is willing to sacrifice everything just to do what is right for the people and the place he loves. Bruce understands that by taking the fall he is no longer acting in concert with the police and must retire his cape once and for all (Allison & Goethals, 2017).

The Return: The Dark Knight Rises

After years of retirement and aging, the hero is hesitant to return to the chaotic world that he once left (Campbell, 1949). However, a hero knows that his duties are never truly finished until all of the enemies are vanquished. In the beginning of The Dark Knight Rises, Bruce is portrayed as obsolete. He is at a state where he cannot fight crime as well because he is older now. He believes that with all that he has done for Gotham, he deserves to be at peace. However, he has a ceremony at his estate each year in honor of Gotham's greatest hero, Harvey Dent. Bruce meets a woman named Selina Kyle on an upper level floor in his house, who swipes his mother's pearl necklace from a safe. She escapes out the window and leaves Bruce dumbfounded. Although this does not contribute to his coming back, she later becomes the woman he loves (Nolan, 2012). As of now he is unaware that he must return due to the city's newest threat whom he has yet to meet.

The Magic Flight

A new threat has emerged that is even greater than the previous one. This is the ultimate challenge for the hero and the last one in the case of Batman. Although he has faced many obstacles before, this is the most formidable one yet (Campbell, 1949).

Bruce is indirectly convinced by Officer Blake of the Gotham Police Department that he needs to return to Gotham as Batman. His reasoning is the looming threat, Bane, a mercenary who once trained with the League of Shadows but was exiled by Ra's al Ghul. In Batman's second encounter with Selina Kyle, he learns that she is a common thief with an advanced skillset. She tricks Batman into going to Bane's underground base where he is waiting for him. A gate drops behind Batman and Selina watches as he meets Bane for the first time (Nolan, 2012). The new villain is younger, bigger, and stronger than Batman and soon he breaks Bruce both physically and spiritually before throwing Bruce into a pit. The pit is a small prison that is located in India. Bane had been in this same prison years before coming to Gotham (Nolan, 2012). The imprisonment of Bruce is similar to the beginning of his hero's journey when he was captive in the Bhutanese prison (Campbell, 1949).

The Road Back

The hero is trapped and must find his way home. For Bruce this means he must regain his physical strength and confidence to be the hero he knows he once was (Campbell, 1949). Even at his lowest point, he must rise to save Gotham.

Bruce is forced to watch his city burn and fall into the hands of Bane. Gotham is completely taken over by the rebel army and they lose all contact with the outside world due to a bomb that will detonate if anyone enters the city from the outside. Almost the entire cities police department have been lured and trapped underground by Bane. Bruce tries to escape the prison by "making the jump"; however, he fails not once but twice (Nolan, 2012). The older wiser prisoners in adjacent jail cells explain to Bruce that he must embrace his fear and fight through it so that he may make the jump. This means that he must remove the safety rope that has kept him safe on the jump and risk it all, for this is what makes life worth living.

During this endeavor Bruce goes through a physical hero's transformation. When he is left in the cell originally, his back is broken and so is his spirit (Allison & Goethals, 2017). He is forced to wait and let his back heal so he can train to get stronger. Once he is healthy, he manages to perform exercises in his cell, such as pushups, pullups, and crunches. He becomes stronger than he was before and even more confident. The third attempt of the jump, he goes without the rope in order to overcome his fear of dying in the prison. On this try he reaches the second ledge and completes the jump to escape the pit and return to Gotham (Nolan, 2012).

Resurrection

his is the final test for the hero, but also the most intense. He must use all the knowledge and skills he has developed over the years to destroy his last enemy (Campbell, 1949). The city is on the line, and Bruce is pushed to his limits to save it from destruction. Batman reenters the city just in time to save Officer Blake from a few of Bane's men. The Gotham Police are secretly released from their underground trap. The force prepares to have one final battle with every-thing they have against Bane's army. Civilians also volunteer from all over to help fight for their city (Nolan, 2012).

Batman is forced not only to face Bane, but also Talia who he believed to be an ally. However, she reveals herself as the daughter of Ra's al Ghul after she stabs Batman in the ribs. She had been working with Bane the entire time. Her plan to destroy the city with a remote detonator fails due to the work of Detective Gordon who stops the signal from reaching the bomb. Nevertheless, Bruce is informed that the bomb has no off switch and will detonate even if the controller is not activated. The bombs clock is ticking and Batman does the only thing he can. Using his plane, he takes the bomb far enough away from Gotham that is will safely explode without killing anyone except the pilot: himself (Nolan, 2012). He appears to make the ultimate heroic sacrifice in the interest of preserving the well-being of society (Efthimiou, Allison, & Franco, 2018).

Batman's transformation from stagnation to growth occurs, here because he has become more than the hero he once was. He has become a legend. A statue is put in place to show the community's ever growing gratitude towards him (Kinsella et al., 2017). This is the final transformation Batman endures in his hero's journey (Allison & Goethals, 2017; Davis et al., 2011).

The hero may live a life of peace and have no fear of death. Often the character lives in the moment, with no regard for what is to come or any regret of what happened in the past (Campbell, 1949). Bruce is finally able to be himself without any concern or worry about his beloved city. The Batman is gone, but Bruce has yet to fall. It is revealed to Lucius Fox, Bruce's equipment specialist, that the autopilot of Batman's aircraft had been installed months before he took the bomb away from Gotham, which means Bruce was never aboard the ship (Nolan, 2012). He is finally at peace in a foreign country with his love Selina Kyle whom he is pictured with at a restaurant in the final scene of the trilogy (Nolan, 2012). Batman's final chapter has finally closed and the end of his hero's journey has finally arrived. While Bruce is not technically known for his heroic actions by the public, his actions as Batman will live on for generations.

CONCLUSION

Throughout his journey, Bruce faces villains who are very similar to him in ways he does not realize. Both the Joker and Bane had troubled childhoods. The Joker was abused by his father, while Bane was put into a prison to serve his father's sentence. Bruce was not abused or imprisoned as a child, but he lost his parents and at a very young age and struggled immensely growing up. The difference between Bruce versus the Joker and Bane is that Bruce made the individual choice to change his life for the better. Instead of allowing the darkness to swallow him whole, he faced his fears and rose to become a hero.

Bruce is a normal human being, a humble hero (Worthington & Allison, 2018) who took a personal oath to become a protector of millions of innocent civilians. He journeys from his comfortable ordinary life to a completely different country just to discern his true path in life. He understands that the world is much broader than he ever imagined and proves that he is committed to only one goal: to keep Gotham safe. His dedication to keeping the people of his city safe is unmatched by any person in his universe. Bruce understands that Gotham city and the world need more than the average hero. They need Batman.

REFERENCES

Allison, S. T., & Goethals, G. R. (2014). "Now he belongs to the ages": The heroic leadership dynamic and deep narratives of greatness. In Goethals, G. R., et al. (Eds.), Conceptions of leadership: Enduring ideas and emerging insights. New York: Palgrave Macmillan.

Allison, S. T., & Goethals, G. R. (2017). The hero's transformation. In S. T. Allison, G. R. Goethals, & R. M. Kramer (Eds.), Handbook of heroism and heroic leadership. New York: Routledge.

Allison, S. T., Goethals, G. R., & Kramer, R. M. (2017). Setting the scene: The rise and coalescence of heroism science. In S. T. Allison, G. R. Goethals, & R. M. Kramer (Eds.), Handbook of heroism and heroic leadership. New York: Routledge.

Campbell, J., & Cousineau, P. (2014). The hero's journey: Joseph Campbell on his life and work. Novato, CA: New World Library.

Davis, J. L., Burnette, J. L., Allison, S. T., & Stone, H. (2011). Against the odds: Academic underdogs benefit from incremental theories. Social Psychology of Education, 14, 331-346.

Decter-Frain, A., Vanstone, R., & Frimer, J. A. (2017). Why and How Groups Create Moral Heroes. In S. T. Allison, G. R. Goethals, & R. M. Kramer (Eds.), Handbook of heroism and heroic leadership. New York: Routledge.

Efthimiou, O., Allison, S. T., & Franco, Z. E. (Eds.) (2018). Heroism and wellbeing in the 21st Century: Applied and emerging perspectives. New York: Routledge.

Eylon, D., & Allison, S. T. (2005). The frozen in time effect in evaluations of the dead. Personality and Social Psychology Bulletin, 31, 1708-1717'

Franco, Z. E., Blau, K., & Zimbardo, P. G. (2011, April 11). Heroism: A Conceptual Analysis and Differentiation Between Heroic Action and Altruism. Review of General Psychology. Advance online publication. doi: 10.1037/a0022672

Goethals, G. R., & Allison, S. T. (2014). Kings and charisma, Lincoln and leadership: An evolutionary perspective. In Goethals, G. R., et al. (Eds.), Conceptions of leadership: Enduring ideas and emerging insights. New York: Palgrave Macmillan. doi: 10.1057/9781137472038

Gray, K., Anderson, S., Doyle, C. M., Hester, N., Schmitt, P., Vonasch, A., Allison, S. T., and Jackson, J. C. (2018). To be immortal, do good or evil. Personality and Social Psychology Bulletin.

Hoyt, C. L., Allison, S. T., Barnowski, A., & Sultan, A. (2019). Implicit theories of heroism and leadership: The role of gender, communion, and agency. Basic and Applied Social Psychology.

Kinsella, E. L., Ritchie, T. D., & Igou, R.I. (2017). Attributes and Applications of Heroes. In S. T. Allison, G. R. Goethals, & R. M. Kramer (Eds.), Handbook of heroism and heroic leadership. New York: Routledge.

M., Jes. (2012, August 01). The Dark Knight Trilogy – A Hero's Journey. Retrieved October 06, 2017, from https://houseofgeekery.com/2012/08/02/batman-heroes-journey

Mercer, R. (2016). The effortless benevolence of heroic figures in Buddhist traditions. Retrieved from https://blog.richmond.edu/heroes/2016/01/08/the-effortless-benevolence-of-heroic-figures-inbuddhist-traditions.

Nolan, C. (2005). Batman Begins. Warner Bros. Pictures.

Nolan, C. (2012). The Dark Knight Rises. Warner Bros. Pictures.

Roven, C., Thomas, E., & Franco, L. (Producer), & Nolan, C. (Directory). (2005). Batman Begins [Motion Picture]. United States: Warner Bros.

Thomas, E., Roven, C., Nolan, C. (Producer), & Nolan, C. (Directory). (2008). The Dark Knight [Motion Picture]. United States: Warner Bros.

Thomas, E., Nolan, C., & Roven, C. (Producer), & Nolan, C. (Directory). (2012). The Dark Knight Rises [Motion Picture]. United States: Warner Bros.

Worthington, E. L, & Allison, S. T. (2018). Heroic humility: What the science of humility can say to people raised on self-focus. Washington. DC: American Psychological Association.

10

HARRY POTTER AND THE HERO'S JOURNEY: AN ANALYSIS OF A WIZARD'S TRANSFORMATION

ANDREW J. GRAHAM

In April of 2010, 30-year old Nikki Carpenter had to make a difficult decision: her life or the lives of her three children. For her, the choice was easy. As a tornado pummeled through their town of Yazoo City, Mississippi, Nikki knew that she had to keep her three boys safe. To that end, she put a mattress on top of them and situated herself on top of it to shield them as their house started coming down (Putnal, 2010). Because of her efforts, her children are alive today even though she had to sacrifice herself. Parental sacrifice may be seen as something that every good parent should do, but it doesn't make the act any less heroic. To give up one's own life so that another can live is a remarkably heroic act, even if it's for one's own child.

Self-sacrifice is a common theme throughout the Harry Potter series, but the first and most notable example of sacrifice is the one that allowed Harry to live. Faced with the same decision that Nikki faced, Lily Potter chose to sacrifice herself in order to create the magic necessary to protect Harry. After Voldemort killed Harry's dad, James Potter, Lily stepped in to save Harry even though it meant her own death. In sacrificing herself, she was able to cast a spell over Harry that was so strong that when Voldemort tried to kill him as well, it merely bounced off and almost destroyed Voldemort himself. This traumatic experience is what primed Harry for heroism. In surviving the attack, Harry became revered by the wizarding world and unanimously decreed "the boy who lived." Before Harry did so much as a heroic deed, there was an expectation from others that he would do great things. But, more importantly, Harry desired something to give his life meaning in order to repay his parents' sacrifice for him, but he didn't know what that was yet. To gain a complete understanding of Harry's transformation as a hero, it is necessary to use the principles of heroism science to explore his role as a hero and how he and society changed because of it.

THE HERO'S JOURNEY

Before embarking on an analysis of Harry Potter's transformation, it is important to first explain his role within the context of the hero's journey as described by Campbell (1949). The hero's journey consists of the hero being summoned to go on a journey that is challenging and compels them to discover a quality they were missing in themselves. Ultimately, at the end of the journey, the hero bestows a boon or gift upon society. This heroic path involves going through three phases of departure, initiation, and return.

Departure

Prior to Harry going to Hogwarts School of Witchcraft and Wizardry, Harry had no idea that he was a wizard and that his parents were murdered by a dark wizard named Voldemort. Instead, until he was 11 years old, Harry lived with his aunt, uncle, and cousin where he was forced to live in a closet under the stairs. Despite receiving letters from Hogwarts for some time, Harry didn't attend until he was 11 because his aunt and uncle intercepted the letters to keep the wizarding world a secret from him. However, that all changed one night when Hagrid appeared and informed Harry that he was a wizard. Of course, this news was met with skepticism from Harry at first, but the notion that he was meant for something better and more purposeful than the bleak life of monotony he had grown accustomed to had already taken root. Thus, Harry left the muggle, magic-less world he was used to and immersed himself into a new world of magic and wizardry, marking the start of his journey.

Initiation

Upon crossing the threshold into the world of wizardry and, more specifically, Hogwarts, Harry was given his first indication of what he would do with his life. By the time the sorting hat placed Harry in the house of Gryffindor, Harry had already made his first two friends: Ron Weasley and Hermione Granger. The process of the sorting hat was an initiation in itself. Harry could have been placed in one of four houses: Gryffindor, Hufflepuff, Ravenclaw or Slytherin, each potentially having a different effect on Harry's maturation as a wizard. If he had been placed in Slytherin, his heroic nature may have never flourished let alone occurred. Gryffindor gave Harry the opportunity to be with his friends who would go on to be significant sources of help for him, and it provided an environment that allowed his hopes for a purposeful life to manifest. To make that happen, though, Harry first had to learn the basics of magic. Although Harry was never able to match Hermione's vast knowledge of spells and magic, he showed great proficiency in the defense against the dark arts magic. By attending Hogwarts and starting his wizarding education, Harry was initiated into the world of magic which made his journey possible.

Return

Along Harry's journey, he faced many obstacles and adversaries but none more sinister than Voldemort. By finally defeating Voldemort, he was able to complete his journey and gain a sense of fulfillment. His journey was not one fueled by a desire for vengeance, as that motive would have made his actions unheroic. He was guided by doing the right thing for others, even if it meant putting himself in harm's way. In doing so, he was able to get the sense of fulfillment that he so yearned for. By the completion of his journey, Harry had gone through major transformation in terms of his moral, mental, emotional and physical capacities (Allison & Goethals, 2017). He went from a position of inferiority in his muggle life to a position of esteem and power that made him a leader in the wizarding world.

Harry began his journey with no knowledge of magic and spells but developed into a powerful wizard with mastery of defense against the dark arts magic. He lessened his dependency on others and became capable of acting independently. Harry developed by becoming more confident in his abilities and in the role of being the hero whom others admired. He also changed from being taught magic to teaching others the necessary spells to defend themselves. These transformations didn't occur overnight or all at the same time; rather, they were part of a long developmental process as depicted by Joseph Campbell's (1949) monomyth of the hero (Allison & Goethals, 2017). By completing his journey, Harry was able to live up to others' expectations of him and his own expectations as well. In killing Voldemort, Harry gave the wizarding world something it hadn't had for a long time: peace.

Mentors and Friends

The peace that Harry bestowed upon the world of magic was not easy to secure. Harry had to overcome tremendous obstacles along the way, each one transforming him in some way and bringing him closer to his goal. In the sense that Harry was transformed by his journey, transformed his society, came from humble beginnings, overcame challenges, and received help from others, he can be seen as a traditional and transforming hero (Allison & Goethals, 2013). In this section of the chapter, the nature of Harry's relationships with his friends and mentors is explored along with how they each played a role in Harry's development as a hero and in the completion of his journey.

Ron and Hermione are perhaps some of the more significant influencers on Harry because they had the most continual interaction with him. Starting out as merely friends when they were 11-years old, the two turned into much more than that for Harry as the years passed. The first instance of the three acting as a team occurred in *Harry Potter and the Sorcerer's Stone*, when Harry and Ron saved Hermione from a troll who had inexplicably gotten into Hogwarts. With very rudimentary training up to that point, the three were able to defeat the troll and establish deep bonds with each other. That moment served to create a foundation for them that established them as a dynamic force to be reckoned with. It was Harry's first heroic deed and it seemed to come naturally to the young wizard. The three don't relent when it comes to doing what's right, even when the odds are stacked against them. This becomes true when the trio learn that the mysterious and terrifying three-headed dog is guarding a valuable object called the Sorcerer's Stone and that a professor is attempting to steal it.

To stop the professor before he takes it, the three must get past the dog and then a series of obstacles designed to keep intruders out. With little magic knowledge between them, they work together to get past these obstacles and, in doing so, they give Harry the support and confidence he needed to face the professor alone. After Harry successfully secures the stone, he is hailed as hero in the school and from that point on, his heroic deeds only continued. Because of this experience, Harry's hero attributes as detailed in "the great eight" (Allison & Goethals, 2011) become clear and continue to develop in subsequent books and movies. Although not all of these attributes are seen to the extent that they are in later movies, Harry demonstrates that he is smart, strong, self-less, caring, charismatic, resilient, reliable, and inspiring. Harry, in some way or another, encompasses all the characteristics of a hero from a young age, making his transition into a hero that people can count on relatively natural for him. This transition is also made easy with the help of Ron and Hermione, whose "active role in selecting and shaping [Harry] into a symbol of the goals of the group" (Adams, 2006; Gardner & Avolio, 1998) helps advance his heroic journey.

As important as friends are in assisting the hero, mentors serve the purpose of guiding and caring for the hero along his journey. One of the most notable mentor figures for Harry is the headmaster of Hogwart's school who is widely considered to be the most powerful wizard: Dumbledore. Dumbledore takes interest in Harry from his first day at Hogwarts, as he knows his past and the fact that he survived an attack by Voldemort. This interest blossoms into a strong relationship between the two that Harry uses in times of distress. Dumbledore offers sage wisdom to the budding hero on his journey whenever it is needed and he believes in Harry's ability to handle situations well beyond the scope of an ordinary pre-teen. His belief in Harry allows him to see past his age and inexperience and see him as the hero he is destined to become.

After Harry witnessed Voldemort murdering Cedric Diggory in The Goblet of Fire, Harry is quick to warn others of the dark lord's return but none in a position of power, besides Dumbledore, believe him. Additionally, Dumbledore entrusts Harry with the monumental challenge of finding all the horcruxes that make up Voldemort's soul, and destroy them. Dumbledore recognizes the good that Harry can do and so he risks his life on multiple occasions to protect Harry so that he can continue fighting the good fight. Dumbledore's belief in Harry and his support of him were invaluable, and this confidence allowed Harry to develop both mentally and morally by giving him knowledge not only of magic, but of right and wrong as well.

Whereas Dumbledore's impact on Harry was obvious, Sirius Black's was less so but still crucial to Harry. Sirius Black was a mysterious character at first; Harry only knew him as the ravenous murderer that escaped the wizard prison, Azkaban. However, when Harry met him for the first time, he found out that he was innocent of those crimes and was also his godfather. This was important to Harry because he believed that all his family was dead -- excluding the Dursley's whom Harry didn't really consider family. There was an instantaneous connection between the two because Harry yearned for family and Sirius wanted a relationship with his godson. Sirius gradually became a father figure for Harry as the years passed, which was important for Harry who felt like he was alone in the world at times.

Although most transformations take a long time, Harry's transformation after meeting Sirius was one that occurred rather fast and intensely (Allison & Goethals, 2017). He no longer felt so alone because he had someone who was family now. Beyond that, Sirius was a mentor to Harry who did whatever necessary to protect him, even if it meant sacrificing his own life in the process. After Sirius was slain by the deatheater Bellatrix Lestrange while protecting Harry, Harry wanted to inflict pain on or even murder her for taking his last remaining family. While these intentions may seem unheroic, it doesn't necessarily entail that his observable disdain and desire to punish Bellatrix are associated with unobservable qualities that aren't aligned with heroism as noted by the costly signaling theory (Kafashan et al., 2017). Not all heroes are perfect semblances of the characteristics they embody, as all people have their flaws. Harry's history of family being taken from him will always be there, but because he doesn't let it take control of him or dictate his decisions, he remains a hero.

An unlikely ally that doesn't make his true intentions known until the last movie is Professor Snape. In the beginning, Harry is untrusting of Snape and believes him to be a deatheater working for Voldemort. As such, the two don't exactly see eye to eye and Harry views him as an enemy. It is not until Snape dies at the hands of Voldemort that his nature is revealed to Harry. All along Snape was doing the most to help Harry by acting as a double agent and pretending to serve Voldemort when in reality he supported Dumbledore as a means of protecting him. He taught Harry how to defend his mind from intrusion by Voldemort and to see into others' minds. He also took the unbreakable vow to assist Malfoy in killing Dumbledore to maintain his cover so that he can keep Harry safe, and let himself be seen as bad while in reality he was a hero in his own right.

Although the focus of this paper is on Harry's transformation as a hero, Snape can be seen as transparent hero whose deeds are unknown and he is unsung until the end (Allison et al., 2019; Goethals & Allison, 2012). Snape risked his own security and reputation to protect Harry all out of love for Lily Potter. After finding out the truth and realizing that he owed a great deal to Snape, Harry underwent an emotional transformation that made him feel foolish for being so short-sighted about Snape and the fact that he was his greatest ally of all.

Hero Functions

In this section it will become evident how Harry fits into the three categories of the heroes function framework (Kinsella et al., 2017). Each category -- enhancing, moral modeling, and protecting -- plays a role in how Harry acts as a hero throughout his journey. Enhancing is associated with how the hero motivates and instills hope in others; moral modelling is related to how he promotes good values and encourages others to follow them and also do good in the world; and protecting is the function of the hero that saves others from forces of evil that will cause harm.

With regard to the enhancing function, Harry is a source of inspiration to the other wizards who fight alongside him against Voldemort. At first, many of the people who are part of his cause, besides Ron and Hermione, are older and more seasoned wizards than he. By virtue of his age and determination, Harry impresses others and motivates them to give their all in their endeavors against the dark forces. As he gets older, more mature, and starts taking on greater responsibility, he earns admiration from wizards his own age and younger. As such, he acts as a role model to them by proving that anyone can help in some way. Harry uses his status to teach other students defensive and offensive magic when Hogwarts is under new rule and won't teach it themselves. By demonstrating to them that they do all have power and can use it for good, he effectively inspires many more young wizards to join him on his journey.

To go along with that, Harry has a strong influence on others in imparting the morals and values he believes in. He does so by continually demonstrating to others the difference between doing what is right and what is not. For example, in *The Goblet of Fire,* Harry partakes in the triwizard tournament representing Hogwarts alongside Cedric Diggory. This competition is centered on winning as many of the challenges as possible to be crowned the winner and prove that your respective school is more superior than the others. In one of such challenges, one of his competitors is unable to rescue her sister from the bottom of the lake. Seeing this, Harry forgoes his lead and rescues Ron along with the girl's sister. In doing so, Harry made it clear to those watching that protecting others is always his priority. Harry consistently exudes empathy for the concerns and interests of the many, not just acting based on his own interests. These qualities make Harry a good model of morals and values that are inherently heroic, which leads many others to act accordingly.

Finally, Harry is above all a protector. He strives to save others when they are in harm's way and often risks his well-being in doing so -- whether one deserves saving or not. One scene in particular in *The Deathly Hallows* epitomizes just what kind of protector Harry is. After Harry, Ron, and Hermione fight Malfoy and his henchmen from Slytherin, one of the henchmen unleashes a fiery serpent that engulfs everything in its path in flames. Just as it looks like they won't make it out alive, Harry finds three broomsticks that they can ride to safety. However, as they are making their escape they see Malfoy and his henchman struggling to climb a mountain of objects while flames nip at their heels. Even though they had just tried to kill Harry and his friends, Harry chooses to go back and rescue them, helping them to narrowly make it out alive. Beyond that, Harry demonstrates the willingness and the capability to defend others from the forces of evil throughout his journey.

Transformation

It is evident that during the course of his journey, Harry changed and developed in a number of ways. In this section the causes of his transformations are explored and whether they are internal, external, or both. Considering he began his hero's journey when he was 11-years old and didn't complete it until years later, he underwent transformation based on natural human development. As he progressed on his journey he got older and more physically fit while also becoming more intelligent and wise in regard to his magic capabilities and decisions as a leader (Piaget & Inhelder, 1958). Moreover, his emotional state altered as he transitioned into his role as a hero because he became more empathetic to others and regarded their problems as his own (Trentacosts & Izard, 2006). Another internal source of transformation that Harry experiences is based on his needs and goals. After accomplishing his goals at lower levels such as destroying Voldemort's horcruxes, Harry was able to reach the highest level by sacrificing himself so that his allies would have the chance to kill Voldemort. He does this because he realizes that he is the last horcrux and that in order for Voldemort to be vanquished, he needed to perish. By sacrificing himself -- as many others did for him -- he was able to reach a state of self-actualization that took place right after he was killed and before he came back from the dead (Maslow, 1943).

Harry also went through transformation because of his transgressions and failures. Although Harry didn't necessarily have many failures of his own, he attributed the deaths around him to his own shortcomings. As his journey went on he put more and more responsibility on himself, which wasn't needed or even helpful. He felt like it was his fault alone that his family and many of his friends died for him which caused him to change his decision making, culminating in him sacrificing himself for the good of others (Rohr, 2011).

On the other hand, there are external forces that caused Harry to change as well. First, there are many situations Harry went through that elicited emotional responses that transformed him (Allison & Goethals, 2017). By being subjected to death all around him, especially the deaths of family and friends, Harry became more determined and focused on completing his journey. Additionally, the series of trials that Harry experienced only furthered his transformation and proved that he was, indeed, capable and willing to complete his task.

In *The Goblet of Fire*, Harry is thrown into an extremely dangerous situation that offers little chance of escape, otherwise known as the "belly of the whale" (Campbell, 1949), when he and Cedric grab the trophy that transports them to Tom Riddle's graveyard. In this situation, Harry witnesses Voldemort rising once again and killing Cedric. The two then battle and Harry is able to escape. This moment was significant for Harry because, even though he was still young and inexperienced, it proved to him that he was the one who had to, and could, defeat Voldemort. The social environment that Harry was in also played a large role in transforming him. He had many friends, mentors, and even his family from beyond the grave, that contributed to his success along the way as detailed above in the mentors and friends section of this chapter.

With regard to transformational arc, Harry most closely falls into the category of stagnation to growth, meaning that Harry was reluctant to change initially but once he realized there was a problem he was able to grow and abandon his false self (Allison & Goethals, 2017). The period of stagnation for Harry occurs before he realizes that he is a wizard. Although he detests the life he has, he accepts it because it is the only one he knows. Even after Hagrid informs him that he is a wizard, he denies it and doesn't believe it to be true. It is not until he attends Hogwarts that he begins to move out of stagnation and into growth mode. However, he doesn't experience real growth until he recognizes how special he is for surviving Voldemort's attack as a baby. His true self is born when he begins to see his potential for what he could do, and then realizes what he should do (Rohr, 2011; Sperry, 2011). As such, it is not immediate change from stagnation to growth, rather it takes Harry the course of his journey until he is fully transformed.

CONCLUSION

Heroes serve an important role in society and act as forces of goodness, benevolence, and well-being (Efthimiou, Allison, & Franco, 2018). Heroes accept great responsibility and the immense risk that comes along with the title. Harry Potter is no exception to this rule. His rise to heroism was paved with death and seemingly insurmountable challenges along the way. He was able to use the deaths of loved ones and friends as motivation to complete his journey instead of letting it ruin him. With his intelligence, fortitude, and magical capabilities -- along with assistance from friends and mentors -- he overcame the significant obstacles that he faced. During the course of his journey he developed and transformed in many ways that made him a hero who was able to defeat Voldemort, create peace in the wizarding world, and instill in others a sense of hope and optimism for the future.

Beyond positively affecting the magical world, Harry also impacted the muggle world through the books and movies about him. Harry Potter has become a household name who is associated with bravery, good moral values, and heroism. Many children and adults, such as myself, have donned their Hogwarts attire and hastily scribbled his signature scar on their foreheads for Halloween and other occasions. It goes beyond just wanting to dress up like Harry, though. The lessons that Harry taught us all and the acts of courage he demonstrated served a broader purpose of inspiring people to act like him in everyday life.

REFERENCES

Adams, P. (2006). Exploring social constructivism: Theories and practicalities. Education, 34(3), 243– 257. doi: 10.1080/03004270600898893

Allison, S. T., & Goethals, G. R. (2011). Heroes: What they do and why we need them. New York: Oxford University Press.

Allison, S. T., & Goethals, G. R. (2013). Heroic leadership: An influence taxonomy of 100 exceptional individuals. New York: Routledge

Allison, S. T., & Goethals, G. R. (2016). Hero worship: The elevation of the human spirit. Journal for the Theory of Social Behaviour, 46, 187-210.

Allison, S. T., & Goethals, G. R. (2017). The hero's transformation. In S. T. Allison, G. R. Goethals, & R. M. Kramer (Eds.), Handbook of heroism and heroic leadership. New York: Routledge.

Allison, S. T., & Goethals, G. R. (2012). Personal versus cultural heroes. Retrieved from https://blog.richmond.edu/heroes/2012/09/12/personal-versus-cultural-heroes

Allison, S. T., Goethals, G. R., Marrinan, A. R., Parker, O. M., Spyrou, S. P., Stein, M. (2019). The metamorphosis of the hero: Principles, processes, and purpose. Frontiers in Psychology.

Campbell, J. (1949). The hero with a thousand faces. NewYork: New World Library

Efthimiou, O., Allison, S. T., & Franco, Z. E. (Eds.) (2018). Heroism and wellbeing in the 21st Century: Applied and emerging perspectives. New York: Routledge.

Gardner, W. L., & Avolio, B. J. (1998). The charismatic relationship: A dramaturgical perspective. The Academy of Management Review, 23(1), 32–58. doi: 10.2307/259098

Goethals, G. R., & Allison, S. T. (2012). Making heroes: The construction of courage, competence and virtue. Advances in Experimental Social Psychology, 46, 183–235. Doi: 10.1016/B978-0-12-394281- 4.00004-0

Hoyt, C. L., Allison, S. T., Barnowski, A., & Sultan, A. (2019). Implicit theories of heroism and leadership: The role of gender, communion, and agency. Basic and Applied Social Psychology.

Piaget, J., & Inhelder, B. (1958). The growth of logical thinking from childhood to adolescence. New York: Basic Books.

Kinsella, E. L., Ritchie, T. D., & Igou, E. R. (2017). Attributes and applications of heroes: A brief history of lay and academic perspectives. In Allison et al. (eds) Handbook of Heroism and Heroic Leadership pp. (19-35). New York: Routledge.

Maslow, A. H. (1943). A theory of human motivation. Psychological Review, 50, 370–396.

Putnal, O. (2015, March 05). Moms Who've Risked It All to Save Their Kids. Retrieved October 06, 2017, from http://www.womansday.com

Rohr, R. (2011). Falling upward. Hoboken: Jossey-Bass

Sperry, L. (2011). Spirituality in clinical practice. New York: Routledge

Trentacosts, C., & Izard, C. (2006). Emotional development. In N. Salkind (ed.), Encyclopedia of human development (Vol. 1, pp. 456–458). Thousand Oaks: Sage Reference.

11

THE QUINTESSENTIAL GREEK HERO: HOW ODYSSEUS FITS THE CAMPBELLIAN MONOMYTH

ANDREW J. GRAHAM

"Humility must always be the portion of any man who receives acclaim earned in the blood of his followers and the sacrifices of his friends."

-- Dwight D. Eisenhower

The 34th president of the United States of America, Dwight D. Eisenhower, is an ideal example of a brave American war hero and a fearless leader during a time of difficulty. Not only was he appointed to the head position of the North Atlantic Treaty Organization under President Harry S. Truman, but during his presidency led America to a Cold War victory ("Dwight D. Eisenhower", 2017). Even amidst his popularity and accomplishments, Eisenhower was always described as a man of humility and principle. His overall successful presidency was fostered by his moral character, much like that of other heroes we see in fiction and pop culture.

Similarly, the story of Odysseus in Homer's Greek epic *The Odyssey* follows the seemingly fearless soldier and leader of Ithaca. Although Odysseus is a hero from thousands of years ago, there are many parallels between his story and Eisenhower's due to the fact that both of them experienced the same proto- typical "hero's journey". Odysseus faces many challenges along his return home after the Trojan War and must put his heroic attributes to the test, all while undergoing a unique self-transformation in accordance with Joseph Campbell's (1949) monomyth. Odysseus specifically endures an "emotional transforma- tion" involving his acquisition of humility, an essential component of the classic "hero" (Allison & Smith, 2015). Joseph Campbell's research on the traditional hero's journey closely aligns with Odysseus' story. *The Odyssey* can be broken down into Campbell's three stages of transformation in order to properly assess the characterization of Odysseus as an archetypal hero.

THE HERO'S MONOMYTH

When studying heroes and heroism science, the analysis of Joseph Campbell's monomyth (Campbell, 1949) is essential in understanding the traditional jour- ney that many heroes undertake. Campbell claimed that the journey can be broken down to three parts: departure, initiation, and return. "Heroes embark on their journeys to achieve a goal that requires the acquisition of an important quality that the hero lacks. All heroes start out "incomplete" in some sense. They are missing some essential inner strength or quality that they must develop to succeed." (Allison, Goethals, & Kramer, 2017) When looking at the journey of Odysseus, it is necessary to use Campbell's monomyth to analyze his heroism and the transformation process that he undergoes. Although Odysseus sets out on his journey as a confident and capable soldier, he can only be properly char- acterized as a hero after proving himself along his journey and experiencing significant psychological development.

Departure

Campbell's (1949) departure phase is often referred to as the call to adventure. "The initial departure phase refers to the forces that set the hero's journey in motion. Heroes embark on their journeys to achieve a goal that requires the acquisition of an important quality that the hero lacks" (Allison, Goethals, & Kramer, 2017). Odysseus experiences his call to adventure when he makes the decision to leave the safety of his home and his family, including his wife Penelope and his infant son. He leaves his flourishing kingdom of Ithaca in order to fight in the Trojan War overseas. Odysseus' role as a king, soldier, and classic Greek hero establishes the call he feels to fight in Troy. "Odysseus is behaving as a stereotypical Greek warrior hero and engaging in the type of behaviour that would have been expected of such a person" (White, 2009). His confidence in the Greek's ability to win the war and reap the rewards provides the incentive he needs in order to leave Ithaca. Yet he is unaware of the trials and tribulations that he will face later on after the Trojan War on his subsequent journey home. Odysseus leaves Ithaca as a confident leader with his troops in tow without any knowledge of the arduous twenty-year journey awaiting him.

Initiation

The second phase of Campbell's (1949) hero journey is the initiation stage. Here the hero must face and overcome numerous adverse circustances and in the process experience a self-transformation (Allison, Goethals, & Kramer, 2017). Over the course of Odysseus's journey back home to Ithaca he must channel his bravery, intelligence, and resourcefulness in order to conquer the hardships that he faces and deal with the losses incurred. A fundamental piece of Odysseus' journey is the transformation he experiences as a result of the challenges that he must overcome. "The second type of transformation is an emotional transformation. These refer to transformations of the heart, and they include heroes who, through adversity, grow in courage, resilience, and empathy" (Allison & Goethals, 2013, 2017). Odysseus experiences an "emotional transformation" specifically in the development of humility and maturity through the consequences he endures and his dependency on his crew to make it home.

The Lotus Eaters

One of Odysseus's first challenges is his encounter with the Lotus Eaters. After nine days of dangerous sailing, Odysseus and his crew land on the shore of an unknown island. The people of the island, also known as the Lotus Eaters, are kind to the exhausted crew and offer them food and drink. Yet after some of Odysseus's men ingest the Lotus flowers that were offered to them, they forget their desire to return home and lose the motivation to continue on their journey

(Reynolds, 2017). Odysseus is faced with a crew that is no longer willing to aid him in the trip back to Ithaca, and thus he must forcefully remove his men from the comfort of the island and its people and strap them to the ship.

The encounter with the Lotus Eaters exemplifies Odysseus's role as a strong leader, which is characteristic of a typical hero. "Then the part of us that is truly hero must take charge forcefully, reimpose the rightful priority, and enforce discipline on the unruly parts who have forgotten" (Hartman & Zimberoff, 2009). He must take control of his men and act in their best interest in order to accomplish their collective goal of returning home. Not only does this challenge exemplify the heroic attributes that Odysseus already possesses, but it also is a catalyst to begin his self-transformation. He must take responsibility for the actions of his men and, in doing so, he realizes the importance of his crew and what his men mean to him. The incident with the Lotus Eaters demonstrates Odysseus's heroic attributes and results in his progression toward developing a more mature version of himself.

Polyphemus the Cyclops

The Land of the Cyclopes brings Polyphemus whom Odysseus must outsmart in order to save both himself and his crew. Polyphemus, the cyclops of great physical prowess, traps Odysseus and his men in a cave after catching them attempting to steal the sheep that he holds there (Wyerson, 2002). Odysseus is unable to rely on physical strength to overcome this challenge and consequently he must depend on his intelligence and quick wit, which are other central characteristics of a hero. He knows that he cannot kill Polyphemus, not only because the cyclops is a larger opponent but also due to the fact that without the cyclops there would be no one strong enough to remove the rock that blocks the opening of the cave. Odysseus and his men would remain trapped and would perish in the cave. When asked for his name by Polyphemus, Odysseus responds by telling him that he is called "Nobody". Once the cyclops falls asleep, the men blind him which results in Polyphemus screaming for help. Thanks to Odysseus' cleverness, when the other cyclops ask what is wrong from outside the cave Polyphemus responds with "Nobody's killing me" (Wyerson, 2002).

The cyclops leave the cave and the next morning when the blinded Polyphemus removes the rock to allow his sheep to graze, Odysseus and his men escape by hanging from the stomachs of the sheep. Odysseus successfully leads his men to safety and is able to continue on his journey back home (Reynolds, 2017). Through his use of heroic characteristics such as his quick wit and intelligence, Odysseus is able to get his crew back on track. One of the most important components to Odysseus' defeat of the cyclops would be his subsequent need to gloat after his victory. This leads to Polyphemus enlisting the help of his father, Poseidon, to curse Odysseus with ten years of bad weather and vicious seas. This curse greatly adds to his difficulties for his return home. Odysseus suffers the consequences of showing a lack of modesty, and with this trial and ensuing punishment he is humbled yet again.

The Sirens

The last challenge of Odysseus's journey that will be discussed here involves his encounter with the Sirens. He is previously warned by a goddess, Circe, that the enchanting songs of the creatures of the sea will be used in an attempt to seduce the men. To be properly prepared to successfully navigate past the sirens and avoid their enticement, Odysseus has his men put beeswax in their ears to block the sound, and he also requests that they tie him up to the ship so that he cannot escape once he hears the siren's melody. While the ship is passing through the siren's waters, Odysseus hears their songs and begs his men to untie him. His crew refuses and keeps him bound to the ship so that they can pass the dangerous creatures and continue towards Ithaca (Reynolds, 2017).

The incident of Odysseus and the sirens is essential to his continued self-transformation because it emphasizes Odysseus' reliance on his crew. While there is no doubt that Odysseus is a capable hero, he would not be able to conquer the seemingly impossible challenges that he faces without the help of his loyal men. "He understands further that this singular drive comes not just from his will alone, but also from all who join him" (Spiegel, 1998). This need for assistance further humbles Odysseus through his acceptance of the fact that he cannot make the journey back to Ithaca on his own no matter how much strength and skill he possesses. He must place his faith in the loyalty of his men in order to conquer the hardships and survive the journey, thereby enabling him to fully develop the trait of humility that he needs to become a true hero.

Return

"From Gilgamesh to Luke Skywalker, from Odysseus to Jane Eyre, heroes set out on a journey, transform into new and improved versions of themselves, and in the process encourage us all to follow in their footsteps" (Allison & Goethals, 2017, p. 1).

The final phase of Campbell's monomyth is the hero's return. Upon their return, the hero has been transformed and bestows some type of gift to the original world from which they came (Allison, Goethals, & Kramer, 2017). To accomplish this feat, Odysseus enlists the help of the goddess Athena to disguise him as a beggar once he returns to Ithaca. This decision can be seen as symbolic of the humbling self-transformation Odysseus has experienced that is imperative to every hero once he has returned to his home. He left as a confident and authoritative king and returns in the form of a lowly peasant, representing the "emotional transformation" that he has undergone. Using his disguise to his advantage as well as the help of his now grown son, Telemachus, Odysseus enters his home and proceeds to kill the nefarious suitors who have encroached upon his kingdom and his loyal wife Penelope.

After they have all been slain and his role as husband and father have been reinstated, Odysseus finds his father Laertes to seek his forgiveness (Hartman & Zimberoff, 2009). With his place in society restored and with Laertes' blessing received, Odysseus has returned Ithaca and its people to the stability it once enjoyed. Odysseus has destroyed the evil plaguing his kingdom which was embodied in the form of Penelope's relentless suitors, and he has once again become the respected king of Ithaca. "He must now introduce the new Odysseus to those he left behind... He is a different person than the one who departed on the journey of self-discovery so many long years before, and they have changed, too" (Hartman & Zimberoff, 2009). By the end of his trip, Odysseus has become a better hero in the sense that his development over the course of his adventure now allows him to continue his life as an improved version of what he was beforehand, not only with regard to being the leader of Ithaca but also within his family. Using Joseph Campbell's (1949) monomyth, one can begin to uncover the deeper meaning to the journey that Odysseus traversed. Both physically and psychologically, Odysseus rises to the challenges that he faces and uses them to transform his identity to that of a humbled, admirable hero (Spiegel, 1998).

JUNGIAN ARCHETYPES

Within heroism science the identification of archetypes imbedded within the hero's journey remains an integral part of research. Archetypes are universal themes and patterns of human experience that according to psychologist Carl Jung are said to be a part of our collective unconscious (Jung, 1969). The Odyssey contains numerous archetypes that can shed light on the heroism of Odysseus. Not only does the general archetype of a classic hero fit the description of Odysseus, but several other archetypes present themselves in Homer's piece as well.

Reunion of Father and Son

The reunion of father and son is a prevalent example of an archetype within Odysseus' hero journey (Lowery, 1970). Odysseus left his infant son Telemachus when he went overseas to fight in the Trojan War. Upon Odysseus' return twenty years later, Telemachus is a young man and is immediately ready to stand by his father's side and aid him in taking back the kingdom of Ithaca and reinstate him as the patriarch of the family. Even when Odysseus is said to have been killed in the Trojan War, Telemachus remains skeptical and accepts the help of the goddess Athena to bring his father back home at whatever cost.

Femme Fatale

Odysseus' seven years of captivity on the island of the goddess Calypso represents a second archetype in the story of his heroism: femme fatale. Odysseus becomes captivated by Calypso's beauty and her care for him which distracts him from his true purpose, which is returning to Ithaca. "This alluring, fascinating femme fatale exists for all men, and we call her the anima... This archetype offers the quicksand of intoxication and complacency when it is approached without intercession..." (Hartman & Zimberoff, 2009). Odysseus must overcome the enchantment of the alluring goddess and reassess his true objective: to reclaim his identity as the heroic soldier and king of Ithaca.

Odysseus' Mentors

A heroic journey, especially when being referenced in regard to the Campbellian monomyth, is not complete without the presence of the "mentor" archetype. Odysseus receives help from the god Hermes, who helps Odysseus accept his "call to adventure", an essential component of the departure phase of Campbell's (1949) hero's journey. Without Hermes' push for Odysseus to accept the trip to Troy, he may have not accepted the journey and he would not have embarked on an adventure essential to the hero's humble transformation. Not only is Hermes crucial in Odysseus' departure phase, but he also comes to help Odysseus during his time on the Aenian island with the goddess Circe. Circe gives Odysseus' men a potion to make them forget their goal of returning to Ithaca. Hermes appears again to assist Odysseus in getting his crew back on track by providing a potion that would reverse the effects of Circe's mischief (Hartman & Zimberoff, 2009). The help that Hermes gives Odysseus on his journey is indispensable to his transformative development along the trip.

The goddess Athena also lends immense assistance to Odysseus throughout his experience. She reaches out to his son Telemachus to support his efforts in locating Odysseus, who is assumed by most people in Ithaca to have been killed sometime during the war. Athena is also the goddess who disguises Odysseus as a beggar upon his return to Ithaca, thereby successfully helping him eliminate Penelope's myriad suitors (Spiegel, 1998). Athena's help is imperative in order for Odysseus to be able to reclaim his position as Penelope's husband and the leader of Ithaca. Without the mentorship of both Hermes and Athena, the course of Odysseus journey, his hero development, and his success might never have transpired.

Suffering

Suffering is an inescapable part of the hero's journey. While suffering is undeniably unfortunate, it can paradoxically result in multiple long-term benefits. Six benefits have been identified as deriving from suffering, with humility being one of the central benefits. Humility is an integral part of Odysseus' personal self- transformation. "Suffering doesn't create anything tangible but creates space for learning and love" (Allison & Setterberg, 2016). Without the trials that Odysseus had to endure alongside his crew, he would not have undergone an intense self-transformation that resulted in the acquisition of a deep sense of humility. While the multiple issues Odysseus faced were undoubtedly difficult, they became beneficial to his psychological advancement by allowing him to develop the modesty that is necessary of a hero.

Social Influence Based Hero Taxonomy

It can be seen that throughout the thousands of years that *The Odyssey* has been heard, read, and analyzed that Odysseus is the consummate hero. There are multiple subtypes of heroism used to classify heroes, especially according to the social-influence-based hero taxonomy proposed by Allison and Goethals (2013). Odysseus is best classified as a traditional hero. "Traditional heroes follow the conventional Campbellian hero's journey" (Allison & Goethals, 2017). The application of Joseph Campbell's (1949) monomyth to the journey that Odysseus undertakes allows him to be seen as a traditional hero whose legacy has been cemented by the passage of time.

ODYSSEUS' ENDING: IS IT HEROIC?

At the conclusion of *The Odyssey* it is said that Odysseus slays numerous men due to their unrelenting attempts at winning over Penelope and assuming the throne of Ithaca in place of Odysseus. It is true that Odysseus kills many men, yet his role as a soldier, king, and the patriarch of his family deems it necessary that Penelope's suitors are removed so that Odysseus may reclaim his throne and his family. The men are unyielding in their efforts to claim Penelope as their own especially due to the fact that the kingdom of Ithaca would then become theirs. Therefore, the only way for Odysseus to reassert himself into his rightful position of power and to earn his title of a hero is to engage in physical combat with the suitors. Odysseus' actions at the end of Homer's epic poem can therefore be seen as a necessary and admirable ending to his hero's journey because it allows him to eradicate the "evil" threats to his home and his family and enables him to reintegrate himself into society as the humbled hero he has become.

Odysseus sets out overseas for Troy to fight in the Trojan War, and he embarks on a journey that aligns with Joseph Campbell's (1949) monomyth and its three distinct stages. He faces myriad challenges and trials of physical and mental strength, all of which are overcome with the help of his crew and his immortal mentors. Throughout his journey and as a result of the many difficulties he encounters along the way, Odysseus experiences a meaningful and significant self-transformation. This supports the assertion that he follows Campbell's monomyth and that he can be classified as a "traditional hero".

Over the course of his 20-year trip back to Ithaca, Odysseus is significantly humbled (Worthington & Allison, 2018). He suffers the consequences of his arrogance and overconfidence, and he also comes to realize and appreciate the indispensable assistance that he receives from his men and mentors. While during the departure phase of Odysseus' journey he can be seen as a somewhat self-righteous character, by the time of his return to the kingdom of Ithaca he has experienced enough challenges and endured enough suffering that his personality is forever altered. This humbling is essential for him to become a true hero. Odysseus is a striking example of a traditional hero whose transformation will no doubt entertain and inspire people for centuries to come.

REFERENCES

Allison, S. T., & Goethals, G. R. (2013). Heroic leadership: An influence taxonomy of 100 exceptional individuals. New York: Routledge.

Allison, S. T., & Goethals, G. R. (2017). The hero's transformation. In S. T. Allison, G. R. Goethals, & R. M. Kramer (Eds.), Handbook of heroism and heroic leadership. New York: Routledge.

Allison, S. T., Goethals, G. R., & Kramer, R. M. (Eds.) (2017). Handbook of heroism and heroic leadership. New York: Routledge.

Allison, S.T., Goethals, G. R., & Kramer, R. M (2017). The Rise and Coalescence of Heroism Science. In S. T. Allison, G. R. Goethals, & R. M. Kramer (Eds.), Handbook of heroism and heroic leadership. New York: Routledge.

Allison, S. T., & Setterberg, G. C. (2016). Suffering and sacrifice: Individual and collective benefits, and implications for leadership. In S. T. Allison, C. T. Kocher, & G. R. Goethals (Eds), Frontiers in spiritual leadership: Discovering the better angels of our nature. New York: Palgrave Macmillan.

Campbell, J. (1949). The hero with a thousand faces. NewYork: New World Library

Davis, J. L., Burnette, J. L., Allison, S. T., & Stone, H. (2011). Against the odds: Academic underdogs benefit from incremental theories. Social Psychology of Education, 14, 331-346.

Dwight D. Eisenhower (2017). Retrieved from https://www.history.com/topics/us-presidents/dwight-d-eisenhower

Eylon, D., & Allison, S. T. (2005). The frozen in time effect in evaluations of the dead. Personality and Social Psychology Bulletin, 31, 1708-1717.

Hartman, D., & Zimberoff, D. (2009). The Hero's Journey of Self-transformation: Models of Higher Development from Mythology. Journal Of Heart-Centered Therapies, 12(2), 3-93.

History.com Staff. (2009). Dwight D. Eisenhower. Retrieved October 06, 2017, from http://www.history.com/topics/us-presidents/dwight-d-eisenhower

Jung, C. G. (1969). The structure of the psyche. In Read, H., Fordham, M., Adler, G., & McGuire, W. (Eds.) (R. F. C. Hull, Trans.), The collected works of C. G. Jung: Vol. 9. The archetypes and the collective unconscious. Princeton, NJ: Princeton University Press. (Original work published 1931)

Lowery, A. (1970). "The Odyssey" as Archetype. The English Journal, 59(8), 1076-1079. doi:10.2307/813516

Odyssey. (2017, October 06). Retrieved October 06, 2017, from https://en.wikipedia.org/wiki/Odyssey

Spiegel, D. (1998). The Odyssey as a Psychological Hero Journey. MIT Alumni

Wyerson, J. (2002). SparkNote on The Odyssey. Retrieved October 3, 2017, from http://www.sparknotes.com/lit/odyssey/

White, J. (2009). The Odyssey: Contemporary Analytic Perspectives. British Journal Of Psychotherapy, 25(4), 493-505. doi:10.1111/j.1752-0118.2009.01144.x

Worthington, E. L, & Allison, S. T. (2018). Heroic humility: What the science of humility can say to people raised on self-focus. Washington. DC: American Psychological Association.

12

Sectumsempra: An Analysis of the Heroic Transformation of Severus Snape

Jake C. Cardwell

> *"You see what you expect to see."*
> --Albus Dumbledore

The sky is grey, the clouds are heavy, and the boy cannot kill him. The Death Eaters taunt him, berate him, but Draco cannot kill Albus Dumbledore. Harry is immobilized with fear, trapped under his invisibility cloak. Suddenly, a figure appears. Snape comes in the door, and Dumbledore pleads with him. With a look of disgust, Severus Snape does the unthinkable. The killing curse is uttered, Dumbledore's body falls from the tower, and my heart drops. In that moment, I hated Severus Snape.

J.K. Rowling, along with help from the great Alan Rickman, created a character who is often loved, sometimes despised, and nearly universally recognized. Severus Snape, a wizard who wears many hats throughout the Harry Potter series, is one of those rare characters that can fill you with love and hate simultaneously. The first time I read *Harry Potter and the Deathly Hallows*, the final book in the series, and Rowling takes us on a journey through Snape's memories, I cried. In that moment, Snape became my hero.

This chapter seeks to examine the character Severus Snape and his heroism. I will go about this task by analyzing Snape's life and legacy, and judging him through several lenses of heroism science. Most importantly, the goal of this discussion is to determine whether or not Snape is truly a "hero." Whether you love him or hate him, Severus Snape is one of the most recognizable literary characters of the twenty-first century, and his morality and merits are still talked about by fans of the Harry Potter franchise. I will use traditional archetypes and theories of heroism science to determine who and what Snape really is: a hero or a villain.

For those of you unfamiliar with the *Harry Potter* franchise, Severus Snape has a very complicated backstory. For the first few novels, Snape is presented to us as the surly Professor of Potions at Hogwarts School of Witchcraft and Wizardry. In later novels, it is revealed that Snape is working as a double agent against the primary antagonist of the series, Lord Voldemort, a sadistic wizard bent on ridding the world of muggles, non-magical humans, and establishing himself as leader. Snape seems to have sided with the antagonist in the sixth novel when he kills Hogwarts' headmaster Albus Dumbledore, betraying the trust of the chosen one, Harry Potter, and many other school children. It is only after Snape's death in the final book of the series that Harry is allowed to look through Snape's memories and see that his true loyalties lied with Dumbledore all along and his death was necessary in order to defeat Voldemort (Rowling, 2017).

Snape and the Hero's Journey

Joseph Campbell, the scholar who anticipated the field of heroism science, described the hero's journey as follows: "a hero embarks on a journey that begins when he or she is cast into a dangerous, unfamiliar world. The hero is charged with accomplishing a daunting task and receives assistance from unlikely sources. There are formidable obstacles along the way and villainous characters to overcome. After many trials and much suffering, the hero learns an important truth about herself and about the world. Succeeding on her journey, the hero is forever changed and returns to her original world. There she bestows some type of gift to that society, a gift that is only made possible by her own personal journey of growth and change. In short, heroes undergo a personal transformation that includes the development of a motive to improve the lives of others" (Allison, Goethals, & Kramer, 2017).

Campbell's monomyth of heroism is seen across myths and tales from countless cultures from around the world and from different time periods in human history (Campbell, 1949). We need to keep this fact in mind when analyzing Snape. He is a literary figure. In analyzing him psychologically, we can forget that he is authored, he is scripted, his journey was laid out purposefully by an author. Does this detract from his impact? Not in the slightest. All this means is that we can hold Snape to a different standard than we could someone's act of heroism in real life. He is a character, and he should be judged as one. Allison and Goethals (2017) point out, the monomyth indicates that three transformations must transpire in order for the traditional heroic archetype to be met: a transformation of setting, a transformation of self, and a transformation of society (Allison & Goethals, 2017; Davis et al., 2011). Snape can be placed against these three criteria to determine whether or not he is a traditional literary hero.

Transformation of Setting

This is the most obvious of the three criteria, in that Snape moves from his muggle life to Hogwarts at a young age, establishing the onset of his journey (Rowling, 2002). He goes from a world without magic to a world with magic. Introduction to the supernatural is in every hero's journey from Odysseus to Luke Skywalker. This change took place early in life relative to many of Snape's endeavors, but it is the catalyst for everything else that transpires later.

Transformation of Self

Throughout his journey, Snape was a member of many groups: the bullies of Slytherin House at Hogwarts, the Death Eaters lead by Lord Voldemort, and finally the Order of the Phoenix, a group of a good wizards fighting against Voldemort. In order to become a member of any one of these groups, Snape had to change himself in some fashion. However, changing his allegiance does not inherently mean that he transformed himself. Changing teams alone does not a hero make. However, if we take into account some viewpoints from Kinsella et al. (2015a) we have a different metric by which to judge Snape: "Consistent with the etymology of the word, heroes are protectors (Becker & Eagly, 2004) and our research suggests that heroic functions reflect this theme: protecting, doing what no one else will, helping, saving, guiding, and acting against evil or danger" (Kinsella et al., 2015b).

Keeping in mind Kinsella et al.'s (2015b) idea of heroes being protectors, it is apparent that Snape does eventually become a protector. Despite all of his hatred towards Harry's father and Snape's former schoolmate, towards himself, and even towards Harry at times, Snape moves beyond his hatred and insecurities to become a protector. In the sequence where Harry goes through Snape's memories, we see Snape's troubled past, his horrifying time with the Death Eaters, and his misery before being rescued by Dumbledore. Most importantly in this sequence, we see an exchange between Dumbledore and Snape where we learn Snape puts his life in danger by being a double agent in order to protect Harry Potter, the only one who can stop Voldemort (Rowling, 2016). This idea of Snape being the protector and Harry receiving the benefits of his protections shows that the subject of Snape's heroism extends beyond himself, as someone else benefited more than the transforming subject (Allison & Goethals, 2016, 2017). The exchange between Snape and Dumbledore demonstrates that Snape in some way has transformed himself by wanting to protect Harry Potter, the son of his childhood rival. Putting aside all his anger and doubt to protect someone else for the greater good seems to fit the idea of transforming oneself, and thus completes the second phase of the hero's transformation.

Transformation of Society

In the society presented in the book, the primary source for most of the magical world's problems is the antagonist Voldemort. To be fair, there are other problems in this world, such as wizard blood purists who hate anyone with muggle blood and obvious political corruption regarding the Ministry of Magic, the governing body of wizards (Rowling, 2002). However, as a large part of the two aforementioned problems stem from Voldemort or are legally enforced by his agents, we can safely assume that removing Voldemort will also slow down many of the novels' secondary conflicts.

The primary hero of the franchise, Harry Potter, undergoes much suffering, the loss of close friends, and self-discovery, eventually defeating Lord Voldemort and effectively saving the wizarding world. Harry however, did not find himself in a position to conquer the Dark Lord all by himself. Only through the help of many allies and sacrifices of others was Harry able to successfully fight Voldemort. As previously discussed, Snape was one of the key players in protecting and training Harry to fight Voldemort. Does this mean Snape himself transformed the society? In a direct sense, no. Given that Snape did not directly defeat Voldemort, he did not directly transform society. However, Snape's actions in protecting Harry do lead to some monumental change in society. If there is a transitive property of heroism, I would argue this applies. Snape is not the protagonist of our story. Therefore, by some metric, he will never fully be "the hero." However, in protecting the hero of our story, his actions and sacrifices ultimately led to a change in society through the peace brought about by Voldemort's death that happened outside of his life span. From this perspective, I argue that Snape has transformed society, and thus fulfilled the monomyth of Heroism.

Other Lenses of Heroism

Rowling's novels give us a phenomenal glimpse into the psyche and motivations of her characters, which gives us a much broader range in which to explore Snape. True, he does meet Campbell's criteria for a "hero," but is he truly heroic? Do his motivations, desires, and actions line up with what we think of as being attributes of heroes? We can analyze him as a literary character easily, but he's robust enough that I thought it would be fun to also analyze him psychologically. On that note, the rest of this chapter will be dedicated to reviewing the psychology of Snape, and whether or not he is a hero in the scientific and perceptional sense rather than strictly through the lens of literature.

WHAT KIND OF HERO IS SNAPE?

There are several taxonomies for classifying heroes, from Franco and his colleagues' situational demand taxonomy (Franco et al., 2011) to Allison and Goethals' social influence-based taxonomy (Allison & Goethals, 2013). The first step in determining if Snape is truly a hero would be to determine what type of hero he may be. These taxonomies provide a great metric for determining hero subtypes. Many of them have caveats, nuances, or places of failure against which we can measure Snape to establish whether he meets the criteria for heroism.

Social Influence Based Taxonomy

Allison and Goethals provide a useful taxonomy for classifying heroes, including trending, transitory, transitional, tragic, transposed, transparent, traditional, transfigured, transforming, and transcendent (Allison & Goethals, 2017). Several of these categories might apply to Snape. The first and most familiar one is the Traditional Hero. This hero's journey corresponds to Campbell's (1949) monomyth, with individuals coming from humble origins, experiencing early setbacks, receiving assistance from unlikely sources, overcoming obstacles, and returning with gifts to society (Allison & Goethals, 2017). Obviously, this sounds much more like the iconic protagonist of the series, Harry Potter, but it can also apply to Snape. He grew up impoverished, went through a phase with the Death Eaters, received help from Dumbledore, overcame trials at Hogwarts, protected Harry, and brought about peace (Rowling, 2017). While this sounds good, there are some counterarguments to be made about his heroism. First, he willingly joined the Death Eaters and terrorized people, so his setbacks are really of his own making. Dumbledore's assistance is not altruistic, as it seems more like Dumbledore is making a plea deal with Snape. Finally, Snape has no traditional, tangible gift to society, but rather Harry benefits from Snape's transformation. Therefore, a different classification might be better.

A second hero subtype category Snape might fit into is that of a Transposed hero, which is a hero who undergoes rapid changes from either villain to hero or from hero to villain (Goethals & Allison, 2012). Snape throughout the series walks a fine line between hero and villain, and at certain points jumps back and forth. The scale of his greater transformation from villain to hero was slow, and some may argue he never fully made that transition with his allegiance to Voldemort being strong for so long.

Finally, Snape may be a Transparent hero, which is an invisible unsung hero (Allison & Goethals, 2017). While working in the shadows and planning on over-throwing Voldemort, he was a real menace to the children at Hogwarts. His time as headmaster was one of hardship and cruelty, and Harry nearly despised him until after his death. While he does appear to be an invisible hero, he was a very visible villain. So if Snape's character defies solid placement in this taxonomy, where else might his journey place him?

Situational Demand: Physical Risk

The first question we need to answer regarding Snape being a physical risk hero is whether or not Snape is duty bound to be put his life on the line. Physical risk duty bound heroes are "individuals involved in military or emergency response careers that involve repeated exposure to high-risk situations. Heroic acts must exceed the call of duty" (Franco, Blau, & Zimbardo, 2011). In the series there are two wizarding wars, and Snape fights in both on different sides. Later in life he does join the *Order of the Phoenix* and work under Dumbledore (Rowling, 2016). While all of these positions do involve physical peril, that's not where the danger that faces Snape comes from. He has not enlisted in a real governmental war, he is not paid to stop evil wizards, and therefore he is not duty bound. Snape works underground as a double agent, and often times because of his treachery and allies needs to fight. Fighting is a consequence, not a requirement, of his actions. He still puts his life on the line but, "the standard for duty-bound and non-duty bound physical-risk heroism differs, but the style of engagement and potential sacrifices are comparable" (Franco et al., 2011). Peril comes to Snape as a result of his allegiance. Snape doesn't go out trying to thwart dangerous wizards from doing harm. Dangerous wizards come to hurt Snape for his intel-ligence. Therefore, Snape is not a physical risk hero.

One could argue that the hex the Death Eaters place on Draco Malfoy eventually does make Snape "duty bound" in a sense. Dumbledore knows Draco must kill him, but he pleads with Snape to do it in order to preserve Draco's innocence. Draco inevitably fails, and Snape is the one who physically kills Dumbledore (Rowling, 2017). However, "It can be argued that the action or behavior ultimately stands as heroic or not in the absence of any social milieu" (Howerth, 1935). Snape knows that killing Dumbledore is a necessary step in defeating the one who placed the hex on him. His loyalties lie not with the Death Eaters, but with Dumbledore. Therefore, Snape is not duty bound to be heroic or villainous because he does it out of love and loyalty to a greater social cause.

Situational Demand: Social

If Snape does not fit into the physical risk hero, then Snape may fit into a few other categories. Under Franco et al.'s social hero taxonomy includes religious figures, politico religious figures, martyrs, political leaders, adventurers, scientific heroes, good Samaritans, underdogs, bureaucracy heroes, and whistleblowers (Franco et al., 2011). The only one of these that really comes close to Snape is a martyr, which is defined as "Religious or political figures who knowingly (sometimes deliberately) put their lives in jeopardy in the service of a cause or to gain attention to injustice" (Franco et al., 2011). Snape lives in proximity to danger in order to fight against Lord Voldemort. However, he is not really a "political figure" as the definition specifies, as he fights for the side that eventually kills him, and his death does not bring light to any social injustice as he dies because Voldemort wants something from him. So, what is Snape?

FINAL THOUGHTS

Snape holds many loyalties to many groups throughout the series. One of his most impactful and relevant to our discussion is his relationship to the Death Eaters and Voldemort. Most of his life as a young adult was spent committing heinous crimes in an attempt to bring Voldemort back to power. Many could look at Snape and say that because he had an allegiance to Voldemort he is disqualified as being a hero. This is in line with Franco and Zimbardo's assertion that "even unvested observers may be quick to negate the hero's acts at the slightest hint of countervailing information about the hero's integrity, motives, or intentions— even if these aspersions have no real bearing on the heroic act itself. There is a constant tension between the desire to elevate and the desire to castigate the actions of heroes— especially social heroes because their actions are easily viewed as threatening, but also with physical risk heroes who have a checkered history" (Franco & Zimbardo, 2006). Snape indisputably has a past lined with bodies and broken promises. However, in the end Snape fights for the good guys, protects Harry Potter, and dies trying to do the right thing. So, does his past besmirch his name so much that he cannot be a hero?

I argue that what would cause one to view Snape as a hero rather than a villain is how much weight one puts on what he did behind the scenes versus what he did publicly. To the wizarding world, Snape was a monster. He personally killed Dumbledore, and by all outward appearances, allowed Voldemort and the Death Eaters to take over Hogwarts. This makes Snape seem cold and against the side of the "good wizards." Snape was mean to Harry, harsh on all his students, and knowingly allowed the suffering of thousands. However, all of these actions represent what Snape did publicly. As we know from the memory sequence, all of this was part of a larger plan to defeat Voldemort; all the suffering and harshness was to some degree necessary for the plan to be executed fully.

In some situations, heroes with negative personal histories can be rebranded as heroes, while in other circumstances context overrides heroism (Franco et al., 2011). This is the inevitable moral paradox we encounter. Does Snape's private history of good override his public actions of evil? Is he an unsung hero (Goethals & Allison, 2012) or a villain who did good things? And truthfully this is where we must let our morality guide us. One thing is clear: Snape, for good and for evil, acted in the long-term best interest of the well-being of the larger society (Efthimiou, Allison, & Franco, 2018).

One final point I will make comes from the argument of failed heroism versus cowardice. The debate is whether or not his decisions stem from the situation, meaning that describing him as a hero would be false, or whether he in and of himself wants to help others, while the situation around him merely activates him (Parks, 2017). Snape agreed to help Harry before we knew the breadth of his assignment. He took on this task before he knew what the risks were. Snape did not think there would be rewards and "...anticipated gain at the time of the act necessarily disqualifies it from being heroic. However, if gains are subsequently accrued without prior anticipation or motivation to attain them, the act should still be upheld as heroic" (Glazer & Glazer, 1999). Snape gained nothing, helped the world, was motivated by love, and in the end lost his life. If that is not a hero, then what is one?

Severus Snape is one of those characters people love to hate. He, along with other compelling characters, is why Harry Potter has such staying power in modern society. Above all else, Snape is emotionally complex, with a past murky enough to be unforgivable and a heart big enough to be deserving of redemption. Through one lens or another, Snape is a hero in the literary sense. He has his initiation, he goes out and transforms himself, and through his transformation bestows a boon on society. Snape's personal transformation is one of the greatest in modern literature, because we learn of it under such sad circumstances. Snape is a great example of how the hero's transformation can take place in a person that many may not find heroic. His actions meet the criteria but his past and morals complicate him in a delicious way. As readers, we cannot definitively classify him as heroic, villainous, or something else, because at a certain point Snape's impact moves out of the scope of the novels and into us. We must judge him by our own sacred values, which will make this argument subjective for as long as morality is subjective.

The goal of this chapter was to present Snape alongside archetypal and scientific heroism studies and give the reader the opportunity to decide whether Snape was a hero or villain with some scientific knowledge. So, which is it?

REFERENCES

Allison, S. T., & Goethals, G. R. (2016). Hero worship: The elevation of the human spirit. Journal for the Theory of Social Behaviour, 46, 187-210.

Allison, S. T., Goethals, G. R., & Kramer, R. M. (Eds.) (2017). Handbook of heroism and heroic leadership. New York: Routledge.

Allison, S. T., & Goethalls, G. R. (2017). The hero's transformation. Handbook of Heroism and Heroic Leadership, 379-400.

Allison, S. T., Goethals, G. R., & Kramer, R. M. (2017). Setting the scene: The rise and coalescence of heroism science. In S. T. Allison, G. R. Goethals, & R. M. Kramer (Eds.), Handbook of heroism and heroic leadership. New York: Routledge.

Becker, S. W., & Eagly, A. H. (2004). The heroism of men and women. American Psychologist, 59, 163–178. doi: 10.1037/0003-066X.59.3.163

Davis, J. L., Burnette, J. L., Allison, S. T., & Stone, H. (2011). Against the odds: Academic underdogs benefit from incremental theories. Social Psychology of Education, 14, 331-346.

Franco, Z. E., Blau, K., & Zimbardo, P. G. (2011). Heroism: a conceptual analysis and differentiation between heroic action and altruism. Review of General Psychology. Advance online publication. doi: 10.1037/a0022672

Efthimiou, O., Allison, S. T., & Franco, Z. E. (2018). Definition, synthesis, and applications of heroic wellbeing. In O. Efthimiou, S. T. Allison, & Z. E. Franco (Eds.), Heroism and wellbeing in the 21st Century: Applied and emerging perspectives. New York: Routledge.

Franco, Z., & Zimbardo, P. (2006 – 07, Fall–Winter). The banality of heroism. Greater Good, 3, 30 –35.

Glazer, M. P., & Glazer, P. M. (1999). On the trail of courageous behavior. Sociological Inquiry, 69, 276 –295

Goethals, G. R., & Allison, S. T. (2012). Making heroes: The construction of courage, competence and virtue. Advances in Experimental Social Psychology, 46, 183–235. doi: 10.1016/B978-0-12-394281- 4.00004-0

Howerth, I. W. (1935). Heroism as a factor in education. Phi Delta Kappan, 18, 18 –24.

Kinsella, E.L., Ritchie, T.D., & Igou, E.R. (2015a). Lay perspectives on the social and psychological functions of heroes. Frontiers in Psychology, 6, 130.

Kinsella, E.L., Ritchie, T.D., & Igou, E.R. (2015b). Zeroing in on heroes: A prototype analysis of hero features. Journal of Personality and Social Psychology, 108, 114-127.

Parks, C. (2017). Accidental and purposeful impediments to heroism. In S. T. Allison, G. R. Goethals, & R. M. Kramer (Eds.), Handbook of heroism and heroic leadership. New York: Routledge.

Rowling, J. K., & Kay, J. (1997). Harry Potter and the Philosophers stone. London: Bloomsbury.

Rowling, J. (2002). Harry Potter and the Chamber of Secrets. London: Bloomsbury

Rowling, J. (2016). Harry Potter and the goblet of fire. London: Bloomsbury.

Rowling, J. K. (2016). Harry Potter and the Order of the Phoenix. London: Bloomsbury

Rowling, J. K. (2016). Harry Potter and the prisoner of Azkaban. London: Bloomsbury.

Rowling, J. K. (2017). Harry Potter and the Deathly Hallows. London: Bloomsbury.

Rowling, J. K. (2017). Harry Potter and the half-blood prince. London: Bloomsbury.

13

The Heroic Transformative Journey of Aeneas, Hero of the Trojan War

> *"He would say that when your mind is telling you you're done,*
> *you're really only 40 percent done."*
> – Finch (2017)

When a person thinks that they have exhausted all of their energy and that they've got nothing left to give, they have truly only burned through forty percent of their "tank". This was a common philosophy that the Navy SEALS called the forty percent rule. When all of the tiny voices inside your mind band together and unanimously call out that enough is enough, that you have no more give, your body is capable of doing things you never witnessed before. This explains why people can achieve extraordinary physical accomplishments and actions some would deem impossible to complete. A 100-mile long race, held in San Diego, was typically run in teams consisting of six men. As impressive of an accomplishment as this is, it is even more impressive when another man runs it alone. David Goggins, a 260-pound retired Navy SEAL, completed the entire race alone, breaking several small bones in his feet and suffering kidney damage along the way. This man figured out he had more to give, and then tapped into his reserve energy.

Aeneas was the protagonist character in the epic story, *The Aeneid*, written by the ancient Roman poet Virgil. The storyline takes place in ancient times that scholars believe to be roughly 1250 B.C.E. Aeneas was widely known as a classic "mythical hero" of that era. The story of *The Aeneid* is told from the point of view of Aeneas, and it captures all the graphic details of his life as a Trojan soldier. The city of Troy was overtaken by the Greeks, which forced Aeneas to flee and build a "new Troy". His journey to heroism begins with his departure from Troy.

Aeneas had a mindset very similar to the retired Navy SEAL. He was given plenty of reasons to quit. Temptation after temptation lured him away from accomplishing his heroic deeds, and yet he managed to navigate his way back toward his goal. The following chapter seeks to answer the following questions: How does Aeneas break through his "40 percent" limit to accomplish his goals? How is Aeneas' journey different from what Joseph Campbell (1949) refers to as the "monomythic journey of the hero"? What distinguishes Aeneas' heroism from other heroes in the ancient world?

LINEAR OVERVIEW OF AENEAS' JOURNEY

The structure of the hero's journey was described by renowned mythologist Joseph Campbell (1949). After researching thousands of heroic stories from around the world, Campbell concluded that all of these stories tended to share a common structure. This pattern is what is referred to as "the monomyth of the hero's journey" (Campbell, 1949). The heroic structure consists of the hero beginning their journey by being called away from their homeland, either by their own choice or some other force pulling them from the comfort of their home. Upon leaving, they will encounter numerous trials and impediments blocking their way toward ultimately accomplishing their goal (Campbell, 1949). Amidst the suffering from these impediments, the hero recognizes their missing dispositional quality. This missing attribute is what hinders the hero from truly becoming "heroic".

Another common theme within the monomyth structure is the hero encountering a wise mentor or some sort of aid. This aid will help lead the hero to their transformation by providing them with wisdom. Upon acquiring their missing quality and triumphing over numerous challenges, the hero undergoes a personal transformation that forever changes them. Possessing this new quality enables the hero to continue their journey and ultimately overcome their villains and other oppositional forces. The hero finally returns to their homeland triumphant and transformed, using their transformation to alter society and essentially give back to the world.

Aeneas' journey to become a hero differs somewhat from what Campbell (1949) calls the monomyth of the hero. The details of this monomythic form of heroic transformation consists of the hero being called away from their present home, an event known as the departure stage. This calling can derive from one of three different sources or some combination of sources. A person can be drawn away by a transcendental force, which is a force acted on a hero by a power greater than themselves; they can depart for the greater good of some entity; or they can be drawn away because of a particular purpose or meaning associated with the departure (Dik et al., 2017).

Campbell (1949) then explains that once the hero has abandoned their home and journeyed to unknown territory, they will then be "initiated" by encountering oppositional forces impeding their path to success. While trying to circumvent these impediments, the hero will often find a "friend" or wise advisor who will help them along their journey. The hero learns of their own weaknesses and strengths, and through their journey they will acquire ways to eliminate their weaknesses. Ultimately the hero should defeat their villains, and with their newfound knowledge and strength they will return to their homeland and use their knowledge to better society. This boon to society lies at the heart of what Campbell (1949) refers to as the final "return" stage.

The Hero's Departure

Aeneas' departure came very abruptly in the middle of the night when the Greeks infiltrated his city and laid ruin to the once beautiful Troy. Aeneas' first motive for departing was for the greater good. Had Aeneas stayed and fought, he would not have been alive to lead the refugees who were looking up to him for answers. Although it might not have been the classic "heroic" method to stay and fight for your land or die trying, Aeneas recognized that the greater good of his fellow Trojans lives were at stake, which inspired him to leave (Dik et al., 2017).

Another motive for fleeing Troy was an outside force. In a dream Aeneas had the night before the Greeks broke into Troy, he was told that he must flee from Troy and take the survivors with him. He was informed that he was destined to build a new city in Italy. This type of calling falls under transcendental forces, because he was urged by a spirit in his dream (Dik et al., 2017).

Element of the Underdog

During Aeneas' departure from Troy, his underdog status became apparent. An underdog is a person or party that is disadvantaged in some way; they are placed against an opponent who is advantageous, thus greatly diminishing the odds of the underdog succeeding (Vandello et al., 2017). Aeneas was compelled to flee Troy because the Trojans were completely and utterly dominated. The Greeks held the element of surprise, they had the man-power, and they possessed superior weaponry. The Trojans were beaten in all facets of war, which made them an underdog.

Interestingly enough, Vandello and his colleagues give four main reasons why people tend to support underdogs and why people revere successful underdogs. We want the underdog to win because we believe it will balance the scales of justice (Vandello et al., 2017). The Greeks dominate the Trojans across the board, and a Trojan victory would engender greater equality with the Greeks. We also route for the underdog because we relate to and identify with the underdog more easily (Vandello et al., 2017). We know what it is like to be disadvantaged and we want an underdog to win because we ourselves desired to win under similar circumstances. Another reason why we want an underdog to win is because of the "thrill of the unexpected". The odds of the Trojans winning over the Greeks were severely small, so a Trojan victory would give us an emotional charge. Finally, we root for the underdog because a victory from them brings us hope (Vandello et al., 2017). If the advantaged party always wins, why even try? When an underdog emerges victorious, we are injected with hope for the future.

Beginning Impediments

Even during Aeneas' initial departure he encounters impediments. Many of his friends are killed in the battle, which can demoralize a hero. His wife, who was with him while Trojans fled, died amidst the chaos. These elements of suffering hold potential benefits, however. Of the ten benefits to suffering, the most pertinent to Aeneas is that pain and suffering can prepare you for glory by giving you a divine purpose. Although this idea is derived from the scripture, the point is valid for almost all heroic suffering (Allison & Setterberg, 2016). Suffering can instill a purpose or meaning into the life of the one who experiences suffering. For Aeneas, it is crucial that he must use suffering to discover his purpose in life.

Villains also emerge as Aeneas leaves Troy. Juno, wife of Zeus, favors the Greek side and poses as Aeneas' most consistent and dangerous villain throughout his journey. Parks (2017) describes numerous purposeful types of impediments that a hero might face, one of which is enacted because the impediment aims to gain a competitive advantage (Parks, 2017). By impeding Aeneas' progression through his journey, Juno gives the Greeks an advantage.

Key Heroic Traits

Even at the outset of Aeneas' departure, he displays some heroic traits. He is a natural born leader, commanding his men effectively and leading them into battle. He also demonstrates deep compassion for his own people. This is evident when he witnessed the death of the Trojan King, Priam, who was slaughtered on his own alter. Aeneas' compassionate leadership is directed toward the good of his comrades and not for himself. He is naturally cooperative in his social values, because while he fights for his comrades, he is also fighting for himself and for the fame he can acquire (Messick & McClintock, 1968). His actions are not entirely altruistic, a downside to Aeneas' heroic makeup.

Allison and Goethals (2011) coined the term, "The Great Eight", to refer to eight attributes that best describe heroes. The qualities that make up the great eight are intelligence, strength, reliability, resilience, care, charisma, selflessness, and inspiration (Allison, Goethals, & Kramer, 2017). Of the great eight heroic attributes, Aeneas at this point in his journey appears to lack wit. His resilience and bravery inspired him to stay in Troy to fight, and it wasn't until he was indirectly forced to flee that he "chose" to leave Troy. This shows that although he is both resilient and selfless, these traits are so abundant that they cloud his judgment and intelligent decision making. This will be Aeneas' missing heroic trait that he is destined to acquire during his journey (Allison et al., 2017).

THE JOURNEY, PART ONE

The story of Aeneas differs from the monomythic heroic adventure that seems most common for heroes (Fuhrer, N.D.). Aeneas actually undertakes two journeys to transform himself and society. He also never returns to his homeland after he departs from it, which differs from most traditional heroic journeys. There are two reasons for this difference. First, Aeneas' homeland is completely overtaken by Greeks, making his return there impossible. Second, a common practice in antiquity was to show pietas, which is strong devotion to the gods, your family, and country. With this in mind, Aeneas must obey the commands of the gods, and this prevents him from returning to Troy. In Aeneas' first journey, he develops more skills to help him during his second journey (Anderson, 2015).

Villains, Obstacles, and Allies

Juno continues to present a threat in Aeneas' life, even after he departs from Troy. As previously mentioned, Juno's intentions reflect the "competitive advantage purposeful impediment" described by Parks (2017). Juno conned the god of wind, Aeolus, to unleash a tornado of winds down on Aeneas' fleet. Many Trojans died as a result of this storm, which served as a formidable obstacle that

Aeneas had to overcome. This incident also threw Aeneas off his course into unknown lands, which compelled him to venture into an unfamiliar world. He is thrown out of his comfort zone and must find a way to lead his men to safety, magnifying his leadership qualities and molding him into a true hero. This first obstacle is also marked by Aeneas receiving his first assistance from an outside source. Specifically, help came from Aeneas' best friend, Ascanius, who offers clarity to Aeneas' emotions by providing unbiased facts to help Aeneas make decisions.

Aeneas did not truly know what his purpose was for enduring all of these events. Many of the friends and mentors described by Allison and Smith (2015) target Aeneas' lack of purpose directly. For instance, Aeneas' mother, the goddess Venus, comes down from Olympus and puts Aeneas in a shroud so that no one on the island can see them. This assistance helps them get into the city of the land on which the Trojans wrecked. Aeneas is thus better able to discern his purpose. Both Ascanius and Venus are examples of our hero receiving outside assistance, which helps trigger the transformation process. Another divine entity who assists Aeneas in his first journey is Jupiter, king of the gods.

While on the island, Aeneas becomes distracted by the Queen of the land and loses his will to continue his journey. Jupiter reminds Aeneas that his journey is meant for much more and he must not remain on the island. This given Aeneas temporary motivation and purpose for continuing his journey, and he thus regains his mental focus and leaves the island. All three of these characters offer assistance to Aeneas and without this help Aeneas may not have completed his journey to heroism. Another friend who aids Aeneas is a man named Nautes (Anderson, 2015). Later in Aeneas' journey, he was presented with a large decision impacting all of his fleet. Aeneas' lack of purpose makes him unable to come to a decision, and Nautes offers a solution. Aeneas adopts Nautes idea, and this aid once again demonstrates how assistance was necessary to guide Aeneas toward his ultimate transformation.

Transformation as Realization

During the first part of Aeneas' journey, his lack of wisdom and knowledge of purpose hinders him, making him dependent on the aid of outside sources.

The transformation and realization of his first journey occurs when he is in the underworld, visiting his father. This pivotal moment is the climax of the hero's journey (Allison & Goethals, 2017). Here Aeneas acquires wisdom. He witnesses all of the souls who have passed away and sees his comrades who died in battle. This builds his compassion for humans, as well as a stronger comradery for his fellow Trojans. His most significant transformation occurs when he meets with his father, who tells him what his true journey will lead to, and what it is all for. Aeneas' first part of the journey was finding the intelligence, wisdom, and clarity of the purpose of his journey. This transformation is what Allison and Smith (2015) describe as being a mental transformation. Such a transformation targets Aeneas' mind and endows him and his men with a true purpose. Now aid is not needed to supply Aeneas with temporary purpose, as he how has generated a purpose for himself.

THE JOURNEY, PART TWO

The first part of Aeneas' journey was about finding his true purpose in his life, as well as obtaining insights and wisdom. Now that he has acquired these traits and transformed his mental state, he must now embark on a second journey to transform his land and people. However, where the typical monomyth of the hero would have Aeneas return to his homeland, Aeneas instead creates a new homeland that is much different from Troy. Some might argue that while he is in a different location, he still has the same men from his homeland, and thus essentially the same society. However, this is not quite true, as Aeneas gathers men from all around the region, making his society extremely heterogeneous. This journey is also Aeneas' final step towards his climactic entry into heroism (Anderson, 2015).

Villains, Obstacles, and Allies

In this part of Aeneas' journey, his goal of creating an empire is halted by a man named Turnus. This is Aeneas' largest mortal enemy and their rivalry, along with the aid of Juno, caused a massive war. The Ascanians were a group of soldiers that came to the aid of Aeneas when he was at war with Turnus. This type of aid is not a "mentoring" aid, because Aeneas has already has undergone his transformation; nonetheless, the Ascanians were crucial to Aeneas' victory over Turnus. Aeneas' mother also has her husband forge Aeneas new god-like weaponry and shields, which helps him in battle. Jupiter indirectly comes to Aeneas' aid by demanding that the gods remain neutral, and no longer intervene in the affairs of the mortals. Jupiter, the Ascanians, and Venus all are allies to Aeneas, and come to his aid on his quest to heroism; however, they do not represent the mentoring aid that Allison et al. (2017) describe as key to the hero journey.

A major obstacle that drives Aeneas away from his new goal is the death of one of his good friends, Pallas. Aeneas is devastated by the loss, and for a moment his old qualities return to him, as he becomes distracted and loses focus toward his goal. This type of impediment is more accidental, as it was not directly intended to pose as a purposeful impediment (Parks, 2017). However, his previous transformation enables him to overcome this setback, and he uses Pallas' death to fight harder and turn the tides of the war. This is a good demonstration of how Aeneas' first transformation helps him on his goal to completing his heroic quest.

Aeneas' Final Transformation

Aeneas' final transformation occurs at the very end of the story. Aeneas stands over Turnus' body and must decide whether or not to kill him. In a moment of weakness, Aeneas feels compassion towards Turnus and wants to spare his life. However, seeing Pallas' dead body draped in the battle field, Aeneas come to his senses and decides to kill Turnus. This pivotal moment completes Aeneas' journey toward heroism. Aeneas has finally defeated the Greeks and all his enemies, and he has realized his true purpose for coming to this new land.

SUMMARY OF AENEAS' HEROISM

Aeneas embodies most of the great eight qualities that Allison and Goethals (2011) claim that a hero should possess. He is a strong leader and courageous in the battlefield. He is selfless, and puts his life on the line, demanding the safety of his Trojans before his own. He is caring, as evident in the way that he reacts over any death that occurs within his army. Aeneas also demonstrates charisma in charming people with his voice. Aeneas even charms a queen into falling in love with him, just by the way he carries himself. The queen even kills herself after he leaves because she has fallen so madly in love with him. Aeneas also represents resilience, reliability, and inspiration for his team, all essential qualities of a war leader. He would never abandon them, nor would he ever quit. The lacking missing quality that Aeneas must find is knowledge and wisdom. He shows intelligence in war tactics; however, he lacks insight about his true destiny as well as the ability to think for the group as a whole. This is the missing quality that Aeneas must journey to find and act upon later.

Missing Character Strengths

From a more general character umbrella, there are 24 character strengths (Peterson & Seligman, 2004). Of these 24, Aeneas seems to lack only two. He lacks self-control at times, which was evident after he saw Pallas' death and went on a rampage killing Turnus' soldiers. Moreover, Aeneas partially lacks forgiveness and mercy. He can display this strength at times throughout his journey, but he lets his other emotions diminish this strength when he experiences immense sorrow.

Why Aeneas was Chosen as a Hero

Aeneas' bloodline gave him a head start to heroism over anyone else seeking such status. Having a mother as a goddess gave him help from the gods, which represents yet another reason Aeneas rose to heroism. A group will designate a hero based on its needs (Decter-Frain et al., 2017). In this instance the Trojans were in disarray and needed both a leader and a hero to drag them out of turmoil. Aeneas was made a hero by the way he commanded his forces. He pitted his troops against the enemy, banding them together and showing tremendous leadership. Aeneas did not need iconic paintings or any other form of media to demonstrate his heroism; his name spread through society on its own. Everyone heard of the great Trojan War, and news of Aeneas' heroism travelled across the land via social contagion, a term defined by Decter-Frain et al. (2017) to explain the spread of heroism.

Heroic Transformation

Of the five types of major transformations, Aeneas' transformation would best be classified as mental or intellectual in nature (Allison & Smith, 2015). He gains knowledge throughout the course of his journey, both about himself and about his destiny. Once he transforms his weaknesses, he then uses his new insights to fulfill his prophecy.

Effect of the Transformation

This transformation helps Aeneas experience personal growth, without which Aeneas would not have been successful (Allison & Goethals, 2017). His transformation also offers healing to him and his fellow Trojans. Being the underdog, they have been broken down by the Greeks. This transformation helps heal the loss that Aeneas has had to face by allowing him to enjoy victory over Turnus. Aeneas lost his home, his wife, and many of his men and friends; this transformation helps heal Aeneas' shattered soul. It also restores his hope, giving him knowledge that he is meant for much more than the present life. His transformation also brings unity and union to his society, another known benefit of transformation (Allison & Goethals, 2017).

Having possessed the knowledge that he needs to establish a magnificent empire, he and the other Trojans were able to band together and work better as a unit. This transformation also allowed Aeneas to advance a new society. With his initial transformation, he was able to gain back his mental focus end the fighting between the Trojans and their enemies. It was this exact transformation that saved Aeneas' society from destruction, in the sense of sparing them from further warfare.

The Aeneid comes to a conclusion after Aeneas stabs Turnus, and so we do not see the full extent of Aeneas' transformation of his society. However, as the Roman Empire will rise in stature to dominate much of antiquity, we know that Aeneas was successful in establishing a new homeland and giving the new society the same knowledge of their destiny that he was given (Allison & Goethals, 2017). Aeneas clearly had a transformative effect on the well-being of his army and his fellow citizens (Efthimiou, Allison, & Franco, 2018).

CONCLUSION

Aeneas was by no means an ordinary individual before his journey to heroism. He fought in the Trojan War and already held many qualities of a hero. What he did not possess was wisdom, as well as knowledge of a greater purpose. These deficits prevented Aeneas from becoming a true hero, as he needed to fully realize his true potential in life. Some would not classify Aeneas as a hero because he murdered many people on his way to achieving legendary status. This chapter has argued that Aeneas was a great war hero, with his actions helping to forever transform society and inspire millions of people for millennia and from all corners of the globe.

REFERENCES

Allison, S. T., & Goethals, G. R. (2011). Heroes: What they do and why we need them. New York: Oxford University Press.

Allison, S. T., & Goethals, G. R. (2016). Hero worship: The elevation of the human spirit. Journal for the Theory of Social Behaviour, 46, 187-210.

Allison, S. T., Goethals, G. R., & Kramer, R. M. (Eds.) (2017). Handbook of heroism and heroic leadership. New York: Routledge.

Allison, S. T., & Goethals, G. R. (2017). The hero's transformation. In S. T. Allison, G. R. Goethals, & R. M. Kramer (Eds.), Handbook of heroism and heroic leadership. New York: Routledge.

Allison, S. T., Goethals, G. R., & Kramer, R. M. (2017). Setting the scene: The rise and coalescence of heroism science. In S. T. Allison, G. R. Goethals, & R. M. Kramer (Eds.), Handbook of heroism and heroic leadership. New York: Routledge.

Allison, S. T., & Setterberg, G. C. (2016). Suffering and sacrifice: Individual and collective benefits, and implications for leadership. In S. T. Allison, C. T. Kocher, & G. R. Goethals (Eds), Frontiers in spiritual leadership: Discovering the better angels of our nature. New York: Palgrave Macmillan.

Anderson, W. S. (2015, November 24). Aeneas. Retrieved October 06, 2017, from https://www.britannica.com/topic/Aeneas

Campbell, J. (1949). The hero with a thousand faces. NewYork: New World Library.

Davis, J. L., Burnette, J. L., Allison, S. T., & Stone, H. (2011). Against the odds: Academic underdogs benefit from incremental theories. Social Psychology of Education, 14, 331-346. doi

Decter-Frain, A., Vanstone, R., Frimer, J. A. (2017). Why and how groups create moral heroes. In S. T. Allison, G. R. Goethals, & R. M. Kramer (Eds.), Handbook of heroism and heroic leadership. New York: Routledge.

Dik, B. J., Shimizu, A. B., O'Connor, W. (2017). Career development and a sense of calling. In S. T. Allison, G. R. Goethals, & R. M. Kramer (Eds.), Handbook of heroism and heroic leadership. New York: Routledge.

Efthimiou, O., Allison, S. T., & Franco, Z. E. (Eds.) (2018). Heroism and wellbeing in the 21st Century: Applied and emerging perspectives. New York: Routledge.

Franco, Z. E., Blau, K., & Zimbardo, P. G. (2011, April 11). Heroism: A Conceptual Analysis and Differentiation Between Heroic Action and Altruism. Review of General Psychology. Advance online publication. doi: 10.1037/a0022672

Finch, S. (2017, October 19). The 40% Rule: A Navy SEAL's Secret to Mental Toughness. Retrieved November 07, 2017, from https://thehustle.co/40-percent-rule-navy-seal-secret-mental-toughness

Furher, T. (n.d.). Aeneas: A Study in Character Development (Rep.). Retrieved from file:///C:/Users/aducci/Downloads/Fuhrer_Aeneas_a_study_in_character_development%20(1).pdf

Kinsella, E. L., Ritchie, T. D. & Igou, E. R. (2017). Attributes and applications of heroes In S. T. Allison, G. R. Goethals, & R. M. Kramer (Eds.), Handbook of heroism and heroic leadership. New York: Routledge.

Messick, D. M., & McClintock, C. G. (1968). Motivational bases of choice in experimental games. Journal of Experimental Social Psychology, 4(1), 1-25.

Parks, C. D. (2017). Accidental and purposeful impediments to heroism. In S. T. Allison, G. R. Goethals, & R. M. Kramer (Eds.), Handbook of heroism and heroic leadership. New York: Routledge.

Peterson, C., & Seligman, M. E. P. (2004). Character strengths and virtues: A classification and handbook. New York: Oxford University Press/Washington, DC: American Psychological Association.

Smith, G., & Allison, S. T. (2015). Reel Heroes & Villains. Richmond: Agile Writer Press.

Vandello, J. A., Goldschmeid, N., & Michniewicz, K.. (2017). Underdogs as heroes. In S. T. Allison, G. R. Goethals, & R. M. Kramer (Eds.), Handbook of heroism and heroic leadership. New York: Routledge.

Why Pain and Suffering? (n.d.). Retrieved November 09, 2017, from http://www.whypain.org/benefits_of_pain.html

SECTION 3: CIVIL RIGHTS HEROES

14

A DREAM BECOMING REALITY: MARTIN LUTHER KING, JR.'S CALLING TO TRANSFORM AMERICA

DANIEL P. GOLDEN

Growing up in Atlanta, Georgia, Martin Luther King, Jr., was already exposed to social segregation daily, but it was not until one life changing day where he finally realized the central issue that would permeate his life. Since a very young age, King had a white playmate with whom he was very close. He did not live in their neighborhood, but his father owned a store across the street from the King's house. They played together almost every day, often creating their own games and going on fun adventures. When it came time for the boys to head to grade school, they both had to attend separate schools. King naturally believed that they would still stay friends considering how convenient and passionate the friendship was, but the boy's father later insisted that the boys could no longer play together.

Questioning why this had to be the case, King received a life-changing response. His parents decided to sit him down and have a long conversation over dinner. They explained to young Martin how the country was "divided" at the time, demonstrating to King for the first the profound impact of race relations in America.

This conversation marked the first "transformation" that King went through in his life, an intellectual transformation that changed his perception of society. This type of transformation is one that changes a person's fundamental insights about the world (Allison & Goethals, 2017), and King evidently saw a new spectrum of the universe that his younger self never realized. It was at this young age that he had his first "calling", and he probably did not even realize it at the time. When he felt the agony of losing his closest friend, he felt a purpose that he had to fulfill to prevent this hatred and inequality from spreading. The hero's journey is one that almost all real life and fictional heroes experience in some way or another. The journey explores how and why a hero transforms into a new person, and the specific steps they must take to do so. The process of the hero's journey characterizes the manner that King not only changed himself, but also found it in himself to change the world.

THE HERO'S JOURNEY: KING'S DEPARTURE

King followed the steps of a hero's journey as described by comparative mythologist Joseph Campbell (1949). The journey begins with a departure, which King experiences at a very early age. He initially departs on this journey through a series of "callings" that prove to himself that he is the one that needs to make a social movement occur. These callings will eventually send him on a quest to transform himself into a better person, and also inspire others to transform themselves into more sympathetic, inclusive individuals.

MLK and His "Calling"

Callings correlate with heroism in three ways: transcendent summoning, using good selfishness to discover a purpose, and finally pro-social greater good (Dik et al., 2017). King's young experience of losing a friend triggered a calling in him, as it was the first time Martin was exposed to the real world. He did not like what he saw. This calling was his first signal that he should make a change, even if he was too young to fully comprehend that concept at the time.

King was born with a bright conscience, and he was raised in a very religious household. His dad was a Christian pastor who had never accepted racial segregation. King adapted to that mentality, witnessing his father boycott businesses, walk out of stores for being treated as a "lesser", and verbally retaliate against people who talked down to him because of his race. A big part of Campbell's hero journey is the presence of a mentor (Allison & Smith, 2015). In King Junior's life, his mentor was his father, as he used his father's values as motivation in pursuing goals that his father admired. Growing up in the midst of the Ku Klux Klan's reign, King already knew not to accept the dominance of white supremacist groups; he was "called" to oppose them and end the racial injustice that had spread so deeply across the south. He had a "transcendent summoning" (Dik et al., 2017) to non-violently fight back against violent acts of racism, and he saw a meaning and purpose behind what he was being called to do. He pursued his goals for the greater good, demonstrating his ability and willingness to act on a calling from a higher power.

King's Heroic Career Path

There may be a direct connection between the selection of career paths and the opportunities those paths give us to become heroes (Dik et al., 2017). King attended Morehouse College at the age of 15, as he skipped two grades in high school. However, after studying hard for several years there, he decided to follow his dad's footsteps and enter into the ministry. He believed that becoming a minister would best help him preach social justice and serve humanity. This spiritual transformation was one that significantly helped him achieve his goals. When he was younger he had gone to church just to follow his siblings and family, not recognizing the importance of religion and often doubting certain biblical claims and stories. Now he was finally appreciating the stories behind the eulogies and wanted to preach them. This substantial conversion in his beliefs shows the impact that his spiritual transformation had on his ideological beliefs. His religious transformation also placed him in a great position to gain the public speaking skills, confidence, and spirituality that he would need to place him on the heroic path of a successful civil rights activist. If it were not for his calling to be a minister, he would not have had the essential tools, platform, and courage to speak up about the social, racial, and economic injustices that he so desperately wanted to change.

This being the case, King's calling enabled him to acquire Zimbardo's (2007) four traits of heroism to perfection. These traits include performing her heroic actions voluntarily; taking a great risk; pursuing the greater good of society; and doing his heroic work selflessly. Outside factors such as his father's career path impacted King's choice to become a minister, yet he made a choice to become a minister completely voluntarily. The choice to become a minister and go down the civil rights activist path put him at great risk socially. He risked hate and retaliation from white supremacists, and he even endured several direct physical attacks. King did his heroic work for the greater good of our nation, striving to create a unified culture and augmenting the well-being of society (Efthimiou, Allison, & Franco, 2018). Also, he did not anticipate any social gain from this calling, as he selflessly placed himself in great danger both socially and physically.

Encounter with "Villainy" and Underdog Status

It is simply an understatement to say that King was an underdog, as nobody expected him to accomplish his ambitious goal of achieving racial equality. Operating in an era in which Jim Crow laws were prevalent in the South, it was considered extremely normal to discriminate in many areas of daily life. The reason we love King's story is not only because of its profound impact on today's society and culture, but also because we are naturally drawn to underdog tales. King is one of the most striking underdog stories in American history. He was just one guy battling an entire society of racist, narrow-minded discreditors.

We can use as an example King's first direct confrontation with villainy involving the Montgomery Bus Boycott of 1955. In this case, blacks were consistently being relegated to the back of public buses. A few outliers like Rosa Parks objected to such cruelty and inequality, and their defiant actions led to imprisonment. Recognizing the Parks incident as a significant social issue, King stood up to the big bus industry by leading a massive bus boycott for all African Americans in Montgomery. This defiance represented King's moral transformation; he had always supported civil rights but now he took that moral code and elevated it by taking direct action. This was the first time he used his beliefs to take initiative against the evil culture of the South, and it was huge step for both him personally and for society more generally. People loved the underdog element of his fight. The progressives in American admired King for standing up to unjust societal laws and norm, and they wanted King to "balance the scales of justice", which is one of the main reasons why people tend to root for underdogs (Vandello, Goldschmied, & Michniewicz, 2017).

Initiation and New Transformations

King did not succeed right away; he had to endure many trials and tribulations, experimenting with different tactics and methods of social activism (Campbell, 1949). The Albany Movement of 1961 is one prime example of how King tried different methods of civil disobedience, some of which did not succeed as he had planned. The Freedom Riders rebelled against bus segregation, as the justice systems were simply dismissing cases that deemed transportation segregation as unconstitutional. When King came into town, he protested with the Riders and found himself thrown in jail several times. The movement stalled, and King realized the movement wasn't working as planned. A central element of Campbell's (1949) hero monomyth involves the hero trying out specific ideas and then making adjustments when they are not working. This is an example of learning from a failed trial because King used this experience to better prepare himself for future movements.

Suffering

Suffering is unpleasant yet offers opportunities to fuel human growth (Allison & Setterberg, 2016). Suffering is often a major turning point in helping people become stronger individuals. There are six benefits from suffering that scholars have identified (Allison and Setterberg, 2016). Martin Luther King, Jr., saw great suffering as a result of discriminatory practices being implemented every hour of every day. Suffering incited a motivational transformation within King, fueling his desire combat the evil that encompassed the South. One benefit of suffering is the idea of redemption, as pain and suffering allow for opportunities for people and society to redeem themselves. Suffering also signifies a crossover point in life, which for King was the point at which he initiated a large social movement. His heart was always in the right place, and he began to gain a truly heroic status when he stood up to unjust social norms. Stimulating compassion, promoting social union, and encouraging humanity were additional benefits to suffering that King realized were largely relevant. He wanted big societal changes to occur not only for the benefit of African-Americans but also for whites to help them find compassion in their hearts that had been missing for centuries.

The Return and Transformation of Society

The hero's journey began with King transforming himself in personal ways. The journey ends with the hero returning home yet seeing it in a whole different way. Dr. King underwent a self-transformation than enabled him to see the world in a new light, thereby enabling him to change everyone else so that they could also envision a much better world with racial equality. King's newly transformed self was instrumental in helping others transform into better people.

"I Have a Dream" Transformation

It was early morning, about 8 AM when the trains started dropping into the Washington Union station. Slowly but surely, buses and trains from across the country started showing up with people, both black and white, filing in front of the Lincoln Memorial on the morning of the historic 'March on Washington". One hundred years after profound hero Abraham Lincoln signed the Emancipation Proclamation to end slavery and free African Americans, there was still racial segregation as Jim Crow laws ensured that blacks were oppressed and equipped with an "inferior" set of rights. After being discussed for years, Civil Rights activists finally made a large, non-violent rally happen and planned to make a statement about how this country had not lived up to its word of being the "land of the free". There were several speakers that day, each getting ready to collaboratively participate in one of the biggest civil rights movements in history. Martin Luther King, Jr., was backstage, still talking with other march heads and making last minute changes to the speech he was about to deliver. Being one of the most charismatic speakers in history, one wouldn't think King would be nervous at all, but this was the first time he had spoken to a crowd this immensely large, and on national TV, with the future of the United States in his hands. King knew what he was getting himself into. He was fully aware that what he was about to deliver to the nation was going to cause extreme pushback and tension, but he simply didn't care. As with all heroes, he knew he had to do what must be done.

That day, about 250,000 people gathered in front of the Lincoln Memorial, and most of them could barely see the podium. King was not giving the speech to transform himself; that had already been done. He was giving it so he could both spiritually and morally enlighten the audience in ways they hadn't experienced before. He was taking everything he had learned and spreading the word to all the white and black people in America, hoping that they would finally see his point, namely, that the current racial structure of the country was unjust and inhumane. King and others had drawn all these people to Washington by setting a common goal. They weren't just unifying the group of people present in Washington; they were also uniting the already "divided" country as a whole, thus impacting the U.S in the largest way possible. "I have a dream" -- the iconic words you hear every January, in every history class, and in every moral lesson, are a brief, but powerful summation of an extraordinarily heroic legacy.

According to Allison and Goethals (2017), the social influence taxonomy of heroes would classify King's heroism under the category of a transforming hero, who is an individual that transforms entire societies. King used several speeches and protests in order to make a statement and initiate a lasting influence. The

Selma Marches are a perfect example of a protest he initiated to stop the government from violating black's constitutional rights. Bringing together many African Americans, he non-violently fought to make equality reign in the South. With the help of many others, including the SCLC, King and his team started a substantial movement that would eventually transform the nation into one with fair voting rights, less repression, and a new sense of empowerment and identity.

Was King a Martyr?

King served the people and our nation, clearly not caring about the risks and dangers in which he placed himself. Does this suggest that King is a martyr? A martyr makes supreme self-sacrifice and is someone who willingly takes physical risk and social risk for the greater good (Franco, Blau, & Zimbardo, 2011). King was indeed a martyr. In momentous events such as the Albany movement of 1961 and the "Bloody Sunday" strive for voting rights in 1965, he publicly stated that he would take any punishment the police would give him to simply make a point.

His tragic death indicated why he was not only a martyr, but both a physical and emotional hero. In 1968, a group of black Memphis sanitation workers felt unjustly treated, as the white workers were consistently getting better working conditions and pay. Several black workers had tragically died as a result, leaving survivors in dismay. They staged a rally and strike, and King came to fight for their cause, but before he could get there his plane was delayed by a bomb threat. He gave what would turn out to be his final speech, "I've been to the Mountaintop", in which he stated: "I would like to live a long life, longevity has its place. But I'm not worried about that now." This line illustrates his selflessness, showing that he does not know what the future has in store for him, but it does not matter because he has done his job. He only cares about the future of the African American community, and the country as a whole.

"I've seen the promised land. I may not get there with you, but I want you to know that we the people will reach the promised land!" Again, these words vividly display his character as a selfless martyr and reveal his transformation into a new man. King had seen the Promised Land, meaning he had made the necessary changes needed to see the world in a new way, and he hoped everyone else could see it that way and would continue to carry the message if anything happened to him.

King's Death and Impact

King arrived in Memphis, Tennessee to help with a protest regarding black sanitation workers. He stayed in a hotel that he had consistently visited during his visits to Memphis, so it had become publicly known where he was, making him a relatively easy target. On April 4, 1968, King was assassinated by James Earl Ray, with the bullet killing him instantly. A great hero was taken from us in the worst way possible. His premature death raises a curious question: Did his dying at such a young age elevate his legacy? In death was he more of a hero than in life?

Allison, Eylon, and their colleagues have argued that the general public tends to exaggerate the heroic features of a human being after they pass away (Allison & Eylon, 2005; Allison et al., 2009; Eylon & Allison, 2005). This "death positivity bias" holds especially true when people die young, as a premature death signifies a tremendous amount of lost potential. In Dr. King's case, his death was a result of massive resistance to his message of racial equality, as well as his resilience and perseverance to achieve his overarching goal. King knew the risk he was taking when he decided to lead a volatile and divisive social movement. This essentially makes him both a physical and emotional hero, a remarkable individual who put himself at physical risk and under social scrutiny. It is reasonable to elevate his heroism to a greater level because he died for his cause, a sacrifice that the vast majority of us are not willing to make.

Adultery Investigations

Frightened that King was going to rip through social barriers and make significant changes, the FBI investigated King's personal life to find some dirt on him that could blemish his lofty reputation and therefore dethrone his heroic status. Not much was found initially, but eventually the FBI discovered evidence that proved that King had several mistresses with whom he had been cheating on his spouse. Being a minister, having extramarital affairs ran counter to his values, and therefore the FBI could make King out to be a hypocrite for preaching morals that he himself did not follow.

Taxonomies of heroes have been proposed with goal of identifying important hero subtypes (Allison, Goethals, & Kramer, 2017; Ritchie, Igou, Kinsella, 2017). We know that King was a transformational hero for his significant contributions in promoting racial equality; however, there are other subtypes that could also describe King. A transposed hero, for example, is a hero who performs some transgression that causes their reputation to become tarnished and destroys their heroic status (Allison & Goethals, 2017). If King were indeed having extra-marital affairs, does it make him a transposed hero? Does it make him make his contributions any less heroic in nature? These questions are left in the eye of the beholder, raising the interesting question of whether it is valid for King to be perceived as a villain. Can everything he did in promoting civil rights be stripped because of an unrelated mistake? Although his controversy can be viewed as a major blemish on his heroic stature, others just see it as a setback he faced on his hero's journey.

CONCLUSION

The hero's journey is a roller coaster ride that is suited for some, but too difficult for many others. Whether heroes transform themselves, and whether they transform other individuals, are two questions that are resolved by the hero's willingness and ability to travel the arduous hero's journey. To transform into a hero, people must be able to handle a multitude of snares and dangers that come their way along the journey. King was ready for those obstacles at every turn; he took every challenge and looked it straight in the eye, not frightened of any threat that confronted him.

King evidently transformed his setting, moving around to several different cities to attend to the different issues. He transformed himself by learning from his failures, and he changed society through his drive to accomplish his goal of ending racial discrimination. These transformations are critical, but aren't the defining factors of his heroism. Heroic status is not necessarily something you can achieve. King is naturally looked at as a hero by many based on how he is portrayed in the media and especially based on his transformative social impact. However, it is always up to the individual perceiving the hero to evaluate whether or not someone is heroic. We all have different views and standard for evaluating heroism, but we can all agree the people who attain that highest level are the glue that is keeping this world together.

REFERENCES

Allison, S. T., & Eylon, D. (2005). The demise of leadership: Death positivity biases in posthumous impressions of leaders. In D. Messick & R. Kramer (Eds.), The Psychology of Leadership: New Perspectives and Research (pp 295-317). New York: Erlbaum.

Allison, S. T., & Goethals, G. R. (2014). "Now he belongs to the ages": The heroic leadership dynamic and deep narratives of greatness. In Goethals, G. R., et al. (Eds.), Conceptions of leadership: Enduring ideas and emerging insights. New York: Palgrave Macmillan.

Allison, S. T., & Goethals, G. R. (2017). The hero's transformation. In S. T. Allison, G. R. Goethals, & R. M. Kramer (Eds.), Handbook of heroism and heroic leadership. New York: Routledge.

Allison, S. T., Goethals, G. R., & Kramer, R. M. (2017). Setting the scene: The rise and coalescence of heroism science. In S. T. Allison, G. R. Goethals, & R. M. Kramer (Eds.), Handbook of heroism and heroic leadership. New York: Routledge.

Allison, S. T., Goethals, G. R., Marrinan, A. R., Parker, O. M., Spyrou, S. P., Stein, M. (2019). The metamorphosis of the hero: Principles, processes, and purpose. Frontiers in Psychology.

Allison, S. T., & Setterberg, G. C. (2016). Suffering and sacrifice: Individual and collective benefits, and implications for leadership. In S. T. Allison, C. T. Kocher, & G. R. Goethals (Eds), Frontiers in spiritual leadership: Discovering the better angels of our nature. New York: Palgrave Macmillan.

Campbell, J. (1949). The hero with a thousand faces. Princeton, NJ: Princeton University Press.

Decter Frain, A., Ruth Vanstone, & Jeremy A. Frimer (2017). Why Groups Create Moral Heroes. In S. T. Allison, G. R. Goethals, & R. M. Kramer (Eds.), Handbook of heroism and heroic leadership. New York: Routledge.

Dik, B., Adelyn B. Shimizu, and William O'Connor (2017). Career Development and a Sense of Calling: A Context for Heroism. In S. T. Allison, G. R. Goethals, & R. M. Kramer (Eds.), Handbook of heroism and heroic leadership. New York: Routledge.

Eylon, D., & Allison, S. T. (2005). The frozen in time effect in evaluations of the dead. Personality and Social Psychology Bulletin, 31, 1708-1717.

Franco, Z. E., Blau, K., & Zimbardo, P. G. (2011). Heroism: A Conceptual Analysis and Differentiation Between Heroic Action and Altruism. Review of General Psychology.

Hoyt, C. L., Allison, S. T., Barnowski, A., & Sultan, A. (2019). Implicit theories of heroism and leadership: The role of gender, communion, and agency. Basic and Applied Social Psychology.

Kafashan, S., Adam Sparks, Amanda Rotella, and Pat Barclay (2017). Why Heroism Exists: Evolutionary Perspectives on Extreme Helping. In S. T. Allison, G. R. Goethals, & R. M. Kramer (Eds.), Handbook of heroism and heroic leadership. New York: Routledge.

Kinsella, E. L., Ritchie, T. D., & Igou, E. R. (2017). Attributes and Applications of heroes: A Brief History of Lay and Academic Perspectives. In S. T. Allison, G. R. Goethals, & R. M. Kramer (Eds.), Handbook of heroism and heroic leadership. New York: Routledge.

Vandello, J., Nadav Goldschmied, & Kenneth Michniewicz. (2017). Underdog heroes. In S. T. Allison, G. R. Goethals, & R. M. Kramer (Eds.), Handbook of heroism and heroic leadership. New York: Routledge.

15

Malala Yousafzai: How One Girl's Heroic Transformation Forever Changed the World

ALEXANDRA M. MALONEY

A 15-year-old, Pakistani girl was being jostled about on a tightly packed van filled with her classmates on the way home from school. She was sitting next to her best friend, chattering aimlessly about only the most important things in a 15-year-old girl's life: exams, friends and boys. The girl knew the route the van took that winded about the lively streets of Pakistan from school to her home well, as she took it faithfully every day. However, on that particular day she was so engulfed in conversation with her best friend, she did not realize how the roads became oddly quiet nor how her bus slowed to a screeching halt in the middle of one of the patchy, dirt roads. Today she does not remember the man jumping aboard the van and repeating her name; demanding to know which seat she was occupying, nor

222

him firing three shots directly into her skull. Three bullets that should have left both her and her campaign for girls' education, dead. But she did survive, and instead of death the bullets brought her resilience and growth. She found clarity and purpose in her life and underwent a transformation so monumental that she impacted society forever.

The purpose of this chapter is to offer an analysis of Malala Yousafzai's transformation, drawing from the literature of heroism science. In doing so, the chapter will explore elements of Malala's heroic traits, calling, suffering, and journey, with an emphasis on how these elements transformed her mentally and emotionally. This chapter will also discuss the implications of being a hero as a woman. The chapter concludes with an analysis of Malala's overall impact on women's rights and the feminist movement.

MALALA'S HEROIC TRAITS EXHIBITED FROM EARLY LIFE

While all heroes possess many attributes that make them heroic in nature, studies have found that there are eight traits that heroes have that are viewed as heroic in the eyes of the public. While it is unlikely that a single person may possess all traits, most heroes have a number of these attributes, which have been coined, "The Great Eight", and they include the traits of smart, strong, resilient, selfless, caring, charismatic, reliable, and inspiring (Allison & Goethals, 2011). Through inspection of Malala's life, it is evident that from both an extremely young age and through her actions now, that she exhibits a number of these traits.

As a young Muslim girl, Malala would frequently tell her parents she planned to defy Muslim culture and not wear a hijab covering her entire face. While she did intend to follow the culture to an extent and dress modestly, she said she would never cover her face as, "her face was hers, and she could do with it what she pleased" (Yousafzai, 2013). Furthermore, Malala outright refused to conform to the stereotypical Muslim women role and stated she would never stay in the home to cook and clean. Rather, she would always continue to learn and grow and reach her full potential. To defy an entire culture in a way as blatant as Malala did categorizes her as strong. As a child, Malala was strong minded and firm in her decision to defy Muslim culture and refused to settle for anything less than what she believed was fair and just, which is why she never felt compelled to conform to gender roles. This behavior has carried over into her activism today, as she continues to be strong in the face of challenge and fights for education rights tirelessly.

Additionally, Malala's attributes of selfless and caring can be seen as early as her elementary school days as well. In one particular incident, Malala recalls seeing young children roughly her age picking through the trash in a Pakistani dump. Upon realizing these young children must sacrifice attending school and receiving an education for rummaging through garbage to help their families, she vowed to help (Yousafzai, 2013). It was at that point in her early life she understood how fortunate she was to have the opportunity to attend school. Although as a child there was not much she could do yet, her pledge to aid suffering children at such a young age is characteristic of a hero. This immense compassion is illustrated today as Malala has followed through on her pledge. It is her mission to ensure no children face the heart wrenching reality of picking through the trash.

Malala is an intelligent young woman and even early on she exhibited her wit and resilience as she organized peace rallies and "spoke out to anyone who would listen" (Yousafzai, 2013). Despite her message not being taken seriously at first, and the size of her audience in her middle school auditorium being notably smaller than her platform that reaches millions today, Malala fought tirelessly for what she believed in with intelligence, leadership and meticulous planning. These traits have carried over into her life today except now, instead of planning school wide peace rallies, she uses her intelligence and fighting spirit to organize world wide fundraisers.

Malala focused on the character traits she felt she were most prevalent in herself and worked to make those her most deep-seated attributes. This has allowed her to develop her heroic traits in such a way that she was able to transform herself from a girl with admirable traits into a political activist. Because of this work and these specific heroic character traits that Malala possesses, she has been able to use the great eight traits of heroes and her self-transformation to make a significant and positive impact on society as a whole.

Still, the fact that Malala simply exhibited many of the great eight traits as a young child did not necessarily make her a hero. Instead, she had to find a calling. All heroes, at some point in their life, receive a "calling" to heroism. Whether it is a literal call to help others or a figurative call, all heroes have some form of summoning that stimulates their heroic potential. There are three different, yet widely accepted, types of calling: transcendent summons, purpose and meaning, and greater good (Dik et al., 2017). Malala Yousafzai has arguably received all three of these types of calling at some point in her life, and they have all fueled her activism.

Malala has received multiple types of callings, none of which is more important than her transcendent summons, which is defined as a calling from a higher power. When Malala speaks about why she fights so hard for all children to have education rights, despite the risks that come along to her own personal being, she says, "There was no decision to make. This was my calling. Some powerful force had come to dwell inside me, something bigger and stronger than me and it had made me fearless" (Yousafzai, 2013). These words were spoken after Malala had been made privy to the fact that her name had appeared on a Taliban death threat list. Despite this intense and frightening realization, Malala felt protected and compelled by a higher calling, almost as if being the voice of those who could not have one was her destiny here on Earth.

By similar means, Malala is a part of the greater good realm of calling, which explains an individual's inner desire to help others and serve society. While Malala did have a role model in her father, the principal of one of Pakistan's only all-girls schools, there was no one telling her she had to do anything more than attend school and receive an education. Malala could have been the same as many of her other intelligent but soft spoken and introverted classmates. The other girls in the school kept their heads down and refused to start conflict, as they already knew in Pakistan girls attending school was conflict. However, Malala felt compelled to go beyond herself and her own education and help the greater good rather than merely reap the benefits she was receiving through her schooling. Finally, it is evident Malala is also a part of the purpose and meaning category of calling. One could argue that she is a member of this grouping of calling in a less definite sense than the other types of calling. Purpose and meaning address calling through obtaining and using a certain skill set; in this sense, Malala can be included in this classification of calling. Speaking about her career goals, Malala states, "I used to want to become a doctor, but after everything we had been through, I began to think becoming a political leader was a better choice. Our country had so many problems. Maybe someday I could help solve them" (Yousafzai, 2013). This sudden shift in career paths caused Malala to begin studying even harder in school and focusing on skills that political figures need, such as public speaking and personal relations, to achieve her goal. Malala molded herself into the type of person that would fit the political job description of an activist and intended to become exactly that. She used her calling for a specific job and purpose in life to uncover and develop a newfound set of competencies to achieve those goals.

Initiation

These various callings in Malala's life were her "initiation" into her hero's journey. The initiation stage of the hero's journey is defined as the point in which a hero encounters certain sets of challenges and obstacles (Campbell, 1949). Malala's initiation did not occur when she was first exposed to the problems Pakistani girls face regarding education, but instead when she became compelled to change these circumstances. This was the beginning of her social activism and where she cultivated her ideas and image to become the hero that she is today.

MALALA'S SUFFERING

Malala hero's journey has been characterized by more suffering than most people experience in an entire lifetime. Regardless of whether Malala became a hero and embarked on this journey or not, as a young Pakistani girl she was already faced with an immense amount of hardships by simply attending school. At the time Malala was growing up in Pakistan, the reign of Maulana Fazlullah was just beginning. Fazlullah was a radio "voice" designed to inspire the people of Pakistan but promoted a total dictatorship over them and instilled fear in every citizen. As this figure joined forces with the Taliban the streets of Pakistan became war zones. Anyone accused of practicing "Western" culture was given a death sentence and the Taliban army regularly followed through:

killing innocent people in the middle of the night, hanging people from trees in the middle of town, and abusing average citizens on the streets for sick amusement (Yousafzai, 2013).

However, as discussed earlier, when Malala received her death threat for her advocacy of girls' education, she was not frightened. Instead, her fearless and resilient nature was revealed as she took this pain and fear and not only refused to stop her fight for equality, but fought harder. She describes how in the face of Taliban violence she would not respond with abomination but instead, "fight with peace, dialogue and dignity" (Yousafzai, 2013). This peaceful and mature approach to the immense suffering she was faced with only demonstrates Malala's heroism; it also proved that she alone could stand up to an army of hate with love.

Her spin of positivity from tragedy does not stop at just a death threat, as Malala was soon shot three times, nearly killing her. She had to relearn basic motor and speech skills like she was a child, her entire face became disfigured and she had to go through countless vital surgeries. Yet remarkably, Malala even grew and benefited from this massive tragedy.

There is an abundance of research that illustrates there are at least six benefits that arise from suffering. These benefits include suffering as redemptive, suffering as a crossover point in life, suffering encouraging humility, suffering stimulating compassion, suffering promoting social union and suffering instilling meaning and purpose (Allison & Setterberg, 2016). Malala, in the wake of her tragedy, took a positive attitude and a forgiving spirit and used this pain to make not only herself stronger, but also her cause stronger.

First, Malala used her tragedy to transform herself from a young girl with a cause to a mature woman with a fight. Her suffering was used as redemption within herself as she realized what truly was important to her in her life. As she says, "when you see death, things change. When you've nearly lost your life, a funny face in the mirror is simply proof you're still here on this Earth" (Yousafzai, 2013). Malala used her tragedy to reevaluate the importance of life and to understand that things that had mattered to her before, things that matter to most teenage girls like appearance, were completely trivial. Now that she was given a second chance at life, she was going to live her life to the fullest extent possible.

Furthermore, Malala used this suffering to further ignite her personal purpose and meaning (Allison & Goethals, 2011, 2017). After her tragedy and recovery, she only became more passionate about the right to education and began to fight even harder than before. She states that, "out of violence and tragedy came opportunity. I never forget that" (Yousafzai, 2013). This personal realization of newfound purpose caused Malala to be able to transform society, as she now understood the opportunity she had been given amidst this tragedy.

Malala further transformed society due to her suffering as she took her tragedy and promoted social union. Instead of becoming afraid of the Taliban and backing down she became stronger: "The Taliban shot me to try and silence me. Instead, the whole world was listening to my message now" (Yousafzai, 2013). As despicable and heart-wrenching as Malala's shooting was, she took it as an opportunity to grow her platform. If she had never got shot, she probably would have never attracted the attention of celebrities and political leaders in the United States who helped her promote worldwide education with donations and resources she could not have obtained herself. She was appreciative, and she knew exactly what to do with this newfound platform because of her personal transformation. Her tragedy transformed society as well, as her cause gained more attention and help than ever before and united the world for women's education rights.

DEPARTURE AND RETURN

This stage in Malala's hero's journey, directly after being shot, can be considered a quite literal departure. The departure stage is typically when the hero leaves their ordinary world for the first time (Campbell, 1949). In Malala's case, she is airlifted out of Pakistan, the place where her cause began, to a hospital in England to recover and escape harm. This literal departure can be seen as Malala leaving Pakistan and everything she knew to continue her fight on a worldwide scale, something bigger than just Pakistan. In Pakistan, there was little she could truly do to promote worldwide education; however, upon being airlifted into the first world, Malala could truly begin to transform herself and society.

Every hero must then complete their journey with some sort of return (Campbell, 1949). Malala never makes a literal return to her home of Pakistan, as it is too dangerous for her to do so currently. Malala's case is unique in that the young activist vows her journey of fighting for education will never stop. She will continue to grow herself and her cause by speaking out against injustices and until her mission is completed, yet it may never be safe for Malala to make a literal return to Pakistan. However, she has made a figurative "return" to her home country of Pakistan through her increasing presence there in social services projects for causes such as ending the domestic child labor of young girls in the Swat district and continually pursuing education for boys and girls alike in Pakistan.

MALALA THE MARTYR

Malala can be classified as one of many different types of heroes, but ultimately Malala is best categorized as a martyr. Martyrs are religious or political figures who knowingly (sometimes deliberately) put their lives in jeopardy in the service of a cause or to gain attention to injustice (Franco, Blau & Zimbardo, 2011). Malala clearly does exactly this, by continually risking her own personal safety to advocate against the injustices of the Pakistani government. This type of person, a martyr, is rare in society as within the social values diagram, most people typically fall within the "cooperative", "individualistic" and "competition" categories. All of these categories, involve some sense of personal gain with varying degrees of helping and hurting others. Malala's form of martyrdom involves helping others and hurting the self; Malala was shot in the name of education for complete strangers. This is a feat many cannot accomplish, as most humans are wired to want some amount of personal gain in any action they pursue (Parks, 2017).

Similarly, Malala can be viewed as both a civil and a social hero within the classifications of the martyr subtype of hero. A civil hero is a person who puts themselves at risk without any formal code nor training and a social hero is one who makes serious personal sacrifice for the sake of others (Kinsella et. al, 2017). These two types of heroes can be seen as specifications of a martyr, as they both involve making sacrifices for others, which Malala has done and will continue to do for the entirety of her life. Furthermore, as a teenage girl in Pakistan, Malala clearly had no training to campaign against the Pakistani government and the Taliban, but she also had no obligation to do so. Yet, she fought anyway, even when she realized this fight would involve making monumental personal sacrifices in the name of the cause. This status as a martyr proves how Malala transformed herself by giving up her entire being to fight for a cause she felt passionate about and transform society as a whole.

Women Prejudice

Malala's cause was not only about advocating for an education for girls, but also about achieving equality for women as a whole. However, as a Muslim, female, teenager attempting to be a leader, Malala had to overcome an immense amount of prejudice to even begin to establish a basis for achieving her goals. Since Malala has clearly exhibited many heroic traits and has continually stepped up and assumed a leadership position throughout her advocacy, it would be logical to assume her as a leader figure and hero in the movement of women's rights. However, because of her gender it was difficult for her cause to be taken seriously and herself to be seen as a leader, even though her cause impacted primarily women and deserved to be led by a woman.

In her book, Malala describes a meeting with a United States ambassador in which she addressed him and said, "I request you help us girls to get an education" (Yousafzai, 2013) and the ambassador laughed in her face. Whether this prejudice was directed at Malala individually because she was a woman asking for change or if it was at the cause as a whole because it was only benefited women, Malala had to overcome the discrimination. It has been established empirically that women are more democratic leaders with better social values and more philanthropy; however, they are often seen as too feminine and not strong enough to be taken seriously as leaders (Hoyt, 2014).

Malala not only had to overcome gender bias within her struggle to gain education rights for girls but also had to overcome racial discrimination, as women who are not of Caucasian descent as widely viewed as even more unfit to be leaders and heroes. These women are typically regarded as "invisible" and hold few leadership positions due to the superficially important combination of gender and race. Malala had to face this abundance of intolerance but she still did not let it stop her; instead she worked harder to achieve her goal for society. Today, Malala is regarded as a role model for young children worldwide. Along with campaigning for the education of young girls Malala is also contributing to the breaking of societal stereotype that only men can lead, as she is now one of the most influential heroines for young boys and girls alike to learn from and admire.

MALALA'S HEROISM AND THE HERO FUNCTION FRAMEWORK

Upon analysis of literature and empirical studies (Kinsella et al., 2015) the idea arose that the functions of heroes can be distributed into three categories. These categories, coined EMP, include enhancing the lives of others (enhancing), promoting morals and virtues (moral modeling) and protecting individuals from physical and/or psychological threats (protecting) (Kinsella et al., 2017). Malala functions as a hero in all aspects of this framework. First, with regard to enhancing, Malala has done enormous work to better the lives of complete strangers. She has started a project in Swat for girls suffering from domestic child labor, and she has arranged various trips to help Syrian refugees. Moreover, she has founded her own charity, the Malala fund, to work for a world where all girls have the opportunity to learn (Yousafzai, 2017).

With regard to promoting morals and virtues, Malala has promoted morality to such an extent that she became the youngest person ever to win a Nobel Peace Prize due to her activism and fight for equality. She promotes nothing but positivity and good morals and was rewarded for her efforts with arguably the highest honor possible. Malala states, "God has given me a responsibility and a gift: the responsibility to make the world a more peaceful place, which I carry with me every moment of every day; and the gift to be able to do so" (Yousafzai, 2013).

It is clear Malala takes her platform and work extremely seriously, which is why she only promotes peace and love and hopes to impact the lives of others by doing so. Finally, with regard to protecting individuals, Malala's work protects those who do not have a voice every day. She has taken on the role of leader and feels it is her obligation to protect children from the streets, to prevent them from skipping school out of fear and to encourage them to arise to their full potential. Malala works to change society, improve the world's heroic well-being (Efthimiou et al., 2018), and protect all of those who must live with injustices.

CONCLUSION

Malala's journey began as a young girl with a love for learning. She knew it was unjust that not everyone could receive an education and she knew she had to do something about the blatant gender discrimination in her society. At first, she did not know how to accomplish her goals. Her commitment to advocacy began in small ways, but enough to get her noticed. When tragedy struck, Malala used her suffering to transform herself as a person. She became a resilient, strong, heroine with a passion. It was through this self-transformation that Malala was able to pursue her fight to its fullest extent and in turn, transform society for the better. Malala is one of the most influential figures in both the fight for women's rights and the feminist movement. As an impoverished, female, teenager living in a developing nation, Malala had to overcome an abundance of challenges.

Her fighting spirit is inspirational to women worldwide, in both privileged and underprivileged nations. It is because of Malala's influence that many other women are reevaluating their personal abilities and places in society and becoming activists. With Malala's guide there is no limits on what other strong, heroic females can do. With all she has accomplished, she remains a humble hero (Worthington & Allison, 2018). The world is thus left to wonder: Under Malala's guidance, what other world issues will be brought to the limelight, challenged, and advanced? Malala is the epitome of a modern-day hero, as she has led remarkable movements in the world of women's education, while also inspiring others to become activists worldwide.

REFERENCES

Allison, S.T., & Goethals, G. R. (2011). Heroes: What they do and why we need them. New York: Oxford University Press.

Allison, S. T., & Goethals, G. R. (2017). The hero's transformation. In S. T. Allison, G. R. Goethals, & R. M. Kramer (Eds.), Handbook of heroism and heroic leadership. New York: Routledge.

Allison, S. T., Goethals, G. R., & Kramer, R. M. (2017). Setting the scene: The rise and coalescence of heroism science. In S. T. Allison, G. R. Goethals, & R. M. Kramer (Eds.), Handbook of heroism and heroic leadership. New York: Routledge.

Allison, S. T., & Setterberg, G. C. (2016). Suffering and sacrifice: Individual and collective benefits, and implications for leadership. In S. T. Allison, C. T. Kocher, & G. R. Goethals (Eds), Frontiers in spiritual leadership: Discovering the better angels of our nature. New York: Palgrave Macmillan.

Campbell, J. (1949). The hero with a thousand faces. New York: New World Library.

Davis, J. L., Burnette, J. L., Allison, S. T., & Stone, H. (2011). Against the odds: Academic underdogs benefit from incremental theories. Social Psychology of Education, 14, 331-346.

Dik, B. J., Shimizu, A. B., & O'Connor, W. (2017). Career Development and a Sense of Calling: Contexts for Heroism. In S. T. Allison, G. R. Goethals & R. M. Kramer (Eds.), Handbook of heroism and heroic leadership. New York, NY: Routledge.

Efthimiou, O., Allison, S. T., & Franco, Z. E. (Eds.) (2018). Heroism and wellbeing in the 21st Century: Applied and emerging perspectives. New York: Routledge.

Franco, Z. E., Blau, K., & Zimbardo, P. G. (2011). Heroism: A conceptual analysis and differentiation between heroic action and altruism. Review of General Psychology, 15(2), 99–113. doi: 10.1037/a0022672

Hoyt, C.L., (2014). Social Identities and Leadership: The Case In Gender. Jepson Studies of Leadership Book Series. Edward Elgar Publishing.

Kinsella, E.L., Ritchie, T.D., & Igou E.R., (2017). Attributes and Applications of Heroes: A Brief History of Lay and Academic Perspectives. In S. T. Allison, G. R. Goethals & R. M. Kramer (Eds.), Handbook of heroism and heroic leadership. New York, NY: Routledge.

Kinsella, E. L., Ritchie, T. D., & Igou, E. R. (2015b). Lay perspectives on the social and psychological functions of heroes. Frontiers in Psychology, 6, 130. doi: 10.3389/fpsyg.2015.00130

Parks, C.D., (2017). Accidental and Purposeful Impediments to Heroism. In S. T. Allison, G. R. Goethals & R. M. Kramer (Eds.), Handbook of heroism and heroic leadership. New York, NY: Routledge.

Yousafzai, M. (2017) What We Do. Malala.org

Yousafzai, M. (2013). I am Malala. Little, Brown, 17-18, 27, 40-44, 102, 106, 112, 118, 119, 127-130, 144, 145, 156, 170, 187, 193, 195, 202.

Worthington, E. L, & Allison, S. T. (2018). Heroic humility: What the science of humility can say to people raised on self-focus. Washington. DC: American Psychological Association.

16

THE GIRL WHO BROKE THE MOLD: MALALA'S INSPIRED HEROIC TRANSFORMATION

WILLIAM A. DELANEY

Living alone in a palm constructed house for an entire year is a common rite of passage for most women within the Tikuna tribe. Spartans in Ancient Greece were forced to live, train, and fight within the compounds of a barracks at the age of 7 for them to become men. Historically, societies across the globe have constructed unique patterns and processes that are geared toward finalizing the transition from childhood to adulthood. In the United States, a common rite of passage for men and women alike is attending college, at which time the children must make decisions independently regarding their future. The "rite of passage" or "coming of age" tale applies to all societies, no matter the period, the place in which one lives, or the gender. This transformation can be traced back thousands of years and has ultimately created many similarly structured metamorphic processes within society.

The primary focus of this chapter revolves around the heroic transformation of Malala Yousafzai. This young woman's story conveys a long-forgotten aspect of the hero's transformation, which is the importance transformation during one's young, formative years. In early societies, heroes were typically associated with being young. Alexander the Great lived to be 33 years of age, and Achilles, the Great Greek Warrior, was in his early 20s to late teenage years. As society has progressed, we have begun to view heroism as a mid-to-late adulthood transformation, suggesting that for an individual to become a hero, they must first become an adult. Malala cracks this new era mold of what constitutes a hero and allows for a proper analysis of her journey through the lens of heroism science. The starting point of this analysis centers on linking the science of childhood development and environmental factors to Malala's initiation phase of her heroic journey.

MALALA'S HEROIC JOURNEY

An average individual between the age of 16 and 20 is either pursuing higher education or just beginning a career. When Malala was between the age of 16 and 20, she was meeting with presidents and dignitaries and becoming the youngest ever winner of the Noble Peace Prize. There are some differences between Malala and the average adolescent, which begs the question: how did Malala become so "heroic" at such a young age? Her heroism can be explained by using the scientific research gathered on cognitive developmental processes in recent years. These processes are essential in a child's transition to an adult and are divided into four subgroups: sensorimotor, preoperational, concrete operational, and formal operational. Within these stages, human beings develop passions and beliefs that will become essential to their identity.

Research on educational processes in industrial cultures (Huit & Hummel, 1998, as cited by Wood & Smith, 2001) found that "only 35% of high school graduates in industrialized countries obtain formal operations; many people do not think formally during adulthood" (Wood & Smith, 2001, 2 - 3). The formal operational subgroup is the fourth stage in the cognitive development process and revolves around the ability to "ponder abstract relationships and concepts such as justice" (WebMD, 2017). Unlike the majority of people in industrialized nations, Malala has a remarkably high ability to understand abstract societal structures. The question asked earlier should actually be rephrased to become: how did Malala develop such a high level of cognitive function a young? These two questions will be correlated and answered later in this chapter, and they will demonstrate that these two processes are pivotal for bringing about Malala's heroic transformation.

Malala's Childhood Environment: Initiation

Research conducted in the field of heroism science has led to the conclusion that an individual's environment directly contributes to the likelihood their heroism will emerge. A person raised by villains will most likely not become a hero. A person raised in a staunchly conservative family will most likely not become strongly liberal. Evidence to support this idea was found by Shonkoff and Phillips (2004) who studied early childhood development patterns. These researchers stated that "human development is shaped by the dynamic and continuous interaction between biology experiences," concluding that "culture influences every aspect of human development and is reflected in child rearing beliefs and practice design to promote healthy adaptation" (Shonkoff & Phillips, 2004). History has proven that this pattern of development has led to many different and equally successful cultures.

Unlike most Pakistani children, Malala grew up a unique social environment. Her father Ziauddin, cited by the Malala Fund as being a lover of education and an educator himself, was "determined to give Malala every opportunity that a boy would have" (Malala Fund, 2017). In accomplishing this objective, her father essentially created two realities in which Malala existed: The family culture which supported her ability to learn, and the larger societal cultural that disapproved of a women's ability to learn. The famous proverb, "do not judge a man until you walk a mile in his shoes" explains the importance of the paradigm. Malala has lived her entire life understanding the difference between being treated equally and being oppressed.

Experiencing this difference is what accelerated Malala's cognitive growth immensely, as not only is she intelligent, but she is uniquely able to see the abstract concepts that are unseen by most people. This leads us to conclude that having been born into "two cultures", Malala experienced an accelerated cognitive growth that revolved around the abstract concept of equality. This egalitarian mindset later proved to be the focal point of her heroic journey.

Malala's Transformation: Childhood to Hero

The hero's journey is cited by Allison and Goethals (2017) as being the centerpiece of the hero monomyth of Joseph Campbell (1949). This transformative journey is marked by a series of stages whose "sequence is critical, with each transformation essential for producing the next one" (p. 381). There is first a call to change, which transitions into departure or "transformation of setting" and "transformation of self," and concludes with the return or "transformation of society" (Allison & Goethals, 2017). Malala as a hero underwent this same transformation process, though as noted above her heroic transformation overlaid her childhood to adulthood transformation. In short, Malala's journey consisted of growing from child to hero. From the time she was born, Malala was exposed to a cultural paradigm that, when paired with standard developmental growth patterns, placed her in a perfect position both socially and intellectually to enact change at some point in her life. With Malala's heroic transformation occurring from the moment she was born, the question becomes: where does her departure begin?

Malala's Departure

Campbell describes departure as the leaving of one's home to grow as a member of society; it is experiencing a journey through the unknown. In Malala's life, departure begins when the Taliban started to assert control over the area of Swat in the year 2007. The Taliban in the few years that followed became even more oppressive to women than what Malala's society deemed to be normal, forcing Malala and countless other young girls out of school. From 2007 to 2012

Malala's story became famous as she began to expose to the world the harsh reality that she and many other women faced while living under Taliban control. Her efforts to reveal the truth are undoubtedly heroic, but Malala's journey was far from over, meaning that she could not formally be classified as a hero until she "returned" from her journey and benefited society. Malala's return did not come until 2012 when a Taliban militant shot her in the head, neck, and shoulder, leaving her at the age of 15 in critical condition.

Malala's Return

In the days following the assassination attempt, Malala was transported to the UK to save her life. Miraculously, she survived her terrible injuries and went through months of rehabilitation, and ultimately she emerged from the hospital a new woman. At this point Malala began to "give back" her experience and wisdom to society. This sharing of knowledge is what characterizes the final stage of the heroic journey. The concept of giving back is evident in all heroic transformations but the means by which it occurs is drastically different case by case. For Malala, the act of giving back was accomplished by meeting with President Obama to raise awareness for women's rights, speaking at the United Nations, having July 12th dedicated in her name to raise awareness for vulnerable girls, and also by starting programs to build schools in areas that have been historically oppressive toward women.

MALALA'S HEROIC JOURNEY: EXPECTATIONS OF HELPING

According to Kafashan et al. (2017), an argument can be made that Malala's original heroic actions, involving the Taliban's vicious attack on her, were not voluntary on her part. Kafashan et al. (2017) describe four levels of expected helping: kin selection, reciprocity, vested interests, and punishments. If a person acts heroically for any reason related to these four expected helping components, then that action is not deemed to be heroic. Malala was technically told by her father to be the blog poster covering the Taliban story, meaning that should Malala have disobeyed she very well may have been punished. This situation places Malala into the category of a brave hero, for when Malala returned to society and began to give back she was doing it voluntarily. Furthermore, her defiant actions led her to become the face of a movement that attracted controversy within her society. She received death threats and hatred to a degree that removes all possibility of her actions as being involuntary. Her father most likely asked Malala to stop making herself a target, as most fathers in this situation would try to protect their children from further harm.

Malala's Dimensions of Transformation

Having blueprinted the three stages of Malala's journey as they correlate to Campbell's (1949) hero monomyth, it is crucial to analyze her transformation strictly through the lens of heroism science. Studies of heroism will conclusively prove that Malala's story is one of pure heroism. Heroism science states that for a hero to be transformed, either the hero or the society must be bettered by the journey. This definition is what Allison and Goethals (2017) refer to as the subject of change, which is one of ten dimensions involved in a hero's transformation. Malala's journey affected change within her society rather than herself, as her journey increased the global awareness regarding the oppression of women. Ultimately, her efforts led a global push toward ending the abuse of women and improving education for women, a task that has since been assisted by the United Nations.

Further analyzing the ten dimensions of hero transformation as they relate to Malala, we see that her growth from child to adult hero was the result of an internal source, referred to by Allison and Goethals (2017) as an enlightened dawning of responsibility. "In a crisis a small but courageous minority of people do step up to do the right thing even when there are strong pressures to avoid assuming responsibility" (Allison & Goethals, 2017). As a woman oppressed by her society and further restricted by Taliban forces, she chose to stand for equal rights. As she was able to understand the magnitude of the gap between women and men within her own culture, Malala took on the responsibility of giving a voice to an oppressed cultural minority. Originally via blog posts posted to BBC and now after her heroic return, Malala has taken up a position as the face for equal educational rights for women, fully exemplifying the concept of "if is to be, it is up to me" (Allison & Goethals, 2017).

Transformation Type: Moral and Intellectual

During her heroic journey, Malala was transformed emotionally and intellectually. Intellectual transformation should come as no surprise, as it was stated earlier that cognitive development defined Malala's entire initiation period of her heroic path. This fact is further supported by Allison and Goethals (2017), who argued that "coming of age stories" are excellent examples of "intellectual transformation" (pp. 385-6). Malala's entire life was spent learning and understanding deep abstract concepts that later enabled her to achieve her larger goal. However, Malala's journey was by no means easy; adversity is seen at every corner of her journey.

Though her ability to overcome daunting challenges, such as death threats and assassination attempts, she embarked on an emotional transformation. motional transformations are described by Allison and Goethals (2017) as "transformations of the heart, and they include heroes who, through adversity, grow in courage, resilience, and empathy." Franklin D. Roosevelt exemplified an emotional transformation because of his ability to function with the debilitating disease of polio. Malala's adversity came in the form of segregation and cultural oppression, which she overcame through her willingness to be the voice and face of a movement that has since changed the world for the better. Also, perhaps most miraculously, she overcame severe, life-threatening injuries from the Taliban's assassination attempt. Her suffering truly transformed her (Allison & Setterberg, 2016).

From Dependency to Autonomy

The final aspect of Malala's transformation that will be analyzed revolves around her heroic journey from dependency to autonomy. Malala in her early years was willing to accept some of her culture's views towards women's rights, meaning that in some ways she became complacent within her role as a woman in society. Allison and Goethals (2017) refer to this as a state of dependency and also propose that "a person's willingness to deviate from the dominant cultural pattern is essential for heroic transformation" (p. 393). Malala's culture held rigid beliefs regarding the treatment of women, especially when it came to women and education. When Malala's ability to attend school became impossible because she was a woman, she was forced into action. Doing the right thing in the face of strong societal pressures to do otherwise is the path toward autonomy (Allison & Goethals, 2014, 2017). "Heroes do the right thing, and do what they must do, regardless of authority, tradition, and consequence," meaning that within her heroic journey Malala exhibited strong signs of a metamorphosis from dependency to autonomy (Allison & Goethals, 2017, p. 393).

Why Does Society Love Malala's Story?

Having discussed and analyzed the critical components of Malala's heroic journey, it now becomes timely to examine the world's view of Malala. As stated earlier, Malala changed society to a greater extent than she did herself, meaning that society benefited more from Malala's heroic journey than she did. This notion leads to the following questions: does society view Malala as a hero? Has an oppressed minority accepted her as leader? And has the world accepted her as woman hero?

Malala as an Underdog

Malala's story of heroism is one that tugs at the heartstrings of millions of people around the world. At the age of 20, she has a global presence and a following that has precipitated massive changes to formally regressive cultural norms. How does such a young person achieve such a monumental impact? To understand such a feat, one must first become familiarized with the idea of underdogs in heroism. Underdogs are defined as a group or individual who beats the predetermined odds of success. Everyone has no doubt witnessed a sporting event during which people desire the underdog team to win. The four major concepts that are laid out by Vandello et al. (2017) as being the reasons society loves underdogs are as follows, "the thrill of unexpected," "hope springs eternal," "identifying with the little guy," and "balancing the scales of justice" (pp. 242–5).

Malala's heroic transformation gives society pieces of each of these four concepts. First, there is the thrill of the unexpected, and Malala's youth certainly made her an unexpected hero. The fact that she was a mere child gave a sense of awe to the world. Vandello et al. (2017) describes hope springing eternal as "the presentation of a compelling underdog success narrative" which causes an increase in personal optimism towards future events (pp. 242-3). Witnessing success from someone who is not supposed to succeed gives hope. This idea resonates with people because at some point in their life everyone has been an underdog.

Related to this notion is our identification with "the little guy". Malala being young, being able to push through adversity, and being a minority gave a large portion of the world the ability to connect with Malala through both hope springs eternal and identification with the little guy. Balancing the scales of justice follows the idea that the prominent, dominant group is picking on the "weaker entity" (Davis et al., 2011; Vandello et al., 2017, 244-5). Malala's story is undoubtedly seen as a balance of justice. Her primary focus revolves around balancing the scales of justice and equality, as she fights against oppressive cultural norms, arguably making Malala one of the best examples of an "underdog hero". She is a member of a minority group from both a racial and gender standpoint, and has almost been killed, and is fighting against the majority of societies rules and norms. Malala is endearing to the public because she is the quintessential underdog who has enjoyed remarkable and unexpected success.

Malala as a Woman Hero

Society has only just begun to accept men and women as equal entities. Historically and in most cultures, only men have been permitted to enjoy the status of "hero". Campbell's entire "heroic journey" model never actually considered women as heroes. In fact, Laura Kerr writes that Campbell's work creates "a somewhat lopsided and masculine view of the role of mythology in personal and cultural development" (Kerr, 2016). These misconceptions held by men such as Campbell were prevalent in pre-21st-century literature. Current research now reveals women to be superior in their leadership skills as compared to men. For instance, Hoyt (2014) reviews research suggesting that "women are slightly more likely to use democratic or participatory as opposed to autocratic leadership styles" (p. 73). This leadership style is arguably one of the most important practices to use when developing cultures.

Malala demonstrated this same style of leadership after her "return" when society established her as a leader in the campaign for women's rights. Evidence of democratic leadership used by Malala is shown in her speeches to and combined efforts with the United Nations. Furthermore, Malala has shown that she is willing to speak to many different nations, such as the United States and many Middle Eastern governments regarding women's equality. Hoyt (2014) advances the discussion of women as leaders by explaining that society looks for an ideal leader to have qualities "such as being determined and influential as well as being caring and open to others' ideas" (p. 75). Malala first demonstrated the attributes of an ideal leader through her determination and resilience during her heroic journey.

Coincidentally, both of these qualities along with many others demonstrated by Malala not only exhibits extraordinary leadership ability but also remarkable heroism. These qualities were originally noted by Kinsella et al. (2017) as including 26 characteristics, ranging from "active, beautiful, brainy" to "skillful, strong, and warrior" (p. 22). This list of heroic attributes contains many characteristics that Malala embodies, such as caring, selfless, brilliant, helpful, honest, and loving -- all of which also correspond to desirable attributes in leaders. These are all characteristics that are universally linked in leaders and heroes regardless of gender. Society's willingness to accept Malala has a hero and leader stems from the transformative impact of her heroic journey (Goethals & Allison, 2014).

CONCLUSION

Malala's heroic journey began when she was exposed to the harsh gap between men and women within her society. From this arduous journey, she developed an immense passion and understanding of abstract concepts such as equality and justice. Malala was pushed into the departure phase of her journey when the Taliban occupied her home region. In the time between her departure and return, Malala risked her life in displaying true heroism and strength by exposing the harsh reality that women in the area were facing every day. Then she was shot and left for dead, truly igniting her heroic journey and strengthening her resolve to change the world.

Malala gave her knowledge and expertise back to the world as gifts to improve society. Malala not only followed the standard heroic journey as described by Campbell (1949) but also demonstrated growth within some of the major dimensions of heroism (Allison & Goethals, 2014, 2016, 2017). Malala transformed from an unknown child to a worldwide hero, becoming a highly recognized champion of women's rights around the globe. She has promoted the well-being of both individuals and society to a remarkably heroic degree (Efthimiou, Allison, & Franco, 2018). Malala stands alongside legendary heroes such as Nelson Mandela, Martin Luther King, and Mahatma Gandhi in having made a positive and immeasurable impact on the world.

REFERENCES

Allison, S. T., & Goethals, G. R. (2014). "Now he belongs to the ages": The heroic leadership dynamic and deep narratives of greatness. In Goethals, G. R., et al. (Eds.), Conceptions of leadership: Enduring ideas and emerging insights. New York: Palgrave Macmillan.

Allison, S. T., & Goethals, G. R. (2016). Hero worship: The elevation of the human spirit. Journal for the Theory of Social Behaviour, 46, 187-210.

Allison, S. T., & Goethals, G. R. (2017). The hero's transformation. In S. T. Allison, G. R. Goethals, and R. M. Kramer (Eds.), Handbook of heroism and heroic leadership. New York: Routledge

Allison, S. T., & Setterberg, G. C. (2016). Suffering and sacrifice: Individual and collective benefits, and implications for leadership. In S. T. Allison, C. T. Kocher, & G. R. Goethals (Eds), Frontiers in spiritual leadership: Discovering the better angels of our nature. New York: Palgrave Macmillan.

Davis, J. L., Burnette, J. L., Allison, S. T., & Stone, H. (2011). Against the odds: Academic underdogs benefit from incremental theories. Social Psychology of Education, 14, 331-346.

Efthimiou, O., Allison, S. T., & Franco, Z. E. (2018). Definition, synthesis, and applications of heroic wellbeing. In O. Efthimiou, S. T. Allison, & Z. E. Franco (Eds.), Heroism and wellbeing in the 21st Century: Applied and emerging perspectives. New York: Routledge.

Fund, T. M. (2017). Malala's Story. Retrieved October 06, 2017, from https://www.malala.org/malalas-story

Goethals, G. R., & Allison, S. T. (2014). Kings and charisma, Lincoln and leadership: An evolutionary perspective. In Goethals, G. R., et al. (Eds.), Conceptions of leadership: Enduring ideas and emerging insights. New York: Palgrave Macmillan.

Kafashan, S., Sparks, A., Rotella, A., & Barclay, P. (2017). Why heroism exist: Evolutionary perspectives on extreme helping. In S. T. Allison, G. R. Goethals, and R. M. Kramer (Eds.), Handbook of heroism and heroism leadership, 36-57. New York: Routeledge

Kerr, L. K. (2016, November 23). "Goddesses" by Joseph Campbell. Retrieved October 06, 2017, from https://www.laurakkerr.com/2014/04/19/goddesses-joseph-campbell/

Kinsella, E. L., Ritchie, T. D., & Igou, E. R. (2017). Attributes of applications of heroes: A brief history of lay and academic perspective. In S. T. Allison, G. R. Goethals, R. M. Kramer (Eds.), Handbook of heroism and heroic leadership, 19-35. New York: Routledge

Rios, F. (n.d.). Coming of age in the Amazon jungle. Retrieved October 06, 2017, from https://matadornetwork.com/read/coming-age-amazon-jungle/

Shonkoff, J. P., & Phillips, D. A. (2004). From neurons to neighborhoods: the science of early childhood development. Washington (D.C.): National academy Press.

Shroff, A. (Ed.). (2015). Piaget stages of development. Retrieved October 06, 2017, from https://www.webmd.com/children/piaget-stages-of-development#1

Vandello, J. A., Goldschmied, N., & Michniewicz, K. (2017). Underdogs as heroes. In S. T. Allison, G. R. Goethals, and R. M. Kramer (Eds.), Handbook of heroism and heroic leadership, 339-355. New York Routledge.

Wood, K. C., Smith, H., Grossniklaus, D. (2001). Piaget's stages of cognitive development. In M. Orey (Ed.), Emerging perspectives on learning, teaching, and technology. Retrieved 10/2/2017, from http://projects.coe.uga.edu/epltt/

17

Thurgood Marshall: A Heroic Influence on The American Justice System

JENNIFER L. KRAMER

"I told myself, 'You either shape up or ship out.' When you
are being challenged by a great human being,
you know that you can't ship out."
--Thurgood Marshall

Thurgood Marshall, the first African American appointed to serve on the U.S. Supreme Court, exemplified the hero's transformative journey as he first developed, and then applied, his sense of idealism to the legal issues surrounding the civil rights movement. In doing so, he became a national inspiration. Marshall was a black man, the great grandson of a former slave, and throughout his upbringing, a witness to, and victim of, inequality and racism. It would be those experiences that would transform him into the American hero that he is remembered as today.

Marshall was America's 96th Supreme Court justice and the first African American justice appointed to the Su-preme Court. "As an associate justice of the Supreme Court… he crafted a distinctive jurispru-dence marked by uncom-promising liberalism, unusual attentiveness to practical considerations be-yond the formalities of law, and an indefatigable willingness to dissent" (History.com Staff, 2009). Principled and confident, Thurgood Marshall would become known as the "Great Dissenter", as he was not afraid to voice his contrarian opinion to represent a suppressed segment of American society. He would emerge as an idealist who fought for equality of all suppressed minorities, and a hero of civil rights advocating for equal protection under the law.

The purpose of this chapter is to offer an analysis of Thurgood Marshall's heroic contribution though an understanding of his own personal heroic transfor-mation. In doing so, I will describe the impact of a mentorship relationship in Marshall's development, and define the ten dimensions of transformation that heroes, in general, may undergo during their journey. I will also discuss the moral, intellectual and emotional transformation that Marshall personally experienced while also evaluating which of the "great eight traits" of heroes Marshall possessed. Finally, I will conclude by discussing his pathway of trans-formation and his personal sacrifice that made him into the American hero he is remembered to be today.

BACKGROUND AND INSPIRATION

Marshall was born to William and Norma Marshall on July 2, 1908 in Baltimore, Maryland. From an early age he developed an interest in the law and was often found listening to cases in the local courthouse. He attended Baltimore's Colored High and Training School, and later attended Lincoln University where he grad-uated cum laude. His crusade on behalf of civil rights may have begun when he applied to the University of Maryland Law School. As the result of his African American heritage, he was denied acceptance to the university, despite the fact that he was, in reality, over-qualified for admission. Such awareness of the implications and limitations imposed by his race would trigger the beginning of his heroic journey. The concept of the "mythic hero's journey" was first developed by mythologist Joseph Campbell (1988) and is described as a transformative jour-ney where "a hero ventures forth from the world of common day into a region of supernatural wonder: fabulous forces are there encountered and a decisive victory is won: the hero comes back... with the power to bestow boons on his fellow man" (Allison & Goethals, 2017). The critical part of this theory is that the hero returns to share his newly discovered knowledge with his community. In Marshall's case, his community would turn out to be 1950s America struggling to come to terms with the civil rights of its minority citizens. Marshall's mythic hero's journey would be result of his moral, intellectual, and emotional transformation that would take place during that time period.

Mentors and Their Role in Transformation

At Howard University, Marshall would meet his greatest inspiration, Charles Houston. Houston served as the dean at the university and immediately took Marshall under his wing, forging a life-long mentoring relationship. Houston was an African American lawyer and a civil rights activist. Every hero ultimately relies on a mentor or a 'sidekick' to teach the hero what they need to succeed (Allison & Smith, 2015). Houston would engage Marshall in philosophical discussions regarding the constitutionality of civil rights and they would debate the founding fathers' intent in their statement that "All men are created equal." Houston would drill into Marshall his view that the law was not just a static set of rules and regulations, but a "force that could be used to promote the rights of African Americans" (Biography.com Editors, 2014).

Houston and Marshall would later continue their relationship while working together at the NAACP. When Marshall was credited with orches-trating the successful outcome of Brown v. Board of Education, he would give much of the credit to Houston saying, "We wouldn't have been anyplace if Charlie hadn't laid the groundwork for it" (Biography.com Editors, 2014). It is well established that heroes who have mentors and are transformed by them, are likely to become mentors to others (Allison & Smith, 2015). "Transformed people transform people," according to Richard Rohr (2014, p. 263). In Marshall's case, he was transformed by Houston and became a guiding light to future lawyers, government officials, and many Americans. Under Houston's guidance and with his encouragement, Marshall graduated magna cum laude and was valedictorian of his class on his road to becoming a civil rights activist.

Ten Dimensions of Transformation

According to Allison and Goethals (2017), "When people embark on the hero's journey, they 'undergo a truly heroic transformation of consciousness' making them think a different way." Although Marshall did not intentionally set out to become a hero, his journey transformed him in-to an influential leader. The "ten dimensions of transformation" describe different ways in which a hero's transformation can differ among individuals (Allison & Goethals, 2017). In Marshall's case, his transformation can be understood by defining the subject that became transformed, and the scale of that transformation.

Subject of Transformation

The first dimension of transformation defines the "subject" to be transformed. The subject can refer to either the hero or to the followers of that hero. "In some stories, however, the heroic protag-onist remains unchanged through-out the narrative but he or she serves as the catalyst for the trans-formation in others" (Allison & Goethals, 2017). Thurgood Marshall was not the only individual who was transformed; all of America was forever changed as the result of his influence. While Marshall may have himself been considered the subject of transformation, his more important he-roic contribution was serving as the catalyst for the transformation of the United States. Determined to revolutionize America, he took on one of the most prominent and influential court cases in American history known as Brown v. Board of Education.

His victory in this 1954 case is considered his greatest accomplishment as a civil rights lawyer. Marshall challenged the Brown v. Board of Education doctrine, suggesting that the "separate but equal" clause was actually unconstitutional. This clause was first established in 1890 in the case of Plessy v. Ferguson when Louisiana established a new law that "provided for 'equal but separate accommodations for the white and colored races' on its railroads" (History.com, 2009). This case was initiated when Homer Plessy refused to sit in the Jim Crow car on a train, and in doing so, broke Louisiana law.

In a 7-1 decision, the U.S. Supreme Court ruled that segregation in this case was constitutional as defined under the "separate but equal" clause, and as such, did not violate the 13th and 14th Amendments. On May 17, 1954 Marshall brought this case before the Court, and this time, in a unanimous decision, the Supreme Court concluded that "separate educational facilities are inherently unequal" (Biography.com Editors, 2017). As the result of Justice Marshall's intervention, segre-gation in public schools was to be considered unconstitutional as a violation of the 14th Amendment (Biography.com Editors, 2017). This victory would propel Thurgood Marshall down his path toward becoming a great American hero. Although it took time to implement the ruling, the Brown v. Board of Education case was a needed push for the American civil rights movement and provided the needed legal foundation for its advancement. "The case established Marshall as one of the most successful and prominent lawyers in America" (Biography.com Editors, 2017) and would establish Marshall as a catalyst for change in American civil rights.

Scale of Transformation

Another component of the Ten Dimensions of Transformation is the "scale," or, understanding who would be the target of the hero's transformation. Scale can either be small, as in a small group, or it can be large, as in the case of an entire society (Allison & Smith, 2015). Marshall be-gan small when he began working on his first court case. His scale increased in 1938 when he was hired as an attorney for the NAACP, where he ultimately founded the NAACP Legal Defense and Educational Fund in 1940. While he argued many court cases, one of his first important "small scale" cases was Smith v. Allwright (1944), which argued that excluding black voters from partic-ipating in the primary elections in Texas was unconstitutional. This was considered small in scale when compared against the ultimate far-reaching effects of Brown v. Board of Education. Yet it did have larger scale implications as it helped to spread his message that there was a need for change, and that there must be more widespread legal arguments on behalf of civil rights. Along with this court case, he would also argue other smaller scale civil rights cases including Morgan v. Virginia, Shelley v. Kramer, and Sweatt v. Painter, among others.

THE GREAT EIGHT TRAITS OF HEROES

Thurgood Marshall demonstrated several of the "great eight traits" as described by Allison and Goethals (2013) and Allison, Goethals, and Kramer (2017). The "great eight" defines several potential traits of a hero including: being smart, strong, selflessness, caring, charismatic, resilient, re-liable and inspiring (Allison et. al., 2017, p. 6). While heroes do not need to possess all "great eight traits," Thurgood Marshall would demonstrate most of them throughout his legal career.

Smart

Graduating with high honors from college, and first in his class from law school, Marshall would become recognized for his brilliant legal mind when he was selected to serve as a judge for the U.S. Second Circuit of Appeals by President John F. Kennedy. While serving in that role, Marshall continued to "issue more than 100 decisions," all of which were passed (Biography.com Editors, 2017). Once President Lyndon B. Johnson took office, he "appointed Marshall as the first black U.S. solicitor general", where he would win 14 out of the 19 cases that he argued before the U.S. Supreme Court (Biography.com Editors, 2017). Marshall's keen legal mind was clearly recognized and sought after by all around him.

Strong

Marshall had a unique combination of intellectual strength and strength of character. His idealism provided him with the courage to stand up to his fellow justices, even if he stood alone in his representation of African Americans during a time of racism and inequality. Along his journey to the Supreme Court, he would witness the inequity of race and he would endure many racist insults directed toward him. However, these prejudices only served to strengthen him and to motivate him to persevere in his calling to end segregation and inequality in America. The work that Marshall immersed himself in was dangerous. He traveled from state to state to ensure that state and federal courts were protecting African American rights, which were supposed to be guaranteed under the Constitution (Biography.com Editors, 2017).

Williams wrote; "The work was dangerous, and Marshall frequently wondered if he might not end up dead or in the same jail helping those he was trying to defend" (Thurgood Marshall, 2004). Decter-Frain et al. (2017) also highlighted the idea of "personal sacrifice." Defending one's beliefs or values can sometimes require a significant sacrifice of time, resources, physical well-being, and personal freedom. Marshall was willing to die for the cause. He recognized the work he was doing was risky and even life threatening, however he knew this was his calling and had no choice but to follow his heart (Campbell, 1991). "Following your bliss" is what Joseph Campbell said each person must do in order to bestow the world with their heroic powers. Similarly, Abraham Maslow (1943) once proclaimed, "What a man can be, he must be," suggesting that an individual in possession of Marshall's heroic qualities must be strong enough to use them.

Selflessness

Marshall's selflessness pursuit of equality for all American citizens can be seen in many people's descriptions of him. For example, his encyclopedia. com entry sings his praises as follows: "Justice Thurgood Marshall built a distinguished career fighting for the cause of civil rights and equal opportunity... Marshall stood alone as the Supreme Court's liberal conscience toward the end of his career, the last impassioned spokesman for a left-wing view on such causes as affirmative action, abolishment of the death penalty, and due process" (Thurgood Marshall, 2004).

His selfless pursuit of individuals' rights guaranteed in the Constitution can be seen not only in his defense of minorities, but also of the rights of criminals themselves. Specifically, he sought the "abolishment of the death penalty and guarantee of due process" for all (Thurgood Marshall, 2004). Although he was victorious in 29 out of 32 cases, he would have to settle with his dissent-ing opinion against the death penalty. Duke University professor John Hope Franklin states:

"If you study the history of Marshall's career, the history of his rulings on the Su-preme Court, even his dissents, you will understand that when he speaks, he is not speaking just for black Americans but for Americans of all times. He reminds us constantly of the great promise this country has made of equality, and he reminds us that it has not been fulfilled. Through his life he has been a great watchdog, insisting that this nation live up to the Constitution." (Thurgood Marshall, 2004).

Putting himself at physical and intellectual risk promoting not only the rights of fellow African Americans, but all suppressed individuals, including criminals themselves, was the ultimate demonstration of Marshall's selflessness in his never-ending pursuit of equality for all under the law. Significant risk-taking is considered to be a hallmark feature of heroism (Franco, Blau, & Zimbardo, 2011).

Charismatic

To achieve the successes that Marshall achieved, he clearly possessed an abundance of charisma. He was the only liberal (not to mention the sole African American) on a nine-member court, representing liberal thought on an otherwise conservative Court. Only a charismatic individual could have swayed the Court to his point of view or delicately dissent when the need arose. The fact that he served as mentor to an entire generation of young attorneys is also a reflection of his ability to communicate effectively and lead charismatically.

Resilient

Perhaps there is no better way to describe Thurgood Marshall than with the trait of resilience. When he was denied admission from the University of Maryland, he learned from the experience and pursued admission to a different school, which turned out to open even more doors for him. He fought his fight for civil rights over and over again as in the case of Morgan v. Virginia. In this case, similar to others, Irene Morgan was an African American woman arrested for refusing to give up her seat on a city bus simply because she was sitting in the "white section." Marshall de-fended Morgan, and, once again, won this case, in a 6-1 decision, on the grounds that segregation in busses was unconstitutional (Catsam & Wolfe, 2014). Resilience implies the ability to fight the same fight over and over until the message takes hold.

Reliable

Marshall was obviously reliable. He was not only loyal to African Americans, but to all Americans, and to the idealism of America as defined by the Constitution. Encyclopedia.com's descrip-tion of Marshall is most apt: "The most important black man of this century -- a man who rose higher than any black person before him and who has had more effect on black lives than any oth-er person, black or white" (Thurgood Marshall, 2004). This description suggests that many recognized what a great leader and hero he was to all of America and the world. He earned the trust of Americans and they knew that he would not let them down.

Inspiring

Marshall was an inspiration to those with whom he worked. He was, perhaps, the most influential African American man in politics, the outsider who dared to transform our history. Professor James Freedman, former President of Dartmouth College and a law clerk to Marshall early in his career, stated in an essay about his mentor that Marshall's achievements "were marked indelibly by Justice Marshall's idealism and courage, his compassion and humanity... The force of his moral example changed our lives utterly, and in ways that have made us better citizens and more reflective lawyers" (Freedman, 2000). Marshall's adherence to a high moral ideal allowed him to serve as a mentor not only to generations of young attorneys (as in the case of James Freedman), but al-so to future generations of civil rights activists looking to the Constitution for a path to true equality. He also served as a leader with the courage to leverage the power of the

Supreme Court to legit-imize the actions of other civil rights activists of the time, including Martin Luther King. Thurgood Marshall's role as a mentor, by definition, served to inspire us all.

TYPES OF HEROIC TRANSFORMATIONS

Despite not going through the typical "monomyth journey" that Campbell (1949) defined previ-ously as a hero setting out on an adventure, overcoming obstacles, and returning to share his new enlightenment with the people (Campbell, 1949), Marshall set out on his own unique journey. He did embark on a mission knowing there was danger, or to specifically save any particular life. His was a transformative journey that began innocently at a very young age when his great grand-father would preach to him the words of the Constitution. Allison and Smith (2015) define five potential transformations that a hero can experience along his journey and that contribute to the emergence of a hero. These transformations include: "moral, emotional, spiritual, intellectual, and physical transformations" (Allison & Smith, 2015). Allison and Goethals however added a sixth transformation referred to as "motivational transformation" (Allison & Goethals, 2017). As the result of his legal education, a keen awareness of the condition of his fellow African Americans, and expo-sure to inspirational African American mentors, Marshall would experience moral, intellectual, and emotional transfor-mations.

Moral Transformation

Marshall began his moral journey to heroism as he became aware of the need to take a stand on the issue of racial inequality within America. Marshall's moral journey began with "self-actualization," defined as "the achievement of one's full potential through creativity, independence, spontaneity, and a grasp of the real world" (Maslow, 1943). He would become open to personal "change and growth" as a result of 'finding himself' (Sedikides & Hepper, 2009). He had grown up in a time of inequality, and his rejection from the University of Maryland was the first real setback that allowed him to come face-to-face with the cruel realities of the world in which he lived. This awareness of the perceptions of the real world, along with his sense of independence and confi-dence, would contribute to his moral growth and transformation as he resolved to pursue his dream of completing his education and having an impact on the condition of his fellow African Americans.

In 1930 Marshall was accepted to Howard University Law School, which was founded in 1867 to help educate slaves and their descendants. Marshall fulfills the requirements of the moral hero because he ultimately became known for both his "agency" and his "communal focus," dedicating himself to bettering the lives of others (Decter-Frain et al., 2017).

Emotional Transformation

Emotional transformation refers to the process by which heroes who, "through adversity, grow in courage, resilience, and empathy" (Allison & Smith, 2015). Marshall grew in courage and resili-ence through the hardships that he experi-enced throughout his life. He grew up in a well-to-do household with a mother who was a teacher in a segregated school and a father who was a stew-ard at an all-white yacht club. What may have tied him emotionally to his African American herit-age was his awareness that his great-grandfather was brought to America from the Congo as a slave. After his rejection from the University of Maryland's Law School, Marshall knew he need-ed to take a stand. This was his first real experience of racism, and through this adversity, he gained the courage and resilience (Allison & Smith, 2015) that he needed to become a hero.

Difficulties and challenges from "outside forces" however can result in an "external source of transformation" (Allison & Goethals, 2017; Worthington & Allison, 2018). Although many may not consider his rejections a "traumatic experience", he was able to change this setback and con-vert it into a strength (Rendon, 2015).

Intellectual Transformation

Intellectual transformation is "a change in mental abilities or fundamental insights about the world" (Allison & Smith, 2015). From a very young age, Justice Marshall knew he was interest-ed in law, visiting the courthouse daily after school. As a "punishment" for occasionally misbe-having as a child, he was made to read the Constitution, and by the end of high school, he knew the entire document by heart (Thurgood Marshall, 2004). Since he was not directly exposed to in-equality or the complexities of the law as a child, his intellectual transformation took place later in life. He studied civil rights and the law at Howard University. He began to favor the liberal side of politics. After Charles Houston took him under his wing, he was able to broaden his knowledge about the law, ultimately getting appointed by John F. Kennedy to the U.S. Court of appeals. Despite being a minority on the court, he did not let that hold him back. He knew he had a voice and wanted it to be heard. He "voted to uphold gender and racial affirmative action policies" (History.com Staff, 2009). Since he was against the death penalty, in every case the Supreme Court did not rule against the death sentence, he dissented:

"No justice has been more libertarian in terms of opposing government regulation of speech or private sexual conduct. Nor has any justice been more egalitarian in terms of advancing a view of the Constitution that imposes positive duties on gov-ernment to provide certain important benefits to people–education, legal services, access to courts–regardless of their ability to pay for them" (History.comStaff, 2009).

In his time on the Supreme Court, he won 29 of 32 civil court cases, an accomplishment that demonstrated his significant intellectual and legal influence on American civil rights law.

Pathways to Transformation

Allison and Goethals (2017) also described three different pathways to transformation that heroes may take: egocentric to sociocentricity, stagnation to growth, and dependency to autonomy. Thurgood Marshall would follow the pathway from dependency to autonomy on his journey to becoming an American hero.

Dependency to Autonomy

Marshall would develop the courage, intellect, and charisma to stand against prevailing social norms and to fight for what he believed. A hero has to be confident in his beliefs to the point that he is willing to defy social norms at great personal cost. Marshall's views could at times have been considered deviant from the norm, a characteristic reflective of his path to autonomy. For example, as already stated, he was not afraid to dissent despite being a minority (in opinion and race) on the court. Heroes do the right thing, and do what they must do, regardless of authority, tradition, and consequence. Maslow (1943) called this characteristic autonomy. "There are the 'strong' people," wrote Maslow, "who can easily weather disagreement or opposition, who can swim against the stream of public opinion and who can stand up for the truth at great personal cost" (Allison & Goethals, 2017). The pathway from dependency to autonomy relates to Maslow's hierarchy of needs because it describes how one must fulfill the lower level needs in order to transcend social norms (Allison & Goethals, 2017)

Personal Sacrifice

According to Decter-Frain et al. (2017), "Enduring personal hardships for the cause may make people seem like moral heroes for several reasons. First, martyrs no longer have the opportunity to fall from grace, and so they cement their legacy when they die." Although Marshall was not a mar-tyr, he cemented his legacy in the law itself, leaving an enduring impact on America. He contribut-ed significantly to the civil rights move-ment by inspiring other leaders to take a stand on the issue of inequality. Regardless of whether he was the sole dissenter, or shared the majority opinion, he never strayed from his own personal high road, despite the potential consequences.

CONCLUDING THOUGHTS

Marshall passed away on January 24, 1993 at the age of 84, leaving behind a great personal and legal legacy. Over eighteen thousand people of all races and different backgrounds came to the Great Hall of the Supreme Court to pay their respects to him -- a reflection of how he unified and inspired not only African Americans, but all Americans. As Thurgood Marshall, remarked, "A child born to a black mother in a state like Mississippi... has exactly the same rights as a white baby born to the wealthiest person in the United States. It's not true, but I challenge anyone to say it is not a goal worth working for." Of course, this ideal vision never came true during his lifetime, but it was an inspiring guiding principle for him.

Marshall was a humble idealist (Worthington & Allison, 2018). He was inspirational to those around him and stood tall as a hero fighting for justice and equality in an unfair and imperfect world (Gray et al., 2018). Thurgood Marshall may have never worn a cape, or personally saved lives, but through his confidence in his himself and his ideals, his ability to inspire others, and his tenacity, he changed the face of America. He represented minorities, the poor, the wealthy, the criminal, and everyone in between, always hoping to end segregation and hate within America, always striving to provide everyone with an equal opportunity. Marshall clearly represents the truism that not all heroes wear capes.

REFERENCES

Allison, S. T., & Goethals, G. R. (2013). Heroic leadership: An influence taxonomy of 100 exceptional individuals. New York: Routledge.

Allison, S. T., & Goethals, G. R. (2014). "Now he belongs to the ages": The heroic leadership dynamic and deep narratives of greatness. In Goethals, G. R., et al. (Eds.), Conceptions of leader-ship: Enduring ideas and emerging insights. New York: Palgrave Macmillan.

Allison, S. T., & Goethals, G. R. (2017). The hero's transformation. In S. T. Allison, G. R. Goethals, & R. M. Kramer (Eds.), Handbook of heroism and heroic leadership. New York: Routledge.

Allison, S. T., Goethals, G. R., & Kramer, R. M. (Eds.) (2017). Handbook of heroism and heroic leader-ship. New York: Routledge.

Allison, S. T., & Setterberg, G. C. (2016). Suffering and sacrifice: Individual and collective benefits, and implications for leadership. In S. T. Allison, C. T. Kocher, & G. R. Goethals (Eds), Frontiers in spiritual leadership: Discovering the better angels of our nature. New York: Palgrave Macmillan.

Allison, S. T. & Smith, G. (2015). Reel heroes and villains. Richmond: Agile Writer Press.

Beggan, J. K., & Allison, S. T. (Eds.) (2018). Leadership and sexuality: Power, principles, and process-es. Northampton, MA: Edward Elgar.

Biography.com Editors, (2014). Charles H. Houston biography.com. A+E Television Networks. Retrieved from https://www.biography.com/people/charles-h-houston-9344795

Biography.com Editors, (2017). Thurgood Marshall biography.com. A+E Television Networks. Retrieved from https://www.biography.com/people/thurgood-marshall-9400241

Campbell, J. (1949). The hero with a thousand faces. New York: New World Library. Campbell, J. (1988). The power of myth. New York: Anchor Books.

Campbell, J. (1991). Reflections on the art of living. New York: HarperCollins.

Catsam, D. C., & Wolfe, B. (2014). Morgan v. Virginia (1946). Encyclopedia Virginia. Re-trieved from http://www.EncyclopediaVirginia.org/Morgan_v_Virginia.

Davis, J. L., Burnette, J. L., Allison, S. T., & Stone, H. (2011). Against the odds: Academic underdogs benefit from incremental theories. Social Psychology of Education, 14, 331-346.

Decter-Frain, Ari, et al. (2017). Why and how groups create moral heroes. In S. T. Allison, G. R. Goethals, & R. M. Kramer (Eds.), Handbook of heroism and heroic leadership. New York: Routledge.

Gray, K., Anderson, S., Doyle, C. M., Hester, N., Schmitt, P., Vonasch, A., Allison, S. T., and Jackson, J. C. (2018). To be immortal, do good or evil. Personality and Social Psychology Bulletin.

Freedman, J. (2000). Idealism and liberal education. Ann Arbor; The University of Michigan Press

History.com, (2009). Plessy v. Ferguson. A+E Networks. Retrieved from http:// www.history.com/topics/black-history/plessy-v-ferguson

Jamar, S. D., (2017). Thurgood Marshall. Howard University Law. Retrieved from http:// law.howard.edu/brownat50/BrownBios/BioJusticeThurgoodMarshall.html

Maslow, A. (1943). A theory of human motivation. Psychological Review, 50(4), 370–396.

Rendon, J. (2015). Upside: The new science of post-traumatic growth. New York: Touchstone.

Sedikides, C., & Hepper, E. G. D. (2009). Self-improvement. Social and Personality Psychology Compass, 3, 899–917.

Thurgood Marshall. (1998). In Encyclopedia of World Biography. Detroit: Gale. Retrieved from http://link.galegroup.com/apps/doc/K1631004311/BIC1? u=s1180&xid=24f87388

Thurgood Marshall. (1998). In J. S. Baughman, V. Bondi, R. Layman, T. McConnell, &

Thurgood Marshall. (2004). In Contemporary Black Biography (Vol. 44). Detroit: Gale. Re-trieved from http://link.galegroup.com/apps/doc/K1606002769/BIC1? u=s1180&xid=b189e44b

Thurgood Marshall Quote, (2017). BrainyQuote.com. Retrieved October 6, 2017, from https://www.brainyquote.com/quotes/quotes/t/thurgoodma821979.html

Tompkins, V. (Eds.), American Decades. Detroit: Gale. Retrieved from http:// link.galegroup.com/apps/doc/K1602000699/BIC1?u=s1180&xid=2b2a4095

Worthington, E. L, & Allison, S. T. (2018). Heroic humility: What the science of humility can say to people raised on self-focus. Washington. DC: American Psychological Association.

18

A Catalyst for Change: How Susan B. Anthony's Heroic Transformation Revolutionized Society

MEGAN G. DORAN

On November 5, 1872, Susan B. Anthony cast a vote in a presidential election 48 years before it was actually legal for women to vote. This incident sparked a massive pushback and controversy, and even led to a highly publicized legal fight. Just days before her vote was cast, Anthony and three of her sisters had gone to a voter registration office in Rochester, New York and insisted on being allowed to register to vote, despite the fact that suffrage for women remained illegal in the United States (Enix-Ross, 2013). The legalities of the issue did not dissuade Susan from casting a vote on election day. She did not care that it was illegal; she knew that it was her right to have her voice heard, to be able to cast a vote to choose who would lead the country, to choose who would lead her country. She also rationalized that the Fourteenth Amendment of the Constitution gave her the right to vote as she was a natural citizen of the United States.

This passion for equality, however, did not leave Anthony unpunished. Thirteen days after the election, a United States deputy marshal came to Susan's home and arrested her for voting illegally. Upon her release from prison, Susan incorporated this incident into her speeches, sharing with her audience why she believed she had committed no real wrong by voting in the election. Susan had hoped this would help her gain the support of some potential jury members. However, Susan was unjustly denied a trial by jury, and ultimately her punishment was to pay a fine of $100 (Enix-Ross, 2013). Recognizing the absence of justice in this outcome, Anthony refused to pay the fine, and instead spoke publicly about her unfair treatment to further spark crowds and get others to rally behind the women's suffrage movement.

Although Anthony's punishment in this case represented a legal setback, her brave actions further advanced the women's suffrage movement and gave Susan B. Anthony the title of the woman who dared (Enix-Ross, 2013). Today, Susan B. Anthony is a role model for feminists everywhere, a symbol of true social change, and a definitive hero. But how did she get there? Transformation is an essential part of a hero's journey (Allison & Goethals, 2017). Through the trials they experience, and the guidance they receive from their mentors, heroes are able to change, to discover in themselves the essential quality they were missing and thus complete their mission. For Susan B. Anthony, this personal transformation was not only essential for redefining her own path and learning more about herself, but also for empowering an entire society to transform as well.

A CALLING FOR ACTIVISM

One could say that Susan Brownell Anthony was always destined for a life as an activist and social reformer. Born on February 15, 1820 to a Quaker family, Susan was encouraged early on to be a free thinker and to partici-pate in activism that would help achieve a greater good (Enix-Ross, 2013). Due to their experience with religious intolerance and injustice, Quakers were large promoters of reform and of supporting different social causes

(Dorr, 1928). Additionally, the Anthony family would host meetings on their farm to help promote these causes. The most notable meetings were about ending slavery through involvement in the abolition movement. During these meetings, Susan was frequently exposed to women and minorities alike being allowed to speak freely and being encouraged to share their ideas. For instance, Frederick Douglas was a frequent visitor to the Anthony farm, and became so close to the Anthony family during their time working on the abolitionist movement that he even gave a eulogy for Susan's father when he passed away (Barry, 1998).

These influences as a child and young adult helped Susan to gain an interest in activism, and helped to show her that part of her calling in life was to play a role in reform. Though she did not yet know what specific cause she would dedicate her life to, Anthony is a clear example of someone who followed a calling. She underwent two of the dimensions of calling: a meaning and purpose call, and a call to help to achieve a greater good (Dik et. al., 2017). Though it seems that answering a call to pursue one's own meaning or purpose can seem inherently selfish, as answering such a call would bring happiness to one's own life, Anthony's call to find her meaning also served to be the call that would lead her to help millions. These callings are what helped set Susan on the path to achieving heroic status.

ANTHONY'S HERO'S JOURNEY

Joseph Campbell (1949), the pioneer of heroism science, found that all heroes undergo the same three steps in their journey, or what he called the heroic monomyth. The hero's journey contains three parts: departure, initiation, and the return (Allison, Goethals, & Kramer, 2017).

Departure

The departure stage is the first step on the hero's journey. It refers to the stage in which the hero is thrown into a new setting and must adapt to the new world around them (Allison, Goethals, & Kramer, 2017). For Anthony, her departure began when she first left her home to teach at a Quaker Boarding school shortly after an economic crisis that occurred in 1837. She took the job to help assist her family financially. This first movement away from her home, however, was not strikingly different to what she had experienced before. Quakerism was still playing a large role in her life, and so she remained relatively unchanged. It was not until a job that she took in 1846 that Anthony experienced a sort of culture shock that heroes typically undergo in the departure stage of their journey. When heroes depart, they are thrown into a situation that they are not familiar with and must figure out how to navigate their new surroundings. For Anthony, this occurred when she was named headmistress of the female department at the Canajoharie Academy (Barry, 1998).

This was the first time that Anthony was away from Quaker influences in her 26 years of life. Thus, she began to dress differently and stopped using the traditional forms of speech common to Quakerism. Additionally, Susan began to notice the lack of equality between herself and the other women and the men they worked with. She astutely noticed that the men and women were being paid different amounts for the same job. Though it would be some time until Anthony began solely focusing on women's rights, this observation remained in the back of her mind and helped remind her of her interests in activism. When the Canajoharie Academy closed in 1849, Anthony moved back to her family's farm and entered the world of reform as an adult member who was ready to make a change.

Initiation

The initiation stage is the second step on the hero's journey. During the process of initiation, the hero is exposed to many trials and challenges that they must learn to overcome. This is achieved by following the guidance of their mentor, and by attempting to learn more about themselves (Allison, Goethals, & Kramer, 2011, 2017). Anthony's early work in reformation largely defines the initiation stage of her hero's journey. During that time, Anthony was learning how to hold her own, and though she did not realize it yet, was slowly being guided toward her true mission.

Anthony's first public speech was in 1849 for a temperance group. Though she found the issue to be of importance, Anthony was frustrated by the lack of a role she could play because of her sex. This was especially frustrating because temperance was not solely a male issue. In fact, many would argue that during Anthony's time temperance was a largely female issue. This is because alcohol often led to destruction in the home and even domestic abuse of wives and children by their alcoholic husbands. Thus, it was surprising and upsetting to Susan that on many occasions when she was speaking at different temperance meetings she received backlash from men in the group who believed they were the ones who should be taking actual action. This was also not something that Susan was used to. As a child, Susan was exposed to women being a welcome part of discussion during church meetings, and now Susan was relegated to choosing between being an audience member at larger temperance movement meetings, or solely being allowed to share her ideas during the Daughters of Temperance meetings where it seemed unlikely that she and the other women could actually help to produce change (Lutz, 1959).

Susan Anthony wanted more, though; she wanted to be able to express her ideas openly, and to be able to participate in reform movements on the national scale. This was simply not something she felt she could accomplish anymore while working only on issues like temperance and antislavery movements. Being a woman limited Anthony's ability to help fight for causes she was passionate about, and suddenly she realized she had a larger issue to fight for that she could play a much larger role in: women's rights. It is important to note, though, that she would still remain semi-active in helping the causes of temperance and ending slavery in the future; however, Anthony would work with females who were supporters of those causes and worked to ensure that female groups could spark a change. Anthony no longer focused on the men who believed they were superior to her while working in activism, but rather worked to establish herself, and the other females who worked with her, as equals in the fight.

Though Anthony's transformation will be more of a focus in later sections, it is important to note that this is where Susan's motivational transformation occurs (Allison & Goethals, 2016, 2017). The moment when she decided to focus her energy on female rights and working with women so she could be more active in making a change is when Susan B. Anthony truly transformed. This transformation was essential to helping Anthony complete her journey and become a full-fledged hero.

Around the same time Anthony was considering pursuing a fight solely focused on women's issues, she became inspired by the radical ideas of Elizabeth Cady Stanton. Though they ended up being partners and sharing a relationship that is more similar to that of two friends, Stanton is someone who fits the mold perfectly of a mentor when it comes to the hero's journey. The mentor's role is to help the hero to find their strengths and to help them use those strengths to achieve levels of greatness (Allison, Goethals, & Kramer, 2017). Anthony is perhaps best known for her work as a suffragette, and she particularly credited Stanton for being the one who led her to this work in the suffrage movement. In fact, the first organized demand for the right to vote for women came from Stanton at the Seneca Falls Convention in 1848. Susan was inspired by this seemingly radical ideal and was thus overjoyed when she got to meet Stanton in person later that year (Anthony, 1954).

It has been thought that the two only needed a single meeting to realize they were meant to form a sort of partnership. Many people later on tried to attack their partnership because it seemed that the two of them working together would make them an unstoppable pair and a formidable opponent to those who did not support their cause (Anthony, 1954). This, however, only further motivated the duo. Stanton would generate a lot of their ideas and turn them into speeches that Susan would then deliver. As a wife and mother of seven children, Stanton did not have the time or ability to travel and spread her message; as a result, Anthony became the one to give those speeches and rally support for their cause. Stanton even wrote in her Reminiscences that "[Susan] supplied facts and statistics, I the philosophy and rhetoric, and together, we have made arguments that have stood unshaken" (Anthony, 1954). In fact, they worked together so often that it even became commonly thought that Elizabeth spent more time with Susan than with any other adult, including her husband (Lutz, 1959). The forming of this partnership, and working with her mentor, proved to be one of the most important steps on Anthony's journey as it led to many remarkable future successes.

Return

The return stage is the final step on the hero's journey. The return stage is when the hero takes what they have learned and what they have gained from their experiences and use these experiences to help serve the greater good, and ultimately produce a boon for society (Allison, Goethals, & Kramer, 2017; Davis et al., 2011). This occurred for Anthony following the forming of her partnership with Elizabeth Cady Stanton. Then, Susan was fully ready to start dedicating herself to the women's movement. Together, they worked to create petitions, groups, and generate more support for their causes. All of these activities were important for allowing their movement to grow and become successful.

One of the most significant accomplishments of this heroic pairing was organizing the first national women's political organization, the Women's Loyal National League, in 1863. The original goal of the founding was to campaign for an amendment to the Constitution that would abolish slavery. In what was the largest petition of that time, the league was able to collect almost 400,000 signatures to abolish slavery (Anthony, 1954). This petition eventually played a crucial role in aiding the passing of the Thirteenth Amendment. Not only was this group doing incredible work for abolitionism, but it also helped to prove that women could play a critical role in the political world. Additionally, the work done by the Women's Loyal National League served to remind the public that if women were given the right to vote, they would be capable of assisting in creating an even greater amount of change. Stanton and Anthony also wanted the league to be able to allow new female leaders and activists to arise and help to expand the talent that would be available to help in the women's suffrage movement and the larger fight for female equality (Lutz, 1959).

Though this is just one example of the work that Stanton and Anthony accomplished together, it is a truly important one. It is also evident of the ways in which Anthony was able to create her legacy, to help spread her cause and charter change, and to inspire other women to rise up and join the fight. The stage of the return for any hero is meant to involve a great deal of sharing one's own experience and using that to help serve one's society and ultimately help aid in the formation of a greater good (Allison & Goethals, 2011, 2014; Allison, Goethals, & Kramer, 2017). This is definitely something Susan B. Anthony accomplished in the later years of her work, and something that even continued to occur following her passing when women and others would act in the name of Anthony's legacy.

Transformation

Transformations are an essential part of the hero's journey. These metamorphoses characterize the developmental growth of the hero. They help to promote healing, to develop social unity, to advance society, and to strengthen spiritual and cosmic understanding (Allison & Goethals, 2017; Allison & Setterberg, 2016). Heroes experience three types of transformation while on their journeys: they experience a transformation of their surroundings in the departure stage, a transformation of themselves caused by either an internal or external force, and a transformation of society during the return stage. The personal transformation of the self is the most important transformative event during the hero's journey. It enables the hero to successfully complete their mission. The untransformed hero is missing an important dispositional quality that they desperately need to accomplish their heroic mission (Allison & Goethals, 2016, 2017; Worthington & Allison, 2018). It is once they are transformed that heroes truly have their largest effect on the world and can be of greatest use to those around them.

Anthony's Transformation

Susan B. Anthony's individual transformation is atypical for a hero. When we think of someone being heroically transformed, they think of the hero gaining one or more heroic traits they had been missing. The acquisition of these traits then helps the hero achieve her heroic mission in life. While this is the narrative of many heroes, this does not characterize the life of Susan B. Anthony was not lacking in any of the Great Eight Traits of heroes as identified by Allison and Goethals (2011). Anthony had lived her whole life as a smart, strong, selfless, caring, charismatic, resilient, reliable, and inspiring person. From the early years of her life, Anthony had obtained these attributes and learned what she did not already have from being around her family and from the influences of Quakerism. Thus, her transformation did not precede her heroism; rather, it followed her heroism (Bronk & Riches, 2017). Her heroic actions did not result from a heroic transformation but rather had a transformative effect on her, instilling her life journey with a clear direction and purpose.

Anthony thus underwent a motivational transformation, which occurs when pivotal events in one's own life alters one's calling and mission (Allison & Goethals, 2017). Anthony had always had a calling to the world of activism and dedicating herself to causes she believed in. Anthony's specific motivations were transformed, however, once she saw how little the female role was valued in many of the movements that she was a part of. She did not simply want to help serve men in changing the world, but rather, Anthony wanted to be the driving force behind the change that was happening.

Susan saw no reason why this direction was something she could not pursue, but society had plenty of reasons. Society's gender roles and mandates for women were getting in the way of Susan pursuing her passion, and thus Anthony's motivations became helping women achieve equality while still working on reform. Further, Anthony was able to see that this goal was achievable once she started hearing about the radical ideas of her soon-to-be mentor, Elizabeth Cady Stanton. Though this transformation seems somewhat slight, if Anthony had not switched her motivations to women's equality, she would not have been able to make as much of a difference. Even if Anthony had continued working on reform, the work that she would have accomplished would have been constantly overshadowed by the work of her male counterparts, and therefore might have gone completely unrecognized.

Society's Transformation

Susan B. Anthony's transformation is particularly notable because it served as a catalyst for society to transform as well. Anthony's new focus on women's issues inspired the burgeoning feminist movement, and ultimately is the reason why women today can participate equally in society and can enjoy the same rights and privileges as men. The most striking example of women's equality is the Nineteenth Amendment to the United States Constitution, commonly referred to as the Anthony Amendment. Though the Amendment was passed in 1920, fourteen years after Anthony's death, it blossomed from the work of Susan B. Antony. In fact, in 1878, Anthony and Stanton had arranged for Congress to be presented with an amendment that would give women the right to vote. This is what laid the groundwork for the actual writing in the amendment and its eventual unanimous passing.

The work Susan B. Anthony was able to accomplish is a clear example of a positive transformative movement. Positive transformative movements are ones that help to stimulate and promote social unity and healthy growth (Allison & Goethals, 2016, 2017). Susan B. Anthony's individual transformation led into the feminist movement, and ultimately promoted social unity in the United States between men and women. This is also an example of how a transformation can involve a change from being egocentric, focused on the self, to becoming sociocentric, focused on society (Allison & Goethals, 2013, 2017). This is truly remarkable; Susan B. Anthony was able to use her transformation to help bring about dramatic change to an entire culture. Additionally, she carved out a legacy ensuring that women would always be able to find their place in our world even after Antony was no longer able to be a direct participant in these efforts.

CONCLUSION

Susan B. Anthony is one of the most influential heroes in US history. Her work to ensure that women were seen as equal to men, her work to promote the idea of women's suffrage, and the other remarkable efforts she made in the temperance and abolitionist movements, represent just some of the reasons why Anthony is and always should be a celebrated heroic figure.

Anthony's individual transformation over the course of her own hero's journey is what helped to give rise to the feminist movement, and it helped to transform an entire society's way of thinking with the eventual passing of the Nineteenth Amendment. However, this is not to say that the issue of gender equality has been completely solved. In fact, we are still working to address some of the problems that Anthony was addressing in her lifetime. One pivotal event that reignited Anthony's passion for activism was the observation she had while working at the Canajahorie Academy. Anthony became aware that male employees were making more money than female employees for the same job (Barry, 1998). This was an issue Susan noticed in 1846, and sadly, it is still an issue almost 200 years later. Women working full time in the United States are paid only eighty cents for every dollar paid to men. For women of color, this wage gap is even larger.

This issue, and the many others facing women, desperately need addressing and require heroes to emerge to do the work necessary to make needed changes happen. Learning about Susan B. Anthony and hearing the stories of other heroes and champions of social issues would help motivate more individuals to become involved in fixing society's shortcomings. For this reason, we should continue to let Susan B. Anthony's own heroic transformation continue to inspire us and lead us to creating more positive changes for society.

REFERENCES

Allison, S. T., & Goethals, G. R. (2011). Heroes: What they do and why we need them. New York: Oxford University Press.

Allison, S. T., & Goethals, G. R. (2013). Heroic leadership: An influence taxonomy of 100 exceptional individuals. New York: Routledge.

Allison, S. T., & Goethals, G. R. (2014). "Now he belongs to the ages": The heroic leadership dynamic and deep narratives of greatness. In Goethals, G. R., et al. (Eds.), Conceptions of leadership: Enduring ideas and emerging insights. New York: Palgrave Macmillan.

Allison, S. T., & Goethals, G. R. (2016). Hero worship: The elevation of the human spirit. Journal for the Theory of Social Behaviour, 46, 187-210.

Allison, S. T., & Goethals, G. R. (2017). The hero's transformation. In S. T. Allison, G. R. Goethals, & R. M. Kramer (Eds.), Handbook of heroism and heroic leadership. New York: Routledge.

Allison, S. T., Goethals, G. R., & Kramer, R. M. (2017). Setting the scene: The rise and coalescence of heroism science. In S. T. Allison, G. R. Goethals, & R. M. Kramer (Eds.), Handbook of heroism and heroic leadership. New York: Routledge.

Allison, S. T., Goethals, G. R., & Kramer, R. M. (Eds.) (2017). Handbook of heroism and heroic leadership. New York: Routledge.

Allison, S. T., & Setterberg, G. C. (2016). Suffering and sacrifice: Individual and collective benefits, and implications for leadership. In S. T. Allison, C. T. Kocher, & G. R. Goethals (Eds), Frontiers in spiritual leadership: Discovering the better angels of our nature. New York: Palgrave Macmillan.

Anthony, K. (1954) Susan B. Anthony: Her Personal History and Her Era. Garden City, New York: Doubleday & Company, Inc.

Beggan, J. K., & Allison, S. T. (Eds.) (2018). Leadership and sexuality: Power, principles, and processes. Northampton, MA: Edward Elgar.

Barry, K. (1998) Susan B. Anthony: A Biography of a Singular Feminist. Pennsylvania: Ballanstine Books.

Davis, J. L., Burnette, J. L., Allison, S. T., & Stone, H. (2011). Against the odds: Academic underdogs benefit from incremental theories. Social Psychology of Education, 14, 331-346.

Dik, B.J., O'Connor, W., & Shimizu, A.B. (2017). Career development and sense of calling. In S.T. Allison, G.T. Goethals, & R.M. Kramer (Eds.), Handbook of heroism and heroic leadership. New York: Routeledge

Doig, L. (2008). Anthony, Susan B. In The Oxford Encyclopedia of Women in World History: Oxford University Press. Retrieved from http://www.oxfordreference.com/view/10.1093/acref/9780195148909.001.0001/acref-9780195148909-e-49.

Door, R. (1928) Susan B. Anthony: The Woman Who Changed the Mind of A Nation. New York: Frederick A. Stokes Company

Enix-Ross, D. (2013). Susan B. Anthony is convicted for casting a ballot. ABA Journal, 99(11),1.

Gray, K., Anderson, S., Doyle, C. M., Hester, N., Schmitt, P., Vonasch, A., Allison, S. T., and Jackson, J. C. (2018). To be immortal, do good or evil. Personality and Social Psychology Bulletin.

Lutz, A (1959). Susan B. Anthony: Rebel. Crusader. Humanitarian. Boston, Massachusetts: Beacon Press.

Society of Friends. (2017). In Encyclopædia Britannica. Retrieved from http://school.eb.com/levels/high/article/Society-of-Friends/109452

Worthington, E. L, & Allison, S. T. (2018). Heroic humility: What the science of humility can say to people raised on self-focus. Washington. DC: American Psychological Association.

Section 4: Entertainment Heroes

19

MUHAMMAD ALI:
HANDS OF STONE, HEART OF GOLD

EVAN B. SHINE

"Why can't I be rich?" asked a young Cassius Clay to his father, who casually gestured at the color of his skin and replied, "Look there. That's why you can't be rich."

It was the late 1940s in the West End of Louisville, Kentucky. A place where segregation controlled daily life to the point where the highest aspirations African Americans had were to become maids, clergyman, or segregated school teachers. Everybody in the West End had dreams, but few ever came to fruition until Clay's parents bought him his "wheels" when he was 12. A glistening red $60 Schwinn bicycle, it was all that Clay had ever wanted growing up as a kid. When Clay found out that his dream bicycle had been stolen at the county fair, he ran with tears streaming down his face to the nearest police offer, Joe Martin, and told him "If I find the kid who stole my bike, I'll whup him." Martin responded, saying that Clay should learn to box before attempting to avenge his stolen bike, and offered to let him join a boxing class he instructed at the local gym. Clay took him up on his offer and six weeks later he got in the ring with a white boy, and defeated him. He never got his bike back, but the feeling he received from his victory in the ring that day assured him that boxing was his life's passion (Thimmesch & Parmiter, 1963).

The purpose of this chapter is to shed light on the life of the late Cassius Marcellus Clay, otherwise known as Muhammad Ali. My goal with this chapter is to elucidate the heroic transformations that Ali underwent in order to become an exalted hero in the sporting realm, and then later in the global realm. No other athlete in history has created as an enduring a legacy as Ali. His legendary status can be explained by the many heroic traits that he came to acquire during his heroic transformation. Ali was not only an icon, but a role model, leader, and inspiration to people of all ethnicities in a time where racial equality was nearly nonexistent.

BEGINNINGS

On January 17, 1942, Cassius Marcellus Clay was born to Cassius Marcellus Clay Sr. and Odessa Grady Clay in Louisville, Kentucky. Clay Sr. Worked as a sign and billboard painter, while Odessa Clay occasionally worked as a household domestic. Clay saw the struggle his parents underwent in order to provide basic necessities for his family, and he vowed that he would be the change that they needed. Clay's ambitions towards escaping the societal structures that were imposed on his family and race is demonstrated when he said, "I'm gonna drive down Walnut Street in a Caddy on Derby Day. And the people will say, 'There goes Cassius Clay.' Pretty girls will be there, and I'll smell the flowers and feel the nice warm night air. Oh, I'm cool then, man. I'm cool. The girls are looking at me, and I'm looking away. I'm wanting to know them worse than they want to know me -- only they don't know it." This quote comes from Clay when he was 21, and on the verge of becoming the world heavyweight champion. This future he's idealized for himself was inconceiva-ble for a man of color during the 1950s and 60s, but

Clay knew that he had what it took to achieve this goal (Thimmesch & Parmiter, 1963).

Clay's first step towards giving himself and his family a better life occurred while he competed at the Olympic World Trials in San Francisco. Clay hesitantly boarded the plane to San Francisco and was unnerved when turbulence occurred. After winning the trials he threw away his plane ticket, borrowed money from a referee, and took a train back to Kentucky. Joe Martin, his trainer, had to convince Clay to take a plane to Rome to compete for the gold medal at the Olympics. Martin gave him an ultimatum when he said, "You'll have to gamble your life, your whole future depends on this one plane ride to Rome. You'll have to gamble your life." Clay conquered his fear of flying due to his trust in his mentor Martin, and took the plane to Rome, giving him the chance to achieve true fame and glory (Thimmesch & Parmiter, 1963).

THE HERO'S JOURNEY OF ALI

Joseph Campbell (1949) described the hero monomyth as consisting of three parts: departure, initi-ation, and return. His hero journey is based the concept of heroic archetypes, which are abundant in mythological tales from around the world. Campbell's idea of the hero monomyth can shed im-portant light on many elements of Ali's heroic journey.

Departure

The departure phase refers to the forces that propel the hero forward on his pathway toward hero-ism (Campbell, 1949). For Ali, this departure could be the moment his bicycle stolen when he was 12. Had his bicycle never been stolen, Ali would not have met Joe Martin, his future trainer and mentor who introduced him to the sport of boxing. Campbell also assumes that the hero starts out incomplete in some manner. In Ali's case, this missing trait may have been humility or resilience. In the beginning of his heroic journey, Ali already possessed intelligence, strength, and charisma, but by the end of the journey it is clear that Ali possessed all of the heroic traits described in Alli-son and Goethals' (2011) "great eight" model of heroism. These traits are intelligence, strength, resilience, caring, charisma, selflessness, and inspiration (Allison &

Goethals, 2017). Consistent with Campbell's model, Ali cultivated these traits from his experiences during the ups and downs of his heroic journey.

Campbell also describes the importance of a good mentor who transforms the hero. In Ali's case, his trainer Joe Martin was an indispensable source of guidance and wisdom. Martin not only exposed Ali to the sport of boxing, but he guided him through the trials and tribulations of his early career. Leadership expert James McGregor Burns describes good mentors as "leaders in the classic sense; they help others discover their strengths and raise them to new levels of competence and morality" (Burns, 1978). Martin certainly guided Ali in this context. He helped Ali to become a hero both inside the ring and outside the ring. The values Martin instilled in Ali early in his career were evidenced in the choices Ali made later in his life, thus reinforcing the pivotal role that the mentor plays in the hero's journey (Allison & Smith, 2015).

Initiation

Initiation, as described by Campbell, refers to the challenges, obstacles, and foes that the hero must conquer in order to succeed (Campbell, 1949). As a boxer, Ali constantly faced challenges and opponents due to his career choice, but these were not the only challenges Ali had to face. Ali had to overcome both tangible and intangible foes to complete his hero's journey. Some of the intangible adversaries Ali had to overcome were race and social class. The tangible adversaries Ali had to defeat were his boxing opponents in the ring. Some of his most difficult challenges came from great fighters such as George Foreman, Sonny Liston, Ken Norton, Joe Frazier, and countless others. Some of these famous fights were the "Fight of the Century" against Frazier in 1971, the "Rumble in the Jungle" against Foreman in 1974, and the "Thrilla in Manilla" against Frazier in 1975 (History.com Staff, 2017). Without his 61 total professional fights, Ali would not have been exposed to the adversities that shaped him into the paragon of heroism that we know him to be today. Had Ali never faced hardships both in and out of the ring, the initiation facet of his heroic journey would have been incomplete.

Return

The final stage of Campbell's description of the hero's journey is the return, where the hero gives back to society after he has been transformed (Campbell,

1949). For Ali, this stage could be seen as the most significant part of his hero's journey. Some of the many heroic things Ali did later in his life were traveling the world to make charitable and humanitarian appearances, meeting with Saddam Hussein in 1990 to negotiate the release of Americans being held hostage, and traveling to Afghanistan in 2002 as a United Nations Messenger of Peace. Ali was named the "Sportsman of the Century" by Sports Illustrated, and he also lit the torch during the 1996 Summer Olympics in Atlanta. In 2005, he contributed 60 million dollars to build the Muhammad Ali Center, a nonprofit cultural center and museum in his hometown of Louisville, Kentucky. He was also awarded the Presidential Medal of Freedom in a ceremony at the White House in 2005 (History.com Staff, 2017). Ali received all of these accolades after he was diagnosed with a debilitating case of Parkin-son's syndrome in 1982. These extraordinarily selfless actions made Ali a true icon, the epitome of a hero, and a champion of the well-being of society (Efthimiou, Allison, & Franco, 2018).

PRE AND POST-TRANSFORMATION HEROIC CHARACTERISTICS

Allison and Goethals (2017), have identified three routes to heroic transformation. These are egocentricity to sociocentricity, dependency to autonomy, and stagnation to growth. While all three types of transformation have their merits, I believe that the concept of egocentricity to sociocentricity best summarizes Ali's personal transformation. A statement from Joseph Campbell in 1988 directly relates to the type of transformation that Muhammad Ali underwent. Campbell said, "when we quit thinking primarily about ourselves and our own self-preservation, we undergo a truly heroic transformation of consciousness" (Campbell, 1988).

Sociocentric Adaptation

Ali's change in consciousness and thought occurred in a very dramatic manner. Remarkably, Ali transformed from a charismatic loudmouth with a desire for material possessions into a social martyr who believed in generosity, tolerance, and open-mindedness. This mental switch was first ex-emplified when Ali became a member of the Nation of Islam in 1964; he was no longer Cassius Clay, he was Muhammad Ali. A year later while the Vietnam War was in full swing, Ali refused to serve based on his religious beliefs. Ali was arrested for draft evasion, his heavyweight belt was taken, and he was banned from the sport of boxing for four years. Most people predicted that this would mark the end of Ali's career and life, but Ali saw this event as an opportunity for growth. His recent transformation enabled him to accept his situation and make the best of it. For three years Ali traveled to college campuses across the country to spread his anti-war sentiments among students. In 1970, Ali's boxing license was reinstated and his conviction was revoked by the New York State Supreme Court. Ali made a resurgence in the boxing realm following his dropped conviction, but it was short lived. Ali retired after four years and directed his energy toward making the world a better place (History.com Staff, 2017).

Awakening

Allison and Goethals (2017) perfectly summarize the transformation that Ali underwent when they write, "the entire point of her hero journey is to awaken her to the larger, deeper task of thinking beyond herself, to developing communion with everyone and with everything" (Allison & Goethals, 2017). Ali's hero journey transformed him from a self-centered man to a global citizen who was willing to sacrifice everything for his beliefs. He made the nearly impossible transition from a dualistic mode of thinking to a nondualistic mode of thinking. Rohr (2011) sees the dualistic mind as being attached to the seven C's of delusion: "it compares, it competes, it conflicts, it conspires, it condemns, it cancels out any contrary evidence, and then it crucifies with impunity" (Rohr, 2011). This transition from a dualistic mode of thought to a nondualistic one enabled Ali to perform the heroic feats that he did. If Ali had not appreciated the complexity of the world around him he would have languished as a self-centered boxer driven by monetary desires.

TYPES OF TRANSFORMATION

Allison and Smith (2015) identified five different types of heroic transformation. These heroic transformations include moral, spiritual, emotional, intellectual, and physical transformations. These five types of significant change coincide with the personal growth and evolved thinking that occurs during the stages of Campbell's (1949) hero's journey. In the case of Muhammad Ali, all five of these heroic transformations are applicable to his journey.

Moral Transformation

Muhammad Ali's newfound sense of morality played a key component in his transformation to-ward heroism. Ali always had a sense of morality, but it wasn't until his religious transformation that it became a significant part of his personal conscience and self-identity. Following his conversion to Islam, Ali had a change in morality that was highlighted by his refusal to fight in the war Vietnam War, and he withstood all the infamy that accompanied this decision. Ali knew he would lose everything by committing to his pacifism, but his new sense of morality allowed him to stand by his convictions. This decision set the stage for a more significant change in Ali's motives. In Ali's circumstances, this change in motives was characterized by a shift from greed and fame to humanitarianism and magnanimity.

Emotional Transformation

Ali's emotional transformation distinctly shaped his acts of heroism. As a boxer, Ali faced signifi-cant adversity that enabled him to develop the key heroic traits of courage, resilience, and empathy (Allison & Smith, 2015). The traits of courage and resilience were not only shown in the majority of Ali's fights, but also in his decisions and actions during and after his career. Ali's high level of courage during his career was displayed in his decision to refuse to fight in the Vietnam War. Ali's courage and resilience following his career in boxing was demonstrated when Ali was diagnosed with Parkinson's syndrome in 1982. Much like the story of Franklin Roosevelt and his battle with polio, Ali persevered through this crippling syndrome to make a noteworthy impact on the world around him. Ali's heightened level of empathy can be seen primarily in his actions later in life. An example of this is seen in his donation of 60 million dollars to build a cultural center and museum with the purpose of educating people about open-mindedness, peace, and social equality (History. com Staff, 2017).

Spiritual Transformation

Allison and Smith's third type of transformation that a hero experiences focuses on spiritual transformation. Ali's spiritual transformation was perhaps most radical transformation that he under-went during his hero's journey (Allison & Smith, 2015). Ali's conversion to the faith of Islam sig-naled a drastic personal change. Prior to his conversion, Ali was spotted in the company of Mal-com X, a notorious Nation of Islam member. Days later it was confirmed that Cassius Marcellus Clay was now Muhammad Ali. This was shocking to not only the boxing world, but to society as a whole (History.com Staff, 2017). Ali's conversion to Islam was life changing due to the fact that it gave him a new perspective regarding his role in the greater world, leading to his impactful life after boxing.

Intellectual Transformation

Of all the transformations that Ali experienced during his heroic journey, his intellectual transformation was perhaps the most gradual and understated. Allison and Smith describe the intellectual transformation as "featuring a change in mental abilities or fundamental insights about the world." This was certainly the case for Ali. As a boxer Ali was never compelled to develop a strong intellect, but in his retirement he underwent a drastic change in his fundamental understanding of the world (Allison & Smith, 2015). By traveling the world on humanitarian missions, Ali gained per-spectives regarding the global political climate, as well as the injustices caused by racial inequality. Ali's transformation from a boxer to an intellectual global citizen can been seen in his actions later in life. Some of these include meeting with Saddam Hussein to discuss the release of American hostages, and traveling to Afghanistan in 2002 as a United Nations Messenger of Peace (History.com Staff, 2017). No other boxer in history has accomplished anything remotely close to Ali's achievements, and his actions clearly showcased the uniqueness and power of his intellectual trans-formation.

Physical Transformation

The last type of transformation identified by Allison and Smith (2015) centers on physical transformation. Ali underwent two types of physical transformation. The first physical metamorphosis occurred when Ali was a young boxer preparing for the first fights of his career. Ali relentlessly trained by hitting the speed bag, jumping rope, and shadowboxing in order to heighten his reflexes and hone his skills as a boxer. Allison and Smith also introduce the concept of physical transformation trig-gering moral transformations. This occurred in Ali's life when he was diagnosed with Parkinson's syndrome. Ali became more intellectually and morally enlightened due to his handicapped physical state (Allison

& Smith, 2015). This mental transformation aided Ali in his achievements that occurred later in his life outside of the boxing ring.

Heroes typically possess unique traits that differentiate themselves from the general population. The most common superficial traits that are associated with heroism are primarily physical traits. Superheroes who are depicted in popular mainstream movies exemplify the unrealistic physical expectations that we as a society have regarding heroes. Classical heroes such as Odysseus and Be-owulf are also examples of the quixotic view that mankind has towards traditional conceptions of heroes. In fact, the majority of individuals whom we associate with heroism do not tend to exhibit physical prowess. Examples of these types of heroes include Martin Luther King and Mahatma Gandhi. Muhammad Ali is unique in this respect because he displayed physical prowess that we associate with fictional superheroes and heroes of antiquity as well as the mental and emotional prowess that we associate with the majority of nonfictional heroes.

Physical Features

Evidence suggests that heroes are perceived as larger-than-life individuals who stand out from the crowd. Some heroes not only appear larger in a physical sense, but also in a metaphorical sense due to their fame and influence (Kinsella, Ritchie, & Igou, 2017). Ali fits both criteria described above. Thimmesch and Partmiter (1963) captured the sense of Ali being larger-than-life when they described his trip to the World Olympics in Rome, "There were times when people wondered if he was real. Crowds stopped to gawk at the tall, brown gladiator as he ambled along the Via Veneto, grinning, waving, talking to everybody whether they understood him or not" (Thimmesch & Par-miter, 1963).

Charismatic Features

One of Ali's most important qualities was his unparalleled charisma. Weber (1919) stated that ex-ceptional men are equipped with charisma. Weber refered to charisma as "a certain quality of an individual personality, by virtue of which he is set apart from ordinary men and treated as endowed with supernatural, superhuman, or at least specifically exceptional powers or qualities" (Weber, 1919). Even as a young child, Ali was a charismatic person, and his level of charisma was only amplified as he grew older and wiser. His ability to craft messages that resonated with people of all races, genders, and socioeconomic backgrounds can be interpreted as an otherworldly gift. After all, the word charisma stems from the Greek expression "divine gift from grace" (Riggio & Riggio, 2008). Ali's charisma showed through in his poetic nature as well. This can be seen in Ali's signature phrase "float like a butterfly, sting like a bee -- his hands can't hit what his eyes can't see."

CONCLUSION

In conclusion, Muhammad Ali was an extraordinary hero whose life accomplishments exemplified the pinnacle of heroic behavior. Ali possessed the many critical heroic traits that allowed him to have an impactful presence in both the world of boxing and in the world at large. Perhaps the most significant heroic traits that Ali possessed were morality, courage, charisma, and selflessness. Ali's heroism is especially compelling given the fact that he defied powerful societal institutions put in place to prevent his success, most especially racism.

In this chapter I have used the literature of heroism science to analyze what makes Muhammad Ali a hero, and to identify the steps and stages that comprised his transformation into a hero. Ali's journey embodied the three key aspects of Campbell's heroic monomyth: departure, initiation, and return. Ali's heroic journey was also shaped by his mentor, Joe Martin. Without Martin, Ali wouldn't have transformed into the beloved iconic figure he became during the second half of his life. Ali's journey also would not have been the same had he never endured the physical and emo-tional hardships of his boxing career and his diagnosis of Parkinson's syndrome later in life. Ali's heroic journey is one that will be remembered for centuries, and I am proud to have been able to offer insights into his development into such a heroic legend.

REFERENCES

Allison, S. T., & Goethals, G. R. (2011). Heroes: What they do and why we need them. New York: Oxford University Press.

Allison, S. T., & Goethals, G. R. (2017). The hero's transformation. In S. T. Allison, G. R. Goethals, & R. M. Kramer (Eds.), Handbook of heroism and heroic leadership. New York: Routledge.

Allison, S. T., & Smith, G. (2015). Reel heroes & villains. Richmond: Agile Writer Press.

Burns, J. M. (1978). Leadership. New York: Harper & Row.

Campbell, J. (1949). The hero with a thousand faces. New York: New World Library.

Campbell, J. (1988). The power of myth. New York: Anchor Books.

Efthimiou, O., Allison, S. T., & Franco, Z. E. (Eds.) (2018). Heroism and wellbeing in the 21st Century: Applied and emerging perspectives. New York: Routledge.

History.com Staff. (2009). Muhammad Ali. Retrieved October 2, 2017, from http://www.history.com/topics/black-history/muhammad-ali

Kinsella, E. L., Ritchie, T. D., & Igou, E. R. (2015a). Zeroing in on heroes: A prototype analysis of hero features. Journal of Personality and Social Psychology, 108, 114–127. doi: 10.1037/a0038463

Riggio, R. E., & Riggio, H. R. (2008). Social psychology and charismatic leadership. In C. L. Hoyt, G. R.Goethals, & D. R. Forsyth (eds), Leadership at the crossroads,Vol. 1: Leadership and Psychology (pp. 30–44). Westport, CT: Praeger.

Rohr, R. (2011). Falling upward. Hoboken, NJ: Jossey-Bass.

Thimmesch, N., & Parmiter, C. (1963, March 22). Muhammad Ali: The Dream. Time Magazine. Retrieved September 27, 2017, from http://time.com/3537815/muhammad-ali-dead-the-dream/

Weber, M. (2015/1919). Politics as Vocation. In T. Waters & D. Waters (eds), Weber's Rationalism (pp. 129–198). New York: Palgrave Macmillan.

20

ALEX MORGAN: THE HERO WHO CHANGED
THE SOCCER WORLD

EMILY R. WIGG

The sky had a warm glow as the sun was setting on a hot August day in 2013. The crowd was cheering, players were in high spirits, and optimism was soaring. It was about eight minutes into the start of the game when the whistle blew for a foul on Portland and a second whistle blew for a player down. At first it was not clear who was injured or how the injury occurred. But within seconds it was clear to all that the player down was Alex Morgan. Commentators could be heard discussing whether it was a knee or ankle injury, and then the replay showed it was a knee injury. In soccer there is always risk in attempting to steal a ball by reaching out with the left knee. Instead of contacting the ball, a player can get tripped by the opposing player causing the left knee to bend back and twist in one fluid motion. For Alex Morgan, the knowledge of what it meant to hear the sound of tearing in the knee was almost more painful than the injury itself. Where once there was cheering, there was now silence, followed by the applause as she was carried off the field on a stretcher. For some this might be the end, but not for a superstar like Alex Morgan. For her, this incident would become a small, short roadblock to overcome.

The purpose of this chapter is to demonstrate the many ways that Alex Morgan is a hero. Moreover, I will outline the ways that Morgan became a hero, focusing on the details of her heroic journey. In discussing her heroism, I will describe her heroic traits and how she developed them. My conclusion will focus on her inspirational qualities and on her powerful role as a mentor to family, team-mates, fans, and followers.

DEFINING A HERO

Who is Alex Morgan? Why is her journey exciting? What makes her so special? Why is she my hero? In today's culture and atmosphere, it is easy to forget what makes a hero. According to Allison, Goethals, and Kramer (2017), there are many different subtypes of heroes: impulsive, reflective, episodic, everyday, personal, cultural, proper, dark, transformed, untransformed, emergent, sustained, civil, martial, brave, and caring. According to Allison et al., social scientists have taken both subjective and objective approaches when defining a hero. The objective approach assumes that a hero will complete a noble action that serves the greater good and is beyond ordinary. Heroes must also make a significant sacrifice and be willing to take risks.

The subjective approach to defining heroism is based on people's perceptions of the hero. Allison and Goethals (2011) adopted a subjective approach by measuring traits that people see in a hero such as: intelligent, strong, reliable, selfless, resilient, charismatic, caring, and inspiring. Summing up all of these ideas, objective and subjective, Franco, Blau, and Zimbardo (2011) define heroism simply as, "the willingness to sacrifice or take risks on behalf of others in defense of a moral cause" (p. 13). When taking this definition into account, I believe Alex Morgan fits this description almost perfectly. In her career as a soccer player, Alex Morgan has achieved great feats and has been viewed as one of the greatest women soccer players in the world. Her greatness stems not only for her abilities and talent on the field but also for her humility and strength of character. Who, then, is Alex Morgan?

Alex Morgan was born on July 2, 1989, and by the age of 14 she was well on her way to making a name for herself in the soccer world. In high school, Alex Morgan was a three-time all-league pick NSCAA All-American. From high school she continued her soccer career in college where she led the Golden Bears of the University of California to the NCAA Tournament all four years she was enrolled. In 2008, at the age of 19, she became a member of the U.S. Women's National Soccer team and assisted in leading them to win the FIFA U-20 Women's World Cup International by scoring the winning goal in the final match against North Korea. The goal was actually named the Best Goal of the Tournament as well as the second-best Goal of the Year by FIFA. By 2009, at the age of 20, she became the youngest member of the U.S. Women's National Football Team.

In 2011, at age 22, Alex Morgan was the youngest player on the team, played in the 2011 FIFA World Cup International, and was the first overall pick in the 2011 Women's Professional Soccer Championship International. In 2012, at age 23, Alex Morgan had success in the U.S. Olympic Women's Soccer Team where she won her first Olympic Gold Medal by assisting her team in winning 2-1 against Japan. The 2012 Olympic Soccer game between the U.S and Japan was the largest soccer crowd in the Olympic history.

Alex Morgan as a Hero

When you examine Alex Morgan's accomplishments and consider the injuries and hurdles she has overcome, it is easy to think of her as almost superhuman. The Merriam-Webster definition of superhuman is "being above human; exceeding normal human power, size or capability." One must acknowledge that Alex Morgan is more of a hero than superhuman as she possesses more hero traits than superhuman traits of speed, strength, endurance. Heroism incorporates the superhuman traits of speed, strength, and endurance, but it goes a step further to include courage, humanity, justice, and moderation. From the large list of traits that Allison et al. (2017) and Kinsella, Ritchie, and Igou (2017) believe are descriptions of a hero, Alex Morgan possesses many of them. Morgan's traits include resilience, intelligence, selflessness, inspiring, bravery, courageous, determination, and compassion. They all combine to describe how Morgan has developed a nearly impeccable character. How an individual elevates her character and maximizes her life transcends her to the level of hero.

Character Strengths and Virtues

Christopher Peterson and Martin Seligman, in 2004 wrote the book *Character Strengths and Virtues* in an attempt to create a classification and measurement scale of positive traits in an "empirical and scientific" manner. In their writings, they describe six virtues that categorically represent 24 character strengths. Alex Morgan not only possesses many of the character traits from all six virtues but also has many traits from the Great Eight list of hero traits discovered by Allison and Goethals (2011).

Six Virtues and Heroic Character Traits of Alex Morgan

Wisdom and knowledge created out of love of learning, perspective, creativity, and curiosity have carried Alex Morgan through her life's journey. Courage born from bravery, persistence, honesty, and zest for life have helped to elevate Alex Morgan in the soccer world. Humility with love, kindness, and social intelligence have helped to make Alex Morgan a success off the field as well as an individual to be admired and respected for her on-the-field accomplishments (Worthington & Allison, 2018). Transcendence with hope, gratitude, humor, and spirituality have helped Alex Morgan face and overcome difficult challenges not only in her professional career but also in her personal life. Justice through teamwork, fairness, and leadership have made Alex Morgan a leader on and off the field. Last but not least, moderation with forgiveness, modesty, and self-control demonstrate Alex Morgan's ability to take life in stride, learn from mistakes, and move forward as a better person.

Alex Morgan Living the Virtues

After graduating from Diamond Bar High School, Alex Morgan graduated a semester early from the University of California, Berkeley with a degree political economy. Morgan has published a middle school book series entitled The Kicks, which has become a live-action comedy series on Amazon Prime. Morgan's book publisher stated that she "wanted her books to inspire young girls and celebrate her love of soccer." In describing the underlying purpose behind the book series, Morgan said, "Kids should take on the responsibility of a teammate and know that being on a team really builds character. It's about the experiences and having it help them later in life, not becoming a professional soccer player" (Morgan, 2015).

The love Alex Morgan has for her fans, especially girls, is inspiring and increases the respect others have of her. Alex Morgan shows respect toward her teammates both on and off the field. When asked about her relationship with the team, Alex Morgan says, "We spend more time with each other than we do with our families so in a way, we're sisters, and with sisters you all respect each other" (Morgan, 2015). The loving respect that Alex Morgan has for her teammates is displayed in the manner in which she treats them, respects them, and competes with them.

Alex Morgan plays as hard as she can and to the best of her ability, and yet she pushes herself for more because she knows that her teammates would do the same for her as well. Morgan inspires young girls and boys through multiple endorsement deals from clothing wear, food, electronics, banks, tires, insurance and health organizations, as well as being a brand ambassador for GNC, a health product company. In 2016 Alex Morgan joined UNICEF Kid Power as a Champion in order to fight global malnutrition and raise awareness among children. Morgan has appeared in magazines, television, and film. These are just a few of the professional accomplishments off the field that Alex Morgan has achieved in her young life; she also has many international, team, and individual awards for her accomplishments on the field.

With all these accolades, adoration, and fan worship, Alex Morgan has remained true to herself, her family, friends, and fans. In December of 2014, Morgan married Servando Carrasco, a soccer player she met in college. Morgan has remained a fierce competitor and devoted to soccer despite multiple knee, ankle, and concussion injuries sustained over the years. She competes hard knowing soccer is the sixth most dangerous sport among all the major sports. Research reveals that more than 22% of soccer players experience a significant injury during their careers (Morgan, 2015).

Morgan not only looks to better herself but those around her. In March of 2016, she and several teammates filed a complaint of wage discrimination against U.S. Soccer for inequities between compensation for women players and the men's national team. Morgan summed up the situation well when she was asked, "What inspires you to stay motivated when times get tough, as far as playing and travel-ing? I find my motivation from everyone who looks up to me and my teammates. From the little girls that look up to me and tell me they want to be like me when they grow up. Sometimes I don't want to get out of bed to do fitness. But I do get up and I have that's in effect why I'm here today" (Morgan, 2015). This desire to be a positive role model for girls no doubt explains, at least in part, why Morgan took the lead in fighting for wage equality with the men's national soccer team.

PEOPLE AND EVENTS THAT SHAPED ALEX MORGAN

In Alex Morgan's memoir, she talks about the support that she received from her parents and mentor. Alex Morgan began playing soccer at the age of five and recalls a conversation with her father when she was complaining about being tired. Alex Morgan stated that her father looked at her and said, "But you gotta work hard every day if you want to be the best. Well, you are the best, but you can be better." He continued: "Come on. We'll get ice cream from 7-Eleven after." Alex Morgan believes that it is important for parents to "push" kids into something "just not too much" and "in the right amount" so they will "naturally gravitate" towards something special. Morgan stated that her father provided this support and appropriate push, which is why she believes they have enjoyed such a great relationship.

At the age of eight, Alex Morgan wrote a note to her mother that simply stated, "Hi Mommy! My Name is Alex and I am going to be a professional Athlete for soccer! Always, Ali Cat". In her memoir, Morgan talks about the sacrifice of giving up so much along the way to become the best. Alex explained, "You just become so committed because you love the game so much." Morgan remarked with regard to the support from her parents, "My parents were very supportive and positive. My mom [Pam] was always the super positive, supporting parent and my dad was the thinker who wanted me to see how I could make myself better and help the team. But at the same time, he would listen to me when I said had enough. When my dad wanted to talk about soccer-specific stuff and I didn't want to hear it -- I would tell him and he'd listen. "I had a good balance and an honest relationship with my parents" (Morgan, 2015).

Abby Wambach

For Alex Morgan, veteran team member Abby Wambach has been a significant mentor for her throughout her national team career. Alex Morgan stated of her mentor Wambach, "it's great to be able to finally get this World Cup, for her, for this team, for this country. She's had the best career, and all she was waiting for was that World Cup title, and she got it. So it was pretty amazing to be on that ride with her."

Alex Morgan on Being Famous

According to Jeri Morgan, Alex Morgan's sister, Alex never wanted to be famous but with her success, she caught on very quickly. Jeri Morgan goes on to say that Alex Morgan works at relating to her fans by letting them know her on a personal side: that she lost her cat Brooklyn, is addicted to Candy Crush, Game of Thrones (her favorite character Daenerys), and Taylor Swift. Stephanie Rudnick, Brand Management and Communications Strategist, emphasizes how devoted Alex Morgan is to her fans: "At every Morgan event, throngs of young girls line up for hours not only to have Morgan sign a book or ball but to have her talk to them. She loves doing that; it's exciting to see. So many young girls drop out of soccer at an early age. To grow the sport you have to get them through that cycle."

Alex Morgan's Thoughts on Being a Mentor

Allison and Smith have argued that "good mentors equip the hero with what he/she needs, but there can also be bad mentors who steer the hero down a dark path of self-destruction (Allison & Smith, 2015)." Allison and Smith believe that mentors play a large role in forming and shaping a hero, as they do anyone. A mentor serves as almost an "advisor" to someone who needs some help or wants to be better. According to Richard Rohr (2014), mentors help heroes become transformed, and later, having succeeded on their journeys, these transformed heroes then assume the role of mentor for others who are at earlier stages of their quests." These ideas are consistent with Campbell's idea that mentors elevate the hero and prepare her for future mentoring duties (Campbell, 1949). When taking this principle into account, Alex Morgan has many mentors in her life that have impacted the person she is now.

While Abby Wambach was a huge mentor for Alex Morgan, it is also true that Morgan looked up to other female soccer players such as Mia Hamm, Brandi Chastain, and Kristine Lilly. Today, reflecting on how she admired these players, Alex Morgan states in her memoir, "it's a little weird to take a step back and think of myself in that way, but at the same time, we have such a big responsibility because so many young girls have such a big opportunity that 20 years ago they didn't have in sports. So I think that's important for me to show them that and help them spark that dream that I had because of these other players" (Morgan, 2015).

Alex Morgan, My Mentor

No matter what goal Alex Morgan sets for herself, she always tries to lead by example and be a positive mentor for others (Allison & Smith, 2015). Over the years she has made many statements that have impacted many young women's personal lives, choices, and priorities – including my own. These statements of Morgan's include the following:

"I want to keep improving, continue to help my teammates improve, make my teammates look good. Continue bringing something new to the game, never getting completely content and always trying to get better."

"Everybody has a talent, but it's what you do with that talent to make it great."

"Always work hard, never give up, and fight until the end because it's never really over until the whistle blows."

"It's great sometimes for parents to talk about the game with their kids. But I think parents sometimes overstep the boundaries and start acting like a coach... And right after a game is not the best time to talk about it."

The above are just a few quotes that have touched my life and the lives of count-less other young women. Learning more about Alex Morgan has shown me that obstacles, roadblocks, losses, and all the bad things in life, combined with the good things in life, help mold an individual into the person they are and the person they were meant to be. They do not define the person. As such, when life knocks us down, we get up, brush ourselves off and learn from the experience. When life is good and things are going our way, it is a time to savor and enjoy but we must stay grounded in our roots and beginnings. This is heroic humility (Worthington & Allison, 2018). Learning about Alex Morgan and her outlook and philosophies made me realize that being on a team is just that: a team, a family. Win or lose, it is the team that wins or loses, it is not one per person or one player that wins or loses the game, but the team.

CONCLUSION

According to Decter-Frain et al. (2017), a hero needs to have a group of follow-ers or supporters that elevate them (the hero) to a status of "superb individual". Decter-Frain also propose other principles and ideas regarding how a hero is created. Once such principle is that the followers or supporters actually create or "manufacture" the perception of moral heroism in ordinary individuals. It is interesting to contemplate whether Alex Morgan represents an example of the first principle, which asks whether she is a hero with followers or whether the followers elevate her to a status of moral heroism. In looking over Alex Morgan's life, it seems highly probable that she is truly a moral hero who has garnered a huge following of supporters.

According to U.S. Soccer, in 2016, the U.S. Women's National Soccer team had a total of 244,132 fans attend the team's 17 games both home and away in large part due to Alex Morgan. People gravitate toward Alex Morgan not just for her superior athletic abilities but for her humility and autonomy in always stay-ing true to her moral character and values. Alex Morgan's family instilled in her values of goodness, honesty, hard-work, and humility to name a few heroic traits. All these attributes helped build her character and serve as a guide for living her remarkable life. We see this in Morgan's interactions with her team, family, fans, and even those whose values and character are not as strong nor as true as hers.

Looking back at Alex Morgan's life, her injuries, obstacles, and setbacks, no one would have blamed her for becoming jaded and bitter or for giving up. Yet, Alex Morgan took each injury, obstacle, and setback in stride, all the while learning, growing, and continuing to move forward with her dreams and goals. Morgan continued to dream and strive to be a hero that young girls could look up to and emulate. Morgan is the hero who treats others the way she wishes to be treated, the hero who supports her team, family, friends, fans instead of breaking them down, the hero who works for the betterment of not only herself but of others through her charity work, books, and leadership.

Alex Morgan, for me, embodies heroic traits and meets the criteria of the classic hero. She is a role model to millions, including me, and her heroism is transcendent (Gray et al., 2018). As a freshman in college, facing not only the stress of adjusting to freedom from parents, rules, and curfews but the stress of learning time management, prioritization, finances as well as the stress of playing for a team sport, there have been times I wanted to walk away and leave it all behind. Learning about Alex Morgan's life, the fortitude she had and still has to always move forward in life with grace and dignity, inspires me to do the same. While Alex Morgan makes the process look so easy, I realize it is not. Without the support of family, friends, teammates, coaches, and fans standing behind Alex Morgan, she may well have had a different path. But heroes always find a way.

REFERENCES

Allison, S. T. (2015). The initiation of heroism science. Heroism Science, 1, 1-8.

Allison, S. T., & Goethals, G. R. (2017). The hero's transformation. In S. T. Allison, G. R. Goethals, & R. M. Kramer (Eds.), Handbook of heroism and heroic leadership. New York: Routledge.

Allison, S. T., Goethals, G. R., & Kramer, R. M. (2017). Setting the scene: The rise and coalescence of heroism science. In S. T. Allison, G. R. Goethals, & R. M. Kramer (Eds.), Handbook of heroism and heroic leadership. New York: Routledge.

Allison, S. T., Goethals, G. R., & Kramer, R. M. (Eds.) (2017). Handbook of heroism and heroic leadership. New York: Routledge.

Allison, S. T., & Smith, G. (2015). Reel heroes & villains. Richmond: Agile Writer Press.

Attendance. (n.d.). Retrieved October 06, 2017, from https://www.ussoccer.com/womens-national-team/records/attendance

Benioff, David.; Weiss, D.B. (Writers), & Sackheim, Daniel. (Director). (2016). Book of the Stranger [Television series episode]. In D. Benioff (Producer), Game of Thrones. New York: HBO Home Entertainment.

Campbell, J. (1949) The hero with a thousand faces. Princeton, NJ: Princeton University Press.

Chat with Alex Morgan. (n.d.). Retrieved October 06, 2017, from
    http://www.espn.com/sportsnation/chat/_/id/47920/us-soccer-alex-morgan

Davis, J. L., Burnette, J. L., Allison, S. T., & Stone, H. (2011). Against the odds: Academic
    underdogs benefit from incremental theories. Social Psychology of Education, 14, 331-346

Decter-Frain, A., Vanstone, R., & Frimer, J. A. (2017). Why and how groups create moral
    heroes. In S. T. Allison, G. R. Goethals, & R. M. Kramer (Eds.), Handbook of heroism and
    heroic leadership. New York: Routledge.

Gilberg, A. (2015, June 07). Alex Morgan's health is going to have a big impact on the World
    Cup. Retrieved October 06, 2017, from http://www.businessinsider.com/alex-morgan-
    injury-health-world-cup-2015-6

Gray, K., Anderson, S., Doyle, C. M., Hester, N., Schmitt, P., Vonasch, A., Allison, S. T., and
    Jackson, J. C. (2018). To be immortal, do good or evil. Personality and Social Psychology
    Bulletin.

Morgan, A. (2015), Breakaway: Beyond the goal, Simon and Schuster.

Mueller, T. D. (2017, April 12). Ranking Sports from Least to Most Dangerous: Includes NFL,
    NBA, NHL and Soccer. Retrieved October 06, 2017, from http://bleacherreport.com/
    articles/876512-ranking-sports-from-least-to-most-dangerous-including-nfl-nba-nhl-and-
    soccer

Top 14 quotes from Alex Morgan. (n.d.). Retrieved October 06, 2017, from
    http://www.azquotes.com/author/23258-Alex_Morgan

U.S. Women's Soccer Team Strikes Deal for Better Pay | Money. (n.d.). Retrieved October 06,
    2017, from http://time.com/money/4726656/u-s-womens-soccer-team-just-scored-a-huge-
    victory-in-the-fight-for-equal-pay/

Wahl, G. (n.d.). Bad news for USWNT: Morgan won't be ready for full-time duty early in World
    Cup. Retrieved October 06, 2017, from https://www.si.com/planet-futbol/2015/05/30/alex-
    morgan-knee-injury-uswnt-womens-world-cup-status

Worthington, E. L, & Allison, S. T. (2018). Heroic humility: What the science of humility can say
    to people raised on self-focus. Washington. DC: American Psychological Association.

21

THE HEROIC TRANSFORMATION OF AN ENTIRE TEAM: HOW THE SWEDISH WOMEN'S NATIONAL SOCCER TEAM BECAME HEROES

OLIVIA SJOEDIN

The atmosphere is heavy with chagrin and the grass field is damp with blood, sweat, and tears. There they stood – the Swedish Women's National Soccer Team had played the final in the Olympic Games of 2016 and it was one of the greatest achievements from the ladies' team in a long time. Nevertheless, history had repeated itself. Sweden had once again suffered a loss against mighty Germany, for the tenth time in a row. They had fought, struggled and yearned for the equalizer; they had climbed a mountain, only to be pushed back down again by the Hector of the soccer world. They said they lost a gold medal, but was that really everything that happened that night?

During the Summer Olympics of 2016, the SWNST (the Swedish Women's National Soccer Team) was considered to be one of the teams with an advantage. They were expected to play well and win games because of previous achievements and the level of skill their team possessed. In the final against Germany, the tables had turned and they were now the underdogs in the game. Despite losing in the finals, many people identified with them because in the SWNST's struggles they could see their own suffering, which is at the core of Vandello, Goldschmied, and Michniewicz's (2017) thesis about how underdogs emerge as heroic entities.

In this case, the reasons why people related to the underdog status of the SWNST probably resides within the thrill of the unexpected. The Swedish team scoring an equalizer would have been against the odds, but it is probable that most people would have cheered for them to score for the game to continue, prolong the experience, and make it more exciting. If they were to have scored an equalizer, they would have been praised for making a heroic effort in keeping the game alive despite the odds being deeply against them. Moreover, if they would have won, they would without hesitation have been considered a team of heroines by the entire Swedish population. The main purpose of this chapter is to analyze, define, and demonstrate what actually makes the Swedish Women's National Soccer Team a group of heroines.

Overview of the SWNST

The first official women's soccer games were played in Sweden, most of which were exhibition games, in the early 1900s (Riksidrottsmuséet, The Swedish Athletic Museum, 2016). However, at that time, women's soccer was denounced and their matches were considered to be ridiculous and petty. These exhibition games they played often had the character of being jesting events where "lads" were posed against "slim girls". In 1973, the SWNST played their first international game in history, and interest would come to increase drastically in 1984 when Sweden won gold medal in the European Championship (Swedish Football Association, 2018).

In 2014, about 150,000 of Sweden's total of 500,000 active soccer players were women, accounting for 30% of Sweden's total of active players. Consequently, soccer was the second most popular sport for women in Sweden, after track and field, which then had about 225,000 active women (The Swedish Sports Confederation, 2018).

Hedvig Lindahl: The Key Hero

One of the key players of the current team is both famed and criticized goal-keeper Hedvig Lindahl. Born in 1983, she is old enough to have spent her entire life following the SWNST's journey from the beginning of their recognition to the present day (Union of European Football Associations [UEFA], 2017). Lindahl appeared in a few matches with the national youth teams, but she made her big breakthrough in the women's national team, which is where she has contributed to the heroine's path to success and heroism (The Swedish Football Association, 2018).

Lindahl wasn't necessarily part of the team's heroic departure, but she has unquestionably been a part of the initiation. She has endured their trials of being under-resourced, as well as being criticized by the media and the fans and being publicly ridiculed. She has had a mentor in the form of legendary Swedish female goalkeeper Elisabeth Leidinge, who took Lindahl under her wings and coached her through her experience with the Swedish youth national team. She has also been a mentor to up-and-coming goalkeeper prodigy Hilda Carlén in the SWNST who is poised to be the one to continue Lindahl's legacy as her successor. Moreover, she has acquired knowledge, wisdom, and new skills with this team throughout these challenges they have faced together (Allison, Goethals & Kramer, 2017).

Experiences with Criticism

In an interview with a respected Swedish sports-site, Lindahl revealed her struggles and the challenges she has faced: "It really was like that [headlines about the smallest things] for a while. People around me would come up and tell me that how I was being treated [by the media] wasn't acceptable. How they are treating you in comparison to your competitors. You can't do anything without having them criticizing you" (Football Channel, 2016). The same interview tells us how during the World Cup 2007 and the World Cup 2011, there was a great deal of criticism aimed at Lindahl.

This difficult time can be recognized as the second phase of initiation in Campbell's (1949) monomyth of the hero. During this initiation stage, Lindahl faced challenges and obstacles that she was compelled to overcome to further advance in her journey toward transforming into a heroine (Allison, Goethals & Kramer, 2017). These trials were at their worst fall in 2012 after the Olympics in London; she considered quitting because of the stress and criticism from others. "It was tough. 2012 was really tough. This led to an injury in my cruciate ligament that same fall. I played very stressed throughout the Olympics and played very stressed in qualifying matches with the national team. [I] felt the competition, and everyone wanted others to play so I became ill when I got back to the club team because I had pushed myself so much. I did not take good care of myself. It was not a good time" (Lindahl, 2016).

Lindahl also explained how close she was to quitting the sport altogether because of the lack of income and lengthy commuting in combination with all the criticism she was receiving. In response to that, she went to see a sports psychologist and then realized that she only played soccer because she thinks it is fun, and not for the fame, fortune, or money. Ultimately, Lindahl went on to participate as a third goalkeeper in the European Championship in Sweden 2013 and then reclaimed her place as first goalkeeper in the World Cup in Canada.

The SWNST's heroic journey has been an involuntary one and they may not follow the monomyth of Campbell's hero (1949) to perfection, but their story is an important one because it is actively changing both Sweden and the world of soccer. The heroic transformation they are undergoing is advancing society by inspiring and guiding us all through our own transformations. Lindahl is a strong, enlightened leader on the team and has helped transform others. A prominent example of Lindahl's impact is seen in the positive influence that she has on the people around her, such as young goalkeeper and SWNST colleague Hilda Carlén. Lindahl has also been an inspiring source for even younger, mainly female but also male goalkeepers, and others who have struggled with public criticism (The Swedish Football Association, 2018).

The Monomyth of the Hero

Consistent with Campbell's (1949) description of the hero's journey in his groundbreaking book, "The Hero with a Thousand Faces", the SWNST's journey was centered on the players' willingness to make sacrifices and commit to something larger than themselves. The players might not have realized it at first, but that is what was required of them and they stepped up to the challenge. They have committed not only to the team of the greatest female soccer players in Sweden, which itself is a challenge, but they have also committed to developing something greater, which in this case is the battle for equality in a patriarchal society.

Recently, Denmark's Women's National Soccer Team protested against the salary differences between the men's and women's team in order for them to get their compensation demands heard from the federation. The did not have any success, However, the Norwegian Soccer Women's Nation Soccer Team took the initiative and fought for equal pay with the men's team. In an act of self-sacrifice, the Norwegian Men's National Soccer Team rejected a portion of their pay so that by 2018 both Norwegian national teams enjoyed equal wages (Svenska Dagbladet [SvD, The Swedish Daily Newspaper], 2017).

Motivation

As mentioned earlier, the SWNST's journey involving the fight for equal salaries was involuntary and perhaps not intended to become what it has become. The team suffered, fought, and endured their challenges; but most importantly, throughout all of this they had love – that is, love for one another and love for their sport. Every person on their roster has followed their bliss (Campbell, 1988), and their love for soccer rose above almost any other source of motivation. Unlike the Swedish Men's National Team, the women's salary is so small that it could not truly serve as much source of motivation. All they have was their love for the sport, which itself can be inspirational to many, and they are the underdogs in this unfair and unequal position (Vandello et al., 2017). Even though succumbing to this unfairness seems like an easy way out, they have chosen to feed from it and fight it, which is an important heroic quality.

Most players on the SWNST probably do not even consider themselves heroines, making their motivations purely genuine heroically humble (Worthington

& Allison, 2018). Soccer players generally have both inner and outer motivations; inner motivations could consist of the will to perform well and to prove something to yourself, while outer motivations could be invisible, such as wanting to make your family proud and wanting to win a tournament. The heroic traits in these players shine through when needed, and their motivations will not change until gender equality is established.

Types of heroic transformation

The main type of transformation that the SWNST has gone through is a suffering transformation (Allison & Setterberg, 2016). Historically, women have been the underdogs in most societies around the world. When the very first women's soccer games were played in Sweden, they were at first considered petty and timid because they were compared to how men's soccer was played. They had to endure these exhibition games where no one took them seriously; they were considered to be these "slim girls" who would play against the big guys, and no one expected them to enjoy success because to the public it was just condescending entertainment. Furthermore, since women soccer players have suffered and through love and compassion for the sport, they have changed the way society views them and gained their respect because today, soccer is the biggest sport for both sexes in Sweden (The Swedish Sports Confederation, 2016).

The Great Eight Hero Attributes

What the SWNST has gained from this type of heroic transformation is a few of the Great Eight hero attributes; they have at least five of the eight characteristics of a great hero (Allison & Goethals, 2017; Allison, Goethals, & Kramer, 2017):

- Strength; they are strong, leading, dominating and courageous while on the field, as well as being courageous and strong when being faced with the inequalities of being female soccer players.

- Selflessness; to become a unified team, they need to be moral, humble, altruistic, and sociocentric, which are qualities they have acquired during their hero's journey.

- Caring; they are caring and compassionate towards one another, and they are also kind, humble, and empathetic. These traits help them be open and straightforward when communicating because they expect each other to be caring and empathetic.

- Resilience; while competing on the field, they are mentally determined to achieve their goals and perform well, and they are as persevering and as accomplished as they can possibly be (Davis et al. 2011)..

- Inspiration; they are inspiring, admirable, and a motivation to not only each other but also to many young soccer players who might already perceive them as their heroes.

Pathway to Transformation

The SWNST's primary pathway to transformation has been the arc from ego-centricity to sociocentricity. When a member of a high quality soccer team, players need to develop a consciousness of the self in combination with a selfless, heroic mindset in order to work for the good of the team (Allison & Goethals, 2017). Sociocentricity is a quality that players partly evolve as they are being socialized at a young age, but it can continue to be developed to the point where you see yourself, the people around you, and the world itself as one great unit (p. 392). In this case, every player in the SWNST must become self-aware as well as aware their own tendencies to unify the team as one. Unity is key when playing soccer, both in a sense of team spirit but it also encourages effective communication on and off the field.

EMP Model of Hero Functions

Referring back to the monomyth of the hero, the return of our heroines leaves them with a function to fill with regarding to helping, inspiring, and guiding the rest of society. The EMP model has been proposed to explain the functions of heroism, with EMP referring to enhancing, moral modeling, and protection (Kinsella et al., 2017). The SWNST best embodies the enhancing aspect of this model.

The players on the SWNST fulfill the enhancing function because they are a source of motivation to many young, aspiring soccer players. They are role models to them, they inspire them, and some players on the team instill hope because of their unique backgrounds and their own personal journeys. In their role as heroines, they have guided other people into believing in something bigger than themselves, which is exactly what the SWNST did when faced with a challenge or a struggle. When they win a game, people experience positive feelings because they feel as if they are a part of the accomplishment since it is the national team of Sweden. They might even be a source of motivation to someone, preferably a soccer player, to become the best version of themselves that they could possibly be.

CONCLUSION

Ths chapter has reviewed the causes, explanations, and motivations of the Swedish Women's National Soccer Team on their journey toward becoming inspiring heroines. The thesis of this chapter is supported because their journey was involuntary; they became part of something bigger than themselves; they suffered significantly; and they fought and endured their challenges as a team. Throughout their journey they demonstrated the admirable trait of love -- love for one another, and love for their sport. They also inspired many people because the team has been seen as the underdogs, as they have been less resourced than men's soccer teams who are essentially performing the same tasks. Although succumbing to this unfairness would be an easy way out, they have chosen to feed from it and do what it takes to make much-needed changes. Doing the right thing no matter the costs is an important, heroic quality.

The heroic journey of the SWSNT started almost a century ago, and the team that represents Sweden's women's soccer today were not there from the beginning of that journey. In fact, they were not even yet born. They are benefiting from the fruits of the labors that their preceding female soccer players reaped for them – although the fruit might not be enough for now, we can be sure that bigger harvests will come in the future assuming the course of female soccer in Sweden continues to progress in the way it is going.

The day will come when an Olympic silver medal in soccer is something to be proud of, but it was difficult for the SWNST to believe that as they stood on the damp grass field with blood, sweat and tears. It hurts when tears fall from the eyes of the fighters – you identify with their struggle and loss. Their fingers trembled as they felt a silver medal hanging wistfully around their throats, glittering more in the eyes than the medals. Their souls burned with disappointment, bitterness, anger, and sorrow – but they were far from losers. They may have lost a gold medal, but to the Swedish public, they were brave fighters who had won a silver because beaten heroes are also heroes. Certainly, it can be debated whether silver medalists are heroines, and this chapter has argued that there are many reasons why they are heroic. After all, the opinion of heroism always lies in the eye of the beholder.

REFERENCES

Allison, S. T., & Goethals, G. R. (2017). The hero's transformation. In S. T. Allison, G. R. Goethals, & R. M. Kramer (Eds.), Handbook of heroism and heroic leadership. New York: Routledge.

Allison, S. T., Goethals, G. R., & Kramer, R. M. (2017). Setting the scene: The rise and coalescence of heroism science. In S. T. Allison, G. R. Goethals, & R. M. Kramer (Eds.), Handbook of heroism and heroic leadership. New York: Routledge.

Allison, S. T., & Setterberg, G. C. (2016). Suffering and sacrifice: Individual and collective benefits, and implications for leadership. In S. T. Allison, C. T. Kocher, & G. R. Goethals (Eds), Frontiers in spiritual leadership: Discovering the better angels of our nature. New York: Palgrave Macmillan.

Campbell, J. (1949). The Hero with a Thousand Faces. New York: Pantheon Books.

Davis, J. L., Burnette, J. L., Allison, S. T., & Stone, H. (2011). Against the odds: Academic underdogs benefit from incremental theories. Social Psychology of Education, 14, 331-346.

Goethals, G. R., & Allison, S. T. (2014). Kings and charisma, Lincoln and leadership: An evolutionary perspective. In Goethals, G. R., et al. (Eds.), Conceptions of leadership: Enduring ideas and emerging insights. New York: Palgrave Macmillan.

Goethals, G. R., & Allison, S. T. (2019) The Romance of heroism: Ambiguity, attribution, and apotheosis. West Yorkshire: Emerald.

Kinsella, E. L., Igou, Eric R., & Ritchie, Timothy D. (2017). Attributes and Applications of Heroes. In Handbook of Heroism and Heroic Leadership (p. 19-35.). New York: Routledge.

Lindahl, Hedvig for the Swedish website "Football Channel" (2016). Lindahl var nära lägga av efter kritiken: "Alla ville att andra skulle spela" (Lindahl was close to quitting after criticism: "Everyone wanted others to play"), by Lundh, Olof. Retrieved from: https://www.fotbollskanalen.se/lundhs-podcast/lindahl-var-nara-lagga-av-efter-kritiken-alla-ville-att-andra-skulle-spela/

The Swedish Football Association (2018). Sveriges motståndare 1973-2016 (Sweden's competitors 1973-2016). Retrieved from: http://do1.fogis.se/svenskfotboll.se/ImageVault/Images/id_1048/scope_0/ImageVaultHandler.aspx161025114306-uq

The Swedish Sports Confederation (2018). Idrotten i siffror: Svensk idrott i samhället (Sports in numbers: Swedish sports in society). Retrieved from: http://www.rf.se/globalassets/riksidrottsforbundet/dokument/dokumentbank/ovrigt/idrotten-i-siffror-2015.pdf

The Swedish Football Association (1904). "Landslagsdatabasen" (The National Team Data Base). (n.d.). Retrieved from: http://svenskfotboll.se/landslag/landslagsdatabas/landslagsspelare/?fplid=99995

Riksidrottsmuséet (The Swedish Athletic Museum). (2016). Damfotbollens historia (The History of Female Soccer). Retrieved from: http://www.riksidrottsmuseet.se/Utstallningar/Tidigareutstallningar/RiksidrottsmuseetpaGloben/Damfotbollenshistoria/

Svenska Dagbladet (SvD, The Swedish Daily Newspaper). (2017). Lika löner för damer och herrar i Norge (Equal pay for female [soccer players] and male [soccer players]), 10/6/2017. Retrieved from: https://www.svd.se/lika-lon-for-norska-damer-och-herrar

The Swedish Sports Confederation (1903). Idrotten i siffror: Idrott och motion (Sports in numbers: Sports and exercise). (n.d.). Retrieved from: http://www.rf.se/globalassets/riksidrottsforbundet/dokument/statistik/idrotten_i_siffror_rf_2016.pdf

Union of European Football Associations [UEFA] (2017). "Hedvig Lindahl: Match Log. (n.d.). Retrieved from: http://www.uefa.com/teamsandplayers/players/player=59877/profile/index.html

Vandello, J. A., Goldschmied, N. & Michniewicz, K. (2017). Underdogs as heroes. In Handbook of Heroism and Heroic Leadership (p. 339-355). New York: Routledge.

Worthington, E. L, & Allison, S. T. (2018). Heroic humility: What the science of humility can say to people raised on self-focus. Washington. DC: American Psychological Association.

22

The Gates to Baseball: Jackie Robinson's Courageous Transformation of an Entire Sport

DUSTIN J. COOK

Jackie Robinson could hear every racial slur and insult from Phillies manager Ben Chapman's large loud lips, but Robinson chose to ignore them in order to not lose all of the racial progress he had made in the sport of baseball. Robinson's newly transformed state of resilience allowed him to overcome his anger from the repetitive abuse that he received. He was now a strong, peaceful activist. Robinson's ability to resist payback dramatically increased the public's respect for him and his goal of breaking the color barrier in Major League Baseball. The goal of this chapter will be to elucidate the origins of Jackie Robinson's heroic transformation.

Born an impoverished black kid, being raised solely by his mother in Georgia, Jackie Robinson was able to overcome tremendous race barriers and change the sport of America's pastime for the better. Robinson was able to overcome financial and racial barriers to break out as an athletic star at Muir

High School. He decided to attend a junior college for a year since his athletic prowess went unnoticed in high school. After being named Southern California Most Valuable Junior College Player, he accepted a scholarship at the University of California at Los Angeles to continue his studies and sports (Daniels, 2017). Jackie's brother, Frank, died in a freak motorcycle accident upon Jackie's start at UCLA. Jackie demonstrated more raw tenacity and devotion as he decided to use this grief to motivate himself in sports, and he became the first UCLA student to earn letters in all four sports that he played. Jackie experienced more inequality in his life after he decided to drop out of college a few months before graduation. He found the task of finding a job as a black man to be increasingly difficult, and his family had financial concerns that needed to be addressed. This adversity paved a path for Jackie Robinson's heroic journey in the world of baseball.

ROBINSON'S HERO'S JOURNEY

Jackie Robinson put forward tremendous social sacrifice while also placing himself in physical peril. He was a civil hero, as he was a non-duty bound civilian vulnerable to physical attack by standing up for something he believed in, and he assisted in ending segregation (Franco, Blau, & Zimbardo, 2011). Robinson constantly tolerated physical and verbal abuse by owners, teammates, fellow players, and most importantly, fans. This abuse represented a strong cultural social environment inhibitor initiating Robinson's transformation (Parks, 2017). He needed special housing by blacks because hotels would not allow him to stay with the white players on his team. Robinson received constant threats from angry civilians. These threats to Robinson's well-being represented his road of trials, and they were clearly the initiation of his hero's journey (Campbell, 1949).

This initiation was necessary for Robinson's transformation, as resilience was needed to successfully overcome these trials and tribulations. Robinson took the form of many different heroic social sacrifice subtypes (Franco, Blau, & Zimbardo, 2011). Robinson could be considered a martyr because he knowingly put his life in jeopardy for the service of broadening the racial barriers of the game of baseball. He also helped bring a spotlight to the injustices facing blacks in America. He was able to bring diversity in the game of baseball during an era of much hatred and racism, and he accomplished this feat by utilizing his qualities of superior athleticism and determination. Finally, Robinson was able to play the role of the underdog in baseball. He overcame detrimental odds of being hated by the overwhelmingly majority of fans. Almost every racist owner did not want to take on the negative publicity associated with signing the first black baseball player. Robinson's boldness and bravery associated with his position as an underdog helped provide a social and moral role model for many people fighting the inhumane racist society (Vandello et al., 2017).

Missing Inner Quality

Jackie Robinson was a man of many great and beneficial traits, but he lacked one of the most important traits when trying to change society: resilience. Robinson struggled to consume the verbal and prejudicial blows from others, and he constantly defended himself. Clearly, it was very hard for him to contain all of his feelings when he had to overcome such tremendous obstacles to be respected in the league. But to become respected, he had to acquire grit. One black writer for the Chicago Defender, a newspaper aimed at campaigning against the Jim Crow era violence, criticized his inability to be tempered. He wrote, "Jackie Robinson ought to behave himself, before he ruins everything for negroes in baseball." Fellow blacks were worried that their chances to finally join the baseball world were threatened by Robinson's inability to stay tempered throughout the immense discrimination he faced. Robinson was being held to a different standard than everybody else, as the New Orleans Times Picayune accused Robinson of doing more to widen the breach between the races than ten of the most rabid segregationists.

Clearly, this is an over exaggeration regarding Robinson's early struggles, but the newspaper clearly highlights the immense publicity and judgment surrounding his behavior. A great example of Robinson's inability to stay tempered is seen in his actions while in the Army. Robinson was drafted into the U.S. Army in 1942, and he was discharged after only two years of service. He was ordered to move to the back of the bus, and Robinson declined knowing that the Army had recently outlawed segregation on its vehicles. He was arrested and tried in a military court, which led to his discharge. Robinson's initial inability to restrain himself from fighting back against racism caused much skepticism and little positive change towards the infusion of blacks in the dominantly white sport during his early days in the league.

Suffering and Response

Before the major leagues. Suffering plays a very large role in initiating the process of transformation, as suffering inspires the hero to transform for the better to overcome barriers (Allison & Setterberg, 2016). Jackie Robinson underwent significant verbal and physical abuse as he tried to break the race barrier in Major League Baseball. Before Robinson was given the opportunity to play in the major leagues, he played for the Kansas City Monarchs in the Negroes League, as playing in the major leagues at that time was not an option for blacks. Racism and poor treatment followed Robinson and his entire team as they were refused service at hotels, bathrooms, and restaurants. Robinson had a famous encounter at a gas station, in which the gas station owner informed Robinson that he was not allowed to use the bathroom at the gas station since he was black. Robinson was furious and told the owner that if he did not let him use the bathroom, the team would take its business elsewhere and not buy gas from the owner. Robinson persuaded the team to make this their policy going forward, a smart and non-violent way to fight back against the racists.

Robinson's skill and ability to play at the major league level was never in question. White Sox manager Jimmie Dykes said of 19-year old Jackie Robinson, "If that Robinson kid was white, I'd sign him right now. No one in the American League could make plays like that." These flattering statements most likely brought negative and unnecessary publicity to the manager. The fact that the manager was willing to take criticism to compliment a black man's skills shows that Robinson truly was very talented. Jackie clearly had the skill to play and excel at the highest level of baseball, but just was not given the opportunity right away because of his skin color.

During the major leagues. Jackie Robinson faced so much pressure as the first black player in the major leagues, and with this spotlight came tremendous scrutiny and abuse. In Robinson's first year in the major leagues, a well-known incident occurred in which Ben Chapman verbally abused Robinson during an at bat. Chapman was the manager of the Philadelphia Phillies and used this position to yell offensive slurs at Robinson while Robison was at the plate. Everybody heard Chapman yelling these degrading and racist insults at Robinson every time Robinson came to bat. Robinson was very used to hearing these types of words coming out of the mouths of racist fans during games, but to be badgered by an opposing manager was not a common incident. It took a long time before a fellow teammate confronted Chapman regarding his inappropriate behavior as a manager. Robinson was able to restrain his emotions during the attack and not fight back, as this would only escalate the situation and give Chapman the satisfaction of rattling him. The consistency of the attacks on Robinson is made clear by an interview with Chapman during which he says, "Sure I did (regarding whether or not he verbally assaulted Robinson). Everyone used those kind of words back then."

Other teams and fans were not the only ones who abused Robinson, as some of his teammates did as well. The overwhelming majority of them were not happy having a black teammate, and it showed in the locker room as Robinson was constantly ignored and treated poorly. Robinson took it upon himself to not make his teammates uncomfortable, as he decided to always wait until after his teammates were done showering before he went in. This continued for most of his first season until Ralph Branca kindly asked him why he did this, with Robinson responding that he did not want to impede on players comfort levels by forcing them to shower with a man of color. Robinson was heroic in his ability to control his emotions and not lash back with the constant abuse that he suffered by pushing the race boundaries that people are comfortable with.

Assistance from Others

Jackie Robinson was brave and courageous in exploring new grounds as the first black player in the major leagues, but the people who aided him through this process were incredibly brave as well. None of these heroic actions by Jackie Robinson would have been possible if it were not for Branch Rickey. Rickey was incredibly courageous and willing to accept great criticism as the first owner to sign a black player to play on his team. He received calls from other owners and powerful people telling him what he was doing was wrong, and that he should get rid of Robinson. Multiple players confessed to Rickey that they would not play on his team if it had a black baseball player on the roster. Instead of letting these people deter him, he traded those players away, sending an even stronger message that he was willing to sacrifice a lot in order to implement integration in the major leagues. It was clear that Rickey really wanted the integration to work, as he would help Robinson through his hero's transformation in becoming more resilient so that the message of integration would be positively received.

Robinson had support from two teammates in particular: Pee Wee Reese and Ralph Branca. Branca showed his support for Robinson immediately by standing with him during the team's introduction on opening day while other players refused to stand with Robinson. Branca's family told him that what he was doing was dangerous and he could easily be collateral damage in an assassination attempt on Robinson's life. Branca chose to disregard the danger of supporting Robinson, and he continued to spread the message of desegregation. Branca also encouraged Robinson to join the other players in the shower and told him that Robinson should not be separating himself unnecessarily from the others because of the color of his skin.

Pee Wee Reese was one of the best players in the major leagues at the time of Robinson's emergence. He was one of the few to reject signing a petition in which players threatened to boycott the team if the Dodgers signed Robinson. Reese first showed his approval of the integration when questioned by the media. The media asked about how he would feel if Robinson took Reese's starting job since they play the same position, to which Reese responded, "If he can take my job, he's entitled to it." Reese publicly showed his support again later in the season when the team was on a road series at Cincinnati. Fans were verbally abusing Robinson, and so Reese decided to walk over to Robinson and put his arm around him while they conversed on the infield. This sent a strong message to the fans that one of the best players in baseball and captain of the team was in full support of Robinson playing in the league. This magical and strong moment was commemorated in the form of a statue to represent Reese's aid of Robinson. All of the people who supported Robinson through the hero's journey were risking their lives and became vulnerable to public hatred by aiding Robinson throughout his transformation of baseball.

Pathways to Transformation

Jackie Robinson's pathway to a heroic transformation was based around the desire to grow from dependency to autonomy (Allison & Goethals, 2017). Robinson was able to resist social pressures in letting Major League Baseball remain solely a white sport, and he was willing to tolerate significant abuse and adversity throughout his journey. He was remarkably courageous as his life was put in danger every place he travelled. The racists who strongly disagreed with integration in baseball would threaten him and his family, trying to scare him into quitting Major League Baseball. Robinson's courageous sacrifices allowed for unfair social norms to be overthrown and represented a positive step towards ending segregation.

The Emotional Transformation

Jackie Robinson underwent a significant emotional transformation throughout his heroic journey (Allison & Goethals, 2017). During Robinson's early days of the major leagues and even before he joined the league, Robinson struggled with temperament. He was naturally a hotheaded individual who was now assuming the role of a man in the spotlight, a person who would be highly scrutinized and judged by his reactions to hate. For the message of integration to be positively portrayed, Robinson needed to show an equanimity even in the face of cruel and unjustified treatment. Somehow, Robinson was able to successfully develop this new emotional approach to life on his journey, allowing him to achieve his goal.

The Result of the Journey

Jackie Robinson's ability to properly navigate his heroic journey allowed for the birth of an iconic civil fights figure and allowed for tremendous progress of desegregation (Kafashan et al., 2017). Not only did Robinson desegregate baseball by being courageous and accepting the hatred that would come with being the first black major leaguer, but he also became a role model for many and gave hope to an entire community of oppressed individuals. Robinson inspired future progression in the game as Roberto Clemente, Luis Castro, and many others followed in his footsteps by being the first player of their race or ethnicity to play in major league baseball.

ROBINSON'S HEROIC TRAITS

Jackie Robinson embarked on his journey with seven of the eight of the "Great Eight" hero attributes (Allison & Goethals, 2011, 2014). By the end of his journey, he possessed all eight. Robinson was exceptionally smart throughout his journey by knowing which battles to pick and which to walk away from. This intelligence was important because he was constantly being judged and held to a whole different standard compared to every other player on the field. Robinson had to be strong just to start his journey, as he was compelled to confront an unprecedented amount of hate and abuse. Nobody really knows whether Robinson knew the severity of negative treatment that he would receive by being the first black major leaguer, but he clearly showed class, strength, and equanimity. Robinson was selfless by being the first black person to play in the major leagues as he was paving the way for racial desegregation. He showed that he cared every day by treating people with kindness though many of them hoped that he was dead.

Robinson showed that he was charismatic by being so passionate every day in his efforts of desegregating the game that he loved. Robinson did not start off being very resilient, as he let the negative emotions surrounding him aggravate him and he would attempt to fight a losing battle. As Robinson's year went on however, he became very resilient by not letting his enemies get to him, and he actually used these negativities towards fueling the greater good. There is no doubt that Robinson was a loyal hero as he fought for all blacks who were being unfairly treated, and he knew that his work could make a difference.

The most obvious of Robinson's heroic attributes was his inspiration. Robinson inspired so many people that there was a clear increase in attendance at the baseball games throughout his first year. Many blacks wanted to come see the first black major leaguer in action. He inspired young black children everywhere who had the hopes of playing baseball at the highest level but thought it would be impossible until they heard about Robinson getting in that Brooklyn Dodgers uniform on opening day. He not only inspired people regarding the desegregation of baseball, but he became a national civil rights figure. People knew that positive change could occur in America once they saw how a black man was successfully able to join an only white league and be one of the best players in it. Robinson's "Great Eight" traits of a hero allowed him to excel throughout his journey and become a national icon who inspired many people who were convinced that desegregation was unattainable.

Transforming Hero

Robinson could fit into many different categories of types of hero, but he benefited society so much that he must be defined as a transforming hero (Allison et al., 2019; Kinsella et al., 2017). He inspired the whole world with the smile he would put on his face every time he ran out of the dugout while being called a multitude of different insensitive racist slurs. He was able to let people know that change was possible, where many had previously thought that they would be oppressed forever.

Six Character Virtues

Jackie Robinson not only finished his journey with all eight of the "Great Eight", but he also finished his journey with all six of the "six character virtues" (Allison & Goethals, 2014). Robinson failed to start with the virtue of wisdom, but definitely ended his journey with it. With help from Branch Rickey and many others, Robinson learned to be wise and recognize when to fight back and when not to respond to abuse. Robinson was courageous by taking on the responsibility of being the first black player in Major League Baseball, and by making the decision to endure many years of unfair verbal and physical abuse. Robinson clearly showed a strong sense of humanity as he used kindness and love in response to hatred, which made his message of love and union with the world even stronger.

Robinson showed transcendence by having hope that the world could change and that his work in desegregating baseball could help the civil rights movement. Robinson was able to show the virtue of justice by fighting for something he knew that he deserved and all blacks deserved. By the end of his career he was a very successful leader in the clubhouse along with leading the civil rights movement on the baseball field. Robinson began his journey with little self-control as he would hurt his image by responding to the negativity of others, but he was able to adopt this virtue as he recognized that showing self-control would send a strong and positive message to the public. Robinson was also the consummate humble hero (Worthington & Allison, 2018).

The impact of Jackie Robinson's love for baseball and desire to play at the highest level was felt around the world. His heroic work resulted in his emergence as an unparalleled figure for justice and civil rights. Don Browning (1980) once said of philosopher William James, "His sense of fragmentation was transformed into a wide and deep sympathy for the vast pluralism of lives which exists in the modern world." This quote is a great description of how Robinson's heroic journey transpired. Robinson was dedicated to enhancing worldwide interracial well-being (Efthimiou, Allison, & Franco, 2018). His ability to expose the sense of fragmentation in society created a strong wide recognition and following for desegregation. People began to realize that this goal was very attainable and would lead to a significantly better life. Through fights with racists such as Ben Chapman, people were able to gain sympathy for Robinson and realize that desegregation needed to be viewed in a new manner. Without Jackie Robinson's heroic journey and transformation of resilience, the civil rights movement may have been significantly delayed.

REFERENCES

Allison, S. T., & Goethals, G. R. (2014). "Now he belongs to the ages": The heroic leadership dynamic and deep narratives of greatness. In Goethals, G. R., et al. (Eds.), Conceptions of leadership: Enduring ideas and emerging insights. New York: Palgrave Macmillan.

Allison, S. T., & Goethals, G. R. (2017). The hero's transformation. In S. T. Allison, G. R. Goethals, & R. M. Kramer (Eds.), Handbook of heroism and heroic leadership. New York: Routledge.

Allison, S. T., Goethals, G. R., & Kramer, R. M. (Eds.) (2017). Handbook of heroism and heroic leadership. New York: Routledge.

Allison, S. T., & Goethals, G. R. (2011). Heroes, What They Do & Why We Need Them. New York: Oxford University Press

Allison, S. T., Goethals, G. R., Marrinan, A. R., Parker, O. M., Spyrou, S. P., Stein, M. (2019). The metamorphosis of the hero: Principles, processes, and purpose. Frontiers in Psychology.

Allison, S. T., & Setterberg, G. C. (2016). Suffering and sacrifice: Individual and collective benefits, and implications for leadership. In S. T. Allison, C. T. Kocher, & G. R. Goethals (Eds), Frontiers in spiritual leadership: Discovering the better angels of our nature. New York: Palgrave Macmillan.

Barra, A. (2013). The Atlantic. What Really Happened to Ben Chapman, the Racist Baseball Player in 42?. Retrieved from https://www.theatlantic.com/entertainment/archive/2013/04/what-really-happened-to-ben-chapman-the-racist-baseball-player-in-i-42-i/274995/

Browning, D. S. (1980). Pluralism and personality. Lewistown: Bucknell Press.

Burns, K. (Director & Producer), & Mcmahon , D. (Director & Producer), & Burns, S. (Director & Producer). (2016). Jackie Robinson [DVD]. PBS

Campbell, J. (1949). The Hero with a Thousand Faces. Pantheon Books

Daniels, P. (2017). ThoughtCo. How Did Jackie Robinson Make History?. Retrieved from https://www.thoughtco.com/jackie-robinson-1779817

Dik, B. J., & Shimizu, A. B., & O'Connor, W. (2017) Career Development and a Sense of Calling. In S. T. Allison, G. R. Goethals, & R. M. Kramer (Eds.), Handbook of heroism and heroic leadership. New York: Routledge.

Efthimiou, O., Allison, S. T., & Franco, Z. E. (Eds.) (2018). Heroism and wellbeing in the 21st Century: Applied and emerging perspectives. New York: Routledge.

Franco, Z. E., Blau, K., & Zimbardo, P. G. (2011, April 11). Heroism: A Conceptual Analysis and Differentiation Between Heroic Action and Altruism. Review of General Psychology. Advance online publication. doi: 10.1037/a0022672

Kafashan, S., Sparks, A., Rotella, A., & Barclay, P. (2017) Why Heroism Exists. In S. T. Allison, G. R. Goethals, & R. M. Kramer (Eds.), Handbook of heroism and heroic leadership. New York: Routledge.

Kinsella, E. L., & Ritchie, T. D., & Igou, E. R. (2017) Attributes and Applications of Heroes. In S. T. Allison, G. R. Goethals, & R. M. Kramer (Eds.), Handbook of heroism and heroic leadership. New York: Routledge.

LarryLester42. 50 Fast Facts on Jackie Robinson. Retrieved from http://www.larrylester42.com/50-fast-facts-on-jr.html

Ofgang, E. (2014). Westchester Magazine. Ralph Branca Recalls Friendship With Jackie Robinson And Baseball's History Of Racism. Retrieved from http://www.westchestermagazine.com/Westchester-Magazine/April-2014/Brooklyn-Dodgers-Ralph-Branca-Jackie-Robinson-Baseball-History-Of-Racism/index.php?cparticle=2

Parks, C. D. (2017) Accidental and Purposeful Impediments to Heroism. In S. T. Allison, G. R. Goethals, & R. M. Kramer (Eds.), Handbook of heroism and heroic leadership. New York: Routledge.

Vandello, J. A., & Goldschmied, N., & Michniewicz, K. (2017)Underdogs as Heroes. In S. T. Allison, G. R. Goethals, & R. M. Kramer (Eds.), Handbook of heroism and heroic leadership. New York: Routledge.

Wikipedia. (2017, October) Pee Wee Reese. Retrieved from Wikipedia website https://en.wikipedia.org/wiki/Pee_Wee_Reese#Jackie_Robinson

Worthington, E. L, & Allison, S. T. (2018). Heroic humility: What the science of humility can say to people raised on self-focus. Washington. DC: American Psychological Association.

23

The Hat Trick Heard Round the World: Carli Lloyd's Journey from Average to Best in the World

CASSIDY N. BENNETTI

"You know how James would always tell me, 'Play every game as if it's the World Cup final?' He doesn't have to say a thing on July 5, 2015 because I am in BC Place in Vancouver, and it is a World Cup final. The stadium in on the north side of False Creek, an inlet that separates downtown from the rest of the city, and it is inundated with true USA soccer fans who are hoping to see the first happy ending to a World Cup since 1999." – Lloyd (2017, p. 205).

The U.S. Women's National Team delivered. Sports Illustrated proclaimed that "it was nothing less than the most remarkable quarter- hour in the history of American soccer" (Wahl, 2015). The team was led to a 5-2 win over reigning champions Japan by their fearless leader, Carli Lloyd, who scored a hat trick in the first 16 minutes of the game. With this remarkable performance, Carli proved herself to be the best player in the world. She said, "I guess it took scoring three goals in a World Cup final for people to start to know my name" (Baxter, 2016). But now, her name will never be forgotten.

The purpose of this chapter is to discuss the heroic journey of Carli Lloyd. I will do so by explaining heroism, transformation, and the hero journey. Carli Lloyd's journey to the top was never a simple or straight path, as you will soon learn, but her love for the game pushed her to become the best in the world.

What Defines Heroism?

When you hear the word "hero", do you visualize Spiderman casting webs across New York City? Or a firefighter saving a child from a burning building? In defining heroism, scholars have adopted two approaches: an objective approach and a subjective approach. The objective approach defines a hero as taking an action which is morally good, exceptional, and requires great risk (Allison, Goethals & Kramer, 2017). In comparison, the subjective approach points out that most of the criteria for heroism is open to vast subjective interpretation. The difficulty of the objective approach lies in establishing what exactly determines the level of good, sacrifice, and risk necessary for an act to be deemed heroic (Allison, Goethals & Kramer, 2017). Although there is no clear answer to what makes one a hero, research has come far in determining what most people would judge to be heroic.

What Characteristics Do Heroes Share?

Allison and Goethals (2011) conducted research on people's perceptions of heroes, identifying "The Great Eight" categories of traits describing heroes. These traits are intelligent, strong, reliable, resilient, caring, charismatic, selfless, and inspiring. To delve deeper, Kinsella et al. (2017) identified twelve central characteristics of heroes, which are: brave, moral integrity, conviction, courageous, self-sacrifice, protecting, honest, selfless, determined, saves others, inspiring, and helpful. They also identified thirteen peripheral characteristics which are, proactive, humble, strong, risk-taker, fearless, caring, powerful, compassionate, leadership skills, exceptional, intelligent, talented, and personable. Heroes all embody some of these qualities, but not always all of them. Carli Lloyd is a striking example of a hero who has many but not all the classic traits of heroes. She was strong, resilient, inspiring, and determined but was lacking in other areas. These are the missing qualities she came to acquire along her hero journey. But just as we know there is no clear baseline for a heroic act, there are no clear baseline characteristics that all heroes must possess.

What Types of Heroes Are There?

We discover new heroes every day and rely on them in a time of need, but who exactly are these heroes? Many researchers have offered categorical schemes of heroes, beginning with that of Franco et al. (2011) who argued that there are three forms of heroism: martial, civil, and social. Martial heroism includes duty-bound heroes, such as a soldier, while civil heroism includes non-duty-bound heroes, such as a bystander. Social heroism is quite different because it occurs over a longer period, is less dramatic, and is private rather than public. Social heroes can be broken down further more into those who defy systems and those who defy reality. Another type of hero is the underdog, defined as the "disadvantaged party facing advantaged opponents and unlikely to succeed" that we love to root for (Vandello et al., 2017). Most people may not have known it, but Carli Lloyd was an underdog hero (Davis et al., 2011).

Who is Carli Lloyd?

Born in 1982, Carli Lloyd was "always a kid in action", "never a girlie girl", and "loved proving people wrong" (Lloyd, 2017, p.11). She grew up in Delran, New Jersey with her parents, Steve and Pamela, and her brother and sister. She started playing soccer at age five and idolized the game from that point until the present day. She covered her bedroom walls with posters of soccer stars Cobi Jones and Ronaldinho. Carli played at Rutgers University before she made her international debut on July 10, 2005, and within ten years she reached the top of the soccer world. She is a two-time Olympic gold medalist, FIFA Women's World Cup champion, and 2015 FIFA Player of the Year (Carli, 2014). All these accomplishments put her at the pinnacle of the soccer universe, but it was a constant uphill battle to get there.

The Hero's Journey

In the 20th century, Joseph Campbell discovered a recurring theme among the events that transpire in all hero stories. This coined the term "hero's journey" and argued that it consisted of the three phases of departure, initiation, and return (Campbell, 1949). This journey reflects an inner, psychological transformation (Allison & Goethals, 2017). The first step, departure, consists of the hero being called away from the ordinary world, "since fantastic quests don't happen in everyday life". Initiation includes challenges that test the hero's endurance, strength, and mettle. To overcome these challenges, many heroes are accompanied by a mentor who imparts wisdom and shows them the way. Ultimately, the purpose of the hero's journey is to foster developmental growth, promote healing, cultivate social unity, advance society, and deepen spiritual and cosmic understanding (Allison & Goethals, 2017). After making new discoveries along the way, the hero reaches the final step: the return. This return occurs when the hero delivers his or her new knowledge or gift to the world.

What Kinds of Transformations Occur?

Throughout the hero's journey, there are three distinct transformations that the hero undergoes. There is a transformation of setting, which occurs during departure; a transformation of self, which occurs during initiation; and a transformation of society, which occurs during the return (Allison et al., 2019; Allison & Goethals, 2014). Each transformation is crucial to move forward to the next. While on this journey, there are different types of transformations of self that can happen. Six types of self-transformations have been proposed. They include moral, emotional, spiritual, intellectual, motivational, and physical (Allison & Goethals, 2017). In addition, there are three pathways to transformation that heroes take: egocentricity to sociocentricity, stagnation to growth, and dependence to autonomy. Carli Lloyd will take the stagnation to growth path, as we shall see next.

Departure: Transformation of Setting

Just like any other hero story, Carli Lloyd was called away from the ordinary world and sent to the unfamiliar world. This transformation of setting occurred in 2003 when Chris Petrucelli, the coach of the U-21 national team, "squashed" her dream by cutting her from the U-21 team due to her "lack of effort and hard work" (Lloyd, 2017, p. 5). On Carli's prior teams, she wasn't always the best player on the roster but this was the first time she couldn't even make the roster. Her dreams of the U.S. National Team seemed to be slipping away.

Missing Qualities

As mentioned earlier, Carli was missing characteristics crucial for her advancement. Allison & Goethals (2017) claimed that heroes must take their heroic journey because they are missing one or more important inner qualities that are necessary to triumph on the quest and to deliver the boon to society. As we discovered in analyzing her departure, Carli was missing hard work. Throughout her aspiring career, she was told, "you didn't work hard enough" (Lloyd, 2017, p. 5) and "It's not a lack of talent; you have plenty of talent. It comes down to a lack of effort" (Lloyd, 2017, p. 35).

Carli also lacked confidence. She found herself saying, "I've often felt overlooked and underappreciated, and at times completely misunderstood" (Lloyd, 2017, p. 5). After having been cut from the team, she lost her self-esteem. Finally, Carli had a tendency to dwell on the past and not look forward. She would beat herself up when she fell short and said, "It is easy for me to hold on to mistakes, keeping them alive in an endless loop of self-criticism" (Lloyd, 2017, p. 7). Her trainer, James, told her stories of the best athletes and said, "the greatest gift an athlete can have is a short-term memory" (Lloyd, 2017, p. 7). Carli was missing this short-term memory quality. As with every human being, Carli needed to traverse the hero's journey to gain these missing qualities and return transformed.

Initiation: Transformation of Self

The next phase of her journey started when the U-21 team was looking for a scrimmage in preparation for the Nordic Cup. They selected a New Jersey team that Carli happened to play on. Carli had the chance to play against the team she was cut from and the coach who told he she was not good enough. This lit a fire under her and she utilized this opportunity to prove how she has improved and developed. Chris Petrucelli saw this change and said, "It was as if Carli had become a different person, her overall commitment to playing the game was way different that night" (Lloyd, 2017, p. 37). He called Carli the next day to inform her that one of the U-21 players had gotten injured and they have an opening on the team. He wanted her to take the spot. She jumped on this offer and became a member of the team who won the U.S.'s "sixth Nordic Cup title in seven years" (Lloyd, 2017, p. 38). She was pleased to be on the winning team but frustrated she did not get much playing time.

Carli spent the rest of her summer training with the Philadelphia Charge of the Women's United Soccer Association, "thinking that this could be an option after I graduate" (Lloyd, 2017, p. 38). Shortly after the summer ended, the league fell apart and she was left with nothing. Carli questioned whether there was a future for her in the soccer world and pondered quitting the beautiful game. This all changed when her dad gave her James Galanis' phone number.

Mentor

James Galantis is an Australian native who resides in southern New Jersey and has had more of an impact on Carli's life than anyone (Lloyd, 2017, p. 2). After putting her through a few trainings, he agrees to train her full time. He composed a three-phase master plan for reaching her goals. James is a crucial element to Carli's hero transformation because without his encouragement, Carli's doubters may have defeated her. As with many effective mentors, Galantis possessed the wisdom Carli needed and gave her the gift of his time and expertise.

Villains

As we discussed before, Chris Petrucelli squashed Carli's dreams but in reality, "he is the guy who's honestly played a key role in saving my career" (Lloyd, 2017, p. 5). This same situation happened in 2007 when Greg Ryan, head coach of the U.S. National Team, degraded her skills and "chuckled" when Carli said that her long-term goal was to be the World Player of the Year (Lloyd, 2017, p.

82). Although they were villains to Carli then, when she thinks back now she believes they are heroes because without their criticism, she may have never worked as hard as she did to rise to the top of the soccer world.

The Game Plan

Now we turn to the game plan that Carli needed to reach the top. James revealed the five pillars that are essential to any world class player, technical skill, tactical awareness, physical power, mental toughness, and character. With brutal honesty, James told her, "you are very strong in the first two but sorely lacking in the other three." He went on to shred her more by telling her she was not fit enough, was mentally weak, lazy, and had a poor character. "You make excuses – You always have a reason why things aren't working, instead of focusing in what you can do to make them work out" (Lloyd, 2017, p. 43). Carli could have absorbed this criticism and given up on the sport, but instead she felt like she has been waiting for someone to say that her whole life (Lloyd, 2017, p. 44).

James made an agreement with Carli that from that day on, soccer would be her number one priority. With the support of James, she felt as though she had gotten "an IV infusion of hope" (Lloyd, 2017, p. 50). She then subjected herself to James' "three-phase master plan". Phase one (2004-2008) consisted of getting her "entrenched with the U-21's and into the mix with the fall national team" (Lloyd, 2017, p. 50). Phase two (2008-2012) focused on improving fitness and sharpening her overall game resulting in a solidity of her standing on the U.S. Women's National Team starting eleven (Lloyd, 2017, p. 50). Finally, phase three (2012-2016) was for Carli to become a dominant player for the U.S. and the best player in the world. (Lloyd, 2017, p. 50).

The Pursuit of the Pillars

From the moment Carli agreed to make soccer her number one priority, she let no time go to waste. She spent countless hours at Laurel Acres Park but she was not there for recreation; she was there to punish her body into shape (Lloyd, 2017, p. 50). She did repeated sprints up the big hill and occasionally ran suicides, all in addition to the distance running she was doing on the streets (Lloyd, 2017, p. 50). Carli finally got a chance to show how much she improved while nobody was watching in 2004 when she was invited to the U-21 camp. It did not take long before Chris Petricelli saw it. He recalled, "A lot of kids say they want to be on the U.S. Women's National team. Then there are kids who are willing to do whatever it takes to be on the U.S. Women's National Team, and that's what Carli was" (Lloyd, 2017, p. 51). Just a year later, she made the U.S. National Team roster (Lloyd, 2017, p. 60). By the 2008 Summer Olympic Games, she was the goal scorer that lead the U.S. to Olympic gold and named Player of the Year (Lloyd, 2017, p. 118). Things were starting to look up, or so she thought.

One Step Back

In late 2008, James began to notice that Carli was not as mentally engaged as she needed to be (Lloyd, 2017, p. 117). All of her hard work and intensity seemed to be missing. Her coach, Pia Sundhage, was not pleased with Carli and decided, along with U.S. Soccer, that she would not be getting her contract renewed for the 2009 season (Lloyd, 2017, p. 118). The hero's journey is never a simple one, and Carli Lloyd's journey had the usual bumps and obstacles. We know Carli loved proving people wrong, and so she responded to this setback with, "It is time to go to work as I never have before" (Lloyd, 2017, p. 120).

One Step Forward

Carli took her training to the next level, pushing beyond thresholds she had not crossed before, acquiring the characteristic of supremely hard work. She was in the best condition of her life, resulting in her confidence rising to new levels. Carli went to training camp in California, determined to gain her contract back. While at camp, she says "My mind is completely clear, unburdened by doubt or complication" (Lloyd, 2017, p. 120), which shows she acquired a "short term memory". Pia Sundhage noticed a major change in Carli's game, just as Chris Petrrucelli did, which resulted in her earning her contract back.

The Grind Continues

It was 2010 and Carli was working towards Phase two of James' plan, which was to further establish herself as a core player with the national team. She worked to build on her aerobic base. "I run the Rocky's steps thirty-five times. Nobody is playing 'Getting Stronger Now' in the background, but that is exactly what I am doing" (Lloyd, 2017, p. 127). The next goal was to win the 2012 London Olympics. Although Carli started the tournament as a reserve, she finished as a crucial player and as a result, the U.S. team became Olympic champions again.

It All Comes Together

Carli wore her captain's armband, her Nike Mercurial Vapor Super Fly cleats, and the words five pillars written on the side (Lloyd, 2017, p. 206). It was the 2015 World Cup final. The whole world was watching, and Carli put on a show. Her first goal came off of a corner kick that she timed just right. The second goal came when she beat two defenders to the ball and easily passed it in the net. And finally, after practicing her midfield shot for 13 years, she found her moment to put it to action and struck the ball from forty-four yards out. It is buried in the goal and the world went wild (Lloyd, 2017, p. 210). The final whistle blew, with the U.S. winning, 5-2. "The coaches and the whole team pour onto the field, running so fast you'd think they were being chased" (Lloyd, 2017, p. 212). Carli was a world hero and the best soccer player in the world. She received the Golden Boot award for the World Cup tournament.

One hundred and ninety days later, she received the FIFA's World Player of the Year award (Lloyd, 2017, p. 215). She said, "When you work toward a goal for this long, you can't even fathom how you might feel once you achieve it. But I don't want to stop here" (Lloyd, 2017, p. 218). That statement is exactly why Carli stands at the top and so many young girls, like myself, idolize her. She continues to put in more work each and every day to push herself to be a better player. And to think she once considered finding a job that didn't involve "cleats and shin guards" (Lloyd, 2017, p. 219).

Return: Transformation of Society

As we saw along her journey, Carli developed hard work, confidence, and a short-term memory. But what did she do with this newfound role as hero? Carli and four other teammates took a stand in fighting for what is right and fair: equal pay for equal play (Lloyd, 2016). Although the United States Women's National Team is the most successful team in the history of U.S. soccer, they were "being treated like second-class citizens" (Lloyd, 2016), and Carli would not stand for it. In 2016, five U.S. Women's National Team players, including Carli, filed a federal complaint with the U.S. Equal Employment Opportunity Commission, accusing U.S. Soccer of "wage discrimination" (Das, 2016). It was established that the women's player earned as little as forty percent of what the men players earned (Das, 2016).

Carli used her own situation to bring attention to the wage gap at large, inspiring young women to follow in her footsteps (Gray, 2016). She wrote, "we are totally determined to right the unfairness in our field, not just for ourselves but for the young players coming up behind us and for our soccer sisters around the world." (Gray, 2016). And because of Carli's fight, changes have been made. After a year of battling, U.S. soccer and the Women's National Team have finalized an agreement with "far more generous terms for players" (Adamczyk, 2017). They received a "sizable increase in base pay and improved match bonuses" (Adamczyk, 2017). Carli was successful in using her clout as a soccer hero to improve the quality of life of the soccer world. In short, she demonstrated how it was her personal imperative to improve the well-being of everyone connected wiith soccer (Efthimiou, Allison, & Franco, 2018).

CONCLUSION

In this chapter we discussed the many facets of the hero's journey by explaining heroism, transformation, and the hero's journey. With this knowledge, we followed all the lows and highs of Carli Lloyd's specific journey to the top of the soccer world. People are drawn to underdog stories because it shows us what we ae capable of and what anyone is capable of becoming. Although research has made tremendous advances in understanding heroes, there is much more to discover about underdogs specifically. For example, what driving forces make these underdogs overcome the disadvantages with which they are faced?

The difference between most soccer players and Carli Lloyd was Carli's willingness to transform, take setbacks, and use them as motivation to achieve greatness. The question confronting all of us is whether we are willing to take the journey and meet the challenges when called. Each of our journeys could start right now, and we will all face struggles and feel like there is nothing more you can do. As Carli Lloyd said, "Nothing in life is worthwhile unless it's kind of hard to get there." We are all called to go on our individual journeys and transform into something greater than we can ever imagine.

REFERENCES

Adamczyk, A. (2017, April 5). U.S. women's soccer team strikes deal for better pay | Money. Retrieved September 20, 2017, from http://time.com/money/4726656/u-s/womens-soccer-team-just-scored-a-huge-victory-in-the-fight-for-equal-pay/

Allison, S. T., & Goethals, G. R. (2014). "Now he belongs to the ages": The heroic leadership dynamic and deep narratives of greatness. In Goethals, G. R., et al. (Eds.), Conceptions of leadership: Enduring ideas and emerging insights. New York: Palgrave Macmillan.

Allison, S. T., Goethals, G. R., & Kramer, R. M. (Eds.) (2017). Handbook of heroism and heroic leadership. New York: Routledge.

Allison, S. T., Goethals, G. R., & Kramer, R. M. (2017). Setting the scene: The rise and coalescence of heroism science. In S. T. Allison, G.R. Goethals, & R.M. Kramer (eds.), Handbook of heroism and heroic leadership. New York: Routledge.

Allison, S. T., & Goethals, G. R. (2017). The hero's transformation. In S. T. Allison, G. R. Goethals, & R. M. Kramer (Eds.), Handbook of heroism and heroic leadership. New York: Routledge.

Allison, S. T., Goethals, G. R., Marrinan, A. R., Parker, O. M., Spyrou, S. P., Stein, M. (2019). The metamorphosis of the hero: Principles, processes, and purpose. Frontiers in Psychology.

Baxter, K. (2016, January 11). World cup champs Carli Lloyd and Jill Ellis win FIFA awards. Retrieved October 05, 2017, from http://www.latimes.com/sports/sportsnow/la-sp-sn-carli-lloyd-jill-ellis-fifa-awards-20160111-story.html

Campbell, J. (1949). The hero with a thousand faces. New York: New World Library.

Carli Lloyd- Alchetron, The Free Social Encyclopedia. (2014, January 18). Retrieved September 20, 2017, from http://alchetron.com/Carli-Lloyd-722736-W

Carlyle, T. (1841). Heroes, hero worship, and the heroic in history. Philadelphia, PA: Henry Altemus.

Das, A. (2016, March 31). Top female players accuse U.S. soccer of wage discrimination. Retrieved September 20, 2017, from http://www.nytimes.com/2016/04/01/sports/soccer/uswnt-us-women-carli-lloyd-alex-morgan-hope-solo-complain.html

Davis, J. L., Burnette, J. L., Allison, S. T., & Stone, H. (2011). Against the odds: Academic underdogs benefit from incremental theories. Social Psychology of Education, 14, 331-346.

Efthimiou, O., Allison, S. T., & Franco, Z. E. (2018). Heroism in the 21st century: Recognizing our personal heroic imperative. In O. Efthimiou, S. T. Allison, & Z. E. Franco (Eds.), Heroism and wellbeing in the 21st Century: Applied and emerging perspectives. New York: Routledge.

Franco, Z. E., Blau, K., & Zimbardo, P.G. (2011, April 11). Heroism: A conceptual analysis and differentiation between heroic action and altruism. Review of General Psychology. Advance online publication. doi: 10.1037/a0022672

Goethals, G. R., & Allison, S. T. (2016). Transforming motives and mentors: The heroic leadership of James MacGregor Burns. In G. R. Goethals (Ed.), Politics, ethics and change: The legacy of James MacGregor Burns (pp. 59-73). Northampton, MA: Edward Elgar Publishing

Gray, E. (2016, April 11). U.S. soccer champ Carli Lloyd writes forceful op-ed on equal pay. Retrieved September 20,2017, from http://www.huffingtonpost.com/entry/carli-lloyd-equal-pay-because-women-should-get-what-they-deserve_us_570bb7b4e4b0885fb50d8342

Kinsella, E. L., Ritchie, T. D., & Iqou E. R. (2017). A brief history of lay and academic perspectives. In S. T. Allison, G.R. Goethals, & R.M. Kramer (eds.), Handbook of heroism and heroic leadership. New York: Routledge.

Klapp, O. E. (1954). Heroes, villains and fools, as agents of social control. American Sociological Review, 19, 56-62

Lloyd, C., & Coffer, W. R. (2017) When nobody was watching: my hard-fought journey to the top of the soccer world. Boston: Mariner Books, Houghton Mifflin Harcourt

Lloyd, C. (2016, April 10). Carli Lloyd: Why I'm fighting for equal pay. Retrieved September 20, 2017, from http://www.nytimes.com/2016/04/11/sports/soccer/carli-lloyd-why-im-fighting-for-equal-pay.html

Schama, C. (2017, August 29). Women's soccer is done playing nice. Retrieved September 20, 2017, from http://www.elle.com/culture/career-politics/a37386/womens-soccer-equal-pay/

Scott, N. (2015, July 06). Carl Lloyd put on the greatest World Cup final performance ever. Retrieved September 20, 2017, from http://ftw.usatoday.com/2015/07/carli-lloyd-put-on-the-greatest-world-cup-final-permormance-ever

Vandello, J. A., Goldschmied, N., & Michniewicz, K. (2017). Underdogs as heroes. In S. T. Allison, G. R. Goethals, & R.M. Kramer (Eds.), Handbook of heroism and heroic leadership. New York: Routledge.

Wahl, G. (2015, July 13). The story behind the goal and the star: Carli Lloyd's rise to World Cup hero. Retrieved September 20, 2017, from http://www.si.com/plant-futbol/2015/07/13/carli-lloyd-usa-womens-world-cup-final-goal

24

ELISABETH SHUE'S HEROIC TRANSFORMATION, AS TOLD THROUGH GRACIE

SYDNEY R. SHAH

"This sounds so dramatic, but really, it happened -- when I first showed up to tryouts, there was a boy that came over to me, stole my ball, and said, 'Girls can't play soccer.'"

Forty-four years later, this is the story Elisabeth Shue told me in an interview I held with her over the phone (Shue, 2017). Intimidation, it seemed, was a recurring theme of her life, yet she never failed to overcome any obstacles that she faced. Whether it was playing soccer with the boys or being the successful actress that she is now, she has consistently proven wrong those who doubted her. She told me about the inevitable challenges she faced back then – some of which she still faces today -- crediting her older brother Will as her inspiration and own personal hero.

She wanted to fit in with her family. She wanted the same level of respect that her brother was getting, the same level of respect that athletes were getting. And, for Elisabeth, soccer seemed like the most obvious choice, regardless of any gender barriers at the time. "[It] occupied practically every conversation at dinner," she said (Shue, 2017). It was a given.

Based on her childhood struggles and experiences, Elisabeth co-produced as well as featured in the movie Gracie, directed by her husband Davis Guggenheim (Wikipedia, 2017). The movie illustrates how a fifteen-year-old girl living in the 1970s is faced with various challenges and tribulations while trying to live out her dream of playing high school varsity soccer. This was a dream that is driven by her greatest suffering: the tragic and sudden death of her older brother.

At first, I think Elisabeth was surprised that I had chosen to write about Gracie as my hero. And truthfully, I went back and forth on my decision. Compared to my classmates' choices to write about Batman, Martin Luther King Jr., Eleanor Roosevelt, and dozens of other names recognized internationally, Gracie was unknown. An unsung hero, perhaps. Not everyone knows Gracie's story -- which, ultimately, is why I wanted to tell it.

I explained to Elisabeth the natural transformation of a stereotypical hero: departure (the forces that set the hero's journey into motion), initiation (the challenges, obstacles, and foes that must be overcome), and return (the hero comes back to his/her original, familiar world and helps transform society) (Allison et al. 2017). Immediately, my choice no longer seemed far-fetched. Elisabeth was able to relate numerous aspects of Gracie's story to this proto-typical outline, helping me draw connections specifically to the call to action, social heroes, underdogs, mentors, and the ability of the hero to acquire her missing inner quality. In this chapter, I will explain why I believe Gracie's fictional story to be an exceptionally heroic one, and the ways in which it related to a personal real-life hero of mine: Elisabeth Shue herself.

"I won't be the shooter; my sister will be."

These were the words uttered by Gracie's older brother Johnny in the opening scene of the movie, just before she was called to kick an empty bottle off the hood of a car with a soccer ball from ten yards away (Gracie, 2007). This is the first glimpse that we, as viewers, get of Gracie's life -- and even better, the first challenge we see her overcome -- as she, despite her brother's friends' torments and her own self-doubt, clears the empty bottle straight off the car. She brushes her talent off as if it's no big deal, because how could a female soccer star exist in a 1970s world that has no place for them?

For a hero to begin her journey, she must be summoned (Campbell, 1949). Of course, this is not to say that her heroic calling is necessarily glorious, enchanting, or other-worldly. In fact, her calling is usually the opposite: upsetting, alarming, and earth-shattering (Allison, 2015; Allison et al., 2019). For Gracie, it was the death of her older brother Johnny. When Johnny dies suddenly in an accident, Gracie's entire world is turned upside-down, to say the least. She loses one of the only people in her life who gave her unconditional support. This earth-shattering loss, however, was the driving point behind her heroic journey.

As Vandello et al. (2017) put it, "struggle is important for growth." In a paradoxical way, the hero's journey is impossible without some form of loss or suffering. The death of one thing -- whether that death be literal or figurative -- allows for the rebirth, growth, and development of another. The memorials held for Johnny opened Gracie's eyes to what life was like as an all-star athlete. Teammates came, along with their families, along with their coaches, along with members of the community who were simply just fans of the game. Soccer brought people together, and the players on the team were the main components that contributed to this unity. They carried higher standards of responsibility, leadership, and respect throughout their everyday lives. They lived the life Gracie knew she wanted; she simply didn't have the right sources or skills to access it.

However, Gracie's call to action was a little more complicated than her simple desires to fit in. Though not explicitly stated, it seems as though her primary motivation for playing soccer was not for a sense of belonging, but rather, as a tribute to her older brother. She knew that he would have wanted to see his team succeed, so she was determined to help make that dream a reality. Playing soccer was her way of paying her brother back, her way of thanking him. The other factors simply came as secondary motivations. And, let's not forget, she swept that empty bottle straight off the hood of a car in one try. It only made sense for her to play soccer and excel at it.

INITIATION

Her father doesn't believe in her, her brothers laugh when the idea is announced, and her mother doesn't want her to get hurt. And at first, she believes them. She quits the idea out of fury, builds a hatred towards her interactions with her family, and ultimately resorts to drugs and alcohol in order to cope with her brother's death. She breaks the law numerous times -- shoplifting and vandalizing the tunnels in the streets by spray-painting Johnny's name. To put an end to her bad behavior, her father eventually agrees to train her. Together the two of them work hard and train often, and despite the physical toll it takes on her, Gracie persists. However, the untouchable challenge remains: there simply isn't a girls' team for her play on. Thus, the school turns her away, and the coaches give her a hard time for even asking, suggesting she plays "field hockey," a girl's sport, instead (Gracie, 2007).

In response to this ridiculous suggestion, Gracie and her father decide to file for a Title IX investigation. This investigation allows her to try out for the boys' team. Although she was not necessarily guaranteed a spot on the roster, this seemingly small victory is still an enormous milestone. She had been spending a series of consecutive months as a female soccer player without an official team to play for -- and though that time period certainly allowed her to showcase her dedication to the sport in general, she knew her talent was never going to be recognized without the official commitment to a team. But now, she had the chance to be a part of a group that brings her one step closer to reaching her goal. The boys prove to be especially rough during tryouts, throwing elbows and pulling jerseys, not only because they want to make the team, but more so because they don't want her to make the team. For any boy on the team to lose his position to a girl would be considered a disgrace at the very least.

Gracie ends up making the junior varsity team, but she still is unsatisfied. She defies the rules of authority and shows up at the varsity practice instead, and she continues to train with them. She pushes the boundaries in order to do what she believes is best. This heroic trait of hers -- the ability to recognize potential outcomes that authority overlooks -- is a trait shared by Rick Rescorla, a hero from September 11th who worked in the Twin Towers for Morgan Stanley, a large and successful organization. Immediately after the attacks on that tragic day in 2001, the Port Authority issued a statement asking everyone in the tower to remain calm and stay put (Carole, 2013). However, Rescorla trusted his gut, and followed his own beliefs. He ordered the employees to evacuate the building, and as a result, saved nearly 3,000 people from burning to death. If he had remained submissive to authority, those 3,000 people wouldn't have gotten the chance to live out the rest of their lives. In a similar manner, Gracie, like Rescorla, was able to trust her own instinct and do what she believed was best, and it ended up benefitting society more than she originally had imagined. It's a crucial characteristic that both Gracie and Rescorla share; their heroic journeys would have not occurred without their willingness to defy the power of authority.

This defiance also contributes well to the recognition of Gracie's "great eight" characteristics. As defined by Allison et al., there are eight defining characteristics collectively found among heroes: intelligent, strong, reliable, resilient, caring, charismatic, selfless, and inspiring (Allison et al., 2017). Gracie embodies strength through her physical toughness, care through her emotional response to her brother's death, and inspiration through her immense dedication to her goal. But her most obvious characteristic is her resilience in response to the many challenges that come her way -- a characteristic that is clearly illustrated here, through her bold Riscorla-like heroic actions.

Fortunately, Gracie's gut instinct to break the rules ends up working in her favor. The varsity coaches find her perseverance and dedication extremely admirable. They, too, have enormous sympathy and sorrow regarding the loss of her brother. So, one of the coaches, after watching all of Gracie's hard work in various practices, invites her to sit with the team at their next game, simply as a spectator. Neither Gracie nor the coach expects her to actually play.

On the night of the game, the coach hands her Johnny's old jersey. When she walks out onto the field, she takes her place on the bench, but not without receiving menacing looks from a number of the boys on the team. She watches the game intently, as the game reaches sudden-death overtime. A few minutes in, there is a slide-tackle penalty made by the other team. A free kick is granted, and despite everybody's expectations -- including her own -- the head coach calls upon Gracie to take it. It is in this moment that we believe our hero has made it. She's on the field as the only girl among boys. This is her moment to prove to herself and to everyone that doubted her that girls can play soccer. But she misses the goal, only to hit the crossbar.

However, for the hero, this is only a minor setback. The game resumes, and she is forced to leave her mistake behind and keep playing. She still has a chance to prove her worth, and she is not going to throw away her opportunity to do so. She continues playing, getting pushed around by her opponents. The crowd is in awe that the coach hasn't taken her off the field at this point. But then, hope rises. Gracie steals the ball and begins taking it down the field. She dribbles past one player, then another, then a third, until she's met with an opportunity for redemption. She makes a move on her final defender, using a trick her father had taught her during training, and scores the winning goal for her team. It is now that our hero has reached her full transformation. All the time she spent training, not to mention the time she dedicated to the various challenges that simply are associated with being a girl in high school, has finally paid off.

Although they are not usually involved in physical danger, social heroes are associated with "considerable risk and personal sacrifice in other dimensions of life" (Franco et al., 2011). It has even been argued that the social hero is more heroic than those who concern themselves with physical danger, as the costs associated with social heroism are almost certain to occur. It's rare to see a social hero that did not have to lose or sacrifice something important to them. For Gracie, it was her social life.

She begins her training months before tryouts begin. From waking up early to go for a run to practicing her penalty shots late at night, there's not a moment she isn't focused on her goal. She's completely dedicated to soccer. There's a specific scene in the movie where her best friend even goes so far as to call it "social suicide" (Gracie, 2007). But the attitude of a social hero doesn't focus on all that she must give up in order to reach her goal. If she focused on these taxing everyday sacrifices, they would inevitably dilute her motivation and ultimately weigh her down. These social heroes must always keep their goals in mind in order to achieve them. Their goals are what make the sacrifices worthwhile.

The social hero is also often seen as suffering "serious financial consequences," "loss of social status," or "social ostracism" (Franco et al., 2011). Gracie is certainly ostracized, first by her family for making such a rash decision, then by the girls in her school for pursuing such a "masculine" activity, and finally by the boys on the team that are driven solely by competition. She has almost no one rooting for her -- that is, until her father comes around and chooses to help her on her heroic journey. And, for the social hero, just that little bit of support can go a long way.

The social hero also unfolds over a much longer time period (Franco et al., 2011). The same holds true for Gracie's story; a full year goes by between the time that her brother passes away and the time that she gets to play on the team. In other words, her initial calling takes place long before her heroism comes full circle. The time that passes throughout her heroic transformation simply helps illustrate her perseverance and commitment to soccer, and her determination to live out her older brother's legacy.

Gracie's parents initially shut her down. Biology simply wasn't in her favor. And even if she could play soccer, her school didn't have the outlets. She completely defied the odds and paved her own pathway to success.

There are a few subtypes of what we consider to be a "social hero," one being the "odds beater," also known as the underdog (Davis et al., 2011). The odds beater is an individual who "overcame... adverse conditions and succeed(s) in spite of such negative circumstances," and can "provide a social, moral model for others" (Franco et al., 2011). Again, Gracie proves to be the perfect example of this hero subtype. Not only did she have to cope with the death of the only family member who seemed to have undying faith in her ability, but she had to fight her way onto the boys' team, through Title IX investigations and aggressive tryouts.

Though these battles were tough, they only help prove her worth as a social hero. As discussed by Franco et al. (2011), the true power and final measure of success for the social hero is whether or not her actions can speak for themselves. And in this case, it is clear that they do. Gracie never refers to herself as a hero; it is her actions that allow her spectators to do so. She remains humble but determined, and her actions never fail to follow the promise of her words (Worthington & Allison, 2018).

MENTORS

Underdogs cannot attain their goals entirely on their own -- at least, not in most cases. Gracie certainly could not have been as successful as she was without her mentors. A mentor can be a friend, a coach, a teacher, or a family member. The role of the mentor "is to help the hero discover, or recover, the missing quality that is needed to overcome challenges and obstacles on the journey" (Allison, 2015; Allison & Smith, 2015). For Gracie, her mentor was her father.

Her father, though doubtful and pessimistic at first, eventually agrees to train her. He shares his knowledge with her through intensive training sessions, giving her the skills and soccer moves she needs to keep up with the boys.

There is one scene that is especially mentor-like, when he teaches her how to cradle a soccer ball through the use of raw eggs. This technique, in a nutshell, is supposed to teach her just how delicate her foot should be when catching a soccer ball out of the air; it should be a soft enough landing that even a raw egg wouldn't crack on it. He demonstrates to Gracie by dropping the egg from about waist-high onto his foot. It stays.

Gracie attempts the task, but of course does not perform it as effortlessly as her father. She cracks about two dozen eggs before she finally lands one successfully. However, her consistent failure to cradle the eggs is what turns this seemingly insignificant task into such a powerful teaching moment. Even though most soccer coaches wouldn't use raw eggs in order to teach young athletes how to cradle a ball, Gracie's father's abstract teaching method is extremely mentor-like, because it possesses a certain unique creativity that can come only from him. Mentors are also strikingly similar to the archetype of the "wise old man," as discussed in Allison et al. (2017).

The fact that her father can perform the task so well certainly gives him this wiser edge, showing that he has obtained much experience and knowledge accumulated over his lifespan (Allison & Smith, 2015). Additionally, her father's position as mentor would not be completed without helping Gracie discover her "missing quality." Specifically, he taught her the move that she used to win the game in overtime. But by doing this, he gave her so much more: self-confidence, recognition from her community, and respect from her family. Without his knowledge and wisdom, Gracie's heroic transformation would not have been possible.

ELISABETH'S REAL-LIFE STORY, AS IT COMPARES TO GRACIE

As the only daughter in a family of three sons, one might say that Elisabeth Shue always had a way of standing out. However, for the first nine years of her life, "standing out" wasn't entirely what she was aiming for (Shue, 2017).

Elisabeth was a soccer player. Her two little brothers were soccer players, her father played for his college team, and, if that wasn't enough, her older brother

Will was the captain of the Columbia High School varsity soccer team in 1978, and led the boys all the way to the New Jersey state championships.

So, yes, Elisabeth was a soccer player, but she certainly faced difficulty being recognized as such. She was a girl soccer player, which was a role in the 1970s that society didn't entirely embrace. Nevertheless, she was determined to follow in Will's footsteps, regardless of the endless comparisons that society would inevitably make. So, at only the age of nine years old, she made the decision to play on a local all-boys soccer team, and thus became the first girl in the South Orange and Maplewood areas of New Jersey to do so (Wikipedia, 2017). When I asked what Elisabeth's inspirations were to try out, she gave the majority of credit to her brother. She said he was incredibly "hard working," always on top of things -- so much so that he earned the nickname "the net" (Shue, 2017). No wonder her brother Will became the inspiration for Johnny, a character with a tremendous amount of faith in his sister.

I chose to specifically focus my paper on Gracie and her fictional transformation because her story includes all the stereotypical parts of the hero's journey. However, Elisabeth's story is undoubtedly heroic on its own merit as well. Although she quit soccer after only a few years after playing with the boys, she still broke the barriers of gender stereotypes. "The movie is really what would've happened if I hadn't quit. I quit because of what people would think of me. The pressure from the boys. The awkward development of my body. I really, really regret it. I wish I'd been brave enough" (Wikipedia, 2017).

Now, Elisabeth spends her days as a well-known actress, continuing to work on new projects. She calls herself the "reluctant hero." Though she began her heroic journey a decades ago, she simply hasn't yet gained all the necessary sources and resources to complete it. Though she has been in the industry for years, she claims that she is still shy in front of the camera. She doesn't love it when all the attention is on her, making her a humble hero (Worthington & Allison, 2018). Thus, she claims to still be searching for her "missing quality," although, as a student studying heroes and their natural transformation, I disagree. She falls into many different subcategories of heroes, making her a transcendent hero (Allison et al., 2017). Like Gracie, she has devoted her life to a cause much bigger than just her own. She makes movies that tell stories that deserve to be heard. This devotion, therefore, makes her a social hero as well.

Elisabeth made the decision to play soccer among boys, drawing attention to herself. After all, she would have been the only person on the field with a ponytail. Everyone would have been able to recognize her. Likewise, being a successful actress comes hand in hand with being recognized; you cannot have one without the other. So, although she claims to be shy despite her many years as an actress, she continues to put herself in positions that borderline on "uncomfortable." She continues to put herself out there, even though it makes her nervous. I'd like to think this willingness to step out of her comfort zone is her missing quality. Although she might get nervous, it's her conscious choice to act in spite of her fears that is not only heroic, but inspirational.

CONCLUDING THOUGHTS

"If you follow your bliss, you put yourself on a kind of track that has been there all the while, waiting for you, and the life that you ought to be living is the one you are living. Wherever you are — if you are following your bliss, you are enjoying that refreshment, that life within you, all the time." – Joseph Campbell

According to Joseph Campbell, the best way to be truly heroic is to "follow your bliss" (Popova, 2017). Much can be said about the genius and authenticity of this statement, as seen through both Gracie and Elisabeth's story. Gracie's bliss is soccer; Elisabeth's bliss is acting. The more a person holds onto the source of their unconditional happiness, the more he or she can achieve.

Gracie and Elisabeth have both accomplished so much, both in the real world and our imaginations, proving themselves to be effective women heroes. Their stories have the power to inspire the girls and women of our current generation to not only be curious of our own potential, but to take the necessary actions to reach it. Gracie and Elisabeth are true humble heroes (Worthington & Allison, 2018). They show us that being in the spotlight won't highlight our flaws; rather, it can bring light to our lives and propel us along our own heroic journeys.

Allison, S. T. (2015). The initiation of heroism science. Heroism Science, 1, 1-8.

Allison, S. T., & Goethals, G. R. (2014). "Now he belongs to the ages": The heroic leadership dynamic and deep narratives of greatness. In Goethals, G. R., et al. (Eds.), Conceptions of leadership: Enduring ideas and emerging insights. New York: Palgrave Macmillan.

Allison, S. T., & Goethals, G. R. (2017). The hero's transformation. In S. T. Allison, G. R. Goethals, & R. M. Kramer (Eds.), Handbook of heroism and heroic leadership. New York: Routledge.

Allison, S. T., Goethals, G. R., & Kramer, R. M. (2017). Setting the scene: The rise and coalescence of heroism science. In S. T. Allison, G. R. Goethals, & R. M. Kramer (Eds.), Handbook of heroism and heroic leadership. New York: Routledge.

Allison, S. T., Goethals, G. R., Marrinan, A. R., Parker, O. M., Spyrou, S. P., Stein, M. (2019). The metamorphosis of the hero: Principles, processes, and purpose. Frontiers in Psychology.

Allison, S. T., & Smith, G. (2015). Reel heroes & villains. Richmond: Agile Writer Press.

Bos, C. (2013, August 29). Rick Rescorla - Saved 2,687 Lives on September 11. Retrieved October 6, 2017.

Davis, J. L., Burnette, J. L., Allison, S. T., & Stone, H. (2011). Against the odds: Academic underdogs benefit from incremental theories. Social Psychology of Education, 14, 331-346.

Elisabeth Shue. (2017, October 27). Retrieved October 30, 2017, from https://en.wikipedia.org

Franco, Z. E., Blau, K., & Zimbardo, P. G. (2011, April 11). Heroism: A Conceptual Analysis and Differentiation Between Heroic Action and Altruism. Review of General Psychology.

Guggenheim, D. (Director). Gracie (film). (2007, June 01). United States. Retrieved October 06, 2017.

Popova, M. (2017, March 26). How to Find Your Bliss: Joseph Campbell on What It Takes to Have a Fulfilling Life. Retrieved October 06, 2017.

Shue, E. (2017, September 26). Phone Interview.

Vandello, J. A., Goldschmied, N., & Michniewicz, K. (2017). Underdogs as Heroes. In S. T. Allison, G. R. Goethals, & R. M. Kramer (Eds.), Handbook of heroism and heroic leadership. New York: Routledge.

Worthington, E. L., & Allison, S. T. (2018). Heroic humility: What the science of humility can say to people raised on self-focus. Washington DC: American Psychological Association.

25

Audrey Hepburn: How a Misfortunate Girl Transformed into a Social Hero

THOMAS J MICHEL

Audrey Hepburn was born in Brussels, Belgium, on May 4, 1929, and died six weeks later from whooping cough. Her heart stopped after a bad coughing fit, only to start beating again when her mother began spanking her. Unfortunately, this was only the start of Hepburn's difficult childhood. At the age of five she was separated from her mother and two brothers so that she could attend a boarding school in England where her father worked as a recruiter for the British Union of Fascists. At the age of six she suffered the worst pain of all when her father, who had made little effort to visit her, officially abandoned the family.

At the age of ten she was flown back to her home in Holland in order to escape World War II, only to have Germany invade and occupy Holland less than a year later. At the age of fourteen she fought through anemia, asthma, and malnutrition when all food imports into Holland halted. The moment that stuck with her throughout her life, though, came in the form of Holland's liberation on May 4, 1945, on her sixteenth birthday (Paris, 1996). This escape from suffering hurled her forward on her heroic journey.

This chapter will offer an analysis of how the misfortunes Audrey Hepburn endured in her youth eventually led her to become a humanitarian hero. Although Hepburn is best known as the leading woman in movies such as *Roman Holiday, Sabrina,* and *Breakfast at Tiffany's,* she eventually cast aside the spoils of her fame in order to pursue humanitarian work for the United Nations International Children's Emergency Fund (UNICEF). The work she did to help disadvantaged children in underdeveloped countries elevated her to the status of hero. The story of her transformation is a fascinating one that spans her lifetime, from six weeks after her birth right up to her death. It seems fair, then, to present her transformation chronologically, describing how each stage in her life eventually contributed to her heroic status.

In this chapter, I examine Hepburn's life with regard to the three basic parts of Joseph Campbell's hero's journey: departure, initiation, and return. The hero's journey is a blueprint for a heroic life that maps out the steps every hero takes on their transition from ordinary to heroic. By breaking her life down into parts and applying this structure to Hepburn's life, her transformation becomes very apparent. It will show how Hepburn's story fits together with stories of other classic heroes throughout the ages (Campbell, 1949). Her story will also demonstrate her relation to the great eight traits of heroes as described by Allison and Goethals (2011), traits that all heroes of fiction and in real life share in common. Specifically, Hepburn's charisma, selflessness, and caring nature, represented through her fame, humility, and empathetic capabilities, all demonstrate why this actress and humanitarian deserves to be considered a hero.

It is important to note, first and foremost, why Audrey Hepburn is a hero. According to Allison, Goethals, and Kramer (2017), "Heroes undergo a personal transformation that includes the development of a motive to improve the lives of others." Before this transformation took place, Hepburn began her long career in Hollywood when she was cast as the star in the movie Roman Holiday. Even during these early years of her Hollywood career she participated in humanitarian efforts, such as her work as a radio narrator for UNICEF in the 1950s, but it was clear that she had not yet turned into a selfless hero. Over the years her motive for heroism developed into a driving force that caused her to give up acting and devote herself to a new career in humanitarian work as a Goodwill Ambassador of UNICEF (Hepburn Ferrer, 2005).

Based on Allison and Goethals' (2013) definition of heroic leadership, Hepburn can be classified as a hero, but not how one might initially think. Her motives for kindness developed slowly over time. Audrey Hepburn's heroic tendencies stemmed from the adversity she endured as a child. Her childhood experiences were only enough to plant the moral values she held, but through the influence of mentors and circumstances her motive and capability to do good grew exponentially. According to Allison and Goethals (2017), this kind of transformation is an emotional one, and it refers to "transformations of the heart, and they include heroes who, through adversity, grow in courage, resilience, and empathy." Because of World War II, Hepburn learned what it was like to be a starving child, inspiring her to eventually devote her career to ensuring that children would not have to endure her same sufferings.

Departure

Departure in the context of the hero's journey corresponds to when the hero leaves her ordinary, familiar world and enters an uncomfortable, unknown one (Campbell, 1949). Hepburn's departure is rooted in the heroic arc of stagnation to growth discussed by Allison and Goethals (2017), which states that a heroic transformation can occur when a person is forced out of their comfort zone, making them realize their true potential. From a very young age, Hepburn dreamed of becoming, and trained to become, a prima ballerina. She told her biographer Barry Paris (1996), "I was going to be a ballerina. I was very fanatic about it." However, because of the physical consequences of the malnutrition she suffered during World War II, she was told that she could never fulfill her dream (Ferrer, 2008). This news was devastating to her, but it forced her to choose a new path that she had never considered before, a path that eventually led her toward helping disadvantaged children. This section of the chapter will discuss how Hepburn's forced departure from her dream and set path eventually led to her moral fulfillment, and how it relates to her importance as a hero.

Stagnation to Growth

The concept of stagnation to growth relies heavily on how disconnected the hero feels from their ordinary world (Allison et al., 2017). Hepburn's ordinary world was that of becoming a prima ballerina, almost to the point where it became an obsession. A ballerina was all she could see herself as becoming, having idolized ballerinas and having taken classes since she was twelve. It is easy to imagine, however, that if she had been allowed to pursue her dream of becoming a ballerina she would have been sent on a different, less heroic path. Paris (1996) wrote that during her ballet years, "the older she got, the more she disliked what she saw in the mirror: Ballerinas were slender with perfect features. She was chubby. She thought her eyes were too big. She hated her irregular teeth." Hepburn herself said "I had an enormous complex about my looks.... I thought I was ugly and I was afraid no one would marry me" (Paris, 1996). Hepburn's ordinary world was one based on vanity and jealousy.

It might have been happy serendipity that forced Hepburn out of her ordinary world, but after she learned that her dream could never come true, she still felt lost. This sort of sudden separation from what was expected is obviously a part of stagnation to growth, but Hepburn's journey was jumpstarted because of her resilience. Others may have settled with living an underwhelming life after having learned their dream could never come true, but Hepburn put what she already knew to good use and went hard at work in the cabaret show *High Button Shoes*. Her strong efforts and unbreakable charm are what stimulated her growth after her departure from the ordinary world, leading her to meet a mentor who would provide her with her first break (Paris, 1996).

Hepburn suffered through and witnessed the worst of humanity during World War II, but this suffering turns out to be the basis of her heroic transformation. Because of her misfortune, Hepburn was able to understand other people's misery for the rest of her life. Allison and Setterberg (2016) describe six benefits to suffering and make the claim that suffering is the necessary ingredient for heroism. In relation to Hepburn, suffering's ability to encourage humility is most important because it explains the origins of her trait of selflessness.

According to Allison and Setterberg (2016), suffering "doesn't accomplish anything tangible but creates space for learning and love." Hepburn often put learning and loving above herself during her humanitarian career, and this notion was instilled in her from a young age. Hepburn often put her humanitarian work above her Hollywood career and even herself. This sentiment is best expressed when she was asked about her stardom: "If people are still interested in me, if my name makes them listen to what I want to say, then that is wonderful. But I am not interested in promoting Audrey Hepburn these days. I am interested in telling the world about how they can help in Ethiopia, and why I came away feeling optimistic" (UNICEF, 1988). I would argue, however, that suffering itself was not enough to instill her with the purpose of putting her needs below others' needs. The sensation of liberation that she felt when the Germans were driven out of Holland was just as important as the suffering she endured. The resolution to her suffering is what drove her to instill the same feeling of liberation in children all over the world.

Hepburn as an Underdog

Vandello et al. (2017) describe the importance that an underdog has in the realm of heroes. Underdogs become successful even though they have faced great adversity. Because of their rags to riches stories, underdogs are much easier to relate to, making their stories more inspirational when compared to other heroes. Audrey Hepburn, going from a misfortunate young girl to an accomplished humanitarian, fits this category well. Often during her life, though, her status as an underdog is not only inspirational to others, but it enhances her ability to do great things. Relating to her trait of caring, being an underdog gives Hepburn a unique position as a hero. Not only can others look up to her and relate to her humble beginnings, but her humble beginnings often allowed her to relate to those less fortunate. This, again, relates to the six benefits of suffering, this time focusing on suffering's ability to stimulate compassion (Allison & Setterberg, 2016). Many times in her life, Hepburn used her understanding of what it was like to be a starving child to expand her capacity for empathy.

Even as a traditional underdog, Audrey Hepburn is peculiar and worth analyzing. Her inspiration is not as widespread as it should be, most likely because her career as an actress outshines her career as a humanitarian. However, even her Hollywood career is not as inspirational as it could be. Many will remember her for her various starring roles in films but not nearly as many will point out how unlikely it was for her to get those roles after her childhood trauma. Her downplayed inspiration, then, may be because of her trait of selflessness. Hepburn's legacy, then, lies within the public. Since she would not promote herself, it is up to all of us to share her inspiring story.

Initiation

Initiation refers to the various trials and challenges the hero encounters after her initial departure from the ordinary world (Campbell, 1949). This portion of the chapter will describe the conditions that came to nurture Hepburn's moral values, eventually leading to her heroic status. Truthfully, she faced few trials once her acting career started, but she also did not fail to learn from the friends she made during this time. She found many people who nurtured the best within her, reinforcing her transition into heroism.

Call to Career

Dik et al. (2017) describe the different ways in which a hero is called to their profession, either through transcendent calling, calling through meaning and purpose, or calling for the greater good. Audrey Hepburn's career can be split into two categories: her acting career and her humanitarian career. Her later years were defined by the latter, which was inspired by a call of greater good, whereas her initial call toward acting came from a transcendent, outer force.

The transcendent call to a career comes from a force outside the self. This call is normally spiritual in nature, but often the transcendent source can be another human being. Hepburn's work at High Button Shoes opened the door to small acting jobs in movies. After she took a small part in the movie *Monte Carlo Baby*, the famous French writer Colette took an interest in her. Colette saw Hepburn and immediately went on to cast her as the main role of Gigi in her Broadway play (Paris 1996). Colette, in this case, was a transcendent source that transported Hepburn on her path towards stardom. Without her,

Hepburn would never have discovered her talent, even saying to Colette when she asked her to play the role of Gigi, "I'm sorry, Madame, but it is impossible. I wouldn't be able to, because I can't act." Despite Hepburn's lack of confidence in her abilities, she was cast, and time with Colette turned out to be more of a trial than mentorship. Tensions were high during Hepburn's time in Gigi, as many of the actors and actresses around her were being fired. Hepburn learned to deal with the tension, though, by constantly practicing and focusing on her dancing (Ferrer, 2008).

Hepburn's call to her career is an important aspect of her transformation because of the new and important role in which she found herself. This was just her start, though, and her later work would only further her moral growth and her capability to do good. This personal evolution, in large part, was due to various friends she met in film.

Friends and Mentors

According to Campbell (1949) and Allison and Smith (2015), people cannot transform into heroes unless they receive assistance from friends, allies, and mentor figures. The people that helped Hepburn realize her passion played an even bigger role in catalyzing her transformation toward heroism. The first person that showed her this kindness was director William Wyler. While casting for the movie *Roman Holiday*, what would be Hepburn's first starring role in Hollywood, Wyler appreciated Hepburn as an underdog and cast her over already respected actress Elizabeth Taylor. The chance that Wyler took with Hepburn when he could have gone for the safer choice in Taylor meant a lot to Hepburn, leading to a lifelong friendship between the two (Paris, 1996).

The next friend and mentor to facilitate Hepburn's growth was her co-star in Roman Holiday, Gregory Peck. After having met Hepburn, Peck insisted that she got top billing on all advertisements for the movie. Peck knew Hepburn had what it took to be a star, and he knew that he'd look like a fool if he tried to overshadow her. This act of kindness and recognition of her talent, again, led to another lifelong friendship that fueled Hepburn's self-confidence and personal growth (Ferrer, 2008).

Many other friends and mentors can be found throughout Hepburn's life, but none are more important than Hubert De Givenchy whom she met on the set of Funny Face. As head designer of the lavish costumes in the movie, he contributed significantly to setting the style of each scene. As Hepburn's friend, he would go on to establish the style that skyrocketed her career. After working together on *Funny Face,* he and Hepburn stayed friends throughout her life. De Givenchy was responsible for creating the look she was most famous for, her little black dress in *Breakfast at Tiffany's,* making her a fashion icon (Paris, 1996).

Overall, the help Hepburn received allowed her the room to expand her morals and elevated her career to the point where she was able to use her influence to help others. If not for the kindness of Wyler and Peck, Hepburn might not have achieved success in Hollywood. Due to their help, though, Hepburn was able to flourish, and she was inspired to show the same kindness to others. Similarly, De Givenchy facilitated the growth of Hepburn's charismatic traits, widening her popularity and influence. All of these actions accumulated to produce the humanitarian hero that Hepburn eventually became.

Return

The return is the part of the hero's journey where the hero uses everything she has learned to help those around her. In a way, the return is a return to the ordinary world, but now with a new moral understanding that will help the hero to do good (Campbell, 1949). For Audrey Hepburn, her return came late in her life, but it came in full force. Her work for her children and children around the world defined her later years, as she used her celebrity status to make a difference in the world (Paris, 1996).

Healing her Childhood Wounds

The return is characterized by the hero going back to the original world from which she came. In Audrey Hepburn's case, the return occurred when she reunited with her father after almost 25 years of separation. Hepburn never knew what became of her father after the war, but that changed when her then husband, Mel Ferrer, reunited the two. Hepburn often called her father's abandonment "the most traumatic event of [her] life," citing it as something she never recovered from (Paris, 1996). Although her father still remained emotionally distant, this reunion marked the beginning of Hepburn connecting her experiences as a child to her now fully developed moral values. After this point, Hepburn's desire to give back to the world is most apparent as her fame and her desire for humanitarian work finally converge.

Semi-Retirement

Not long after reuniting with her father, Hepburn put acting on the backburner in order to focus on her family. Her new role as a mother was another new beginning, as it signaled her priority of putting others above herself. The trauma of her youth, now fully resolved, could be put to good use. Because she wanted to give her children the childhood she was not allowed to have, Hepburn gave up acting for nine years in order to spend time with her two sons in her country home in Switzerland. She only partially went back to work once her sons were happily attending school (Ferrer, 2008).

Hepburn willingness to step away from her acting career was one of the greatest markers of her heroic transformation. Although her acting career is what set her up to be able to do great things, her withdrawal from it shows that she really did wish for more than fame. She was a humble hero (Worthington & Allison, 2018), and focusing on her children was the start of her emotional transformation. Her strong empathic concerns, especially toward children, gave Hepburn a drive to do more with her life. This aspect of Hepburn's life relates back to Dik et al.'s (2017) notion of being called to a career path. This time, though, Hepburn is called by the greater good. This call is one that comes from the inner desire to bring make the world a better place by doing good to other people. This new call led to Hepburn's truly heroic years: those working for UNICEF.

Audrey Hepburn stated multiple times that her work as a UNICEF International Goodwill Ambassador was what she was most proud of. She was invited to do this work in 1988 along with five other celebrities, in hopes that her influence combined with this work would create a large change in the world. As a Goodwill Ambassador, she traveled to various underdeveloped countries so she could report what she saw back to the United Nations. She traveled to over twenty countries in the four years she worked for UNICEF, often reporting back abysmal conditions in which children were forced to live. Due to her work, the United Nations sent food and supplies to where they needed to go (Hepburn Ferrer, 2005).

For Hepburn, this work was her most important contribution to society, and it marks the end of her heroic transformation. Having transformed herself, she was now committed to promoting the well-being of the world (Efthimiou, Allison, & Franco, 2018). After living a life based on the misfortune of her youth, Audrey Hepburn became a truly selfless, heroic figure through the help of friendship and extraordinary circumstances. Unfortunately, right as her career as a great hero was starting, she was diagnosed with colon cancer at the age of 63. Even with four months remaining to live, she was still working for UNICEF in Somalia (Hepburn Ferrer, 2005).

CONCLUSION

Audrey Hepburn's early life experiences should have truly limited her heroic potential. The fame she achieved through determination and talent, though inspirational, is hardly heroic at first glance. This fame, though, is what allowed her to make great change in the world. As with many notable heroes, her story is deeply rooted in her humble beginnings (Worthington & Allison, 2018). She made it well known that her passion for saving starving, ill-fated children came from her experiences during World War II, but it would be unfair to say her years as an actress were superficial. She used her luxurious career in Hollywood as a springboard for her fulfilling work with UNICEF. The position her fame put her in allowed her to do more good than someone with less influence. Her story serves as evidence that great financial success in the first part of adult f life can lead to even greater success in heroic endeavors later in adulthood. Audrey Hepburn represents the best of what humanity has to offer. She cherished what liberation felt like when it saved her life as a child to the point where her whole life became a journey to discover how she could give that same liberation to other children around the world.

REFERENCES

Allison, S. T., & Goethals, G. R. (2011). Heroes: What They Do and Why We Need Them. New York: Oxford University Press.

Allison, S. T., & Goethals, G. R. (2017). The hero's transformation. In S. T. Allison, G. R. Goethals, & R. M. Kramer (Eds.), Handbook of heroism and heroic leadership. New York: Routledge.

Allison, S. T., Goethals, G. R., & R. M. Kramer (2017). The Rise and Coalescence of Heroism Science. In S. T. Allison, G. R. Goethals, & R. M. Kramer (Eds.), Handbook of heroism and heroic leadership. New York: Routledge.

Allison, S. T., & Goethals, G. R. (2013). Heroic leadership: An influence taxonomy of 100 exceptional individuals. New York: Routledge.

Allison, S. T., & Setterberg, G. C. (2016). Suffering and sacrifice: Individual and collective benefits, and implications for leadership. In S. T. Allison, C. T. Kocher, & G. R. Goethals (Eds), Frontiers in spiritual leadership: Discovering the better angels of our nature. New York: Palgrave Macmillan.

Campbell, J. (1949). The Hero with a Thousand Faces. NewYork: Pantheon Books.

Dik, B. J., Shimizu, A. B., & W. O'Connor (2017). Career Development and a Sense of Calling: Contexts for Heroism. In S. T. Allison, G. R. Goethals, & R. M. Kramer (Eds.), Handbook of heroism and heroic leadership. New York: Routledge.

Efthimiou, O., Allison, S. T., & Franco, Z. E. (Eds.) (2018). Heroism and wellbeing in the 21st Century: Applied and emerging perspectives. New York: Routledge.

Ferrer, S. H. (2005). Audrey Hepburn: an elegant spirit. London: Pan Books.

Ferrer, S. (2008). Life & Career. Retrieved October 07, 2017, from http://www.audreyhepburn.com/menu/index.php?idMenu=84

Paris, B. (1998). Audrey Hepburn. London: Orion.

UNICEF. (1988). Profile: Audrey Hepburn, UNICEF Goodwill Ambassador[Profile of Audrey Hepburn by UNICEF].

Vandello, J. A., N. Goldschmied, & K. Michniewicz (2017). Underdogs as Heroes. In S. T. Allison, G. R. Goethals, & R. M. Kramer (Eds.), Handbook of heroism and heroic leadership. New York: Routledge.

Worthington, E. L, & Allison, S. T. (2018). Heroic humility: What the science of humility can say to people raised on self-focus. Washington. DC: American Psychological Association.

26

THE HEROISM OF SIDDHARTHA: A JOURNEY TO ENLIGHTENMENT

ISABEL R. NONEMAKER

"Enlightenment is the key to everything, and it is the key to intimacy, because it is the goal of true authenticity."
-- Marianne Williamson

A man once came to see the Buddha to get help with his problems. After the man had told the Buddha one of his problems and asked for help, the Buddha replied: "I cannot help you get rid of that problem."

The man was surprised that the Buddha could not help him in this regard, but he told the Buddha about another problem; he thought to himself that the Buddha should at least be able to help him with that problem. But the Buddha told him "I cannot help you with that problem either."

The man started to get impatient. He said: "How can it be that you are the perfectly Enlightened Buddha, when you can't even help people get rid of their problems?" The Buddha answered: "You will always have 83 problems in your life. Sometimes a problem will go, but then another problem will come. I cannot help you with that."

The baffled man asked the Buddha: "But, what can you help me with, then?" The Buddha replied: "I can help you get rid of your 84th problem." The man asked: "But what is my 84th problem?" The Buddha replied: "That you want to get rid of your 83 problems" (Anderson, 2012).

- - - -

For generations, humans have been faced with an inescapable thirst for material, social, and political perfection. Many modern heroes fulfill these wants through the glory of their physical risk and victories. But there is another type of hero: the kind that does not care about being viewed as ideal but focuses on their bliss, calling, and unbreakable contentedness. This hero, the Buddhist hero, takes risks and experiences victory internally and religiously.

Buddhism is the practice of finding pure contentment and enlightenment (Tucci et.al., 2017). The central goals for followers are to lead a moral life, to be mindful and aware of thoughts and actions, and to develop wisdom and understanding (Mittelman, 1991). The creator of this religion, the Buddha, is considered a hero by many because he founded the idea to escape mentally from social pressures of perfection, and he emphasized self-acceptance (Tucci, 2017). A 1922 novel written by Hermann Hesse features a young boy who realizes the importance of resisting social pressure and an unpurposeful lifestyle. Siddhartha goes on a life-altering endeavor at a young age and displays all of the qualities that heroism entails; he continues his mission until he finds his awakening, following the pattern of the distinct hero's journey.

Siddhartha is the main character in the novel Siddhartha by Hermann Hesse. He is a young boy who grows up and faces the common internal struggle of finding himself, his values, and his life's purpose. While many people would accept the comfortable and affluent life he was born into, Siddhartha calls on himself to reject the lack of ambition he believes he has (Hesse, 2005). Readers can notice Siddhartha's capability of becoming a hero through his growing awareness of the importance of enlightenment at such a young age. It is very rare to read a story about a child who voluntarily calls on himself to endure a heroic journey, especially in his unforceful circumstances. The only motivation behind making a change in his life was Siddhartha's desire to experience true happiness and disconnect from the material world.

Siddhartha is considered a religious figure who undergoes a spiritual transformation, as this is a fictional novel about his path to becoming submerged into Buddhism. A religious figure is someone "dedicated to life-long religious service embodying highest principles or breaking new religious/spiritual ground" (Franco, Blau, & Zimbardo, 2011). A spiritually transformative hero experiences a life changing conversion in beliefs about God and the universe (Allison & Goethals, 2017). However, he is not necessarily a creator of a religion like some heroes. Instead, he demonstrates to others how one person can adopt values and reject a life of wealth while gaining bliss and purpose. Siddhartha follows all the steps of the hero's journey, experiences a heroic transformation, makes sacrifices, and does everything he can to benefit himself and educate others.

Siddhartha's heroic cycle begins with his call to action. Enjoying an abundance of wealth and no problems to endure, Siddhartha becomes bored with his life and believes his purpose is nonexistent. He decides to leave his home because of his desire to find meaning and reject the status quo (Hesse, 2005). Siddhartha's courage is impressive, as the places he intends to visit are dangerous and unpredictable. There is no external pressure for Siddhartha to change his lifestyle or go anywhere; the exact opposite in fact is true. Siddhartha's parents and friends encourage him to stay in Brahman territory, persuading with statements regarding his family's money and all the material goods he has. Siddhartha continues to reject his loved one's requests and leaves to find enlightenment. It can be expected for a teenager to be drawn to materialistic incentives and the comfort of relying on parents. Siddhartha's persistence and his voluntary departure is extremely rare and displays the signs of a future hero.

The second phase of the heroic cycle is the initiation stage. During this part of the journey, a hero must face and defeat challenges, obstacles, and foes (Campbell, 1949). Heroes cannot overcome these obstacles without help from others, and these people emerge as their friends and mentors (Allison & Goethals, 2017). Govinda is Siddhartha's best friend from home and his side-kick. He does not encourage Siddhartha to leave for his journey but accepts the fact that Siddhartha does not want to adopt an ordinary and unfulfilling life. Govinda follows him to the Samanas, Siddhartha's first attempt at enlighten-ment. Govinda is essentially Siddhartha first student, as he learns two lessons from Siddhartha: that adapting to a Brahman lifestyle is unfulfilling, and there is more to one's life than money. Eventually, Govinda and Siddhartha reunite at the end of the novel. Govinda has been on an enlightenment journey of his own, yet he has continued to fail in awakening. Siddhartha gives him advice, listens to him speak, and ultimately encourages his transformation. Although Govinda did not directly teach Siddhartha, he allowed him to experience the status of a leader and an archetypal wise man.

The Samanas are Siddhartha and Govinda's first stop on their journey toward finding enlightenment, and they teach Siddhartha what he does not want. The Samanas are a Buddhist group who believe that there is a purpose in self-harm and negligence of the body's natural wants and needs. The group's rituals included fasting, dehydration, cutting themselves, and staring into the sun for long periods of time. They act as a mentor for Siddhartha, not because they taught him how to awaken, but instead showed him that Samana Buddhism is not the correct method for him. Joseph Campbell's monomyth explains that one of the key steps of the heroic journey is overcoming obstacles and sometimes facing failures (Allison, Goethals, & Kramer, 2017). Challenges are an essential part of every hero's journey, and this was Siddhartha's first of many.

Gautama Buddha is one figure who has found full enlightenment. Siddhartha and Govinda hear about him and go to watch him speak. The Buddha lives in an effortlessly peaceful world, and he tells the two children that enlightenment must be experienced, not taught. Siddhartha declares that he must resume his journey independently. Gautama Buddha's advice is simple but makes a large impact on the rest of Siddhartha's conquest. Independence allows Siddhartha to follow his instincts without another person holding him back.

Siddhartha eventually runs into a ferryman, Vasudeva, and befriends him. Vasudeva gives him a straightforward piece of advice: to learn from the river. This advice initially sounds unhelpful, but it is later shown that the river is the answer to Siddhartha's enlightenment. Vasudeva is a minor mentor to Siddhartha at first, and he returns later on to assist him further. Another influencing figure comes along immediately afterward. Kamala is a woman who encourages Siddhartha to adopt a wealthy lifestyle of his own, one similar to the one from which he escaped. Their relationship was extremely counterproductive to his journey, but he becomes blinded by love. Siddhartha realizes that he needs to leave this life indulged in greed. Although Kamala is not a mentor in his enlightenment tactics, she is another form of failure that Siddhartha encounters. He falls victim to emotions, and Kamala ultimately slowed down his enlightenment process. Despite this, Kamala also made Siddhartha stronger. She forced him to face the lifestyle he tried to leave; he caved into it, ultimately regaining his original motivations to awaken himself. He failed, yet he also learned from his mistakes and rejected the easy escape from hardship, which is an essential aspect of becoming a hero.

Return

Siddhartha leaves Kamala and returns to the ferryman, Vasudeva. When returning to the water, Siddhartha has an epiphany and realizes that enlightenment lies within the concept of a river; the water is everywhere at once yet still living presently. The acceptance of how something is, rather than how something should be, is the sign of an enlightened mind. Siddhartha finally gains this knowledge through his long experimental and experiential journey.

Siddhartha does not return to his Brahman country, but instead becomes a ferryman himself. In this role, he boats people across the river and quietly listens to their stories. He officially willed his life to be a supporter of others seeking their enlightenment, similar to how his mentors supported him in his journey. Siddhartha is not a direct hero to his future mentees, but he acts as a guide and listener. The belief that enlightenment must be an independent discovery remains with Siddhartha, but he knows guidance and advice remain helpful.

When one experiences a truly heroic transformation, they acquire a new mind-set and perspective on life. Siddhartha undergoes an extreme self-transformation throughout his journey, and his changes accurately describe those of a hero. He becomes awakened and enlightened, able to see the world through the lens of wisdom and compassion (Allison et al., 2019).

Purposes of Transformation

A hero's transformation is purposeful to both the hero and to the society in which he lives. Siddhartha develops as an individual throughout his story using his newfound present mindset and eternal contentedness. One of the central motivations for his entire journey is that Siddhartha feels he has no purpose as a wealthy Brahman's son. By the end of the novel, he found that guiding people is his mission, and living on the river is his bliss.

Transformations are also essential to healing and cultivating social unity (Allison & Goethals, 2017; Efthimiou, Allison, & Franco, 2018). In the religion of Buddhism, these purposes complement each other. Siddhartha undergoes a religious conversion and wishes for a community in which he can feel comfortable. It is believed that telling the stories of hero transformations can result in many of the same benefits as group therapy (Allison, 2015; Allison & Goethals, 2017). Some of these benefits include the fostering of self-awareness, the relief of stress, and the development of a sense of meaning about life (Allison & Goethals, 2017). Siddhartha's enlightenment and heroic journey heal his inner pain and feelings of confusion while integrating him into a religion that he later promotes to others. Siddhartha's internal pain eases, and he learns how to be a mentor in cultivating a community of Buddhism and supporting others' enlightenment journeys.

The most prominent purpose of Siddhartha's transformation is that it promoted a spiritual change in him. He now has a more profound spiritual and cosmic understanding. Joseph Campbell (1949) mentions that the hero's transformation involves "experiencing the supernormal range of human spiritual life" and "brings us into a level of consciousness that is spiritual" (Allison & Goethals, 2017). These changes characterize Siddhartha's journey perfectly, as his spirituality is at first nonexistent, slightly develops, diminishes again through his time with Kamala, and eventually, blossoms into his Buddhist enlightenment. A central reason for his transformation can be found in his determination and self-will.

Dimensions of Transformation

The term "hero" has an ambiguous connotation to it, as all heroes vary along ten dimensions of transformation (Allison & Goethals 2017). Siddhartha, a spiritual hero, will have many differences from a physical or militia hero within these realms of categorical measures. Siddhartha's main aspects that set him apart from a stereotypical hero are the scale, whom his transformation affects, speed, his speed of transformation, timing, the permanence of the transformation, and whether his transformation stems from internal or external sources.

Siddhartha's scale of heroism reaches to himself individually and to a group of potential enlightenment seekers. The novel was based primarily on a boy seeking an individual transformation and adventure to find purpose. The result was both his success in finding a meaning and developing into a mentor for many people in the future, similar to how the ferryman guided him. Siddhartha learned about himself, and he learned how to help others by being a person listens and dispenses advice.

The speed of Siddhartha's metamorphosis severely lengthens due to his downfall into a seemingly inescapable love for a woman. His multiple failures, however, were essential to the outcome of his journey. Without visiting the Samanas, he never would have discovered the type of Buddhism to which he did not belong. Without Kamala, he never would have gained a sense of self-empowerment. He fell victim to her femininity, but in the end Siddhartha's self-control became unmatchable. His transformation consumed years and encased many failures, but his altered mindset stuck with him longer than his journey set him back.

The timing is one of the most impressive parts of Siddhartha's transformation. When Siddhartha leaves his family and home, he is in his teenage years. As a teen, it is not uncommon to take advantage of the simple life, relying on parents and avoiding responsibility. Siddhartha is also the son of a very wealthy Brahman, a member of the highest Hindu caste, that of the priesthood. However, Siddhartha does not aspire to become a Brahman himself. Despite having the social, material, political, and cultural dreams of many, he still recognizes that lacking ambition is unfulfilling. It could be argued that older people are more "ready" to embark on such a transformative journey. Siddhartha's youthful willingness to leave the safety and luxury of home to become transformed truly underscores his willpower and determination to improve himself.

The source of Siddhartha's heroic journey is purely internal and in a way counter-external. His cause of motivation to change resides in the natural needs to pursue goals. Maslow's (1943) hierarchy of needs reveals that an individual is motivated to fulfill higher level needs once lower level needs are satisfied. Once the needs at the four lower levels are satisfied (physiological, safety, love, and esteem) one is no longer concerned with them (McLeod, 2007). One eventually is drawn to achieve self-actualization, which is Siddhartha's ultimate destiny, as he acquires meaning, beauty, truth, and a sense of oneness with the world. The component of Siddhartha's situation that most sets him apart from others resides in the fact that he rejected eternal material wealth and social status to embark on a self-enhancing journey. Siddhartha does follow the hierarchy of needs, climbs to the top, then dismisses the first four levels. This is psychologically rare and unnatural, but a hero should never be ordinary.

Overall, Siddhartha transforms from a lost and curious boy to a wise and content Buddhist man. His spiritual journey was challenging and unique, as it involved a calling, many mentors, failures, resurgences, and return. Siddhartha is the epitome of a changed man by the end of his story, and he fulfilled his goals exceptionally well.

SIDDHARTHA'S HEROISM

Heroism is a very ambiguous term in the explicit classification of who is a hero in contrast to who is not a hero. One reasonable objective definition of a hero is that a hero is a person who takes risks to help others without self-gain as motivation (Kafashan et al., 2017). A subjective hero is determined by a person's opinions or experiences; this type of hero may be one person's role model, but an ordinary figure to someone else (Kinsella, Ritchie, & Igou, 2017). Siddhartha and his heroic journey can fit into both classifications. Siddhartha took risks by leaving his comfortable lifestyle and financial conditions to embark on an unpredictable and dangerous journey. He leaves to find self-awakening, and at first he was oblivious as to how, where, and when he would find it. Additionally, Siddhartha later becomes a ferryman and mentor for future persons on their enlightenment endeavors.

Although he fits most of the objective hero's requirements, he did not explicitly take a risk to help others. The reason he embarks on his heroic journey was for himself, and in doing so he left many people who cared about him. It is a subjective view on whether he still qualifies as a hero after considering this self-seeking motivation. From a subjective standpoint, Siddhartha is rightly a hero to anyone who perceives him as such. Because subjective heroism is based purely on perception and opinions, Siddhartha fits into the heroic realm easily. Siddhartha would be objectively regarded as a hero to those whom he mentored, and he is a hero because he served as an inspiration and role model to countless people over the centuries.

The Great Eight

The great eight traits are essential to a hero's success and qualification. These features are: intelligent, strong, reliable, resilient, caring, charismatic, selfless, and inspiring (Allison & Goethals, 2011; Allison, Goethals, & Kramer, 2017). Siddhartha fulfills all eight of these characteristics, but four of them, intelligence, resilience, selflessness, and inspiring, are most prevalent throughout the novel. Siddhartha is intelligent because he has benefited from growing up as a Brahman's son who had access to schooling. However, Siddhartha is also emotionally wise as he can recognize his unhappiness and how to cure it. Resilience is displayed after he falls into a wealthy life because of Kamala. Although Siddhartha is in love and is strongly suppressed by his romance with Kamala, he reminds himself that returning to an affluent, unenlightened lifestyle is not what he intended on doing. He uses his resilience to ignore his temptation and re-embark on his adventure to awakening. Selflessness becomes apparent near Siddhartha's heroic return, once he becomes a wise riverman he devotes his life to helping others find spirituality like Vasudeva did for him.

Siddhartha did not begin utterly selfless because he left his family and community to find himself, but concurrently he left many material goods and his position of high status to do so. His selflessness was key to his transformation as well, as he went from only being occasionally selfless to a man who devoted his entire life to being content with minimalism and helping others. Lastly, Siddhartha was an inspiring man to those whom he mentored and to readers of this novel. He encouraged people to change their mentality and spirituality if they felt they had no purpose in life. As a riverman, Siddhartha inspired people to continue with their journeys despite their possible frustration and impatience; those feelings dissipate with enlightenment.

Suffering

Siddhartha's suffering leads him into the intense and long journey that gives his life purpose. Many obstacles are faced during his journey, but Joseph Campbell explains "Where you stumble, there lies your treasure" (Huffington Post, 2017). Siddhartha stumbled in his sense of self and purpose, and instead of allowing this suffering to suppress him, he found his treasure. The heroic journey he undertook was unpredictable and challenging, but because he faced his difficulties, Siddhartha found success. Siddhartha gains enlightenment, contentedness, spirituality, and his ability to guide others as a Buddhist mentor. Siddhartha's suffering and treasure tie into the six benefits of suffering and how one's pain can turn into a success story. These six benefits are that suffering is redemptive, signifies a crossover point in life, encourages humility, stimulates compassion, promotes social union, and instills meaning and purpose (Allison & Setterberg, 2016). All of these positive outcomes of suffering depict Siddhartha's transformation extremely well.

First, he is redemptive because he uses his story to mentor people at the end of his adventure. Siddhartha saves people from their lack of self-acceptance and feelings of being lost, much like how he felt initially. Suffering also signifies a crossover point in life, a benefit that correlates closely to Siddhartha's situation. Siddhartha finds himself as a result of his spiritual journey, and such spiritual growth is often life-changing. Evolving from a Brahman's son to a Buddhist is an extreme inflection point in his life, and the largest change he has and will experience. Siddhartha's suffering also injected meaning and purpose in his life. Without his transformative heroic journey, Siddhartha would not be any different than any other Brahman. He would have no true sense of self beside the facts that he was well liked, wealthy, and labeled. Finding enlightenment was Siddhartha's most central goal, and he accomplished it by successfully completing his journey. By acquiring his spirituality and later spreading his considerable wisdom to others, Siddhartha found meaning and purpose in his life, and he found meaning and purpose in his suffering by using it as motivation.

CONCLUSION

Hermann Hesse wrote this bildungsroman novel inspired by the Buddha and the struggles one can face when trying to adopt a new spiritual lifestyle. Siddhartha's initial situation, hardships, unpredictable journey, and singular outcomes combine to reveal him to be a striking hero. Although many people struggle to find themselves and then adopt a religion, they are not all heroes. Siddhartha's tale encases the journey, transformation, return, and qualities that a hero must have. By teaching himself how to view the world in a different, relaxed, accepting way, Siddhartha is a role model for millions of people who are struggling with self-image. Relating Siddhartha's story to real life phenomena, we see that it is not uncommon for people to have a sense of confusion when navigating through our complex world. People today question their purpose more than in any time in human history. Siddhartha's story demonstrates to readers that if one is feeling lost and meaningless, the only person that can fix the feeling is oneself. Siddhartha's ambition, persistence, and courage contributed to his enlightenment and goal fulfillment. Siddhartha is destined to exert heroic influence on readers worldwide for many years to come.

REFERENCES

Allison, S. T. (2015). The initiation of heroism science. Heroism Science, 1, 1-8.
Allison, S. T., & Goethals, G. R. (2011). Heroes: What they do and why we need them. New York: Oxford University Press.
Allison, S. T., & Goethals, G. R. (2016). Hero worship: The elevation of the human spirit. Journal for the Theory of Social Behaviour, 46, 187-210.
Allison, S. T., & Goethals, G. R. (2017). The hero's transformation. In S. T. Allison, G. R. Goethals, & R. M. Kramer (Eds.), Handbook of heroism and heroic leadership. New York. Routledge.

Allison, S. T., Goethals, G. R., & Kramer, M. (2017). Setting the scene: The rise and coalescence of heroism science. In S. T. Allison, G. R. Goethals, & R. M. Kramer (Eds.), Handbook of heroism and heroic leadership. New York: Routledge.

Allison, S. T., Goethals, G. R., Marrinan, A. R., Parker, O. M., Spyrou, S. P., Stein, M. (2019). The metamorphosis of the hero: Principles, processes, and purpose. Frontiers in Psychology.

Allison, S. T., & Setterberg, G. C. (2016). Suffering and sacrifice: Individual and collective benefits, and implications for leadership. In S. T. Allison, C. T. Kocher, & G. R. Goethals (Eds.), Frontiers in spiritual leadership: Discovering the better angels of our nature. New York: Palgrave Macmillan.

Anderson, R. L. (2012). Moving mountains: The journey of transformation. Authorhouse publications.

Crandell, S. (2012, December 18). 'Where You Stumble, There Your Treasure Is'. Retrieved from http://www.huffingtonpost.com/steven-crandell/treasure_b_2317215.html

Efthimiou, O., Allison, S. T., & Franco, Z. E. (Eds.) (2018). Heroism and wellbeing in the 21st Century: Applied and emerging perspectives. New York: Routledge.

Eylon, D., & Allison, S. T. (2005). The frozen in time effect in evaluations of the dead. Personality and Social Psychology Bulletin, 31, 1708-1717 Allison, S. T., & Goethals, G. R. (2011). Heroes: What they do and why we need them. New York: Oxford University Press.

Gregory-Guider, C. C. (2017, March 16). Siddhartha. Retrieved from https://www.britannica.com/topic/Siddhartha

Hesse, H. (2005). Siddhartha - Hermann Hesse. New York: Spark Publishing.

Kinsella, Ritchie, and Igou (2017). 'Attributes and Applications of Heroes'. In S. T. Allison, G. R. Goethals, & R. M. Kramer (Eds.), Handbook of heroism and heroic leadership. New York: Routledge.

Kafashan, S., Sparks, A., Rotella, A., and Barclay, P. (2016). Why Heroism Exists, Evolutionary Perspectives on Extreme Helping. In S. T. Allison, G. R. Goethals, & R. M. Kramer (Eds.), Handbook of heroism and heroic leadership. New York: Routledge.

McLeod, S. (2016, September 16). Maslow's Hierarchy of Needs. Retrieved from https://www.simplypsychology.org/maslow.html

Mittelman, W. (1991, January 1). Maslow's Study of Self-Actualization. Retrieved from http://journals.sagepub.com/doi/abs/10.1177/0022167891311010

Tucci, G., Lopez, D. S., Kitagawa, J. M., Reynolds, F. E., Nakamura, H., & Snellgrove, D. L. (2017, July 18). Buddhism. Retrieved from https://www.britannica.com/topic/Buddhism

U. (2017, January 15). Problems. Retrieved from http://www.philosophyworks.org/problems/

27

DESMOND DOSS: THE TRANSFORMATION OF THE HERO OF HACKSAW RIDGE

MARK D. WHITE

A gunshot cracks nearby. A grenade is set off just a matter of feet away, decimating whomever and whatever is around the explosion. Planes buzz overhead, bringing nothing but more destruction with them. The surrounding men are all either dead or dying. The day is May 5, 1945, and the battle of Okinawa, one of the deadliest battles of World War 2, is just beginning. During the battle, an American combat medic named Desmond T. Doss, a man who has almost been discharged from the military for his beliefs several times, earns the Congressional Medal of Honor.

The purpose of this chapter is to provide an analysis of the heroic transformation of Desmond Doss. In doing so, I will focus on his transformation as it pertains to Joseph Campbell's hero's monomyth (Campbell, 1949). I will also analyze several other areas of heroic transformation such as the categorical shift from dependence to autonomy (Allison & Goethals, 2017), and his status as an underdog (Vandello et al., 2017), a transcendent hero (Goethals & Allison, 2012), and a martial hero (Franco, Blau, & Zimbardo, 2011). My analysis will also explore the benefits of suffering undergone by Doss and his fellow soldiers (Allison & Setterberg, 2016). This chapter will conclude with a brief description of the heroic characteristics that aided Doss on his journey, with emphasis on the "great eight" traits most commonly found among heroes (Allison et al., 2017).

Background on Doss

Doss, a Seventh-Day Adventist Christian from Lynchburg, Virginia had not always planned on joining the military. He was raised by his family to be as peaceful as possible, helping people in any capacity and keeping the Bible and religion above all else. When Desmond was a child, his father bought a framed picture of the Ten Commandments with illustrations. Doss took the Commandments to heart, especially the sixth: "Thou shalt not kill." When Japan attacked Pearl Harbor in 1941, Doss was working at the Newport News Naval shipyard, and it was on that day that he decided to go above and beyond for his country.

Rather than request a deferment, he joined the Army as a medic with the belief that he would not have to bring a weapon into combat, and could therefore uphold his nonviolent values. This mindset, however, caused several problems on his journey to actual deployment. During training, his commanding officers tried – unsuccessfully -- to court martial him for not following their direct order to carry a firearm. Moreover, his fellow soldiers threatened and ostracized him for his refusal to even touch a gun.

Things began turning around when the men discovered that this quiet unassuming medic had a way to heal the blisters on their march-weary feet. And if someone fainted from heat stroke, this medic was at his side, offering his own canteen. Desmond never held a grudge. With kindness and gentle courtesy, he treated those who had mistreated him. He lived the golden rule, "...do to others what you would have them do to you..." (Matthew 7:12 NIV) (Desmond Doss Council, 2004).

Doss's selfless willingness to help others before considering the consequences to himself was exactly what earned him the Medal of Honor during the Battle of Okinawa. After securing the rockface known as Hacksaw Ridge, the Allies were surprised by a vicious Japanese counterattack, prompting the Officers to order an immediate retreat. Less than one third of the Americans reached the bottom of the cliff alive. Disobeying orders, Desmond stayed in the firefight, singlehandedly saving at least 75 Allied soldiers (he was credited for 75, but the Army estimated over 100) by going directly back into enemy gunfire, dragging each man to the cliff, then lowering them to the safety of the Allied camp below.

Desmond's actions on Hacksaw Ridge were a culmination of great physical and mental strength along with a calling from his God and country to help set the world right again by saving lives, rather than taking them. The events of Hacksaw Ridge marked the culmination of Desmond's journey as a hero (Campbell, 1949), thus solidifying his journey from dependency to autonomy (Allison et al., 2019; Allison & Goethals, 2017). His heroic actions proved everyone wrong by illustrating that he could be an effective soldier without carrying a weapon, that he could save lives in his role as a disadvantaged underdog. This combination of transformative characteristics also contributes to his classification as a transcendent hero (Allison & Goethals, 2013; Goethals & Allison, 2012).

Doss' Journey as a Hero

According to the hero's monomyth, there are three main stages of any hero's journey: departure, initiation, and return (Campbell, 1949). In the departure stage, the hero embarks on a journey as a result of some outside force leading or inspiring him to leave the safety of home. In Desmond's case, the departure occurred when he left the Newport News Naval shipyard to begin training with the Army. In the initiation stage, the hero is presented with a set of challenges or enemies who hinder the completion of the heroic journey. According to Campbell, heroes need the help of mentors to aide in accomplishing their heroic goals and advancing to the next stage. Desmond did not have a direct mentor during his training to help him through the process, but his parents were indirect mentor by instilling in him lessons that he carried with him to training. Consistent with his faith, Desmond arranged to attend church once a week as well as read the Bible during training so that he could maintain a strong relationship with his God, who served as the ultimate moral mentor throughout his journey.

Desmond faced many obstacles on the way to completing his journey, including his time at boot camp where he was almost court martialed and was consistently ostracized by his fellow soldiers for his anti-violence beliefs and his status as a conscientious objector. His true personal mandate, as it pertains to his personal hero's journey, was to save as many lives as possible. He accomplished this feat heroically during the battle of Okinawa, thus marking the physical completion of his journey and providing a boon to society by saving 75 lives and inspiring millions of people with his efforts. Aside from the battle of Okinawa and his tour there, Doss also served in Guam and Leyte, continuing the service he provided in Okinawa and saving even more lives. These continued services after the completion of his journey represent additional gifts to society after his initial distinguishing heroic act. He used what he learned from his journey and continued to apply it to other areas of his life, thus positively serving humanity as a whole.

Without his childhood experiences and strong faith, his heroic journey would likely not have been completed. During the return stage of the journey, the hero returns to his original world, bestowing upon it a boon or reward as a result of his accomplishments. Desmond's boon was obvious given that he saved the lives of 75 others, but he also served as an inspiration for heroes of the future by setting an example of what true valor and courage looks like. He also continued to give back to the world after he retired from the military, speaking internationally to youth groups on character development (Desmond Doss Council, 2004). It is clear that Desmond Doss not only successfully completed the hero's journey on an individual level, but also completed the journey holistically, as the entire country benefited and continues to benefit from Doss's heroic actions.

For his heroism, Doss was awarded the Congressional Medal of Honor, which did not change his priorities later in life but definitely solidified the country's appreciation for his remarkable feats. In addition to his Medal of Honor, he earned "a Bronze Star for valor with one Oak Leaf cluster (signifying he received two Bronze Stars); Purple Heart with two Oak Leaf clusters (signifying he received three Purple Hearts); the Asiatic-Pacific Campaign Medal with three Bronze Stars, a beachhead arrowhead (signifying he served in four combat campaigns including an amphibious landing under combat conditions); the Good Conduct Medal; the American Defense Campaign; and the Presidential Unit Citation given to the 1st Battalion, 307Inf, 77th Infantry Division for securing the Maeda Escarpment" (Desmond Doss Council, 2004). Even with all these recognitions, Doss remained a humble hero throughout his life (Worthington & Allison, 2018).

These many recognitions have been shown to have a minimal impact on the awarded individual, but they do serve as a method for a hero's followers to build them up as the moral hero they perceive them to be (Decter-Frain et al., 2017). These awards and the legendary status they bestow upon a hero may also serve as an example of Doss being a transfigured or constructed hero. The abundance of awards he received, as well as the popular documentary about the battle and Doss' actions, clearly helped build his legacy as one of the greatest military heroes ever (Goethals & Allison, 2012). I am not implying that his awards were not warranted; he most certainly deserved every award he received. However, he may not have received the same amount of appreciation and recognition from the general public for his actions had it not been for his highly publicized awards and for the movie made based on his life.

Transformation into the Role of Combat Medic

There are three main categories of transformations that heroes may undergo throughout the course of their journey: egocentricity to sociocentricity, stagnation to growth, and dependence to autonomy (Allison & Goethals, 2017). Desmond's journey resulted in a transformation of dependence to autonomy. Autonomy is defined as "a person's willingness to deviate from the dominant cultural pattern... [which is] essential for heroic transformation. Heroes do the right thing, and do what they must do, regardless of authority, tradition, and consequence," and applies directly to Desmond Doss (Allison & Goethals, 2017).

Before Desmond embarked on his journey, he showed signs of autonomy through his unbreakable faith established from a very early age. As a child, when he saw his father's picture of the 10 Commandments, he would ask himself, "why did Cain kill Abel? How in the world could a brother do such a thing?", thus exhibiting his distaste for violence even at a young age. Being brought up in a non-violent household obviously had a tremendous influence on him (Desmond Doss Council, 2004).

By ignoring the norms of the culture surrounding him, bearing the pressure of not carrying a firearm, and remaining a devout Christian, Desmond showed that he was willing to disregard the dominant normative pattern and remain faithful to his religion. Consequently, he became able to thrive on his own and maintain his values as an independent person even when his beliefs countered those of the majority. This marked his transformation to autonomy. He also risked his own life despite being told to retreat on Hacksaw Ridge, once again illustrating his disregard for the normative behavior of his peers and allowing him to save the lives that earned him his Medal of Honor.

Doss as an Underdog

The classic underdog tale of an unlikely hero rising to the occasion to conquer challenges that faces him has become a favorite in pop culture and storytelling in general. As the story of Hacksaw Ridge pans out, it's nearly impossible to not root for Desmond's success, and Vandello et al. (2017) provide several reasons why we love underdogs such as Doss. First, it is easy to identify with an underdog because almost every individual has been an underdog at some point; we all come from unexpected places to reach our goals. Second, it is extremely thrilling when the underdog finally achieves success, as people tend to see it as "due justice" when underdogs reach their goals or win. Successful underdogs, in other words, balance the scales of justice. Finally, underdogs also provide inspiration and give us hope when they do well. This inspirational quality of underdogs may stem from how much we all can easily relate to underdogs (Vandello et al., 2017). Desmond's story is that of an underdog to its core, with his humble beginnings, his unwillingness to arm himself in combat, and his courage in saving at least 75 lives under the most dangerous circumstances of war.

The Benefits of Suffering

Along with his fellow soldiers deployed at Hacksaw ridge, Desmond Doss exemplified several of the benefits of suffering (Allison & Setterberg, 2016). The soldiers surrounding Doss all showed much more humility and compassion, and were much more united socially as a result of the suffering they endured together. His allies showed a much greater appreciation for him after he risked his life to save so many of their own, and many of them were inspired, prompting them to follow in his footsteps and help save lives of others in future battles.

Continued Service and Heroic Subtype Categorization

Several days after the events of Hacksaw Ridge, Doss was badly wounded in an unsuccessful night raid by a grenade detonating near him, tearing into his leg all the way up to his hip. During his efforts seek safe shelter from the attack, he was struck by a sniper's bullet which shattered his arm. After he treated his own wounds, he ordered the litter-bearers who were sent to rescue him and bring him to safety to take other men out before him. Nearly bleeding out, Doss was once again willingly disregarded his own life to save the lives of others, demonstrating his unrelenting selflessness in every situation (Desmond Doss Council, 2004).

Due to his position as a member of the Army, Doss fits the category of a martial hero as he was bound by a code of conduct to be a hero and went above and beyond the call of duty (Franco, Blau, & Zimbardo, 2011). As a martial hero, Doss was duty-bound to perform heroic acts and was repeatedly exposed to high-risk situations. For his actions to be considered heroic, he had to exceed the call of duty (Franco et al., 2011). The Medal of Honor is awarded to soldiers who demonstrate conspicuous gallantry and intrepidity at the risk of life above and beyond expectations. Doss's achievement of such an award thus fulfills Franco et al.'s classification of a heroic act for a martial hero.

Doss as a Transcendent Hero

According to the social influence-based taxonomical structure of heroes, there are 10 types of heroes: trending, transitory, transitional, tragic, transposed, transparent, traditional, transfigured, transforming, and transcendent (Goethals

& Allison, 2012). Within this taxonomy, Doss would be considered a transcendent hero due to the fact that he demonstrates the attributes of several different types of heroes, thus "transcending" the other categories of heroism. The main attributes he exhibits from the various categories of heroes come from those of the transparent hero, the traditional hero, and the transforming hero. Doss exhibits the unseen component of a transparent hero as he wasn't widely known before he received a Medal of Honor or until the movie Hacksaw Ridge was released. It can also be argued that

Doss was a transfigured, or created hero due to the exponential rise in popularity he experienced after the movie Hacksaw Ridge came out, despite the movie being released several years after his death. As a traditional hero, Doss mostly represents the moral heroic subtype as his faith is what inspired him to save lives, serving as a moral exemplar for others. A transforming hero is defined as one who transforms societies, and Desmond managed to transform societies as his actions led the capturing of the Maeda escarpment and eventually the city of Okinawa, playing a large role in the Allies' victory in the war. Aside from these attributes, Doss also displayed several traits that aided in his heroic performance.

Characteristics that Contributed to Doss's Heroism

Doss exemplified each of the "great eight" traits derived from studies of people's perceptions of heroes. The great eight includes the following: intelligent, strong, reliable, resilient, caring, charismatic, selfless, and inspiring (Allison & Goethals, 2011; Allison et al., 2017). The story of Doss's actions on Hacksaw Ridge is a great example of an individual demonstrating every trait at once or at varying times throughout the battle. He was intelligent enough to be able to diagnose and treat each of the 75 men, strong enough to carry each of them back on his own, reliable and resilient enough to keep coming back until he could not find anyone else to help, caring enough to put others' lives ahead of his own in order to save them, charismatic in a bit of a unique way by remaining modest after his accomplishments, and inspiring to anyone who follows in his footsteps, including followers he gained as a result of his awards. Doss's embodiment of all eight of the necessary characteristics of heroism illustrate yet again that he is the quintessential hero, and especially is one that deserved all the recognitions he received.

I have argued in this chapter that Desmond Doss represents the textbook definition of a hero. With regard to his heroic journey, he transformed from a young Christian boy to a protagonist who is arguably the most selflessness and courageous man in American wartime history. The most important part of his journey, the return, yielded many boons to the rest of society, most notably in the saving of over 75 of his fellow soldiers' lives. The inspiration provided by his story and his speeches that followed it no doubt exerted a remarkably positive effect on audiences worldwide.

Doss died on March 23, 2006 at the age of 87, and he was buried in the National Cemetery in Chattanooga, Tennessee. His story remains alive via the documentaries The Conscientious Objector and Hacksaw Ridge. If every individual had a mindset similar to that of Doss, the mindset that they will change the world for the better no matter the personal costs and that they will save lives despite seemingly insurmountable odds against them, how different would the world be? What kind of inspiration can everyday people take away from Doss's actions in their day-to-day lives, and how might they apply this inspiration? There is no doubt that Desmond Doss has provided the ultimate example of how ordinary people can become exceptional.

REFERENCES

Allison, S. T. (2015). The initiation of heroism science. Heroism Science, 1, 1-8.

Allison, S. T., & Goethals, G. R. (2011). Heroes: What they do and why we need them. New York: Oxford University Press.

Allison, S. T., & Goethals, G. R. (2013). Heroic leadership: An influence taxonomy of 100 exceptional individuals. New York: Routledge.

Allison, S. T., & Goethals, G. R. (2017). The hero's transformation. In S. T. Allison, G. R. Goethals, & R. M. Kramer (Eds.), Handbook of heroism and heroic leadership. New York: Routledge.

Allison, S. T., Goethals, G. R., & Kramer, R. M. (2017). Setting the scene: The rise and coalescence of heroism science. In S. T. Allison, G. R. Goethals, & R. M. Kramer (Eds.), Handbook of heroism and heroic leadership. New York: Routledge.

Allison, S. T., Goethals, G. R., & Kramer, R. M. (Eds.) (2017). Handbook of heroism and heroic leadership. New York: Routledge.

Allison, S. T., Goethals, G. R., Marrinan, A. R., Parker, O. M., Spyrou, S. P., Stein, M. (2019). The metamorphosis of the hero: Principles, processes, and purpose. Frontiers in Psychology.

Allison, S. T., & Setterberg, G. C. (2016). Suffering and sacrifice: Individual and collective benefits, and implications for leadership. In S. T. Allison, C. T. Kocher, & G. R. Goethals (Eds), Frontiers in spiritual leadership: Discovering the better angels of our nature. New York: Palgrave Macmillan.

Campbell, J. J. (1949). The Hero with a Thousand Faces. New York: MJF Books

Davis, J. L., Burnette, J. L., Allison, S. T., & Stone, H. (2011). Against the odds: Academic underdogs benefit from incremental theories. Social Psychology of Education, 14, 331-346.

Desmond Doss Council (2004). Desmond Doss: The Real Story. Retrieved from https://desmonddoss.com/bio/bio-real.php

Decter-Frain et al. (2017). Why and How Groups Create Moral Heroes. In S. T. Allison, G. R. Goethals, & R. M. Kramer (Eds.), Handbook of heroism and heroic leadership. New York: Routledge.

Eylon, D., & Allison, S. T. (2005). The frozen in time effect in evaluations of the dead. Personality and Social Psychology Bulletin, 31, 1708-1717.

Goethals, G. R., & Allison, S. T. (2012). Making heroes: The construction of courage, competence and virtue. Advances in Experimental Social Psychology, 46, 183–235. doi: 10.1016/B978-0-12-394281- 4.00004-0

Gray, K., Anderson, S., Doyle, C. M., Hester, N., Schmitt, P., Vonasch, A., Allison, S. T., and Jackson, J. C. (2018). To be immortal, do good or evil. Personality and Social Psychology Bulletin.

Kinsella et al. (2017). Attributes and Applications of Heroes. In S. T. Allison, G. R. Goethals, & R. M. Kramer (Eds.), Handbook of heroism and heroic leadership. New York: Routledge.

Vandello et al. (2017). Underdogs as Heroes. In S. T. Allison, G. R. Goethals, & R. M. Kramer (Eds.), Handbook of heroism and heroic leadership. New York: Routledge.

Worthington, E. L, & Allison, S. T. (2018). Heroic humility: What the science of humility can say to people raised on self-focus. Washington. DC: American Psychological Association.

28

SULLY SULLENBERGER: AN INSPIRING TALE OF TWO HEROIC TRANSFORMATIONS

KARA E. CROMWELL

Mason Wells is an ordinary American teen who has transformed into an extraordinary survivor. Wells is only 19 years old but he has survived three different terrorist attacks within three years: the Boston Marathon bombings, the Paris attacks, and the Brussels Airport attack. He was not injured during the first two attacks, but suffered second and third-degree burns, a ruptured Achilles tendon, and shrapnel wounds in Brussels (Mohney, 2016). Wells was only a block away from the finish line of the Boston Marathon, waiting for his mom to cross the line, when the bombs exploded. Wells' father tells interviewers: "[the blast] had shaken their bodies" (Mohney,

2016). During the interview, Wells' parents do not go into much detail about the Paris attack, but they confirm that he was there.

Wells was at the Brussels Airport on the day of the attack with two other Mormon missionaries. They were dropping off a colleague at the ticket desk when the bombs exploded, and were essentially at ground zero (Mohney, 2016). All survived, but they had injuries and burns comparable to Wells. Wells told CNN that when the first blast happened, "my body was actually picked off the ground for a moment... and I was covered in a lot of fluids, a lot of blood, and a lot of blood that wasn't mine" (Pearson, 2016). Mason and his parents both state that each event prepared him for the next and that Mason is unbelievably lucky to be alive (Mohney, 2016). At some point though, Mason's life experiences cannot be attributed to just luck. The probability of dying in terrorist attack is 1 in 20 million ("Deadly Statistics", 2010). While there is no statistic for the probability of being near or injured in a terrorist attack, one can reasonably predict that it would be a similar number. We can thus extrapolate that the chance that Mason was in three terrorist attacks is about 1 in 8 sextillion. People like Mason who experience unlikely things multiple times are few and far between.

Sully Sullenberger can be added to this short list of rare people. Sully is the pilot who famously landed US Airways Flight 1549 on the Hudson River after a dual engine loss. He saved the lives of all 155 people on board. On the surface, this appears to be just one rare act of heroism, but an in-depth study of Sully's life shows that like Mason, he has been through multiple heroic transformations.

The goal of this chapter is to apply the science of heroism to analyze the life of the hero Sully Sullenberger. I will demonstrate that Sully went through not one, but two hero transformations. Both of his transformations align with Bronk and Riches' (2017) paradigm of purpose-guided heroism and heroism-guided purpose. In describing these transformations, I will offer an analysis of the definitions of heroism and the hero classification taxonomies that can be applied to Sully. I will then examine Sully's life before, during, and after his heroic actions using Joseph Campbell's (1949) monomyth. Finally, I will explore the implications of this argument for society and for future research.

Historically, heroism was associated with many masculine characteristics such as strength and bravery (Houghes-Hallet, 2004). Hero worship was compared to divine worship and classical heroes were thought to possess god-like qualities (Carlyle, 1841). Today, scholars in the field of heroism science do not agree on a single, all-encompassing definition of heroism, but most have proposed definitions include the same basic criteria. Allison, Goethals, and Kramer (2017) distinguish between two definitional categories of heroism. There is the objective approach in which people must meet certain standards to be considered a hero, and the subjective approach which takes on the idea that "heroism is in the eye of the beholder" (Allison & Goethals, 2011, p. 196).

Some examples of characteristics that are required in objective definitions include: taking great risk for a socially valued goal (Becker & Eagly, 2004), no possibility of external gain (Franco, Blau, & Zimbardo, 2011), and actions that serve the greater good (Allison et al., 2017). Sully can be considered a hero through the objective approach because his action of landing Flight 1549 on the Hudson River serves the greater good by saving the lives of everyone on board and required Sully to take a tremendous risk. Sully is also a hero through the subjective approach, because the people who were on Flight 1549 were directly impacted by his heroism and regard him as a hero for saving their lives.

Heroes can be classified into various subtypes according to several different taxonomies. Franco, Blau, and Zimbardo (2011) offer a situational demand-based classification in which heroes are considered either military heroes, civilian heroes, or social heroes. The social heroes are further divided into ten categories: religious figures, politico-religious figures, martyrs, political leaders, adventurers, scientific heroes, good Samaritans, underdogs, bureaucracy heroes, and whistleblowers (Franco et al., 2011). Sully can be classified as a civilian hero for landing the plane on the Hudson River, because it was a physical heroic act. Goethals and Allison (2012) developed a social influence-based taxonomy which includes the categories: trending, transitory, traditional, tragic, transitional, transparent, transposed, transfigured, transforming, and transcendent. Sully is a transparent, or every day hero during his first transformation because of his profession as a pilot. Allison and Smith (2015) use a social structure-based taxonomy, which focuses on the types of transformations the heroes experience: emotional, mental, moral, physical, or spiritual. Sully experiences a spiritual transformation during his second transformation because of the new sense of purpose he develops after landing the plane on the Hudson. Taxonomies are critical to analyzing heroes because they help create a deeper understanding of the experience of each individual hero.

Purpose-Guided Heroism and Heroism-Guided Purpose

Bronk and Riches' (2017) theory of purpose-guided heroism and heroism-guided purpose creates the lens through which Sully's two transformations can be understood. Bronk and Riches use three criteria to define a life purpose. First, a person must have a meaningful, long-term goal which guides short-term behavior; second, the person must be actively engaged in pursuing his goal; and third, the goal must impact the broader world. Purpose-guided heroism occurs when people with an established purpose in life use that purpose to do something heroic. The reasoning behind this is that people with a purpose are better prepared to act heroically when the opportunity arises. On the flip side, heroism-guided purpose occurs when people discover their purpose after acting heroically. They see the world with a new perspective and become aware of injustices. Bronk and Riches' (2017) theory distinguishes Sully's two transformations: the first is purpose-guided heroism and the second is heroism-guided purpose.

ONE MONOMYTH, TWO TRANSFORMATIONS

Joseph Campbell's (1949) monomyth is the structure through which all heroic transformations occur. Even individuals who do not necessarily engage in an extravagant act of heroism can traverse the hero's journey (Solomon, 2011). The journey begins with the departure. There must be some event, either a voluntary decision or an involuntary force, that propels the individual into his journey (Goethals & Allison, 2019; Solomon, 2011). Everyone enters the departure stage with a missing quality, and the goal of the journey is to develop that quality (Campbell, 1949). The physical or metaphorical death of some element of the hero's previous life is a common phenomenon during the departure stage (Allison & Goethals, 2016; Solomon, 2011). After people pass through the departure, they enter the initiation stage, where the specific transforming or heroic act occurs (Campbell, 1949). The hero is typically accompanied by a mentor and displays a level of deviance during this time (Allison & Goethals, 2017).

The mentor's guidance and insight, and the hero's newfound ability to deviate from societal or cultural norms, help the hero acquire his missing quality (Allison & Smith, 2015). The initiation is also marked by obstacles and villains that the hero must face, which brings about suffering that the hero must experience. In overcoming these obstacles, villains, and suffering, the hero further develops his missing quality. Finally, the hero enters the return stage and brings back everything he learned on his journey and thereby helps society itself transform (Campbell, 1949).

Transformation 1: Purpose-Guided Heroism

Sully is famously known as a hero for landing a commercial airplane on the Hudson River, but in his life leading up to that public moment, Sully held the role of a transparent hero. Sully's ability to fly members of his family and, eventually, military planes and commercial planes, classifies him as an everyday hero because he sacrificed many things such as family time to serve others in a dangerous profession. Campbell's (1949) monomyth helps show that Sully underwent a transformation to become a transparent hero (Goethals & Allison, 2012) before landing the plane on the Hudson River.

In Sully's autobiography, Sully: My Search for What Really Matters, he writes that he discovered his calling to be a pilot at age 5. This sense of calling to be a pilot became his purpose in life. He spent countless hours each week reading everything about airplanes that he could get his hands on. Finally, when he turned 16, his parents let him begin taking flying lessons and flying went from a fantasy to a tangible passion (Sullenberger, 2009). Sully's desire to be a pilot serves as the force that propels him into the departure of his first hero's transformation. During Sully's childhood, he lacks confidence, not just in his ability to fly a plane, but also in his identity. This is the missing quality that his transformation serves to remedy.

Shortly after beginning lessons with Mr. Cook, Sully is exposed to the wreckage of a plane crash, and this event serves as a metaphorical death in his hero's transformation. One of Mr. Cook's friends accidentally approached the landing strip too early and too low, and unfortunately died on impact. When Sully examines the wreckage, he describes it as "a sobering moment" (Sullenberger, 2009, p.11). He forced himself to investigate the wreckage and look at the cockpit of the destroyed plane. In this moment, Sully began to comprehend the dangers associated with flying. Just as his calling to be a pilot matriculated into a passion when he had the opportunity to actually fly a plane, Sully's understanding of the risks associated with flying became tangible when he witnessed the wreckage.

After seventy hours of mentored flying, Sully was ready to take his private pilot license test (Sullenberger, 2009). This test, and particularly his success taking the test, serve as the back-bone of the initiation stage. A private pilot license allows Sully to take passengers on flights. He develops the confidence that he was previously lacking when he receives his license because it is physical verification that he is a capable and competent pilot. It also gives him the self-confidence to ask a girl out on a date and take her on flight (Sullenberger, 2009). His license represents his deviance from society. Sully writes in his autobiography that he was considered an outcast in high school because no one else had any interest in airplanes and pilots (Sullenberger, 2009). While his passion for flying has always made him different from his peers, the license was physical proof of his deviance. Dik et al. (2017) suggest that it is likely that a sense of calling or purpose is linked to the status of transparent hero, and Sully's transformation corroborates this hypothesis.

Sully's flying instructor, Mr. Cook, serves as his mentor for this transformation. Mr. Cook fits the wise, old man Jungian archetype, which is a common theme among mentors in hero stories (Allison et al., 2017). Cook was a crop dusting pilot who also served as a military training pilot during World War II. Sully describes Cook as a man of few words, only speaking when he needed to give a command and, on the rare occasion, compliments (Sullenberger, 2009). Sully states that during his first solo flight, "it was as if I could hear his voice... even though he wasn't with there in the airplane, his words were still with me" (Sullenberger, 2009, p. 8). This phenomenon of hearing a mentor's voice is very common in hero's transformations. The classic example comes from Star Wars when, on the Death Star and facing imminent danger, Luke Skywalker hears Obi-Wan Kenobi's voice saying: "use the Force, Luke" (Allison & Goethals, 2017). Allison and Smith (2015) argue that mentors help their heroes develop their missing qualities, and that these transforming mentors are a "pivotal component of the hero's journey" (Allison et al., 2017, p. 3). Mr. Cook can be accredited with helping Sully develop his confidence because he taught him everything he needed to know to be successful on the private pilot license test, and, therefore, has transformed Sully's life by serving as his mentor. Even now, after 19,700 hours of flying time, Sully still looks to Mr. Cook as an influential and transforming mentor (Sullenberger, 2009).

After Sully receives his license, he enters the return stage. With his new ability to fly passengers, Sully can bring his knowledge and skills back to his community to benefit society. Sully begins by taking his family members up in Mr. Cook's one passenger plane. As time goes on though, his contributions to society increase exponentially. Sully attended the Air Force Academy for college, receiving formal military pilot training. After earning a graduate degree from Purdue and completing further pilot training, he served his country in the US Air Force for 5 years with the rank of Captain (Sullenberger, 2009). Although he never saw combat, being a member of the armed forces is the most noble way an individual can give back to society. After serving in the Air Force, Sully became a commercial pilot and continued to give back to society. Sully comments that being a commercial pilot allows him to "share [his] passion for flying" (Sullenberger, 2009, p.18). Sully's first private license set him on a path of further education and helping society.

Sully's first transformation fits into Bronk and Riches' (2017) classification of purpose-guided heroism. Sully's calling to be a pilot fits the criteria that Bronk and Riches (2017) define for having a purpose in life. His long-term goal is to have a career as a pilot and this guides his behavior of reading about airplanes, taking lessons, and attending the Air Force Academy. His short-term behaviors also demonstrate that he is engaged in his long-term goal nearly every day of his life. Sully's goal impacts the broader world, as evidenced by his return stage. Since Sully has a purpose in life, the heroic act that he completes during the initiation stage is purpose-guided heroism. His purpose in life of being a pilot is what leads him to take his private pilot license test.

Transformation 2: Heroism-Guided Purpose

On January 15, 2009, Sully successfully landed US Airways Flight 1549 on the Hudson River, propelling him to national fame. Sully risked his life, along with all of those on board, to attempt something that was deemed impossible and save everyone on the plane. His experience and knowledge that he developed through his first transformation as a transparent hero allowed him to take calculated risks to land the plane. This heroic act is more in line with objective definitions of heroism. Unlike Sully's first transformation which was guided by a purpose to be a pilot, this heroic act creates a new purpose in life for him.

The initiation stage of Sully's second transformation is the same time period as the return of his first transformation, but analyzed under a different context. Sully was 57 years old when he landed the plane on the Hudson and airlines require pilots to retire at age 65, so during the months and years leading up to this event, Sully was struggling with what he wanted to do with his life after retirement (Sullenberger, 2009). Sully lacked courage, not in the conventional sense of taking physical risks, but rather he did not have the courage to end the life that he has known and take up something new. Sully started a company called Safety Reliability Methods Inc. to help other industries implement some of the safety tactics used by pilots, but he was not ready to give up being a pilot and switch over to being a CEO (Sullenberger, 2009). Even though his family was beginning to struggle financially, he could not find the courage to change his life. Sully's transition from departure to initiation is marked by an involuntary force: Sully did not choose to lose thrust in both engines on that day, but this event placed him in a situation to develop courage.

The initiation stage includes Sully's heroism on Flight 1549 and the obstacles he faces in the immediate aftermath of the event. After the birds flew into the engines and the plane lost thrust, Sully was instructed by air traffic control to immediately return to LaGuardia Airport for an emergency landing. When he said that was impossible, they suggested another airport nearby in New Jersey. Sully defied both orders from authority and decided to attempt a water landing on the Hudson River instead (Sullenberger, 2009). Sully's deviance is what enables his heroic act. Had he followed the directions of the air traffic controller, the plane would have crashed into a building in New York City, offering no chance of survival and killing lives on the ground. It takes extreme courage to defy orders and follow one's instincts, so Sully's heroic act developed his missing quality of courage. Mr. Cook continued to serve as Sully's mentor during the emergency landing. Sully claims that "Mr. Cook's lessons were a part of what guided me on that five-minute flight" (Sullenberger, 2009, p. 15).

A hero will often face obstacles, such as villainous characters, that make their journey more difficult (Allison, 2015; Allison et al., 2017). Sully's "villain" was the National Transportation Safety Board (NTSB). The role of the NTSB was to investigate the crash and ensure that Sully did not unreasonably put the lives of his passengers at risk to land the plane on the water. The film Sully depicts the NTSB as more villainous than they really were, but there were some aspects of the investigation that threatened to ruin Sully's reputation and caused him to channel even more courage (Epstein, 2016). The NTSB ran simulations to figure out if the plane could have made it back to either of the airports safely. Originally, eight out of the fifteen simulations showed a successful landing (Epstein, 2016). Sully, however, showed defiance and defended his decision, claiming that the simulations did not properly account for the real-life reaction times of pilots. In the one simulation where a time delay was added, the plane crashed on its way back to LaGuardia (Epstein, 2016). The obstacles presented by the NTSB caused a level of suffering for Sully, but through the suffering, Sully became more courageous.

The return stage of Sully's second transformation is what characterizes the transformation as heroism-guided purpose. Sully retired in March of 2010, and he found a new purpose in life as a safety advocate (Sullenberger, 2009). He authored two books, Sully: My Search for What Really Matters and Making a Difference: Stories of Vision and Courage from America's Leaders. The first chronicles his experience with Flight 1549 and divulges many details of his personal life and why he is the person he is today. The second looks at the nature of leadership and how it can be developed through the stories of many top leaders (sullysullenberger.com, 2016). Sully also created a video training program called "Miracle on the Hudson: Prepare for Safety" which is used by organizations worldwide to teach employees a commitment to safety (sullysullenberger.com, 2016).

Sully speaks at educational institutions, corporations, and nonprofit organizations about "aviation and patient safety, crisis management, life-long preparation, leadership and living a life of integrity" (sullysullenberger. com, 2016). He is regarded as an expert in the field of aviation safety and has been called to testify in front of Congress. Recently, he was asked to serve on the Department of Transportation's Advisory Committee on Automation in Transportation (sullysullenberger.com, 2016). The return stage requires that hero gives a "gift" to society after their transformation (Campbell, 1949). Sully's accomplishments after Flight 1549 not only represent his "gift" to society, but also his new purpose of safety advocacy. In alignment with Bronk and Riches' (2017) theory, Sully's heroism allowed him to see the world in a new light and develop a new purpose (Davis et al., 2011). Sully uses his newly developed courageousness to make this change in his life purpose.

Allison et al. (2017) propose that all heroes have at least one characteristic on a list termed the Great Eight. Sully possesses two of these characteristics: intelligent and inspiring. Sully is very knowledgeable on aviation and safety because of his experience in the field and his devotion to his purposes in life. His intelligence is why he is regarded as an expert and is sought after by top officials. Sully is also inspiring, not just because of what he accomplished with Flight 1549, but for his whole life story because he represents the pinnacle of human accomplishments. Sully was ranked number two in TIME'S "Top 100 Most Influential Heroes and Icons of 2009", proving that society views him as inspirational (sullysullenberger.com, 2016).

CONCLUSION

This chapter has demonstrated that Sully Sullenberger underwent two heroic transformations, in accordance with Bronk's and Riches' (2017) theory of purpose-guided heroism and heroism-guided purpose. His life experiences can be classified under Joseph Campbell's (1949) monomyth to emphasize the two distinct transformations. Sully's first transformation is centered around his missing quality of confidence and his status as an unsung hero. His second transformation is characterized by Flight 1549, his development of courage, and his gift back to society.

The realization that people can undergo multiple hero transformations and have multiple purposes throughout life, has important implications for society. Adults in today's world constantly ask kids, "what do you want to be when you grow up?" The expectation is that the child will provide one answer. While their answer may change over time, they never say something such as, "I want to be a doctor and a teacher." In reality though, a child could grow up to be a doctor and a teacher. A person's first purpose in life could be to save lives by being a doctor, but then down the road their purpose could shift and they could become a teacher. However, Americans do not typically think this way, and children are raised to believe that while they can become anything, they cannot become multiple things.

Statistics show that only 49% of Americans are satisfied with their career, and only 51% feel they get a sense of identity from their job (The State of American Jobs, 2016). While there are many reasons for discontentment in the work-place, if people can have a heroic role model like Sully who developed the courage to shift purposes and follow a new career path, people may be more inspired to discover a new purpose and transform their own lives. Role models can help create a growth mindset because people are motivated to change and develop. Kinsella et al. (2015) refer to this phenomenon as the enhancing function of heroes. Future research can investigate how role models and heroes with a sense of calling or purpose impact people's perspectives on, and feelings about, their careers. If more people can develop the courage to shift careers like Sully did, the overall well-being of society (Efthimiou, Allison, & Franco, 2018) would be enhanced immeasurably.

REFERENCES

Allison, S. T. (2015). The initiation of heroism science. Heroism Science, 1, 1-8.
Allison, S. T., & Goethals, G. R. (2011). Heroes: What they do and why we need them. New York: Oxford University Press.
Allison, S. T., & Goethals, G. R. (2016). Hero worship: The elevation of the human spirit. Journal for the Theory of Social Behaviour, 46, 187-210.
Allison, S. T., Goethals, G. R., & Kramer, R. M. (2017). Setting the scene: The rise and coalescence of heroism science. In S. T. Allison, G. R. Goethals, & R. M. Kramer (Eds.), Handbook of heroism and heroic leadership. New York: Routledge.
Allison, S. T., & Goethals, G. R. (2017). The hero's transformation. In S. T. Allison, G. R. Goethals, & R. M. Kramer (Eds.), Handbook of heroism and heroic leadership. New York: Routledge.
Allison, S. T., & Smith, G. (2015). Reel heroes & villains. Richmond Agile Writer Press.
Becker, S. W., & Eagly, A. H. (2004). The heroism of women and men. The American Psychologist, 59, 163–178.

Bronk, K. C. & Riches, B. R. (2017). The intersection of purpose and heroism: A study of exemplars. In Allison et al. (eds) Handbook of Heroism and Heroic Leadership, pp. (495-506). New York: Routledge.

Campbell, J. (1949). The hero with a thousand faces. New York: New World Library.

Carlyle, T. (1841). Heroes, hero worship, and the heroic in history. Philadelphia, PA: Henry Altemus.

Davis, J. L., Burnette, J. L., Allison, S. T., & Stone, H. (2011). Against the odds: Academic underdogs benefit from incremental theories. Social Psychology of Education, 14, 331-346.

"Deadly Statistics". Lifeinsurancequotes.org. Lifeinsurancequotes.org, 2010. Retrieved from http://www.lifeinsurancequotes.org

Dik, B. J., Shimizu, A. B., & O'Connor, W. (2017). Career development and a sense of calling: Contexts for heroism, pp. (316-338). In Allison et al. (eds) Handbook of Heroism and Heroic Leadership. New York: Routledge.

Efthimiou, O., Allison, S. T., & Franco, Z. E. (Eds.) (2018). Heroism and wellbeing in the 21st Century: Applied and emerging perspectives. New York: Routledge.

Epstein, A. "US aviation investigators say they're unfairly villainized in Clint Eastwood's film "Sully"". Quartz Media LLC. Atlantic Media Inc., 9 Sept 2016. Retrieved from: https://qz.com

Eylon, D., & Allison, S. T. (2005). The frozen in time effect in evaluations of the dead. Personality and Social Psychology Bulletin, 31, 1708-1717.

Franco, Z. E., Blau, K., & Zimbardo, P. G. (2011). Heroism: A conceptual analysis and differentiation between heroic action and altruism. Review of General Psychology, 15, 99–113.

Goethals, G. R., & Allison, S. T. (2012). Making heroes: The construction of courage, competence and virtue. Advances in Experimental Social Psychology, 46, 183–235. doi:10.1016/B978-0-12-394281- 4.00004-0

Goethals, G. R., & Allison, S. T. (2019). The Romance of heroism: Ambiguity, attribution, and apotheosis. West Yorkshire: Emerald.

Hughes-Hallett, L. (2004). Heroes. London: HarperCollins.

Kinsella, E. L., Ritchie, T. D., & Igou, E. R. (2017). Attributes and applications of heroes: A brief history of lay and academic perspectives. In Allison et al. (eds) Handbook of Heroism and Heroic Leadership pp. (19-35). New York: Routledge.

Mohney, G. (2016, March 22). American teen survives attack in Brussels, his third brush with terrorism. ABC News. Retrieved from http://abcnews.go.com

Pearson, M. (2016, March 26). 'I'm very lucky' – Brussels attack survivors tell their stories. CNN. Retrieved from http://www.cnn.com

Solomon, P. T. (Director). (2011) Finding Joe [Motion Picture]. United States: Distribber.

The state of American jobs. (2016, Oct 6). PEW Research Center. Retrieved from http://www.pewsocialtrends.org

Sullenberger, C. B. & Zaslow, J. (2009). Sully: My search for what really matters. New York: HarperCollins

SullySullenberger.com (2016). Retrieved from http://www.sullysullenberger.com

Worthington, E. L, & Allison, S. T. (2018). Heroic humility: What the science of humility can say to people raised on self-focus. Washington. DC: American Psychological Association.

.

29

ELEANOR ROOSEVELT'S HEROIC AND TRANSCENDENT ROLE AS FIRST LADY

JOANN CHONGSARITSINSUK

Nothing came easy to her. In fact, disappointment became the norm. Dark clouds surrounded her all the time. Father: an alcoholic. Mother: depressed. This seemed to be just the tip of the iceberg for the troubles that she would face throughout her life. By the time she was ten, she had lost both her mother and father. She now claimed the status of "orphan". She was passed off to her grandmother and had no one except her two younger brothers. Essentially, she was left to traverse adolescence and young adulthood by herself. Tragedy after tragedy, there seemed to be no end to her misery. It seemed unlikely that she would ever get past these setbacks she faced at an early age. This could be the beginning of the rest of her life, but in the end, she did not let her struggles define her. She was Eleanor Roosevelt.

Eleanor was born into a rich upper-class family. Her father, Elliot, was the younger brother of Theodore Roosevelt, and her mother Anna came from a wealthy New York family (Black, 2017). Anna especially valued "feminine qualities" and beauty. She was considered one of New York's most stunning beauties. She constantly made young Eleanor self-conscious of her demeanor and appearance (Black, 2017). Eleanor was even nicknamed "Granny" by her mother for her plain, old fashioned, and serious demeanor (Black, 2017). Eleanor was very mature for her age during her childhood and to others; she seemed like a little old woman trapped in the body of a ten-year-old girl.

During a time when women were valued for their physical appearances and beauty, Eleanor believed that beauty was unimportant in the grand scheme of things. There were more important qualities in a person that took precedence, such as intelligence and profound passion about a topic of interest to the person. As a result, she gained another nickname. Her peers called her "ugly duckling" which highlighted how she stood out from everyone else her age. When she was around her friends, Eleanor always faded into the background. This continued for most of her childhood, but she learned to live with others outshining her, especially when there were more important things on her plate.

When Eleanor was just nine years old, she experienced her first tragedy. In 1892, she lost her mother to diphtheria, and the loss took a large toll on Eleanor (History.com, 2009). She became steadfastly devoted to her father despite his constant absence. When he was present, Elliot adored his daughter and loved her with uncritical abandon. Elliot always referred to Eleanor as his "darling little Nell" (Black, 2017). Regrettably, nineteen months later Elliot died from depression and alcoholism. He had attempted suicide by jumping from a window but survived that fall. His death came a couple of days later when he was hospitalized for the injury and suffered a deadly seizure. After her father died, her grandmother Mary Hall became her legal guardian. Eleanor lived with Mary until she was fifteen years old, at which point Mary sent Eleanor off to a private boarding school called Allenswood Academy in London (History.com, 2009). There she met her influential mentor and teacher, Marie Souvestre, who was the school's headmistress.

Eleanor's Return to The Big Apple

Eleanor stayed at Allenswood Academy for three years until her grandmother believed it was time for Eleanor to "come out as a woman" to society. She returned to Manhattan, New York, at the age of eighteen in 1902 (Caroli, 2017). During her time at home, she became actively involved with social reform work and joined a number of organizations including the National Consumers League and the Junior League for the Promotion of Settlement Movements. She became actively with these organizations and also served as a volunteer teacher for impoverished immigrant children at a nearby settlement house in her spare time (History.com, 2009). She was dedicated to her work and soon became known for her activism.

Later that summer, she met her future husband. In July of 1902, Eleanor took a train back home to Tivoli to visit her grandmother. Franklin Roosevelt, her father's fifth cousin, was also on the same train as Eleanor. At the time, he was a student at Harvard. They continued to meet after their chance encounter on the train. After a year of "dating", they became engaged on November 22, 1903 and got married on March 17, 1905 (Black, 2017). Eleanor was now only years away from becoming First Lady.

Becoming First Lady

In 1911, Dutchess County elected Franklin Roosevelt to the New York Senate. Shortly after, Franklin joined Woodrow Wilson's administration and was later appointed Assistant Secretary of the Navy in 1913 (Black, 2017). By this time, Eleanor had become accustomed to the expectations that came with being the wife of a politician. She acted as Franklin's eyes and ears and as a trusted and tireless reporter (Anna Eleanor Roosevelt, 2017). During World War I, Eleanor found that she enjoyed a more public political role contributing valuable service to projects such as the Navy Relief and Red Cross (History.com, 2017). Although being Franklin's wife had propelled her into the public eye, Eleanor had stepped into the public eye long before through her work with the National Consumer League and volunteer work. Nevertheless, once Eleanor was officially dubbed first lady, she stepped into a powerful role that would provide a strong base for her to continue her activism.

During her time as First Lady, Eleanor was an active champion of civil rights for African Americans, and an advocate for women, American workers, the poor and young people. Roosevelt encouraged her husband to appoint more women to federal positions and held hundreds of press conferences for female reporters during a time when women were typically barred from White House press conferences (History.com, 2017). These were just some of the things Eleanor Roosevelt did that paved the way for the contemporary views present in society regarding sex and civil rights today.

Ring Ring: Her Call to Heroism

During her time at Allenswood Academy, Eleanor's headmistress Souvestre proved to be a great mentor to Eleanor. Souvestre was a noted feminist educator who sought to cultivate independent thinking in young women, and she took a special interest in Roosevelt who became passionate about feminism as well (Black, 2017). Souvestre played a key role in shaping Eleanor's social and political development. She was considered one of the three most important influences in Eleanor's life. After leaving Allenswood Academy, Eleanor continued to emulate Souvestre by joining the Women's Trade Union League and chairing the League of Women Voters Legislative Affair Committee (Black, 2017). Eleanor was profoundly passionate about gender equality and realized that fighting for this cause was her purpose in life.

By meeting Souvestre, Eleanor had found her call to heroism and her meaning in life. It is suggested that people experience meaningful work when they find congruence between the components of their global meaning and their daily work experiences. They achieve this aim through a process of fitting their global beliefs, goals, and values with their work activity and career decisions (Dik et. al., 2017, p. 329). Eleanor certainly experienced this sense of self-efficacy once she became more active in politics by supporting Franklin's political endeavors. Although Eleanor's focus was on Franklin, she realized that she did not have to follow his political agenda and could also advocate for her own ideas. Eleanor used her powerful position to empower and advocate for the "little people". Eleanor had found an alignment of work that satisfied her with a broader sense of purpose in life. This calling, which she accepted, allowed her to transcend into the hero she was destined to become.

Several contemporary investigators have proposed taxonomies of heroism based on the situational demands of the heroism, the social influence exerted by the hero, and the social structure of heroism (Allison, 2015; Allison, Goethals, & Kramer, 2017). These taxonomies help us classify heroes into categories and thus shed light on the dynamics of their transformation. In the context of Eleanor's early life, she was an "underdog" but her growth transformed her into a "traditional hero". Eleanor Roosevelt's rise and ascendance to heroism occurred as a result of situationally-based heroism.

When Eleanor's mother died, her father demanded that Eleanor take special care of her younger brother, Hall. At the time, Hall seemed to be treading the same path that Eleanor's father had: alcoholism and depression. Eleanor's father thrust her into a heroic position in which she had to grow up quickly. Her father commanded Eleanor to be the motherly figure that Hall needed in his life. Therefore, she became responsible for both herself and Hall. The same expectations were pushed upon her once she married Franklin Roosevelt.

As the wife of a politician, she had to act the part and was given tremendous power to champion whatever causes she wanted alongside Franklin. As "First Lady", Eleanor realized that she had a duty to the citizens of the United States, as well as to her beliefs. She used her position of power to direct her heroism towards social issues such as breaking the barriers of racism and sexism, fighting for civil rights, and promoting world peace. Eleanor's steadfast devotion to her core values meant she always stood up for what she believed in with strength and integrity, two common "heroic traits".

All heroes are said to exemplify eight specific characteristics which verify or validate their heroic status. Eleanor Roosevelt possessed all of "The Great Eight" characteristics which are attributed to heroes: smart, strong, selfless, caring, charismatic, resilient, reliable, and inspiring (Allison & Goethals, 2011). Eleanor used all of these characteristics throughout her life, and especially during her time as First Lady on a day-to-day basis. For example, in 1939 when the Daughters of the American Revolution (DAR) refused to let Marian Anderson, an African American opera singer, perform in Constitution Hall, Eleanor resigned her membership in the DAR and arranged to hold the concert at the nearby Lincoln Memorial (Caroli, 2017). In this case, Eleanor was exemplifying her selflessness and her zealous compassion for those who were disenfranchised. She was a believer in equality for all and that could be seen in her deep-rooted passion.

On another occasion, when local officials in Alabama insisted that seating at a public meeting be segregated by race, Eleanor carried a folding chair to all sessions and carefully placed it in the center aisle (Caroli, 2017). Her defense of the rights of African Americans, youth, and the poor exemplified her empathy for others. Her actions and commitment to the overall well-being of the community communicated her dedication to inspiring and being an admirable role model for others. She continued to have a strong and charismatic persona throughout the rest of her life. In the last decade of her life, she remained an active part in the Democratic Party, having not strayed away from her core values.

The Butterfly Emerges from Its Cocoon

Early life transformations usually occur in heroic stories involving calamitous or severely challenging childhood circumstances (Allison & Goethals, 2017). In Eleanor's situation, she was transformed early on by life-changing external events. Eleanor's trajectory followed the classic heroic arc; she began life as a relatively ordinary individual and was thrust into the journey by the external circumstance of the loss of her mother and father. Eleanor faced trials and tribulations (her family troubles and her outcast status) which were examples of suffering caused by external forces. Her journey could be split into three parts which Campbell believed all heroes experienced: a transformation of setting, a transformation of self, and a transformation of society (Allison & Goethals, 2017, p. 381). She transformed into a highly moral or competent hero by the story's end or the end of her life (Allison & Goethals, 2017, p. 385).

In the hero cycle which Joseph Campbell created, Eleanor can be seen to have entered the "belly of the whale" when she was shipped off to boarding school. This represents the change in setting that is required for the hero to change. Eleanor was truly on her own with no one there to guide her. The unknown and new environment that Eleanor had found herself in fostered change and allowed her to discover who she really was independent of the influence of others. At last, no one was defining her and thrusting social cues or roles upon her.

At Allenswood Academy, Eleanor was no longer expected to be the pretty debutante that her mom so desperately wanted her to be. She no longer had to be the mother to Hall that her father expected her to be. She simply had to be herself and she was given free range to discover what that meant to her. Today, this is similar to the adolescent's transition from high school to college.

For my entire life, I was shaped by my parents and peers back home without realizing it. When I arrived at college, I found that I would have to discover who I was without my friends or parents. This would allow me to cultivate a new friend group in college, giving me a sense of where I fit into the community at the University of Richmond and what my contribution to the world would be. This was unnerving for me because it is so easy for us as humans to fall into a daily routine or to conform to what others want us to be. I was so used to categorizing myself by my friend group at home and defining myself as part of that "in-group" that I did not really know who I was anymore. Eleanor Roosevelt experienced a similar identity shock. She had played the role of mother for Hall because it was what her dad wanted her to do. Daughters try to be dutiful and obedient because that is what their mothers or fathers want and expect them to be. Without those external expectations pushed upon her, she was lost and had no idea what "role" she was supposed to play now.

As Eleanor began to discover her true self, her actions transformed her and the world in which she lived. She became self-aware of her calling to social activism and she utilized her calling to give back to society. The culmination of the hero's journey is the hero's boon, or gift, to the world (Allison & Goethals, 2017, p. 382). Although Eleanor did not give back to society immediately after returning from Allenswood Academy, the growth she experienced afterwards eventually led her to complete her heroic journey sometime during her role as First Lady. As First Lady, she used her gained self-confidence and self-awareness to improve the lives of others, to make a difference and to better the world around her. Yet even with her newfound self-confidence, she always remained a humble hero (Worthington & Allison, 2018).

According to Campbell (1949), during the process of experiencing personal transformation, the hero obtains the "elixir" that empowers and enables her to help guide others on their personal transformative journeys (Allison & Goethals, 2017, p. 383). This elixir is designed to improve the well-being of individuals and society (Efthimiou, Allison, & Franco, 2018). Eleanor's elixir was the sense of achievement and fulfillment she received from pursuing social activism, and this new sense allowed her to create a following which would help guide others on their personal transformations as well. She inspired other women to support the cause of women's right, instead of tearing each other down. She also inspired others to support the civil rights movement which propelled society towards greater levels of compassion, tolerance, and understanding.

Coming Out on Top

Despite Eleanor's successful quest and completion of her hero's journey (as indicated by the social boon she exhibited to society), Eleanor's early life contrasted starkly with the person and hero she ended up becoming. If we just looked at the beginning of her life, we might assume or expect that she would never become a hero. As a young woman she would become extremely depressed or suicidal, inhibiting her ability to be successful, but that did not turn out to be the case. Eleanor was pushed and battered down but nevertheless she rose to the top.

As humans, our feelings about disadvantaged competitors such as Eleanor Roosevelt are shaped by moral considerations and motivations to see the world as just (Vandello et al., 2017, p. 345). One of the reasons that people would root for an underdog is that they not only want them to succeed, but they feel it is right and just for them to do so (Vandello et al., 2017, p. 385). The suffering that underdogs experience is critical to their heroic transformation. Although it is important to face obstacles, it is not always the act of overcoming these obstacles that defines an underdog. People create narratives of underdogs such that, whether they ultimately win or lose, they demonstrate bravery and heart because they are able to stand up to a more formidable opponent (Vandello et al., 2017, p. 347). Thus, it is more significant that Eleanor faced obstacles in her life and experienced these setbacks.

By perceiving struggles and failings in this way, there is room for everybody to become a hero. A hero does not have to be someone who is capable of overcoming the most challenging obstacles. A hero can be someone who learns from their setbacks, something that is more applicable and more achievable for the average citizen. As humans, we face obstacles every day and it is how we deal with those obstacles that make us "heroes". Failings or setbacks are blessings because they move us as humans toward improvement and self-realization, as well as pushing us to reach the fullness of our creation (Allison & Setterberg, 2016).

In Eleanor's case, her suffering had redeemed her and instilled meaning and purpose, two of the benefits that heroes are said to experience as a result of suffering (Allison & Setterberg, 2016). Eleanor had seen those closest to her suffer from various diseases and psychological problems during her childhood, and this led her to believe that she had a responsibility to help contribute to the world to make a difference in others' lives. Her desire to change the world could be seen in her fervent activism efforts and she became one of the world's most widely admired and powerful women. Today, many consider Eleanor Roosevelt a hero and a trailblazer.

While Eleanor's heroic journey started out with her taxonomic classification as an underdog hero, her fate and taxonomic classification did not remain static. She rose up from the low ranks and overcame all the hardships life had to throw at her. As a result, we look at her today through a highly favorable lens.

Heroism is in the eye of the beholder (Allison & Goethals, 2011). Although most of society believes that Eleanor was heroic, there are others who would disagree. Research has shown that people will often imbue underdogs with heroic qualities in order to see them as morally just. As a result, people often believe underdogs have positive personal characteristics (Vandello et al., 2017, p. 351). Today, Eleanor Roosevelt is a widely known name and is known for her activism but the theory that society perceives underdogs with positive heroic qualities could have indeed contributed strongly to her success.

Movement for Feminism

All hero narratives consist of the hero leaving her common world of everyday existence, embarking on a journey in which powerful forces are encountered and painful challenges are endured. The hero then returns to her original world forever changed or transformed, with new insights or powers to share and improve life for everyone (Dik et al., 2017, p. 317). Eleanor experienced all of these elements of the hero narrative and ultimately returned with a "boon" which she had acquired and was more than willing to give to society. While

Eleanor was a superb social activist and as a woman during that time, she made an even bigger splash in history with her deep passion for gender equality. Today, many support this social cause and refer to it as "feminism". Although women experience a greater level of equality today than they did a century ago, there is obviously still room for progress to be made. Eleanor would no doubt know that the movement she championed still has a long way to go.

As feminism and its goals have become more mainstream over the past few decades, it is important to consider whether current feminists are still considered heroes today and whether they attract the same respect as heroic leaders such as Eleanor Roosevelt. It is also important to consider whether the gender of feminists can cause others to overestimate a person's heroic qualities, similar to how followers of moral heroes create or uplift the moral hero's status. Research has shown that if a person's actions have larger costs than benefits, our perception of the person as a hero increases markedly because it is a signifier of their "selflessness" (Kafashan et al., 2017, p. 40). For a man to have supported gender rights during Eleanor Roosevelt's time would have been considered very heroic because there was a large externality or social cost that came with that action; it was considered controversial and counter to social norms at that time. This man might have been considered more heroic than a woman who supported gender rights, considering the larger social cost he would have incurred in the form of being ostracized or shamed by other members of society, family, and friends.

Therefore, external and internal effects such as societal norms and our definition of a hero, respectively, both come into play when we distinguish or perceive someone as a hero. The difference that heroes make in their current society and the actions they take are compared to the status quo in that society. This can indicate or create a "threshold level of heroism" that the hero is said to be exhibiting which can define the true magnitude of someone's heroism. A hero's impact or their perceived heroism is thus affected by the era in which they live along with the status quo norms in place during that era.

Can Eleanor Roosevelt can be considered more heroic than current feminists because she was a pioneer who broke barriers and paved the way for women today? Although Eleanor paved the road for today's women to enjoy more equality, girls like Malala Yousafzai are incurring physical costs due to the hate that is still present in many global societies. Malala, who is an extremely well-known hero, turned her dire situation into something extraordinary and is now an idol for girls all around the world. She might even be considered more heroic than Eleanor Roosevelt due to the physical suffering that she incurred. Therefore, as time passes and heroes are replaced by new heroes emerging, there will always be a natural tendency to compare current heroes to past heroes. What is most certain is that people who make great sacrifices to improve the quality of life for historically subjugated segments of society will always be deemed heroic.

REFERENCES

Allison, S. T. (2015). The initiation of heroism science. Heroism Science, 1, 1-8.

Allison, S. T., & Goethals, G. R. (2011). Heroes: What they do and why we need them. New York: Oxford University Press.

Allison, S. T., & Goethals, G. R. (2017). The hero's transformation. In S. T. Allison, G. R. Goethals, & R. M. Kramer (Eds.), Handbook of heroism and heroic leadership. New York: Routledge.

Allison, S. T., Goethals, G. R., & Kramer, R. M. (2017). Setting the scene: The rise and coalescence of heroism science. In S. T. Allison, G. R. Goethals, & R. M. Kramer (Eds.), Handbook of heroism and heroic leadership. New York: Routledge.

Allison, S. T., & Setterberg, G. C. (2016). Suffering and sacrifice: Individual and collective benefits, and implications for leadership. In S. T. Allison, C. T. Kocher, & G. R. Goethals (Eds), Frontiers in spiritual leadership: Discovering the better angels of our nature. New York: Palgrave Macmillan.

Anna Eleanor Roosevelt. (2017, March 08). Retrieved October 04, 2017, from https://www.whitehouse.gov/1600/first-ladies/eleanorroosevelt

Black, A.M., Ph.D. (2017). Biography of Anna Eleanor Roosevelt. Retrieved October 04, 2017, from https://www2.gwu.edu/~erpapers/abouteleanor/erbiography.cfm

Caroli, B. B. (2017, September 08). Eleanor Roosevelt. Retrieved October 04, 2017, from https://www.britannica.com/biography/Eleanor-Roosevelt

Davis, J. L., Burnette, J. L., Allison, S. T., & Stone, H. (2011). Against the odds: Academic underdogs benefit from incremental theories. Social Psychology of Education, 14, 331-346.

Dik, B. J., Shimizu, A. B., & O'Connor, W. (2017). Career development and a sense of calling. In S. T. Allison, G. R. Goethals, & R. M. Kramer (Eds.), Handbook of heroism and heroic leadership. New York: Routledge.

Efthimiou, O., Allison, S. T., & Franco, Z. E. (2018). Definition, synthesis, and applications in the practice of heroic wellbeing. In O. Efthimiou, S. T. Allison, & Z. E. Franco (Eds.), Heroism and wellbeing in the 21st Century: Applied and emerging perspectives. New York: Routledge.

Eylon, D., & Allison, S. T. (2005). The frozen in time effect in evaluations of the dead. Personality and Social Psychology Bulletin, 31, 1708-1717.

History.com Staff. (2009). Eleanor Roosevelt. Retrieved October 04, 2017, from
http://www.history.com/topics/first-ladies/eleanor-roosevelt

Kafashan, S., Sparks, A., Rotella A., & Barclay, P. (2017). Why heroism exists. In S. T. Allison,
G. R. Goethals, & R. M. Kramer (Eds.), Handbook of heroism and heroic leadership.
New York: Routledge

Kinsella, E. L., Ritchie, T. D., & Igou E. R. (2017). Attributes and applications of heroes.
In S. T. Allison, G. R. Goethals, & R. M. Kramer (Eds.), Handbook of heroism and heroic
leadership. New York: Routledge

Vandello, J. A., Goldschmied N. G., & Michniewics K. (2017). Underdogs as heroes.
In S. T. Allison, G. R. Goethals, & R. M. Kramer (Eds.), Handbook of heroism and heroic
leadership. New York: Routledge

Worthington, E. L, & Allison, S. T. (2018). Heroic humility: What the science of humility can
say to people raised on self-focus. Washington. DC: American Psychological Association.

30

"This was a man": Julius Caesar's Sociocentric Transformation as a Hero

JACK R. BERGSTROM

"καὶ σύ, τέκνον"? These were the last words spoken by Julius Caesar before twenty-three stab wounds put him to death. Some say he should have seen this betrayal coming, as his cows were said to have been weeping that morning, a bird flew into the Theater of Pompey carrying a sprig of laurel and was eaten by a larger bird, and his wife had had a foreboding dream the night before. These omens were no match for Caesar's confidence. He wielded an empire; how could a Senate meeting turn into a massacre? As he asked Brutus, "You, too, my child"? Caesar was met with a final dagger to the groin.

Julius Caesar's demise was monumental. Not only was a mere individual murdered, but a figure of power, a monument, was thrust from his throne atop the Roman empire and executed at the feet of an old enemy's memorial. Caesar's death signified the end of a dictatorship overflowing with the conquering of nations, killing over two million people and fighting at least fifty battles. Despite the tragedy that this powerful leader brought upon civilization, his military and humanitarian accomplishments deemed him a hero among Roman citizens and named him an influential figure in politics and many other issues currently in society. The tragic death of this figurehead exemplifies the significance of his presence within his era. His death was that of a martyr, more of an event and execution than that of a killing, even glamorized by the likes of Shakespeare himself. Julius Caesar's status as a hero to some, and villain to many, will forever remain a true story of power's hand in heroic transformation.

This chapter explores the life, perils, and achievements of Julius Caesar. My central focus is on offering an analysis of how events throughout his journey influenced his heroic transformation. Drawing from many different articles and relevant sources, I will examine the effect of different factors on heroic transformation, assessing Caesar's responses to each factor and the ultimate outcomes of these actions.

A HERO'S BEGINNING

According to Allison and Goethals (2017), "Early human societies recognized the value of initiation rituals in promoting the transition from childhood to adulthood" (p. 381). Today, these rituals are prevalent in a child's development. Through Jewish tradition, a son's Bar Mitzvah marks the transformation of an individual's journey from adolescent to adult. Just as this culture has traditional ceremonies to celebrate one's coming of age, tribes throughout Africa and Australia have performed rites and rituals to and for their young men. One ritual performs tortuous acts involving wooden splints and pulleys to raise a boy into the air. Once unconscious and reawakened, he sacrifices his pinky finger. The pain and suffering he endures is a sign that the young male is now ready to become a man.

Despite the obvious differences between Western society's initiation rituals and those of other societies, there is a strong connection focusing on obstacles each child must overcome to earn the respect he needs to be viewed as an adult. Some may point out that owning a car, working a full-time job, or losing one's virginity are all signs of adulthood; however each of these has its own merit. They are stepping stones in life which grant more responsibility.

Similarly, our hero's journey does not begin at birth. Julius Caesar encountered many different blockades on his road to heroism. Circumstances surrounding his birth and family of origin were complicated. His father was the husband of the current Roman republic's leader's sister, making our hero's family very influential. During his childhood, Marius, the leader, was involved in many discords, starting with a civil war brought upon him through the disagreement of a general named Sulla. As Marius was driven out of the empire, Sulla went on to fight and claim victory over a sworn enemy of Rome. His success did not sit well with Marius, who went back to his land, murdered of all Sulla's comrades and claimed his seat as consul, soon after dying of natural causes. This, along with Julius's father's death, and the return of Sulla from battle left Julius's family extremely vulnerable.

Although granted a prestigious education and a wife named Cornelia with whom he had a child, Julius never truly enjoyed any security. Sulla's return gave him the status of dictator in which he exercised his power to exterminate all the supporters of Marius. Julius, however, was granted a much easier punishment: divorce his wife. This did not sit well with the young hero, who disobeyed his orders, an act of defiance which Sulla respected. Sulla repealed his initial order, stating that "in this young man there is more than one Marius."

Met with his first initiation into adulthood, Julius Caesar triumphed over his first of many enemies, denying temptation to take an easy path and a quicker means out of harm's way. He did not have an effortless early life, and soon, the young man would have his call to adventure through external pressures. Sent as a missionary to King Nicomedes IV of Bithynia, Caesar encountered two bands of pirates from which he paid ransom to escape. After the second account, he sent ships after the villains to crucify them. The many obstacles that our young hero overcame reinforced his reputation of strength and determination. His unwavering charisma had been jousted, each time remaining victorious.

As Allison & Goethals (2017) argue, "While the transformed hero enjoys union with the world she remains an autonomous individual who can establish her own path in the world that is unfettered by the patho-adolescence all around her" (p. 394). Caesar was not one to falter in the face of the fear. Villains were looked upon as games that he would win and notch into his belt after every victory. His rejection of authority and decimation of his foes reflected individualistic growth ideologies young Caesar possessed. The thirst for knowledge was not outshone by the power-inducing behaviors he presented. A hero must thrive to benefit society to earn that status while still acting individually, and this is the path that Julius Caesar began to carve for himself.

After his assassination of the pirates, Caesar continued his studies, furthering his education and drive to become a more informed leader. The senseless acts of violence were tests which influenced him to make change, in a way mentoring Julius. His reputation proceeded to grow as he was halted from learning by Mithridates of Pontus when he attacked Asia Minor. Standing for his own nation and the pride of his homeland, Julius created a militia on his own dime to hold off the destruction of small towns. This not only protected the people but also gave the official commander of Rome the time to destroy the threat. Caesar's noble act was not one of a bystander watching villages burn, but one of great heroism, selflessly contributing to society from which only the union could benefit.

With his war hero status, Caesar quickly grew in popularity and rose through the ranks of politics, becoming high priest and further establishing trust with the people of the Roman republic through his denouncement of the death penalty. This issue was brought about by Catilina and others who attempted to overthrow the government. As Caesar grew older, his wisdom and knowledge grew exponentially. His very humane opposition of capital punishment was seen as a step in the right direction, that of internal maturation and development. Popular policy was one of Julius's many strengths, revealing his motive to benefit the people and the state using his heroic status.

His well-known reputation had preceded him when Caesar had finally run out of money, spending too much of his budget on praetorship and pontificate.

Hoping to gain a popular politician by his side and helping a hero get back on his feet, Marcus Licinius Crassus paid off all of Caesar's debts and appointed him the governor of Baetica. In this new position, along with a new-found ally, he obtained much more power. As an autonomous being, Caesar performed many acts to aid humanity around him, but the introduction of power and political gain would soon catalyze a new approach to his mental transformation.

THE HEROIC TEST

Overall, Caesar's whole career succeeded through his high expectations of himself, as he adopted an all or nothing risk-taking mindset. In electoral politics, he had spent far too much money beyond his means, indebting himself to the point of criminal liability, but somehow managed to always be redeemed by an electoral or military success. Marcus Licinius Crassus's bailout was just the beginning. Caesar decided to divorce his newly obtained wife, Pompeia, because of rumors indicating that she might have been with another man, although the mysterious other lover had been acquitted in the courts. Caesar declared, "The wife of Caesar must be above suspicion," hinting that anyone associated with him must be upstanding and enhancing of his reputation.

At this point power's hand starts to reveal itself. The newly acquired governorship had supplied Julius Caesar with a position in which he could continue his status build, creating a potential conflict in our hero between pursuing his own well-being versus that of the people. Popularity among the citizens was gained through his acts of selflessness and heroism that he had displayed during the siege of Mithridates and his opinion of capital punishment. As power is introduced into the internal equation, Caesar abruptly recedes into an egocentric state. This is his heroic ordeal. According to Campbell (1949), the prototypical heroic path, which he called the hero monomyth, consists of three parts: departure, initiation, and return" (Allison, Goethals, & Kramer, 2017, p. 3). Deviating from this heroic path, Julius Caesar takes a detour after his initiation. His struggle with autonomy and power coincide to create a much larger internal conflict. It is clear that the initiation from youth to adulthood spurred a state of heroism within young Julius, but instead of maintaining his benevolent status, he undergoes a struggle. As Campbell explains, a hero's quest consists of stepping stones along the journey, but Caesar not only skips a few, he steps into the murky waters below, blurring the line between hero and villain.

Julius Caesar furthers this controversy with his actions while holding a newly appointed position as governor, or propraetor. His character strayed from the heroic side, as Caesar's Spanish War broke out. It began with initial unrest in a province of Spain. Slowly growing worse over time, Caesar had had enough and kicked the hornet's nest, capturing several towns, looting them, and continuing his rampage along the western coast which is now modern-day Portugal. He went on to plunder the silver mines of Gallaecia, granting him an extreme amount of wealth, increasing his overall stock as a grand leader of the Roman republic. These villainous acts of murder and destruction seemingly diminish Julius Caesar as a hero, but while they may cause much suffering, Duntley and Buss (2005) states that, "Some homicides...are considered excusable, justifiable, or even altruistic-for example, killing in self-defense, killing to protect a family member from harm, or to prevent a helpless stranger from being raped" (p. 105).

Arguably, Caesar had prevented further civil wars and the harming of future citizens by shutting down an uprising among the Spanish people. Plundering and pillaging are not selfless acts and in no way represent qualities of heroism, but it is still the duty of a leader to protect the land and its posterity. Caesar slides down the steep slope of questionable activity as he returns to the courts. Once elected consul, he was appointed to a smaller province for which he would not be allocated an army to command. Counteracting this purposeful measure from the Senate, Caesar created an alliance with his old friend Crassus, the wealthy banker who secured his spot in Spanish command while paying off his debt, and Pompey, Rome's leading general. Together, the triumvirate, the three most respected men in Rome, held power over the Senate of Rome and would greatly influence Caesar's transformation.

JULIUS CAESAR'S ORDEAL

Caesar's pursuit of political change and wealth of his nation was sought out by ignoring many conventions and rules, even laws that strained his autonomous goals. His approach was to achieve said goals without the dependence of the state. As he grew physically and mentally, the young hero took it upon himself to right any wrongs he encountered. The determination of success which ensued significantly correlates with the claim that Allison and Goethals (2017) make when they observe that "the hero must leave home and venture on the journey to obliterate a status quo that is no longer working" (p. 394). But Caesar continued to resort to actions that painted him as both hero to some and villains to others. The repetition of illegalities committed by our yearning anti-hero led others to prosecute him politically. To escape the ever-present threat to his political career, along with his military status, Julius Caesar was required to move up in position to free himself from scrutiny, or to let go of his ambitions. This was the trap in which he found himself.

Originally, Caesar did not intend to attack Gaul, but it had blossomed into a golden opportunity. He could impress the Senate and People's Assembly which would give him more immunity for possible future controversial actions he might take to promote change within the Roman Empire. Beside this advantage, there were reports about Germans who were attacking the Aedui, a Gallic tribe in alliance with Rome. A victory over the Germans would advance Julius Caesar to the same rank his uncle Marius once acquired before his untimely death. Of course, given Caesar's skills as a combatant and leader, the Germans were defeated. Caesar could have easily led his troops back home due to the cessation of the threat, but our hero changed his mind; he aspired to conquer all of Gaul. This decision showcases the great struggle Julius had with power. It intoxicated him. Given a little bit of what it was like to be a war hero and great leader, he had to have more, once again paving the way for his transformation from hero to villain.

After his return home from battle, this time as a politician, Caesar is tempted with more power than he can handle. After Crassus' death, the triumvirate consisted of only Caesar and Pompey; the Senate feared a civil war from which a dictator would arise. An overwhelming majority in the Senate, 400 against 22, formally insisted both leaders sacrifice their commands before the consular elections for the sake of the political peace. Because Pompey obeyed the Senate, he stood in better stead with the Senate than did Caesar. This was the easy, cowardly way out. If the latter obeyed, Julius would no longer be immune to prosecution. If Caesar refused the order, he would be declared an enemy of the state.

This choice would be the turning point at which Julius Caesar would be rewarded or punished. The power at stake was that of his initial goal to change the way Rome was governed. Everything he had strived for was at risk. Preferring the dignity of war, standing up for his views, and refusing submission, Caesar chose to rebel. In response to the Senate's mandate, he quoted the poet Menander, "alea iacta est" (the die is cast). In doing so, he crossed the river Rubico, thereby invading Italy and provoking the Second Civil War.

PAINTING THE BIGGER PICTURE

While this act of treason would lead to the deaths of many civilians, Julius Caesar exemplifies qualities that a great hero would possess. He not only gives his life for a greater cause, but he also displays the perseverance and optimism, allowing his strength to prevail. Two of the seven important character strengths of a hero are presented through just one act of Caesar, marking the point in his transformation from anti-hero to martyr, creating a new physicality and morality of his heroism. His life and goals had turned from those of internal value to that of a movement. The change of setting in which Julius Caesar was operating, from war to a rebellion against a higher, unjust order, can be summed up by Dik et al. (2017): "Some types of work environments increase the odds of experiencing work as meaningful -- in particular, those that offer autonomy; a chance to use one's skills; recognition of how one's work contributes to a tangible product" (p. 329).

As one can conclude, Julius's early life was a stepping stone to his hero's transformation upon which he obtained many skills to build and succeed. His scholarly teachings, battles fought in, and political status represented an effort to gain a position high enough to begin reformation of the Roman empire. These early steps were for mere egocentricity, but arguably the act of denouncing and opposing the government marked a pivotal moment in Caesar's journey. No longer volatile was his trend line on the hero's market; he would now begin to act to benefit a cause greater than himself. He aspired to selflessly sacrifice his life to draw attention to the corruption of the Senate. Because of the major shifts Caesar creates due to the extremity of his many operations, Goethals and Allison (2012) would categorize him as a member of "trending heroes, for example, those heroes whose impact is rising or falling" (p. 24), furthermore reinforcing the structure of heroism rooted within his activities.

Caesar was first appointed dictator in 49 BC after he had crushed the last resistance of Pompey's army and the Senate's weaker legions. Although typically ruthless and brutal, dictators in antiquity could be acceptably pleasant, as it was much more common to have a single, strong leader who would rule the land. Despite owning all of the power in the Roman empire, Julius Caesar finally harnessed his self-control and thirst for domination, a major change from his previous heroic challenge. Allison and Goethals (2017) claim that, "transformations advance society. The culmination of the hero's journey is the hero's boon, or gift, to society. This gift is what separates the hero's journey from simply being a test of personal survival" (p. 382), which is precisely how our hero proceeded (Allison & Goethals, 2013).

Through trials and tribulations as a war commander, scholar, politician, and martyr, Caesar had gained great skills in which he would apply to those of his new, rightfully owned kingdom. He founded new settlements for the veterans of his army along with the distribution of land to around 20,000 poor families who had three or more children. To deal with widespread unemployment, he offered many citizens jobs in public works involving the reparation of ancient cities. Accumulating enough workers in need of employment, Carthage and Corinth were both rebuilt. Also, he mandated that landowners were required to have at least one-third of their laborers as freemen instead of slaves, thus reducing unemployment and creating a significant change in human rights. Introducing a new and likeable taxation system, Julius increased tax on luxury imports to receive more money from the rich and to encourage domestic production.

These, along with many more reforms to the old, unfit government of Rome significantly enhanced Julius Caesar's popularity. He endowed people with many more rights, helped the poor immensely, and ultimately improved conditions in which many people lived. His promotion of the general well-being of his society was heroic (Efthimiou, Allison, & Franco, 2018). Caesar went on to publish and speak to promote a more humane style of government, appealing to the people, not the state. His influence in politics can be seen today.

Kafashan et al. (2017) sum up the success of a hero's journey by declaring that "the costs of providing help are less than the fitness benefits received, and we can expect that benefits would be directed towards those whose well-being is valuable to the helper" (p. 39). As explained in Presenting Elixir to Society, Julius Caesar greatly contributed to the lives of many Roman citizens, as well as to politics and human rights. The perils in which our hero traveled and the obstacles he overcame eventually molded his character into one of great leadership and wisdom. Beginning as a member of a wealthy family, Julius sought to improve his life after the death of his beloved father and uncle.

Through initiation into adulthood and learning from many tests, Caesar claimed allies with the likes of Crassus and was mentored by the battles he commanded along with the spats he endured with members of the Senate. Eventually, as he struggled with power's influence and the state's suppression, our young, aspiring, egocentric hero transformed into the heroic leader of a movement. This is what spurred his mental and moral transformation, along with the creation of a physical rebellion. His pathway from egocentricity to sociocentricity finally concluded once Julius Caesar claimed his goal: to change the way Rome was governed through dictatorship (Allison & Toner, 2017). The impact of his career and accomplishments greatly influence our society today, further emphasized and solidified by many stories told, myths created of our ambitious hero, plays written, and his famous words upon his infamous death, "et tu, Brute?"

REFERENCES

Allison, S. T. (2015). The initiation of heroism science. Heroism Science, 1, 1-8.
Allison, S. T., & Goethals, G. R. (2013). Heroic leadership: An influence taxonomy of 100 exceptional individuals. New York: Routledge.
Allison, S. T., & Goethals, G. R. (2017). The hero's transformation. In S. T. Allison, G. R. Goethals, & R. M. Kramer (Eds.), Handbook of heroism and heroic leadership. New York: Routledge.
Allison, S. T., Goethals, G. R., & Kramer, R. M. (2017). Setting the scene: The rise and coalescence of heroism science. In S. T. Allison, G. R. Goethals, & R. M. Kramer (Eds.), Handbook of heroism and heroic leadership. New York: Routledge.
Allison, S. T., & Toner, A. C. (2017). Radical heroic leadership: Implications for transformative growth in the workplace. In R. A. Giacalone, & C. L. Jurkiewicz (Eds.), Radical thoughts on ethical leadership (pp. 151-168). Charlotte: Information Age Publishing.

Duntley, J. D., & Buss, D. M. (2004). The evolution of evil. In A. G. Miller (Ed.), The social psychology of good and evil (pp. 102-123). New York, NY, US: Guilford.

Efthimiou, O., Allison, S. T., & Franco, Z. E. (2018). Definition, synthesis, and applications of heroic wellbeing. In O. Efthimiou, S. T. Allison, & Z. E. Franco (Eds.), Heroism and wellbeing in the 21st Century: Applied and emerging perspectives. New York: Routledge.

Eylon, D., & Allison, S. T. (2005). The frozen in time effect in evaluations of the dead. Personality and Social Psychology Bulletin, 31, 1708-1717

"Julius Caesar." Biography.com, A&E Networks Television, 25 Aug. 2017, www.biography.com/people/julius-caesar-9192504.

McKay, Brett & Kate. "Male Rites of Passages From Around the World." The Art of Manliness, International News Feed, 15 Nov. 2017, www.artofmanliness.com/2010/02/21/male-rites-of-passage-from-around-the-world/.

McManus, Barbara F. Julius Caesar: Historical Background. The College of New Rochelle, Mar. 2011, www.vroma.org/~bmcmanus/caesar.html.

"The Murder of Julius Caesar." Ancient History Encyclopedia, Donald L. Wasson, 15 May 2015, www.ancient.eu/article/803/the-murder-of-julius-caesar

Vogler, Christopher. "The Hero's Journey Outline." Hero's Journey, www.thewritersjourney.com/hero's_journey.htm.

31

THE LIST THAT SAVED A THOUSAND LIVES: OSKAR SCHINDLER'S HEROIC TRANSFORMATION DURING WORLD WAR II

ALLYSON S. MANER

Ask yourself: have you ever been responsible for saving another person's life? Are you able to say you are the reason that another person still walks this earth? How about two people? Ten people? Oskar Schindler would be able to say over 1,200. Incredibly, more than 1,200 people and their families and descendants exist because of this one man and his actions (Jackson, 1988). This almost incomprehensible number of lives is still a remarkably small fraction of how many Jewish people perished in the Holocaust. Imagine if there had been a few dozen Schindlers, a few more people working for the right thing against all odds. Although Oskar Schindler's story might not be the most well known, his heroic light shines brightly in the darkness of the horrors of the holocaust.

In this chapter, the heroic transformation of Oskar Schindler during World War II will be discussed. First, a brief background of his life will be provided including information on his early life and "The List". The events of Schindler's life during World War II will be recounted throughout the entire chapter. Next, the specific events that molded Schindler into the hero he became will be highlighted according to the "hero's journey" as described by Joseph Campbell (Campbell, 1949). These include Schindler's summons to heroism, his initiation through trials and tribulations, and his return to society with newly acquired heroic status.

Finally, Schindler's heroic nature will be analyzed through a series of taxonomies and ideas provided by a multitude of scholars in the field of heroism science. This chapter's central thesis is that Oskar Schindler is a true hero, and that his legacy will endure long after the remaining "Schindler Jews" have passed. After all, how many people can say that they were the cause of over one thousand people dodging the grips of death?

SCHINDLER'S BACKGROUND

Oskar Schindler was born to Hans Schindler and Franziska Luser on April 28, 1908, in the Sudeten town of Svitavy, Germany. He was the eldest of two children, and his family was in the farm machinery business. His father was known to be an abuser of alcohol and a womanizer, which presumably had later influence on Schindler's behavior as an adult. It is well known that he was strikingly close with his mother. Schindler graduated high school, but never attended university, and instead enrolled in various trade schools (Crowe, 2004). He later married Emilie Pelzl at the age of twenty, but the couple did not have any children until three years into their marriage (Wundheiler, 1986).

As he grew older, Schindler began to take his father's shape. He had many girlfriends throughout his life (even during his marriage), and was known for frequently abusing alcohol. He was very intent on creating profit, and desired high social status as a businessman. He had many jobs during his life, and often switched employment impulsively. The story of Schindler's life through the war is explained at length throughout the different sections of this chapter.

In 1944, the Nazi Party began the "relocation" of many labor camps, including Schindler's factory, to Auschwitz (Crowe, 2004). This struck panic in the hearts of the workers in Schindler's factory. Although this announcement rattled Schindler deeply, he knew it was bound to happen. All he had to do was figure out how to maneuver his way out of it, just as he had done in every situation leading up to this point. With much clever thinking, efficient planning, bribery, and convincing, Schindler was able to exempt the majority of his factory and be relocated to a safer area in Czechoslovakia rather than the death camps. He was permitted to take 700 men and 300 women, but required to give the Germans a list of the names he would be taking with him. He tried to protest, claiming that he needed many more in order to build up his new factory in Czechoslovakia, but it was risky to ask for more privilege than he had already been granted (Crowe, 2004).

With the help of two very important people in his life, Issac Stern and Marcel Goldberg, both "Schindler Jews", Oskar Schindler was able to compose a list of people whom he was allowed to take with him. Stern had been Schindler's accountant for the entirety of this complicated process, and they formed a close personal bond. He was a mentor to Schindler, and was very familiar with him, as well as the costs of what it was going to take to save all of these people once and for all. Marcel Goldberg was asked to write The List himself for Schindler to accept (Wundheiler, 1986).

Cunningly, Schindler was able to re-route one of the railcars headed to Auschwitz that was filled with women, Instead of Auschwitz, the new destination was Brünnlitz, where Jews would be safer. Because of the recent relocation news, Jewish prisoners were beginning to attempt more escapes from the camps. This prompted Schindler to make secret agreements with the police officers in Brünnlitz, mostly through bribery, to turn in all escapees of the camps to him. This is how many more people were saved than were allowed on The List (Crowe, 2004).

The ideas explained below of departure (summoning), trials and tribulations (initiation), and return as the cycle of the hero's journey were constructed by Joseph Campbell (1949) in his iconic treatment of heroism, *The Hero with a Thousand Faces*.

Departure: The Summoning

Many people believe that all heroes have a calling to perform their heroic work. This calling consists of an inner sense of purpose and destiny that sometimes leads individuals to sacrifice their own well-being for the well-being of others. Heroic calling provides meaning for the individual's life and could lead them to consistently seek out heroic acts (Dik et al., 2017). Schindler's summoning arose from discovering his missing inner quality. This idea of the missing inner quality stems from the idea that heroes typically have some missing quality that they must obtain in order to reach heroic status, and the quality can only be acquired by pursuing heroic deeds (Allison, Goethals, & Kramer, 2017).

Schindler discovered his missing inner quality during a very difficult time in his life in the year 1935. In that year, the family farm machinery business when bankrupt, and Schindler's father left his mother, which caused severe anger within Oskar. He turned his back on his father for good, and soon afterward his mother passed away (Wundheiler, 1986). In this sense, Schindler experienced suffering through the many losses that he experienced with the family business, his father emotionally, and his mother physically. Through all of this struggle, he developed the quality he had been missing: compassion for others. In the years before 1935, he only had some compassion for himself and people he knew personally. But after experiencing so much loss, his eyes were opened to a new understanding of empathy and understanding for those dealing with loss. This is the trait he needed to overcome the many obstacles on his long heroic journey (Allison, Goethals, & Kramer, 2017).

Oskar Schindler joined the Nazi party in 1938, hoping to expand his job as a salesman for the Moravian Electrotechnic Company. He realized that it was much easier to make sales in these times if one was a member of the party, although he did not agree with or believe in their policies (Wundheiler, 1986). In 1939,

Germany invaded Poland and opened many forced-labor camps (United States Holocaust Memorial Museum, 2017). Schindler watched as more and more Jews were persecuted and carted away to theses camps. He observed the great losses occurring among these people, and identified with them deeply: his calling had arrived. Using his recently developed inner trait of compassion for others, he decided to take action by purchasing an enamel factory in January of 1940. He employed both Polish and Jewish workers, with the number of Jews rising from 190 in 1941, to 550 in 1942 (Wundheiler, 1986) and finally, just before the war ended, in 1944 he employed 1,000 Jewish people (Crowe, 2004).

Trials and Tribulations: Initiation

The trials and tribulations that Schindler experienced in his journey to heroism were significant, and put him in a position of high risk. One of the largest obstacles was the Nazi party, who were constantly on Schindler's back, questioning him about his true motives. Technically, he was a part of this group, which made the Germans skeptical of him because he wished to keep so many of these people alive, when the desire of the Party was total extermination. His excuse became that they were cheap labor, but in 1941 when it was established that Jewish people were not allowed to receive wages anymore, the excuse was no longer justified. Schindler was then required to pay agreed upon sums of money to SS soldiers for each individual Jewish worker he kept (Wundheiler, 1986). Now, Schindler needed a new argument as to why he had to retain his Jewish workers.

Schindler was constantly interrogated by German officials, especially because he was always asking that more Jews from the death camps be sent to work in his factory, claiming he "desperately" needed more workers. The amount of money Schindler spent feeding "his Jews" with food from the black market, housing them, and keeping them alive was another obstacle in Schindler's path (Jackson, 1988). But in 1944, Schindler's factory, along with other labor camps in the area were called for "relocation", meaning transportation to Auschwitz and other death camps. The special permissions he had to obtain and connections he had to make almost destroyed his cause. Eventually, he was able to convince the authorities to transfer his factory to Brünnlitz in Czechoslovakia on the condition that he could only bring a certain number with him (Crowe,

2004). This trial of Schindler's heroic ability was perhaps the largest and most difficult to overcome, and its result: The List.

Return: Why Did He Do It?

There are many speculations about why Schindler might have performed such an impactful feat and risk everything he had socially and financially. Oskar Schindler was known to be a man of few words, and somehow instead became a man of action. This is perhaps why, when he did speak, he was so charismatic. He chose his words carefully in order to leave the most impact on people and get what he wanted. This explains Schindler's actions and what he did for his people; he saw suffering, identified with it, and answered it. As with many heroes, he did not think; he just acted. His impulsivity allowed him to simply react and respond to something he saw that upset him. This heroic way of thinking was developed through Schindler's discovery of his missing inner quality and calling to a situation of suffering, trials and tribulations, which led to his return to impact many people's lives in a positive manner. Even though the techniques he used to perform this heroic act were not necessarily moral, they were what had to be done in order to achieve his end goal.

Hero Analysis of Oskar Schindler

Although Schindler had some times in his life when his morality was questionable, and when his path to heroism were not entirely ethical, he still is deemed a hero by millions of people around the world. What other term besides 'hero' would be used by the 1,200 people that he saved to describe him? Through much research on this ideology of heroism, and what constitutes a true hero, there are many theories and explanations for the different dimensions of heroism. In this portion of the chapter, I will explain how Oskar Schindler fits into the several different categories of heroism according to research in the field of heroism science (Allison, Goethals, & Kramer, 2017).

Social Influence-Based Heroic Taxonomy of Schindler

According to Goethals and Allison (2012), a taxonomy of heroism can be developed that is based on the view that the influence of heroes can vary across many different situations. Goethals and Allison have proposed ten separate subtypes of heroes to emphasize the variety of heroic social influence. Schindler falls under four of these subtype categories: transposed hero, transforming hero, transfigured hero, and transcendent hero.

A transposed hero is one who has experienced a role reversal, either from hero to villain, or villain to hero. It could be argued that Schindler started out as a villainous individual, with his dishonesty, con artistry, self-interested nature, and involvement in the black market. He was known for committing adultery and was never short on his supply of alcohol (Wundheilier, 1986). He is also criticized for being a member of the Nazi party, but research shows he was doing this presumably to hide his true intentions from the unforgiving Nazis, and to make being a salesman in those times easier. After all, his connection to higher authority in the German army through the Nazi party is what allowed him to finagle his way to getting what he wanted with the goal of saving many Jewish people (Jackson, 1988). In this way, it is clear that Schindler went from being a villain in many eyes, to a hero in even more eyes. He gained desirable, heroic traits that overrode the traits from his past self.

Next we can argue that Schindler was a transforming hero, one who transforms not only themselves in the heroic process, but the entire societies in which they function. Considering the fact that there were many transforming heroes during World War II, it would be an overstatement to claim that Oskar Schindler was the ultimate transforming hero during that time, but he was definitely a member of this grouping of heroes. Schindler took part in the transformation of a remarkable number of lives during the Holocaust, and in the process he was able to transform himself. He gained the missing inner quality he was seeking, along with many other heroic traits. These allowed him to affect the lives of so many people in unimaginable ways.

A type of hero that is constructed over time and whose final reputation is exaggerated into legend is called a transfigured hero (Goethals & Allison, 2012). Schindler was definitely a hero who had to be constructed, considering his initial personality traits and concern only for people he knew personally. Through his heroic transformation cycle, he was able to overcome these characteristics and perform in ways that made him subject to heroic entitlement. Although he is not the most well-known hero in history, the impact he made on so many lives weighed greater than many known in the past.

A hero that fits into many different subtypes within Goethals and Allison's taxonomy of heroes is called a transcendent hero (Allison & Goethals, 2013). This type of hero demonstrates that not only are heroic situations diverse, but also the type of influence they have on people is diverse and assumes many forms. This subtype is very important in showing how heroes are contributors to a wide variety of social influence, as highlighted by the taxonomy (Goethals & Allison, 2012).

Heroic Subtypes of Situational Heroism

Franco, Blau, and Zimbardo proposed a taxonomy of heroes in a situation-based context (Franco, Blau, Zimbardo 2011). These twelve categories of heroes vary from martyrs to scientific (discovery) heroes. There are two subtypes in which Oskar Schindler fits nicely. The first is the "Good Samaritan", described as "individuals who are first to step in to help others in need" (Franco et al., 2011, p. 4). These types of situations are not considered to be necessarily under threat of physical risk. Although Schindler was not particularly threatened by physical risk, he was definitely threatened by emotional, social, and financial risk. He and his family had valuable social status, despite their reputations, and it was a very courageous and heroic act to go against the norms of his current society. As soon as Schindler arrived in Cracow and realized there was the potential save people from a government he disagreed with, he jumped right into action. He was able to use his social status and his Nazi party membership to mask his true motives. Putting his well-being on the line for others in need definitely meets the definition of a Good Samaritan.

Schindler is also called a "Bureaucratic" hero, one who is known to "stand firm on principle despite intense urges to conform or blindly obey higher authorities" (Franco, Blau, Zimbardo, 2011, p. 4). These are heroes in the context of large organizations who are typically controversial. Schindler is no doubt a part of this category, considering the extreme stress he was put under to participate in the dark movement of the rest of Germany. It was risky and difficult to oppose his own country and patriotism and stand up for people who were being treated as less than human. There were many pressures and higher authorities that Schindler had navigate carefully for his cause to succeed. It took considerable heroic savvy and boldness to achieve this high goal, especially with most everyone around him conforming blindly to the higher authority.

Bronk and Riches questioned the topics of purpose and heroism, and how they related to one another (Bronk & Riches, 2017). The authors produced two "routes" to heroism and purpose in their framework that describe how the two converge. The first has been coined "purpose-guided heroism" and the second is "heroism-guided purpose". The former is defined as, in accordance to the name, purpose coming before (and therefore causing) heroic action, and the latter is the opposite, namely, heroic action preceding (and therefore causing) the emergence of purpose (Bronk & Riches, 2017).

Purpose-guided heroism refers to pre-constructed values developed earlier in the hero's life playing the central role in producing the heroic act. From this perspective, there is already an existing purpose on which the hero bases their actions. Because of this realization of purpose in the individual's life, they are mentally and physically prepared to perform designated heroic actions. Purpose helps them to be more aware and more inclined to step in and be heroic. The hero must be completely devoted to this sense of purpose in order to achieve the path of purpose-guided heroism.

In contrast, heroism-guided purpose refers to occasions when an individual performs a heroic deed which in turn illuminates their life purpose. This purpose would not have been evident and could not later have been developed if the individual had not accomplished the heroic act. Heroic achievement can allow individuals to see the world in which they live in a whole new perspective. This newfound sense of purpose in the hero's life can help the hero be guided to execute more heroic acts in the future. Essentially, the individual must have enough courage to commit to a heroic deed in order to reveal their purpose and pursue the course of heroism-guided purpose (Bronk & Riches, 2017).

Oskar Schindler is one hero who clearly fits into both of these frameworks. We first turn to the heroism-guided purpose element of the Bronk and Riches (2017) framework. Schindler's calling to save as many Jewish people as he could in their time of crisis was the pinnacle of his transformation and the heroic act that required him to grasp his true purpose in life. Before his heroic deeds, he did not have this sense of purpose. He was mostly focused on himself and only the people he knew personally. His realization that he had the ability to assist others in need, even if he did not know them, was the key to realizing that this was his true purpose. He gave up many of the undesirable character traits he possessed in his earlier life, traits such as womanizing and heavy drinking. But he also realized that he could put some of his more questionable traits, like his experience in lying and deception, and his charisma, to good use.

We also see evident of purpose-guided heroism as well. The losses he suffered early in his life transformed him into a compassionate individual whose purpose was to help others also experiencing loss. It was clear to Schindler after gaining his missing inner quality of compassion for others that he could use his own resources, such as money and social status, to help people who had neither of these things. He spent the years of his life during the war dedicated to this purpose after his realization. It changed him as a person, and pushed him to work for the greater good against many odds. His dedication to the well-being of humanity is a key component of heroism (Efthimiou, Allison, & Franco, 2018). It is clear that both purpose-guided heroism and heroism-guided purpose elevated Schindler to heroic status.

Personality Traits: "The Great Eight"

In their research on heroism, Allison and Goethals discovered eight character traits that typically come to mind when people think of the prototypical hero (Allison & Goethals, 2011). The authors collected a multitude of opinions about the traits of heroes, and then systematically narrowed them down to produce "The Great Eight" (Allison & Goethals, 2017). These traits include: smart, strong, caring, charismatic, selfless, resilient, reliable, and inspiring. Heroes do not necessarily embody all of these traits, but they must have some, because they are what people consistently think of when they identify a hero (Allison & Goethals, 2011).

Oskar Schindler possessed some of these traits even before his heroic transformation. Because of his experience as a salesman, in the black market, and in interactions with many different kinds of people in the social hierarchy, it is clear that Schindler was a very smart and savvy man. He was able to deceive people to get what he wanted with his charismatic nature. During the tough period of time when the family business went bankrupt, his father left his mother, and his mother passed (Wundheiler, 1986), Schindler was forced to remain strong and resilient in order to keep himself and his family going.

After Schindler's calling and transformation to heroism, he gained many more of these "Great Eight" traits. He kept his trait of being smart, as he was intelligent enough to outmaneuver the Nazis, with the help of his extreme charisma. These traits allowed him to get out of any situation, and what helped him convince German leaders during the war to give him the permissions necessary to carry out his secret operation. The suffering he went through from the losses he experienced in his family helped him remain strong. Through Schindler's discovery of his missing quality of compassion not only for people he knew, but for complete strangers, he was able to gain the trait of selflessness. This is shown through his dedication and work by pouring his social status, time, energy, and life's savings into protecting as many people as he possibly could. This also shows how caring he was about his work and about the people he was saving. He stood up against the Nazi's Final Solution and did everything in his power to stop it.

Oskar Schindler risked so much for people he did not even know. This deed made him exceptionally inspiring, a trait he gained after becoming a hero. People relied on this man, a complete stranger, to save their lives, some never even meeting him (Jackson, 1988). He not only became a reliable person, but also an incredibly resilient one. There were many situations Schindler had to navigate successfully in order to carry out his goal. There were many bumps in the road for Schindler and "his Jews," but with his newfound resilience, he was able to push through and bounce back in every circumstance presented. In these ways, it is argued that Oskar Schindler, after his heroic transition, actually embodied all eight of the "Great Eight" traits (Allison & Goethals, 2011).

CONCLUSION

The awe-inspiring heroic work of Oskar Schindler during the Holocaust is one of great significance when discussing a hero's journey. His life experiences leading up to the war compelled him to feel the need to answer his call to heroism. If he had ignored this summoning, imagine the repercussions; over one thousand additional innocent people would have died in the deadly concentration camps. The impact Oskar Schindler has made on history because of his heroism is one that will be remembered forever. We end with a very telling quote from Oskar Schindler himself that features the essence of heroism in its simplest form. "If you were to cross the street, and there was a dog in danger of being run over by a car, wouldn't you try to help?" (Wundheiler, 1986). Would you?

REFERENCES

Allison, S. T., & Goethals, G. R. (2011). Heroes: What they do and why we need them. New York: Oxford University Press.

Allison, S. T., & Goethals, G. R. (2013). Heroic leadership: An influence taxonomy of 100 exceptional individuals. New York: Routledge.

Allison, S. T., & Goethals, G. R. (2014). "Now he belongs to the ages": The heroic leadership dynamic and deep narratives of greatness. In Goethals, G. R., et al. (Eds.), Conceptions of leadership: Enduring ideas and emerging insights. New York: Palgrave Macmillan.

Allison, S. T., & Goethals, G. R. (2017). The hero's transformation. In S. T. Allison, G. R. Goethals, & R. M. Kramer (Eds.), Handbook of heroism and heroic leadership. New York: Routledge.

Allison, S. T., Goethals, G. R., & Kramer, R. M. (2017). Setting the scene: The rise and coalescence of heroism science. In S. T. Allison, G. R. Goethals, & R. M. Kramer (Eds.), Handbook of heroism and heroic leadership. New York: Routledge.

Bronk, K. C., & Riches B. R. (2017). The Intersection of Purpose and Heroism. In S. T. Allison, G. R. Goethals, & R. M. Kramer (Eds.), Handbook of heroism and heroic leadership. New York: Routledge.

Campbell, J. (1949). The hero with a thousand faces. New York: MJF Books.

Crowe, D. M. (2004). Oskar Schindler: the untold account of his life, wartime activities, and the true story behind the list. Westview Press.

Davis, J. L., Burnette, J. L., Allison, S. T., & Stone, H. (2011). Against the odds: Academic underdogs benefit from incremental theories. Social Psychology of Education, 14, 331-346.

Dik, B. J., et al. (2017). Career Development and a Sense of Calling. In S. T. Allison, G. R. Goethals, & R. M. Kramer (Eds.), Handbook of heroism and heroic leadership. New York: Routledge.

Efthimiou, O., Allison, S. T., & Franco, Z. E. (2018). Heroism in the 21st century: Recognising our personal heroic imperative. In O. Efthimiou, S. T. Allison, & Z. E. Franco (Eds.), Heroism and wellbeing in the 21st Century: Applied and emerging perspectives. New York: Routledge.

Franco, Z. E., Blau, K., & Zimbardo, P. G. (2011, April 11). Heroism: A Conceptual Analysis and Differentiation Between Heroic Action and Altruism. Review of General Psychology. Advance online publication. doi: 10.1037/a0022672

Goethals, G. R. & Allison, S. T. (2012). Making heroes: The construction of courage, competence and virtue. Advances in Experimental Social Psychology, 46, 183-235.

Jackson, M. (1988). Oskar Schindler and Moral Theory. Journal of Applied Philosophy, 5(2), 175-182. Retrieved from http://www.jstor.org/stable/24353520

United States Holocaust Memorial Museum. Oskar Schindler. Retrieved October 06, 2017, from https://www.ushmm.org/wlc/en/article.php?ModuleId=10005787

Wundheiler, L. (1986). Oskar Schindler's Moral Development During the Holocaust. Humboldt Journal of Social Relations, 13(1/2), 333-356. Retrieved from http://www.jstor.org/stable/23262673

OTHER BOOKS IN THE PALSGROVE SERIES

Allison, S. T. (Ed.) (2017). *Heroes of Richmond: Four centuries of courage, dignity, and virtue.* Richmond: Palsgrove.

Allison, S. T. (Ed.) (2018). *Heroes and villains of the millennial generation.* Richmond: Palsgrove.

Allison, S. T. (Ed.) (2019). *Heroic transformation: How heroes change themselves and the world.* Richmond: Palsgrove.

Allison, S. T. (Ed.) (2020). *Core concepts in heroism science: Volume 1.* Richmond: Palsgrove.

Allison, S. T. (Ed.) (2020). *Core concepts in heroism science: Volume 2.* Richmond: Palsgrove.

THE SERIES EDITOR

Scott T. Allison has authored numerous books, including *Heroes* and *Heroic Leadership*. He is Professor of Psychology at the University of Richmond where he has published extensively on heroism and leadership. He has co-authored articles and chapters with 35 of his current and former students. His work has appeared in USA Today, National Public Radio, the New York Times, the Los Angeles Times, Slate Magazine, MSNBC, CBS, Psychology Today, and the Christian Science Monitor. He has received Richmond's Distinguished Educator Award and the Virginia Council of Higher Education's Outstanding Faculty Award.

www.ingramcontent.com/pod-product-compliance
Lightning Source LLC
Chambersburg PA
CBHW031422270326
41930CB00007B/534